Community Psychology
Theory and Practice

Community Psychology
Theory and Practice

JIM ORFORD
University of Exeter, UK

JOHN WILEY & SONS
Chichester · New York · Brisbane · Toronto · Singapore

Copyright © 1992 by John Wiley & Sons Ltd,
  Baffins Lane, Chichester,
  West Sussex PO19 1UD, England
  National Chichester (0243) 779777
  International +44 243 779777

Reprinted March and October 1993, May 1994

Other Wiley Editorial Offices

John Wiley & Sons, Inc., 605 Third Avenue,
New York, NY 10158–0012, USA

Jacaranda Wiley Ltd, G.P.O. Box 859, Brisbane,
Queensland 4001, Australia

John Wiley & Sons (Canada) Ltd, 22 Worcester Road,
Rexdale, Ontario M9W 1L1, Canada

John Wiley & Sons (SEA) Pte Ltd, 37 Jalan Pemimpin #05-04,
Block B, Union Industrial Building, Singapore 2057

Library of Congress Cataloging-in-Publication Data:

Orford, Jim.
  Community psychology: theory and practice/Jim Orford.
    p. cm.
  Includes bibliographical references and index.
  ISBN 0-471-91147-X (ppc)
  ISBN 0-471-93810-6 (paper)
  1. Community psychology. I. Title.
  [DNLM: 1. Community Mental Health Services—Great Britain.
  2. Psychology, Social. WM 30 067c]
  RA790.55.O74 1992
  155.9'4—dc20
  DNLM/DLC
  for Library of Congress   91–30651
                                                        CIP

British Library Cataloguing in Publication Data:

A catalogue record for this book is
available from the British Library.

ISBN 0-471-91147-X (ppc)
ISBN 0-471-93810-6 (paper)

Typeset in 10/12 Times by Mathematical Composition Setters Ltd, Salisbury, Wiltshire
Printed and bound in Great Britain by
Biddles Ltd, Guildford and King's Lynn

Contents

To my mother
Margaret Orford (née MacKeown)
a fellow writer
for her 80th birthday
14 February 1992

Preface

Community psychology is about understanding people within their social worlds and using this understanding to improve people's well-being. It is about understanding *and* helping. Thus it is both an area of research and a branch of the academic study of psychology and at the same time a branch of a helping profession. It stands, too, on a bridge between the psyche and the social, the private and the public. These are uncomfortable positions to occupy. In many ways it is easier to commit oneself to being either an academic *or* a practitioner. Similarly most people lean towards one side or other of the psycho-social divide, interested more in the emotions, thoughts and actions of individual people or in people as social and political animals.

I was attracted to the bridging position that community psychology occupies during the ten years, from the mid-1960s to the mid-1970s, that I spent working at the Addiction Research Unit at the Institute of Psychiatry/ Maudsley Hospital in London. This is and was then a unit devoted to the academic study of alcohol and other drug problems, but it had many practical and policy connections. It was there that I became interested in community-based houses as alternatives to hospital, and from this grew an interest in organisational processes and organisational change. It was there, too, that new ideas on the importance of primary care in the treatment of alcohol and drug problems were first developing, and from this source developed my interests in alternatives to specialist treatment, such as consultation and the role of volunteer counselling. At the same time the nature of the subject we were studying forced me to reconsider the person-centred or individually oriented psychology with which I had been equipped as a clinical psychologist. There was no escaping the fact that problems relating to the use of alcohol and other drugs had to be understood within a wider framework that included the peer group, the neighbourhood, attitudes and norms prevailing within a community, as well as the biological and psychological make-up of individual people. We discussed everything from the potency of opiates to motivate animal behaviour and the likelihood of there being an 'alcoholic personality', to the prescribing habits of general practitioners and the history of the British public house. It was also accepted that in this field prevention was at least as important as treatment.

It was with this background that I went to Exeter to run the Masters course in Clinical Psychology. Exeter Health Authority was one of the first in Britain to close its mental handicap and most of its mental illness hospital provision and to move over to community-based residential units and specialist support teams. The clinical psychology training there developed a marked community emphasis both in terms of its academic side and in terms of the supervised placements that were available for student-trainees. In 1988 the course title was changed to 'clinical and community psychology' (the first in the UK), and in 1991 a new journal was launched—the *Journal of Community and Applied Social Psychology*—co-edited from the universities of Exeter and Kent. None of these achievements necessarily means that we are yet matching up to the theories and practices described in this book. They do indicate, however, that we are moving in that direction.

I owe a great debt of gratitude to the many colleagues of mine in London and Exeter, too numerous to mention individually, who have influenced and encouraged me along the way. I should also like to acknowledge the influence on my thinking of those community psychologists who have been writing about their work in the USA over the last two decades or more. It is a distinctive form of community psychology that is developing in Britain, and the same will be true in other parts of Europe and elsewhere in the world, but without the lead that has been set in North America it is unlikely that the present book would have been written, at least in anything like its present form.

My special thanks are reserved for Liz Mears who during the time this book was written has been Administrator to the MSc in Clinical and Community Psychology and without whose help in preparing the manuscript and support in countless other ways, this book would never have been written.

I am pleased to acknowledge that the following figures and tables that appear in this book have been reproduced by permission of the publishers:

Figure 2, Tavistock Publications; Figure 4, Archives of General Psychiatry; Figure 5, Academic Press; Figures 6 and 7, The American Psychological Association; Figure 11, Plenum Press; Figure 15, *Administrative Science Quarterly*; Tables 2, 6 and 12, John Wiley & Sons; Table 13, Heinemann.

Jim Orford
Exeter
June 1991

Part I

THEORY

1 What is Community Psychology?

The term 'community psychology' will be unfamiliar to many, perhaps most, readers. Few will claim to know at all precisely what it means and many will, quite rightly, approach the subject with some scepticism. Do we really need another specialised branch of psychology? Is it just following fashion by thoughtlessly adding the word 'community' to create an imperious-looking subject but one which on closer inspection turns out to be naked of any substance? Is it a typical creature of the later years of the twentieth century when limits on expenditure for public services are severe and any suggestion about 'the community' taking responsibility for itself or providing its own care is welcome? Is it academic enough, sufficiently rigorous and based on empirical research, to stand alongside other more familiar branches of psychology?

It is the task of this book to convince the reader that community psychology is sufficiently distinct, and crucial to the development of psychology in the future, that it warrants separate treatment. Not that it would be altogether new. Although community psychology is just emerging in Britain and else-where in Europe, it has been part of the North American psychology scene for a number of years. There has been a Community Psychology Division of the American Psychological Association since 1966, and two journals published in the USA, the *American Journal of Community Psychology* and the *Journal of Community Psychology*, first appeared in the early 1970s. By contrast, the British Psychological Society has no division of Community Psychology and the first British-based journal with the expression 'community psychology' in its title—the *Journal of Community and Applied Social Psychology*—appeared for the first time in 1991.

A number of textbooks on the subject appeared in the USA in the 1970s and 80s. Amongst those the present author has found particularly useful are Zax and Specter's (1974) *Introduction to Community Psychology*, Rappaport's (1977) *Community Psychology: Values Research and Action*, Heller, Price, Reinharz, Riger, Wandersman and D'Aunno's (1984) *Psychology and Community Change*, and Levine and Perkins' (1987) *Principles of*

Community Psychology: Perspectives and Applications. In Britain, Bender's (1976) *Community Psychology* and Koch's (1986) edited volume *Community Clinical Psychology* contain useful examples of applied psychological work in community settings although neither drew upon the rich background of ideas in North American community psychology. In an emerging sub-discipline such as community psychology it is important to have models of good practice, but in the long run it is more important to have a core foundation of ideas which provide the driving force for the development of the subject. As Kurt Lewin—the pioneering social psychologist of the 1920s, 30s, and 40s to whom community psychology owes so much—is reputed to have said, 'There is nothing so practical as a good theory' (de Board, 1978).

What, then, constitutes the subject of Community Psychology? Does it really represent, as some would claim, a 'paradigm shift', a veritable scientific revolution (Kuhn, 1970) in the way psychology might be applied? Table 1 lists some of the main ideas and topic areas that will be dealt with in this book. This table is taken, much modified, from one in Rappaport's (1977) book. His table contrasted dimensions of *community mental health* versus clinically oriented services. This immediately underlines one important point about the origins of community psychology ideas—many of them have come from the mental health field. The present author's background is in clinical psychology, and many of the illustrations of background knowledge and of community psychology practice to be found in this book have been taken from mental health. Community psychology cannot simply be identified with community

Table 1. The principles of community psychology

---

1. Assumptions about causes of problems
   An interaction, over time, between person and social settings and systems, including the structure of social support and social power.
2. Levels of analysis
   From micro-level to macro, especially at the level of the organisation and the community or neighbourhood
3. Research methods
   Include quasi-experimental designs, qualitative research, action research, and case-study methods.
4. Location of practice
   As near as possible to the relevant, everyday social contexts
5. Approach to planning services
   Proactive, 'seeking out', assessing needs and special risks in a community
6. Practice emphasis
   On prevention rather than treatment
7. Attitude to sharing psychology with others
   Positive towards formal and informal ways of sharing including consultation
8. Position on working with non-professionals
   Strongly encouraging of self-help and non-professionals and seeks to facilitate and collaborate

---

mental health however (Cowen, 1980). For one thing, community mental health is not in itself an academic or scientific discipline with a base of theory and knowledge upon which to build practice. In fact developments in community mental health in the last few decades have been criticised for lacking the vision that community psychology could have helped to provide (Ramon, 1988, and see Chapter 11). Furthermore, the principles of community psychology once they are translated into practice result in ways of applying psychology which no longer fit neatly into the present, compartmentalised and fragmented approach to applying psychology. Once psychology is practised outside the clinics, schools and penal establishments in which it has found its institutional homes in the past, and emerges into the community (principle 4 in Table 1), then the familiar separations of clinical, educational, occupational, criminological and legal, and other branches of applied psychology, make less and less sense. The central ideas of community psychology transcend these artificial boundaries as do many of the most exciting innovations in practice.

PERSON-IN-CONTEXT: THE FUNDAMENTAL PRINCIPLE

The first principle shown in Table 1 is the most important. Community psychology endeavours to take seriously Lewin's (1951) famous equation $B = f(P, E)$, that is behaviour is a function of the person, the environment, and the interaction between the two. There has been a bias in psychology generally, even within social psychology (Turner and Oakes, 1986), and certainly within applied branches of the subject (J. Tizard, 1976), towards the P component of Lewin's equation. The almost exclusive emphasis has been upon assessing and modifying the behaviour, emotions and cognitions of *individuals*. In our practice and in our research we work principally with individuals. We think largely in terms of what is wrong with people, and how we can help them change themselves. It is very personal, private and individualistic. Occasionally, our thinking is one notch up, in terms of family systems, but we rarely extend this to consider seriously the workplace, the school, links between home, school and work, the neighbourhood or community, media influences, housing conditions, the state of the labour market, or social stratification and other aspects of the wider social structure. At best we pay lip service to these things. As Heller (1989) put it:

> Our professional traditions tell us to attend to symptoms of depressed affect, such as the number of days when it was hard to get up in the morning, and to ignore signs of political apathy, such as the number of years of not registering to vote. We ask about queasy stomachs, sleepless nights, and family conflicts, but not about feeling safe in the streets, the number of persons on our block that we know by first name, or the availability of recreational centers for teens. We ask our teenagers about their experiences with drugs, alcohol, and sex, but do not ask them about their hopes for the future, the community attributes they value, or whether they

believe that they can make a personal impact upon the way they, or others, will live 10 years from now. (p.12)

Community psychology aims to correct this individualistic bias by aiming always to consider people within the contexts of the social settings and systems of which they are parts or which influence them. This is no easy task for a number of different reasons. For one thing, if we seriously wish to consider person-in-context we have a great deal of complexity to deal with. The relationships between people and their environments almost always turn out to be reciprocal. We shall meet many examples of this later in this book: Is mental illness the cause or consequence of living in poor city areas? Does social support aid well-being for people under stress, or does well-being result in better use being made of social support? Is the climate of a rehabilitation house in the community affected more by the personalities of its residents, or is the stronger influence in the reverse direction from climate to residents' behaviour and experience? The most likely answer in all cases is that people and their settings constitute a totality, an indivisible whole (Marsella, 1984), with *mutual influence* between one and the other. Furthermore, this system of person-in-context has some continuity over time, often over a very long period of time in the case of the kinds of phenomena with which community psychology deals. Hence people are continually being changed by their settings, and settings by people, so that a new state of the system emerges as a result of the transaction (Seidman, 1988). This world of transactions and emergent properties of person-in-context systems is difficult to conceptualise and assess, let alone to try and modify, and this is surely one of the reasons why we are more comfortable with a more individualistic approach.

Another difficulty in the way of fully achieving this ambitious aim of considering the totality of individuals in their settings has been the lack of leading theoretical ideas around which this new field might coalesce. It is for this reason that considerable space has been devoted here to examining some of the many ideas out of which a leading theory for community psychology might be fashioned. These include the concept of *social support* (Chapter 4), the related ideas of *power, control and empowerment* (Chapters 5 and 11), Barker's (1968, 1978) concept of *behaviour settings* (Chapter 2) and Bronfenbrenner's (1979) model of *micro-, meso-, exo- and macro-level systems* (Chapter 2). The latter is a particularly important set of ideas since it defines the scope of community psychology and sets its limits very wide indeed. The idea of a system, with reciprocal and continuing influence between component parts, is familiar to family therapists for example (Vetere and Gale, 1987), but the family is just one, albeit very important, micro-level system. Community psychology is about the interdependence of individuals and their settings and systems at many levels including the 'highest' or macro-level. At this level it is concerned, to take what is probably the most general and important example, with social stratification, particularly stratification by socio-economic status but also by factors of gender, race, age and disability (House and Mortimer, 1990).

It follows that those who use a community psychology orientation should be free to move as required from one level of thinking to another. Someone working with physically disabled people should feel comfortable counselling a young person who needs to use a wheelchair to move around the neighbourhood, and lobbying local public and commercial enterprises to make sure that they provide adequate wheelchair access to buildings (Yates, personal communication, 1989). Someone working with older adults might apportion time both to working individually with them, and attempting to influence local authority housing policy regarding low-cost housing for older people (Twining, 1986). Whatever level we are working at we should be alert to the influence of factors operating both at higher and lower levels:

> we can and should always be ready to look 'beyond' and 'within'. ... If we see husbands and wives in conflict over lost income, we need to look beyond to the economy that puts the husbands out of work and now may welcome the wives into the labour force, as well as to the culture that defines a person's personal worth in monetary terms and that blames the victims of economic dislocation for their own losses. But we must also look within to the parent-child relationships that are affected by the changing roles and status of the parents. In addition, we must also look across to see how the several systems involved (family, workplace, and economy) adjust to new conditions over time. (Garbarino, 1982, pp. 21–22)

Rappaport (1977) warned that intervening at an inappropriate level runs the risk of neglecting the most important causes of a problem. It is certainly a central tenet of community psychology that interventions at the individual level, which have tended to be the rule in applying psychology, run the risk of appearing to *blame* the individual who might more appropriately be seen as the victim of forces operating at a higher level (Ryan 1971). Thereby the intervention and those employing it may unwittingly help to maintain the status quo rather than being a force for changing it.

It is, of course, when taking into account the interdependence of individuals and aspects of social structure that community psychology most clearly ceases to be exclusively involved with the private and personal and enters the arena of the public and the political. Indeed much of the motivation for forming a community psychology specialty in the US in the mid-1960s was a desire to reduce social inequality and to right social wrongs. There was great concern with issues such as poverty, educational deprivation and racial tension, and a sense of dissatisfaction with the apparent irrelevance of individual therapy as a way of relieving such problems (Levine and Perkins, 1987; Heller, 1989). A related theme has been the need for community psychology to be *culturally relative* rather than absolutist, respecting diversity between, for example, men and women and different ethnic groups rather than imposing one dominant set of norms (Rappaport, 1977). There are many commonalities between feminism and community psychology. For instance, both seek to link the personal and the political, recognise the importance of inequality and power relations and value empowerment (Mulvey, 1988).

TOPIC AREAS IN COMMUNITY PSYCHOLOGY

If person-in-context is the overarching philosophy of community psychology, what is its substance? How is this translated into practice? What do people actually do when they are doing community psychology? Table 1 (principles 3 to 8) provides one answer in brief, and the remaining chapters of this book (particularly Chapters 6 to 11) provide the same answer at much greater length. Principle 3 (and Chapter 6) refers to the types of research method that may be particularly useful for community psychology. The need to find research methods that do justice to the complexity that has already been referred to is vital. Community psychology is an applied subject. In other words, it is a practical subject, concerning itself with trying to change things at one or more level, from micro to macro. But it is a branch of psychology, and it is therefore as thoroughly committed to the building up of theory and knowledge through research, and the sound evaluation of practice, as are all other branches of psychology. It is committed to empiricism and *the scientist-practitioner model* (Barlow, Hayes and Nelson, 1984). There are, however, many definitions of the word 'science', some of them too narrow and restricting to allow a number of the research methods (qualitative and case-study methods for example) which the present author believes to be necessary for community psychology (see Chapter 6).

Principles 2 and 4 in Table 1 refer, respectively, to the location of community psychology practice, and to two common levels of practice which receive attention in this book. Although location away from large institutions—for example in community mental health centres—does not *guarantee* that a person-in-context philosophy is being used, or that community psychology is being practised (Rappaport, 1977; Ramon, 1988), it is a general principle of community psychology that practice should take place within the relevant social context or as close to it as possible. Anyone with a community psychology orientation is likely, therefore, to feel frustrated working in a clinic, hospital or penal establishment. Not only is the prevailing ethos likely to be an individualistic one, but the individuals concerned are extracted from their normal habitats and therefore it is difficult to understand and help them in their normal contexts. Indeed these special settings often confound the picture by adding complicating factors that are more to do with the institutions themselves than with the people they are trying to help. The ideal is not always possible, but working with a community psychology orientation one is always attracted to working in peoples' own homes, at their places of work, in their neighbourhoods and with their social networks.

One of the principal levels at which community psychology is practised is that of the organisation. Keys and Frank (1987) have argued that the linking of community psychology and the study of organisations can be a particularly fruitful one. Organisations are, after all, settings with which everyone becomes familiar at one time or another. They are diverse, often large enough to contain multiple behaviour settings, systems and inter-system linkings, and they probably have major impact on the well-being of member individuals (Warr, 1987). Many who have practised in a more individualistic manner have had to grapple with organisational functioning in the schools, hospitals and hostels in which they have worked. Once the focus is upon understanding and changing the organisation itself, then community psychology is being practised (see Chapter 9).

At least some community psychology—although to date a disappointingly small proportion—has been at the level of 'the community' itself. Quite apart from the practical difficulties of working at this level, there are two conceptual problems to overcome. Firstly, how is the term 'community' to be defined? The term has been used in at least two different senses: community defining a geographical area, locality or neighbourhood; and community as a network of social interaction and support (McMillan and Chavis, 1976; Heller, 1989). The two are by no means necessarily the same. The second difficulty, which is related to the first, has been the absence of a leading psychological theory or set of constructs to guide work at this level. One of the most promising ideas has been the concept of a *psychological sense of community* (Sarason, 1974), although in practice this has proved a difficult idea to pin down. One of the points discussed in Chapter 11 is the possibility that sense of community has a greater reality in relation to smaller geographical units such as neighbourhoods or even 'blocks' in urban areas.

One of the implications of the basic community psychology way of thinking is that the practitioner is bound to want to reach out beyond individual psychological difficulties, not only in thinking about higher levels of influence but also in trying to bring about changes at these levels. In Table 1, principles 5, 6 and 7 address this proactive stance. It has been referred to as a *seeking* mode of working in contrast to a reactive mode of *waiting* (Rappaport, 1977). Working with a community psychology orientation, the practitioner is not content to wait for individuals to make contact, but rather wishes to understand how problems have been generated in the community, to find out what needs exist and which of them are not currently being met, and to anticipate problems and to prevent them where possible. Thus community psychology draws heavily upon *epidemiology* and *needs assessment* (see Chapters 3 and 6), favours *consultation* and other less formal ways of sharing psychology with those in contact with problems in the community (Chapter 7), and places much more emphasis upon *prevention* (the subject of Chapter 8) than upon treatment of individual disorder.

A further consequence of taking the kind of view of the world outlined above is a wish to share the fruits of psychological understanding and knowledge as widely as possible within the community. This is partly on practical grounds, since the numbers of trained mental health workers, let alone psychologists, is nowhere near adequate to deal directly with those psychological problems already known to exist (Albee, 1968; Hawks, 1973). This is true even in countries with relatively well-developed higher education and health care systems, and it is far more the case in third world countries where people trained in applied psychology and related disciplines may be almost non-existent.

The predilection for sharing psychology derives mostly, however, from the strongly held belief in community psychology that psychological expertise resides principally amongst the residents of a community themselves and amongst the many *human service workers* who have special helping roles within the community but who have little or no special training in psychology. This perspective is very different from that adopted in many of the other branches of psychology and in professions generally, and is bound to be controversial. Suffice it to say that someone with this orientation will always tend to be positively disposed towards sharing psychology with other workers, either through formal consultation or in other ways (Chapter 7) and towards the psychological work of people in the community with little or no formal training as well as towards mutual aid or self-help approaches (Chapter 10). Psychology has often taken a guarded or patronising view of this work, believing that its role is limited or merely supportive of real psychological intervention which can only be carried out by trained people. This is in marked contrast to the enthusiasm felt by those with a community psychology viewpoint who are likely to hold quite the contrary belief, namely that real psychology is largely practised by those *without* special training, and that it is the work of psychologists and others with such training that is supportive. The converse of this is that psychologists with a community orientation are likely to be amongst the least enthusiastic when it comes to licensing or chartering of psychologists and other moves towards increased professionalisation (Rappaport, 1977).

PROGRESS TOWARDS ACHIEVING COMMUNITY PSYCHOLOGY'S GOALS

The aims and aspirations of community psychology are far from modest. Community psychology is new and progress has been slow and to some, disappointing. Rappaport (1977) was of the opinion that the shift to community mental health in the USA had not been accompanied by a move from working in a waiting mode to a seeking mode, that values were no more tolerant of diversity and cultural relativism than they had been formerly, and that ideas were still individually oriented rather than system oriented. Ketterer (1981) reported that consultation and prevention represented very small proportions of community mental health workers' schedules and that this proportion was scarcely increasing.

Although there is encouraging evidence that at least some community mental health services in the USA are significantly more responsive to the needs of ethnic minority groups than they were (O'Sullivan, Peterson, Cox and Kirkeby, 1989), the point has already been made that community mental health cannot necessarily be equated with community psychology. We are dealing here with organisational systems and the difficulty of changing them. Activities such as prevention and consultation have not been afforded a high priority within mental health care, educational or criminal-legal systems, or within branches of applied psychology or in related professions. The same processes that operate to produce group conformity in any setting have operated within these human service systems to perpetuate an almost exclusive concentration upon individual treatment, and topics such as prevention and consultation have been neglected. These processes include selection: individuals with certain interests and aptitudes are attracted towards, and selected for, training, whilst others are not so attracted or are not selected. This is likely to have resulted in a concentration of professionals who are inclined towards an understanding of problems in individualistic terms, who may prefer a reactive, responsive or waiting mode of working rather than a more forceful, proactive or seeking one, and who may be fearful of becoming too 'political' or 'social activist' in style. Training courses then compound these biases by giving novice practitioners skills that make them feel confident to carry out individual treatment procedures, but which leave them feeling unskilled, or even that they would be wasting what skills they have, when it comes to prevention or organisational change. Once in practice, these biases will be reinforced by some employing authorities which appear to value and to reward a large and often exclusive commitment to individual work at the expense of prevention. Heller, Price, Reinharz, Riger, Wandersman and D'Aunno (1984) pointed out how clinical psychology, for example, had followed the tradition of psychiatry, despite the evident dissimilarities between these two professions, in holding individual treatment in the highest esteem.

Even in the research and writings of those most committed to the perspective outlined in this chapter, however, it seems to be difficult to escape an individualistic approach. A content analysis of over 700 research articles that appeared in the *American Journal of Community Psychology* and the *Journal of Community Psychology* between 1973 and 1982, produced some surprising and disappointing results. In only 8 per cent of the projects reviewed had a level of analysis been employed that was beyond the individual, although the responses of individuals had often been aggregated to the level of programmes or organisations. It was for the latter level that many of the implications of the research were drawn, only 12 per cent drawing implications at the level of community or society as a whole. In terms of research methods, most had used paper and pencil tests, questionnaires or inventories, and only 7 per cent had used two or more methods to measure the same construct. In general it was concluded that community psychology researchers were using methods of low complexity in an area where the situation was inherently complex. The general conclusion was: 'We feel uneasy about the lack of a community perspective in most of the research articles we examined ... [and] the nearly exclusive focus on the individual as the unit of analysis' (Lounsbury, Cook, Leader and Mears, 1985, p. 95).

Although there are encouraging signs that this stage of affairs is changing—for example most of the February 1990 issue of the *American Journal of Community Psychology* was devoted to citizen participation, voluntary organisations and community development—others have been dismayed at the extent to which research in community psychology still focuses upon the individual. Often they find that constructs that could serve a valuable role in linking the individual and the micro- and macro-environments have been commandeered by, or have remained trapped in, an individualistic perspective (Seidman, 1988; Heller, 1989). We will come across a number of examples of this in later chapters. Social support provides perhaps the best example (see Chapter 4) and powerlessness and empowerment are others (Chapters 5 and 11).

Indeed, the struggle to establish an *action science* (Argyris, Putnam and Smith, 1985) which matches up to the ideal of person-in-context will be apparent to the reader in the chapters that follow. In some chapters, the material will be found to fall far short of the ideal. This is probably true of Chapter 3 which rests heavily upon excellent British work in social psychiatry, where, although findings are often aggregated to the level of community, many of the central ideas remain individualistic. It is probably true also of much of Chapter 8 where many of the examples of preventive work are still individualistic in conception.

Although the distinction is not totally clear-cut, theoretical background ideas are mostly presented in Part I of this book and examples of practice mostly in Part II. Otherwise, the main feature of the organisation of the book to note is the choice and ordering of chapters in Part II. This is a reflection of the author's background in an individualistically-oriented branch of applied psychology. A writer with a different background—such as applied social psychology—might have started with, and much expanded, the contents of Chapter 11. The present author's more cautious approach has been to commence with a form of practice (sharing psychology through consultation and other means—Chapter 7) which is closest in style to that of practitioners who have been brought up as he has, and to move gradually through Chapters 8 to 11 towards the kind of practice that is most radically different from it.

At this stage in the development of what is still a new subject, there are many different choices that could be made about the content of a book on community psychology, reflecting the different origins of community psychology and the various options for the direction of its future development. Heller and Monahan (1977) saw a number of possible ways in which the subject might proceed organisationally. It might develop as a branch of clinical psychology. There are many training courses in the US and one in Britain in community clinical or community *and* clinical psychology (*The Community Psychologist*, 1987). This supposes that the more individualistic orientation of clinical psychology can combine with the person-in-context orientation of community psychology in a harmonious and productive way. There are certainly encouraging developments in clinical psychology in Britain that suggest that this might indeed be the case. These developments have often been led by those working with disadvantaged groups such as people with learning disabilities or those with long-term needs for mental health care.

Alternatively, community psychology might develop as an orientation within a number of branches of psychology, or as a separate specialty of its own within psychology (Heller and Monahan, 1977). The latter approach, embodied in the many community psychology training courses that exist in North America (*The Community Psychologist*, 1987), assumes that the subject will better develop unhampered by the need for theory and skills in individual assessment and therapy. This direction is perhaps more likely to be followed in those parts of the world where clinical and other branches of psychology rest most heavily upon individualistic models of peoples' behaviour and experience. Particularly in places where social problems are most pressing and inescapable (see Chapter 11), forms of psychology that are too exclusively oriented towards the person may not find it easy to adapt to meet the challenge that these problems pose.

Finally, Heller and Monahan suggest that community psychology might develop as an inter-disciplinary subject linking psychology with other disciplines with an equal interest in such subjects as community mental health, health promotion, organisational change, and community development. This is a suggestion with which the present author has a great deal of sympathy. Very few of the topics dealt with in this book are the exclusive province of psychology, and if the ideas and knowledge generated are to lead to any benefits for the human condition, they will surely do so only through joint efforts with many colleagues and collaborators who come from other traditions.

2 Theories of Person-In-Context

Community psychology is about understanding and helping individual people in their natural settings and social systems. It is this concern with people within the context of their own settings and systems that is community psychology's hallmark. It is not, as so much psychology has been, about people extracted from their natural environment. Neither is it about environmental settings or social collectivities without regard for the individuals who inhabit or comprise them. This would be to depart the realms of psychology altogether. Our subject is located at the interface between person and social context. More accurately, it is about an indivisible *gestalt*, or whole, which can be termed 'person-in-context'.

The point has been made that no unifying or leading theory yet exists in this field although one is badly needed. This chapter presents a number of theoretical concepts which the present author believes to be amongst the most promising for the development of community psychology theory. These will be dealt with under two main headings: Settings and Systems. Under Settings will figure the work of Barker, of Moos, and of the environmental psychologists. Under Systems will be considered the ideas of Bronfenbrenner, of the interpersonal behaviour theorists, and of the ecological psychology school.

SETTINGS

The theme running through the ideas presented in this section is that individuals are in a state of continuing *transaction* with the various settings in which they spend time as part of their everyday lives. This state of transaction is characterised by reciprocal influence. Not only are the experiences and forms of behaviour of individuals profoundly affected by characteristics of the settings in which they find themselves, but so too are settings created and shaped by their occupants.

BARKER AND THE CONCEPT OF BEHAVIOUR SETTINGS

Barker's (1968, 1978) approach is a potentially important one for community psychology, and it will be described in some detail. Barker was very critical of the way in which psychology had become, 'a science of the laboratory and the clinic ... more and more removed from settings that are not arranged by scientists' (1978, p. 39). Unlike chemists who know about the distribution of elements in nature or zoologists and botanists who know about the distri- bution of animal and plant species in their natural habitats, psychologists know very little about how human behaviour occurs naturally, without their interference, in 'the real-life settings ... the mealtimes, ... offices, airplanes, ... arithmetic classes, ... streets and sidewalks' (1978, p. 38). Barker's unique solution to this problem was to set up what he called a Psychological Field Station in a small town (Midwest) of about 800 inhabitants in Eastern Kansas, and to study in painstaking detail the naturally occurring public behaviour of its children and later in equal detail the 884 public behaviour settings in which all its inhabitants, adults and children, partook during one year.

Behaviour settings consist of standing patterns of behaviour-and-milieu. This idea that action and the environment in which it takes place are inseparably bound up together is a crucial one for understanding Barker's concept of behaviour setting. The milieu may be formed from natural features of the landscape, but it is much more likely to consist of parts of the built environment: a room, a sportsground, a classroom. Whatever it is made up of, milieu is circumjacent to behaviour: it encompasses it, surrounds it, encloses it—behaviour occurs within it. The expression, 'within these four walls', neatly captures the idea of behaviour having a spatial boundary. Behaviour settings also have a temporal boundary: a shop opens for cus- tomers at a particular time of day and closes at a later time; a meeting lasts for an hour or two. Only a very few of Midwest's behaviour settings were available all the time: the streets of the town constituted one such setting.

Barker's key insight was that behaviour and milieu are in synchrony within behaviour settings; or as he put it, that milieu and behaviour were *synomor- phic* one to another. There was a *fit* between behaviour and its milieu: they were inseparable. Behaviour-milieu units, which he called *synomorphs*, had both physical and behavioural attributes. He identified a number of sources of this synomorphy. Some constraints on behaviour in a setting are built in to the structure: for example the pews in a church are in fixed rows and face the pulpit in a way that demands that the congregation face the minister. Other sources of synchrony between behaviour and milieu consist of social forces to conform, explicit teaching about appropriate conduct within the set- ting, selection of individuals by the setting (for example a proportion of set- tings in Midwest required the presence of children, whilst others prohibited their presence), and self-selection *out* by individuals who are unwilling or unable to conform. A most important general point is that this synchrony or synomorphy is by no means to be interpreted merely as the direct influence of the physical environment upon behaviour. Most of the settings studied by Barker and his colleagues were deliberately created to serve human needs and interests. However, once they are firmly established, 'behavior settings ... are stable, extra-individual units with great coercive power over the behavior that occurs within them' (Barker 1968, p. 17).

When Barker studied the behaviour of children in Midwest, he found:

> that some attributes of behavior varied less across children within settings than across settings within the days of children. We found, in short, that we could predict some aspects of children's behavior more adequately from knowledge of the behavior characteristics of the drug stores, arithmetic classes and basketball games they inhabited, than from knowledge of the behavior tendencies of particular children. (1968, p. 4)

The people who occupy a behaviour setting are to a degree, 'interchangeable and replaceable' (1968, p. l7). In other words people to an extent lose their individuality within behaviour settings.

Of course people do not lose their individuality altogether in the kinds of everyday behaviour settings that we have been discussing, nor did Barker suppose that they did. Nevertheless, although he recognised that most behaviour settings were created by people, and that social forces were amongst those that constrained behaviour within them, his work is particularly strong on the importance of the physical environment, and he probably underplayed two aspects which have been stressed by other ecological and community psychologists. One of these is the importance of change and of adaptation to change (Heller *et al.*, 1984). Perhaps in a tiny county town in Kansas in the early 1960s stability of behaviour settings was more apparent than change; but settings are probably constantly changing in response to changing needs, perceived pressures, or simply the individuality of new occupants of a setting. The other aspect that receives little attention in Barker's works is the way in which individuals perceive, interpret, or make meaning out of a setting. Indeed Barker made no pretence of studying the subjective environment, or Lewin's (1951) *lifespace*, in which perceptual and interpretive aspects are all-important. He was concerned, rather, with the objective, pre-perceptual or 'ecological' environment.

By concentrating on the more objective aspects of peoples' immediate environment, Barker was able to highlight a number of interesting things about life in Midwest which could easily have been overlooked otherwise. He developed a number of measures to describe individual behaviour settings and the totality of Midwest in terms of its constituent settings. Many of these measures were highly complex and need not concern us here, but others are potentially of great relevance. A particularly insightful observation was that individuals can *penetrate* a behaviour setting to a variable degree: Barker identified six *zones of penetration* ranging from mere passive onlooking (zone

1) to being the single leader in the setting (zone 6). By this means he was able to show that certain groups (e.g. children or women) were excluded from being active performers (zone 4 or above) in a certain proportion of settings. A particularly striking finding was that a mere 3 per cent of all Midwest settings were without clearly identified leaders (either a single leader, zone 6, or joint leaders, zone 5). Another interesting measure was the *richness* of a setting, which was based upon a complex combination of the number of different age, gender, social status and racial sub-groups that were able to penetrate the setting, the number of different types of *action pattern* (business, education, nutrition, recreation, etc.) and *behaviour mechanisms* (talking, thinking, motor activity, etc.) which were displayed in the setting, and the total amount of time that the setting was 'open'. According to his measure the local drug store was the 'richest' setting in town. Although this fact may have been appreciated by many of Midwest's inhabitants, it may be particularly important for social planners and policy-makers to appreciate this kind of finding. Otherwise it may be difficult to comprehend the strength of feeling engendered, for example, by the threat to close a village school or post office. In Barker's terms these are likely to be rich settings serving as focal points for a wide diversity of community members.

Barker and his colleagues were also able to use the concept of behaviour setting and the detailed methods of observation that went with it to make an interesting cross-cultural comparison between Midwest and a small town in Yorkshire, England, which they called Yoredale. The latter was slightly larger than Midwest but had fewer behaviour settings. Yoredale was also more controlling of its children in terms of entry to behaviour settings: the proportion of settings in Yoredale which required the presence of children was twice as great as in Midwest and the proportion that prohibited the presence of children was also greater.

Another idea that was derived from this work, and from Barker and Gump's (1964) comparison of large and small high schools, is that of *responsibility theory* (originally termed 'manning' theory). This is the theory that when there are relatively few individuals available for a certain number of settings—as in Midwest compared with Yoredale, or in small schools compared to large—then there is greater opportunity and felt pressure for individuals to take on roles or positions of greater penetration or responsibility (these settings are underoccupied or 'undermanned' in terms of the original theory). In line with these predictions, Barker and Gump found that students in small schools participated in a greater range of behaviour settings, and were twice as often active performers in their settings. Willems (1967) showed how this affected the integration of students who might otherwise be relatively uninvolved. Whereas middle-class students of relatively high IQ felt equal pressure to engage in extra-curricular activities in schools of different sizes, those of lower social class *and* who had relatively low IQs felt four times as much pressure in small schools than in large.

Responsibility theory has also been used to help integrate findings of research on the effects of size of organisation upon socio-emotional aspects of life in work settings. O'Donnell (1980) reviewed the evidence suggesting that there is a greater opportunity for social interaction in small work units, that there is a greater chance of the development of a sense of obligation to other members, and that members participate at a higher level in smaller organisations.

Wicker (1969) found much the same with church groups: small groups were associated with great involvement as shown by more attendance, more involvement in more behaviour settings, more taking of positions of responsibility, and more donating of money. There is presumably an optimal level of person occupation for any given setting; it must not be so well-occupied that opportunities do not exist for all to participate and take responsibility, but at the same time must not be so underoccupied that the demands upon members exceed their capacity to cope (Bechtel, 1984).

Small residential hostels are further examples of behaviour settings which generally give residents far greater responsibility than the alternative large institutions for the mentally ill or handicapped (see Chapter 9). Numerous further examples could be given of behaviour settings and their importance for human well-being. Whether or not public buildings provide wheelchair access is an obvious example of a setting characteristic which makes all the difference to the ability of people with physical disabilities to 'penetrate' community behaviour settings of importance to them.

ENVIRONMENTAL PSYCHOLOGY

Barker's ecological psychology was one amongst a number of broad conceptions of settings and systems that were useful as a background to planning social and community interventions according to Rappaport (1977) in his book on community psychology. Environmental psychology was another.

Environmental psychology has appeared to hold out great promise, as its name suggests, for revealing those aspects of the physical or designed aspects of the world which may have a direct causal influence upon human health and well-being, and hence for the possibility of designing or redesigning environments to prevent human problems. In fact very few such simple prescriptions have emerged. This is hardly surprising in view of the complexities of person and environmental interaction. After all, Lewin's (1951) dictum was that behaviour was a function of the *interaction* between person and environment, not that each alone had simple and straightforward effects upon behaviour. Nevertheless there do exist areas of environmental psychology where powerful and relatively uncomplicated effects of the physical environment can be demonstrated. We shall examine two such areas: the effects of design in psychiatric hospital wards, and the effects of high-rise dwellings.

One of the simplest and most convincing demonstrations of the effects of part of the physical aspect of behaviour settings is provided by the work of Sommer and Ross (1958) and Holahan (1972) who adopted the simple expedient of altering the arrangement of seating in the day rooms of a ward for elderly patients and of a general psychiatric ward. Dramatic increases in the amount of social interaction were achieved by altering seating from an arrangement they termed *sociofugal* (chairs placed in a large continuous square or oblong around the edges of the day room) to one they called *sociopetal* (seats arranged in a number of small, separate groups around focal points such as coffee tables).

Holahan and Saegert (1973) took this line of research much further by helping to completely redesign a psychiatric admission ward and by comparing the results on patients' behaviour and attitudes with those of a control group of patients who had been randomly assigned to a ward that was otherwise very similar, but which had not been redesigned. The remodelled ward was painted in bright off-white (compared with dull tan in the other ward) and the deteriorating brown marble that had covered the lower half of the corridor walls was covered with bright blue paint. In addition all doors and one wall in each room were painted in bright colours, and doors were colour coded according to the function of a particular room. In the control ward walls and doors were marred by scribbling that was rarely cleaned; in the remodelled ward when this did occur scribbles were cleaned off quickly by the staff. Attractive comfortable modern furniture was added to the day room, and this was arranged in a sociopetal fashion. Bedrooms on both wards were large dormitories, but on the redesigned ward a private section was created by installing six-foot high partitions which created a number of two-bed cubicles in each dormitory. A table and two comfortable chairs were placed in a screened-off area in each bedroom and brightly coloured bedspreads were substituted for the old ones. A second day room was arranged to facilitate watching TV or playing games, and new games equipment was supplied.

Time-sampled observation periods on the two wards showed significantly more social behaviour on the part of the patients in the remodelled ward, and significantly less 'isolated passive' behaviour. There was more socialising with other patients, with staff and with visitors, and the effect occurred in all four areas of the ward that were sampled (day room, dining room, bedrooms, corridors). When interviewed about the ward, patients on the redesigned ward described it as more attractive and stimulating, but the expected differences in positiveness of attitude towards staff and other patients were not found.

This, then, was an environmental manipulation which fairly convincingly had at least some of the desired effects. We can be fairly certain, however, that the effect was by no means as simple and straightforward as it appears. Holahan and Saegert refer to the fact that the university environmental psychology programme for which they worked had permission to plan, finance and direct the ward remodelling, and that they consulted with patients and staff about the changes that might be made. Thus their intervention had, from the beginning, some of the desirable, *social* features of organisational change interventions which will be discussed in Chapter 9. They also waited for six months after the remodelling of the ward had taken place before observing and interviewing patients. This was to make sure that any significant results produced could not be attributed to an immediate and short-lived effect of change on ward routine or staff behaviour or attitudes. One of the problems that had been found with simply changing the seating arrangement of an area, had been that the arrangement tended, in the natural course of events, to revert to its previous shape within a short time. In the case of Holahan and Saegert's redesigned ward, the changes introduced were multiple, they could not all easily be undone, and their effects appear to have lasted. The changes clearly had an effect upon social processes: for example they describe the way in which patients, especially the women, personalised their bedroom spaces by lining the window ledges near their beds with personal articles—something that did not happen on the control ward although identical ledge spaces were available.

Thus personal and social processes occurred as a result of the remodelling of the ward and these then helped to reinforce the hoped-for effects The final results were predicted but were by no means assured and the outcome would not necessarily be so favourable under other circumstances. This project, along with other work in environmental psychology, was one of the factors that contributed to a widespread move for upgrading psychiatric wards in the late 1970s. The fact that in many parts of the world these desirable changes were rapidly overtaken by the move to deinstitutionalise psychiatric hospital patients and to close hospital wards and whole hospitals altogether, is an illustration of the obvious but often forgotten fact that a small system such as a hospital ward is part of the larger hospital system and thence part of much larger social and political systems.

It is also the case that the effects produced by Holahan and Saegert can be brought about equally effectively in quite other ways. In fact Fairweather (1964) did just that. He produced dramatic changes in the social interaction of patients in a psychiatric ward, in comparison with that of patients on a physically identical ward, not by repainting and introducing other new design features, but rather by altering the social rules and routines.

Fairweather designed a 'small group' regime which involved some modifications to the traditional pattern of daily activities, but more important were changes in patient and staff role. Patients were divided into small groups which had responsibility for welcoming new patients, carrying out housekeeping tasks as a group, and monitoring each other's progress and making recommendations about privileges and even about the timing of fellow patients' discharge. Time was scheduled for these groups to meet together each day to discuss and make decisions. These changes in social structure had dramatic effects upon social behaviour in the ward in much the same way as did Holahan and Saegert's changes to the physical environment. Time-sampled observations showed, in comparison with the traditional ward, significantly more talking, more occasions when three or more people were interacting together, less inactivity and fewer incidents of symptomatic behaviour.

Hence, this first example of environmental psychology in action demonstrates two things. Firstly, it shows the dramatic effects that are possible as a result of the kind of environmental manipulation that Holahan and Saegert made. It also shows, however, the complex link that exists between the intervention and its results. Between the two intervenes a complicated social process, and the fact that two very different kinds of intervention can lead to similar outcomes is illustrative of this. We shall return to this point later in the chapter when considering the systems approach to person-in-context.

Our second comparatively clear-cut example, high-rise dwellings, also illustrates the complex and uncertain linkage between aspects of the physical environment and human behaviour and experience. It cannot easily be demonstrated that living in such an environment is causally related to a particular health or social outcome. As Kasl, White, Will and Marcuse (1982) put it: 'Residential variables [are] richly embedded in a large matrix of individual and social variables that condition and attenuate the impact of the residential environment' (cited by Freeman, 1984a, p. 221). Freeman's (1984a) review of the link between high-rise housing and mental health describes a number of studies which find the predicted effect. For example Hannay (1981) found a higher than average level of psychiatric symptoms amongst people living on the fifth floor or above of a high-rise block in Glasgow. But several other studies have found more complicated results. For example Ineichen and Hooper (1974) found a higher rate of symptoms in women living in houses in a redeveloped central area of Bristol than was the case for those living in high-rise flats, but the former had the largest number of children, and unsatisfactory environmental aspects of the area in which they lived could be held accountable for their relatively poor health. In London, Richman (1974) found a higher rate of depression amongst mothers living in flats compared to houses, but surprisingly the highest prevalence was found amongst those living in low-rise flats. Child-care and social contact appeared to be made more difficult by flat dwelling, whether high- or low-rise.

Apart from the complexity of the variables involved, another element making research difficult in this area is the fact that many people do not stay in high-rise flats very long, thus making it difficult to demonstrate an adverse effect on health (Freeman, 1984a). Even more insurmountable difficulties have surrounded other topics within environmental psychology and mental health. The possible effect of urban density is just one of these. Freeman's (1984b) review of this field suggests that a number of complexities have conspired to bring about a general verdict of 'not proven' where density and mental health are concerned. The complicating factors include: collinearity of variables (high density tends to correlate with poverty and lower socio-economic status for example); combined with the importance of mitigating factors (stability and homogeneity of the population seem to make high densities easier to bear for example); cultural relativity (one study found an increased rate of illness in France at a density that was associated with *low* rates of illness in Hong Kong); and the familiar question of whether it is objective density or *perceived* overcrowding which is most important. Each of these, and more, are likely to be relevant in the case of high-rise dwellings also.

It may be unreasonable to expect to discover simple relationships between a measurable aspect of housing environment, such as height above the ground or square metres per person, and the development of a particular type of ill-health or social disorganisation. The process that must be presumed to link the two, housing and health, contains so many steps (e.g. living in a high-rise dwelling—practical difficulties—feelings of isolation—vulnerability to stress—depression) that the relationship is bound to be at best a modest one and is certain to depend upon other circumstances. A more realisable aim may be to demonstrate predicted differences in the feelings and attitudes of those who dwell in different types of housing. This was the approach very successfully adopted by McCarthy and Saegert (1978) in their comparison of the experiences of tenants of 14-storey and 3-storey buildings in one low-income housing project in the Borough of Bronx in New York City.

Tenants in their study were selected from waiting lists and assigned to apartments at random as they became available. The only exception was that large families were not assigned to the high-rise building. The effect of family size was partialled out statistically and was found not to affect the results, which were extremely convincing. The main differences concerned perceptions of, and feelings about, the more public areas such as the lobby, lift and stairs, and about the project as a whole; there were no differences concerning the tenants' own apartments. The tenants of the high-rise buildings reported a lower *feeling of control* in the public areas and felt less safe there at night. They felt these areas were less private. They were less likely to identify with the whole project and they expressed more agreement with the statement, 'I don't feel there is much I can do to affect decisions made by the management'. They thought they were less likely to come to the aid of another tenant who was being attacked in the building, or to interfere in an act of vandalism. They reported less use of a bench area outside the building and less socialising generally.

MOOS AND THE CONCEPT OF CLIMATE OR ATMOSPHERE

It could be said that the tenants in the McCarthy and Saegert study were able to describe different *atmospheres* associated with their apartment buildings depending upon whether their buildings were high-rise or low-rise. This concept of perceived atmosphere or *climate* was taken much further by Moos in a sustained programme of research and action (e.g. Moos, 1974; Cronkite, Moos and Finney, 1984). By collecting perceptions of a particular setting by those who lived or worked in it or who were taught or treated in it, he was able to provide a profile which represented the participants' consensus about the atmosphere or climate of the setting. Although the process involved averaging the responses of individuals, like Barker and the environmental psychologists he was interested in providing a description at the level of the setting itself.

The method for obtaining a measure of perceived climate is a questionnaire and the results are expressed in terms of around nine or ten separate dimensions. The first such questionnaire to be developed was the Ward Atmosphere Scale (WAS) which was designed to collect the perceptions of patients and staff on psychiatric wards. There followed a similar questionnaire for assessing perceived environment of Community-Oriented Programmes (COPES), a similar scale for describing perceived family environment (FES), and others for assessing work settings, schools, penal institutions, and groups of various kinds.

The dimensions covered by the scales for assessing the climates of eight different types of environment are shown in Table 2. It was Moos's contention that the *relationship* dimensions of importance were more or less identical across a wide variety of different types of setting. In practice, these dimensions assess the degree to which participants feel positive about their setting. Moos made the same claim of universality for the *system maintenance* and *system change* dimensions. The *personal development* dimensions, on the other hand, vary more widely from one type of setting to another. For example, whereas *task orientation* and *competition* are thought to be dimensions relevant to the personal development of pupils in schools, in families the relevant dimensions are *independence, achievement orientation, intellectual-cultural orientation, active recreational orientation*, and *moral-religious emphasis*. It is likely that the relevance of these dimensions varies not only from setting to setting but also from one socio-cultural group to another.

Much less well known than the work of Moos, but in this author's opinion with very considerable potential for the development of theory in community psychology, is the idea of *primary emotional responses* to the environment. This concept, put forward by Mehrabian and Russell (1974), may have been neglected because it appears oversimple. They suggested that the emotional response evoked by a setting was crucial in understanding how people would behave in that setting. For example, if the setting evoked pleasure there would be a tendency to remain in the setting or to approach it in the future; if the setting produced feelings of arousal, people would be active in the setting; and if the setting gave people a sense of dominance, then individuals would demonstrate commitment and take responsibility. Emotions that people experience in settings would be partly an individual matter but would be equally powerfully determined by characteristics of the settings themselves. The

Table 2. Dimensions of perceived climate in eight types of setting (reproduced by permission from Moos, 1974)

Type of environment	Relationship dimensions	Personal development dimensions	System maintenance and system change dimensions
Treatment			
Hospital and community programmes	Involvement Support Spontaneity	Automony Practical orientation Personal problem orientation Anger and aggression	Order and organisation Clarity Control
Total institutions			
Correctional institutions	Involvement Support Expressiveness	Autonomy Practical orientation Personal problem orientation	Order and organisation Clarity Control
Military companies	Involvement Peer cohesion Officer support	Independence	Order and organisation Clarity Officer control
Educational			
University student living groups	Involvement Emotional support	Independence Traditional social orientation Competition Academic achievement Intellectuality	Order and organisation Student influence Innovation
Junior high and high school classrooms	Involvement Affiliation Teacher support	Task orientation Competition	Order and organisation Rule clarity Teacher control Innovation
Community settings			
Work milieus	Involvement Peer cohesion Staff support	Task orientation Competition	Work pressure Clarity Control Innovation Physical comfort
Social, task-oriented, and therapeutic groups	Cohesiveness Leader support Expressiveness	Independence Task orientation Self-discovery Anger and aggression	Order and organisation Leader control Innovation

(continued)

Table 2. (*continued*)

Type of environment	Relationship dimensions	Personal development dimensions	System maintenance and system change dimensions
Families	Cohesiveness Expressiveness Conflict	Independence Achievement orientation Intellectual-cultural orientation Active recreational orientation Moral-religious emphasis	Organisation Control

theory largely concerned responses to physical features of environments, but can equally be applied to reactions to social aspects of settings.

Mehrabian and Russell suggested that primary, emotional responses to the environment could adequately be described in terms of three dimensions: pleasure, arousal and dominance. Each is important in understanding the impact of settings but the emotional dimension which they termed 'dominance' is the most original and is one with obvious application to the social environment. Their concept of dominance was linked by them with variability in behaviour and with freedom of choice. A person is likely to feel more dominant in a setting where there is privacy or where personal territoriality operates, or where the person feels unrestricted or free to act in different ways. Mehrabian and Russell predicted that submissive feelings would be associated with physical stimuli that are rated as more intense or more ordered, and with formal social occasions, and with settings where the person is in the presence of others of higher status.

They commented that this dimension of emotional response had received little attention from investigators; nor has it received a great deal of attention since. Yet it may serve to link a number of aspects of environmental influence that are of interest to community psychologists. As Mehrabian and Russell noted, people are likely to feel more dominant in their own homes, and in settings where they have more behavioural independence. Dominance feelings may equate with a sense of personal control and freedom of choice. Some of the changes that occur when a psychiatric ward is remodelled, as in Holahan and Saegert's (1973) study, may be thought of in this way. Many of these changes are designed to increase privacy and a sense of personal territory.

INTERPERSONAL SYSTEMS

BRONFENBRENNER AND NESTED SYSTEMS

Although Barker (1968, 1978), whose work was discussed earlier, is principally remembered for his detailed descriptions of behaviour settings, he also thought in terms of systems. It is clear that he was very alert to the problem that has taxed the minds of many biological and social scientists, namely: When is a system to be thought of as a system in its own right, and when is it best thought of as part of a larger system or better thought of in terms of several, smaller component systems? This question of the appropriate level of analysis is a particularly important one for community psychology because of the tension, discussed in Chapter 1, between a traditional, individual level of analysis within psychology and the higher levels of person-in-environment, setting, or community, with which community psychology is concerned. For Barker: 'The unity [of a behaviour setting] is based ... upon the interdependence of the parts; events in different parts of a [setting] have a greater effect upon each other than equivalent events beyond its boundary' (1968, p. 17). Thus part of Midwest which had the appearance of a setting was not in fact a single behaviour setting if it contained parts that fell below a certain threshold of interdependence: the exact means of determining this was complex, and depended upon similarity and difference in terms of occupants, leaders, physical space, behaviour objects, etc. For example, the school system of Midwest did not qualify as a setting because it contained individual schools which were sufficiently independent. Indeed some individual classes within the schools were considered sufficiently independent to constitute behaviour settings: the secondary school Latin class was one, whereas all the primary school eighth grade academic classes together constituted a behaviour setting—details perhaps, but points which are very revealing about degree of integration or independence of different components of school life at different ages.

Person-milieu units might be sufficiently independent in day-to-day operation to be counted as separate behaviour settings, and yet clear authority relationships might exist between them. Barker identified a number of clear *authority systems* in Midwest. The greatest authority in the town seemed to be vested in the Elementary and High School Board meeting which had authority (i.e. 'direct and intentional intervention') over no less than 228 of the town's behaviour settings. At the other extreme, the Beauty Shop had authority over no other setting than its own! To describe relationships between systems at different levels, Barker used the analogy of nested assemblies—systems within systems, like Chinese boxes, each nesting within one slightly larger than itself. The same analogy was used and taken further by Bronfenbrenner (1979).

Bronfenbrenner is another influential writer who has remarked upon the imbalance in psychology between the close attention that has been paid to concepts of individual personality and developmental stages and the relative neglect of the environmental side of Lewin's classic equation. In the field of child development, which is the focus of Bronfenbrenner's interest, he pointed out that often little more is said about the environment than that a family is of a particular size, from a particular social class, or is of a particular ethnic background. Such undifferentiated concepts and categories, important though they are, are in contrast to the rich array of personality typologies and developmental stages which psychologists have developed.

The core of Bronfenbrenner's theory of development-in-context, or ecology of human development, is a set of nested structures which he refers to as the micro-, meso-, exo- and macro-systems (see Table 3). A micro-system is any context, such as a child's school or a person's home, of which the developing person has immediate experience. It includes the objects or people with whom he or she interacts in the setting, as well as the complex set of connections between other people there. Hence, the micro-system corresponds roughly with Barker's behaviour setting, although it is much less precisely defined and some of Bronfenbrenner's micro-systems (e.g. a whole school) would have been broken down by Barker into a number of relatively independent behaviour settings.

In fact Bronfenbrenner's and Barker's approaches complement one another well. Although Bronfenbrenner provided much less in the way of detailed description of his micro-systems, he added a number of vital ingredients for an ecology of human action which can form an adequate basis for community psychology. One was his insistence on the importance of *perception* of the environment and the person's evolving construction of reality—an aspect

Table 3. Systems at four levels (based on Bronfenbrenner, 1979)

Micro-level
　　Systems of which the individual person has direct experience on a regular basis, e.g. home, school, work group, club
Meso-level
　　System consisting of two or more of a person's micro-level systems and the links between them, e.g. home—school, hospital—patient's family, mother's family—father's family after separation
Exo-level
　　Systems that influence the person and the person's micro- and meso-level systems, but which the person has no direct experience of him/herself, e.g. a school governing body, a parent's place of work, the county transport department
Macro-level
　　Systems on a larger scale which determine the prevailing ideology and social structure within which the individual person and his/her micro-, meso- and exo-level systems operate, e.g. current rate of unemployment, other conditions of the labour market, gender roles in society

which Barker deliberately avoided. Second, was his overriding concern with *change*: indeed his interest in environmental systems lay in the capacity which he saw them as having for assisting change and development particularly in children. Third, although like Barker he recognised the importance of the physical and material characteristics of a setting and the activities and roles experienced by people therein, it was with the interpersonal relationships that the developing person experiences within the setting that he was principally concerned. Dyadic relationships involving joint activities and mutual positive feelings were thought to be the most important ingredient of a micro-setting for encouraging learning and development. He was also insistent on the importance of *second-order effects*. This refers to the enhancement of the potential of a dyad (e.g. mother–child) for aiding development if each partner has mutually positive relationships with third parties (e.g. father) who are supportive of the dyad's activities. Amongst other work, he cited in support a study by Hetherington (1972) showing the importance of continued, non-conflictual, contact with the father in avoiding some of the otherwise harmful effects of divorce upon children. An additional, important feature of Bronfenbrenner's view was the reciprocal nature of influence within micro-systems: developmental changes occur not only in children but also in their caregivers as a result of their dyadic interactions.

The meso-system, which has a particularly important part to play in the theory, is defined as the set of linkages that exist *between* micro-systems or settings which the person enters or will enter later in development. Bronfenbrenner formulated a number of hypotheses about the meso-system which together propose that development will be enhanced if two settings in which the developing person is involved are strongly rather than weakly linked.

By including exo- and macro-systems in his theory, Bronfenbrenner recognised the influence upon human behaviour and development of the wider environment and of higher-order systems. The exo-system consists of interconnections between those systems of which the person has direct experience (the micro- and meso-systems) and those settings which the person may never enter but which may nevertheless affect what happens in his or her immediate environment. The school board or governing body would be a good example, as Barker showed. A parent's place of work might be another. A macro-system consists of the wider pattern of ideology and organisation of the social institutions common to the particular social class, ethnic group, or culture to which the person belongs. Thus Bronfenbrenner recognised socio-cultural influence and the importance of social change. As an illustration he cited work by Luria (1976), suppressed in the Soviet Union for many years, which documented changes in individual cognitive processes (from concrete, concerned with practical activities, to the theoretical and abstract) which took place alongside a rising literacy rate in some of the remoter areas of the USSR during a time of rapid economic development and cultural change. This illustrates the influence of the macro-system upon an aspect of human functioning which has generally been considered on an individual level. War, the condition of the labour market, energy generation methods, and modern transport systems are other features of the macro-system which create the conditions for crises and disasters which in the end manifest themselves in individual disorder or distress (see Chapter 3 for the effects of unemployment, and Chapter 11 for responses to disasters).

The following quotation from Bronfenbrenner's book neatly sums up the field with which he was concerned:

> The ecology of human development involves the scientific study of the progressive, mutual accommodation between an active, growing human being and the changing properties of the immediate settings in which the developing person lives, as this process is affected by relations between these settings, and by the larger contexts in which the settings are embedded. (1979, p. 21)

THE INTERPERSONAL BEHAVIOUR THEORISTS

The nested systems model of Bronfenbrenner provides a structure within which many of the subject areas of community psychology can be located. In itself however, it has little to say that is systematic about the content of social interaction. For this, we can look towards interpersonal behaviour theory, and in particular towards those who have depicted interpersonal behaviour in terms of a circumplex such as that shown in Figure 1 (Leary, 1957; D. Kiesler, 1983; Strong and Hills, 1986). A number of variants of the interpersonal circumplex have been produced in the last 35 years. The one shown in Figure 1 is a slightly modified version of the Strong and Hills (1986) version. Basic to all such systems is the arrangement of codeable or rateable types of interpersonal behaviour (sometimes 16 in number, sometimes 8) around a circle, each type being represented by a point on the circumference or by a sector of the circle. Underlying this arrangement is the notion of there being two fundamental dimensions to human social behaviour: most commonly referred to as Dominance-Submissiveness and Hostility-Friendliness. There is strong evidence that two such dimensions exhaust a very great deal of the variance when people describe their own interpersonal behaviour or that of others, and when attempts are made to code objectively interpersonal behaviour occurring in a variety of different social contexts. Triandis (1977), for example, reviewed a wide range of psychological and anthropological evidence which included observations of the behaviour of children in different cultures, observations of mothers' behaviours, observations of leaders' behaviours, self-reports both within and across cultures, and peer ratings. The two basic dimensions, which he termed Superordination-Subordination and Association-Dissociation, were almost universally found in the studies he reviewed, and he concluded that they were cultural universals.

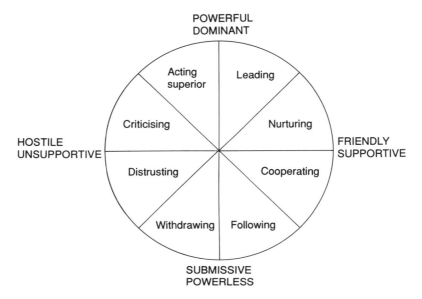

Figure 1. The interpersonal behaviour circumplex (based on Strong and Hills, 1986)

Leary's (1957) original use of the circumplex was to categorise deviant personalities—the aggressive-sadistic and the docile-dependent personalities for
example— but the principal use of the circumplex since then has been as a
framework to record, utterance by utterance, the interactions that take place
within micro-systems such as husband—wife and psychotherapist—client dyads
in terms of coding procedures derived from the circumplex model (e.g. the
Interpersonal Communications Rating Scale: Strong, Hills and Nelson, 1988).
The circumplex model of interpersonal behaviour is linked to a theory of
complementary action which in its simplest form states that action tends to
elicit similar behaviour along the horizontal axis of the circumplex (i.e.
friendly behaviour will tend to elicit friendly behaviour in return, and hostile
action will tend to be followed by hostile reaction), but *opposite* behaviour
along the vertical axis (i.e. dominant action tends to pull submissive reaction,
and vice versa). The present author has reviewed the evidence (Orford, 1986)
and has found that although there is general support for complementarity, the
exact directions in which it operates do not conform very closely to these
simple predictions.

The potential for community psychology of this type of model of interpersonal behaviour lies in the varied levels of analysis of social action to which
it has been or could be applied. In addition to its application at the level of
personality and the study of unit by unit sequences of interaction, this model
may equally be used to conceptualise and record social attributions, interper-

sonal perceptions, and attitudes towards the self as a social interactant (Leary, 1957; D. Kiesler, 1983). The circumplex also readily lends itself to role analysis. Terms used to describe behaviour and role often have the same derivation: managerial and manager, nurturant and nurse, critical and critic, for example. Through the chapters of this book we shall meet many roles and role relationships which can usefully be conceptualised in terms of the circumplex—a leader in a multidisciplinary team; consultant and consultee; advocate and partner; service user and service provider; action researcher, to name but a few.

Because of its ability to span levels of analysis from the personal to the social structural, the circumplex model lends itself particularly well to the study of interpersonal behaviour and relationships within social structures which ascribe or at least invite certain individuals to adopt an interpersonal style characterised by a predominance of certain behaviours. Behaviour in families and behaviour in organisations constitute two obvious fields of application. However, the use of circumplex theory and method to study the interface between interpersonal behaviour and personality on the one hand and social structural relations on the other, need not stop at the micro-level. Inter-group relations (for example relations between different professional groups who contribute to a multidisciplinary task), as well as relations between groups with common cause in society (e.g. based upon ethnicity, class or gender identity), as well as relationships between nations, are characterised by varying degrees of hostility or cohesion, dominance or dependence.

Finally, the circumplex approach to social relations underlines the importance of the two major social resources which are dealt with in detail in later chapters. Corresponding to the two dimensions of interpersonal behaviour, which some have claimed are universal and fundamental, are the social resources of *support* and *power*. There is a correspondence between the provision of social support within social systems and friendly behaviour at the level of individual action. Likewise there exists a correspondence between the granting of power and autonomy within social systems and the practice of dominant action on the part of individuals. It is this interface between individuals and systems (at the various levels of which Bronfenbrenner has written) that constitutes the very stuff of community psychology.

INTERACTIONISM AND PERSON–ENVIRONMENT FIT

There are numerous possible examples that could be given to illustrate Lewin's (1951) point, which is so central to community psychology, namely that human behaviour is a function of the interaction of person and environment. The first illustration of this theme is taken from a report by Raush (1965) of the behaviour of boys who were undergoing residential treatment on account of their aggressive conduct. It is an instructive illustration because the boys' bad past conduct—they were referred to as 'hyperaggressive'—would naturally lead to the expectation that personal or individual characteristics would be predominant, and also because their behaviour and also that of two control groups was observed and coded carefully. Each boy was observed for two separate periods of time in a number of different settings: all interactions with other boys and with adults were coded as either 'hostile' or 'friendly'. As expected, the hyperaggressive boys in treatment showed more hostility than control boys. However, Raush was able to show that slightly better prediction could be obtained by knowing in which setting the behaviour was occurring irrespective of which type of boy was being observed: for example whether boys were observed having breakfast, having a bedtime snack, during a structured games period, or doing arts and crafts. Knowing something about the person and in addition something about the setting gave the best prediction.

There have been many demonstrations that variables, such as aggression or anxiety, previously treated solely as properties of individuals are in fact a complex result of both person and setting in combination and in *interaction* (i.e. some settings are relatively more anxiety-provoking for some individuals, whilst other settings induce more anxiety in others). This is the interactional model of personality (Endler and Magnusson, 1976). This has led on to the adoption of ideas and terminology from ecology: for example the idea that adaptation is related to the goodness of *fit* between person and habitat.

For example, French, Rogers and Cobb (1981) adopted an interactional concept of stress using the idea of person-environment fit. Their prediction was that strain, and hence an increased likelihood of ill-health, would occur when there was an absence of fit between the two. This might take two forms: an individual's needs might not be met by the environment, or the demands of the environment might not be matched by the individual's abilities. For example, in the work setting, strain might result because an individual was unable to respond to a very high workload, or because the job was unable to provide a sufficient workload to satisfy the person's needs. Thus strain is a function of both the personal and environmental. Another way in which personal factors entered into their model was in terms of the individual's perceptions of self and environment—the *subjective* person and environment as they termed them. Strain, they predicted, would be a function of absence of fit between these two subjective perceptions, as well as being a function of the discrepancy between objective environment and objective person. Bronfenbrenner's (1979) principle, it will be recalled, was that what matters most for development is the environment as perceived rather than as it exists in supposedly objective reality. Indeed in practice, it was subjective fit that French, Rogers and Cobb measured in most of their studies. As predicted, they found evidence that such measures of fit could account for additional variance in strain, 'which cannot be predicted by linear relationships with the E or P components, either singly or in additive combination' (p. 43).

In their book on community mental health and behavioural ecology, Jeger and Slotnick (1982) also stressed the importance of the fit between the demands and resources of the environment setting on the one hand, and those of the person on the other hand, as a central feature of the ecological approach. The links between P and E are reciprocal, integrated parts of a system. Hence the relationship between the two is to be understood in terms of a continual, reciprocal *transaction* rather than as a matter of simple cause and effect operating in one direction or the other. This idea of transactional influence is a central one, to which we shall return often.

One of the consequences of complex, transactional influence is that outcome is difficult to predict. This is well captured in the two general systems theory (GST) principles of (i) *equifinality*, that is that the same outcome may be reached from different starting points and by different routes, and (ii) *multifinality*, that is that similar initial conditions can lead to different end states (Buckley, 1980). The example of changing patterns of behaviour on psychiatric hospital wards which was described earlier offers a good example. The same result—improved social interaction—could be brought about by very different means (the physical design approach of Holahan and Saegert or the social engineering approach of Fairweather), whilst the link between a planned change and the expected outcome is fraught with complex transactional processes and the hoped for result cannot be guaranteed.

There are other features of general systems theory which are in keeping with the ecological approach adopted by many community psychologists. One is the principle of *interdependence* which leads to the expectation that change in any one part of a system will alter the relationships between other parts, and that interventions in systems are therefore certain to have effects elsewhere, not all of which will have been intended or desired (Barker, 1968; Jeger and Slotnick, 1982). In practice, however, systems theorists have stressed the needs of systems to maintain themselves rather than the needs of individuals which may be to change the systems they are part of (Bowey, 1980). They have emphasised *morphostasis*, that is 'those processes in complex system-environment exchanges [which] tend to preserve or maintain a system's given form, organisation, or state' (Buckley, 1980, p. 39) to the relative neglect of *morphogenesis*, that is 'those processes which tend to elaborate or change a system's given form, structure, or state' (p. 39). The analogy which GST draws between social psychological and biological systems is only helpful up to a point (Buckley, 1980; Katz and Kahn, 1978) and community psychologists are much more inclined to stress the naturally occurring processes of change and the natural resources that members of communities and other social systems have for producing change.

Furthermore, whilst systems theory has principally been of value in applied psychology by exploring interdependencies within systems at one level—particularly family systems (Vetere and Gale, 1987)—community psychology is first and foremost about interdependencies *between* levels. In particular it deals with the transactions between, on the one hand, the individual and the micro-systems of which he or she is a part and, on the other hand, the wider meso-, exo- and macro-systems (to use Bronfenbrenner's terms) which influence and are influenced by the person.

The bias in psychology has been towards an exclusive focus upon the individual or at most the micro-system of the family. If, as J. Tizard (1976) suggested, applied psychology has concentrated on formulations of human problems and ways of treating them which focus on individuals without paying due attention to the wider systems that may have affected them, we run the risk of 'blaming the victim' (Ryan, 1971; Mitchell, Davidson, Chodakowski and McVeigh, 1985) and of intervening at the wrong level and hence becoming 'part of the problem' (Rappaport, 1977).

Such dangers may exist with all manner of problems and all social groups, but they are perhaps most obvious in the case of adolescents in trouble with authority. Rappaport cited the example of residential treatment which was designed to prevent the institutionalisation of young boys in trouble, but which in fact *increased* later institutionalisation compared with boys in a neighbouring control town: an outcome which Rappaport attributes to blaming the boys rather than their environment. Brown (1986) also criticises the medico-psychological model that has prevailed in the area of services for adolescents, and has taken psychologists in Britain to task for working more in institutions and rarely close to the communities in which young people live.

The characteristic neglect of higher system levels on the part of 'helping agents' was well demonstrated by Whittle's (1984) study of an Observation and Assessment Team for youths who had been in trouble with the police or who had had difficulties at home or at school. Part of his evaluation of this team involved asking four of the team's staff members (three social workers and an educational psychologist) to describe what they felt to be the causes of the young peoples' difficulties. The largest category, making up nearly 65 per cent of all the causes mentioned, referred to the micro-system of the youths' families, for example unrealistic parental expectations, parents reinforcing immaturity, absent or ineffectual father, inconsistent rules between parents. A further 25 per cent were intrapersonal, referring to the individual youth, for example immature, plays off parents, unpredictable mood changes. Almost all the remainder, a relatively small number, referred to school influences. No references at all were made to higher order influences such as home–school links (Bronfenbrenner's meso-system), local Council decisions about leisure facilities (the exo-system), or the national climate of expectations and opportunities for young people of that generation and socio-economic status group (the macro-system). The kind of psychology that has influenced that team of human service workers and countless others is one that has focused heavily on the intrapsychic and the small-scale interpersonal. This has not been true of psychology's companion discipline, anthropology, and a comparison between the two is instructive.

In his intriguing book, *Psychology and Anthropology*, G. Jahoda (1982) pointed out that psychology, which on the whole has ignored the ordinary behaviour of persons in their social settings, and anthropology, which has on the contrary provided, 'a unique fund of information about the lives of people in an enormous number of eco-cultural settings' (p. 3), have common roots and were at one time much more closely associated than they have been in recent years. Seminal anthropological ideas can be seen to have great relevance now for community psychology. They include Durkheim's discovery that there were social regularities in rates of suicide, his idea of *collective representations* (see Moscovici's, 1981, modern variant of *social representations*); Radcliffe Brown's central idea of the social system—as a set of relations amongst events, actions, interactions and transactions; Malinowski's belief that peoples' own views about their actions, their beliefs and their ideas must be collected (caught in his famous phrase, 'to grasp the native's point of view'); and the functionalist dogma that, 'cultural details must always be viewed in context, that everything is meshed with everything else' (Leach, 1976, p. 5, cited by Jahoda). In fact Jahoda was critical of Durkheim and some anthropologists for ignoring the individual level totally: according to Jahoda, Durkheim believed that collective representations could not be accounted for at the individual level, and some anthropologists have written as if: 'Man is infinitely malleable and plastic, so thoroughly shaped by his social milieu that his influence, singularly or in aggregate, can be discounted' (Murphy, 1971, p. 68, cited by Jahoda).

As illustrations of the interlinking of the environmental and the personal, Jahoda asked, rhetorically, whether the almost universal tension between men and their mothers-in-law, and the traditional preference for cross-cousin marriage in some parts of West Africa are to be taken as examples of psychological causation in terms of motives, or of the importance of socio-economic factors. His answer was that: 'The relationship is best regarded as a dialectical or feedback process, whereby social system and psychological factors are in continuous interaction' (1982, p. 49). A consequence of continuous feedback and the transactional nature of the systems we are considering, is that they change over time, in a way that makes it even more difficult to unravel the threads of causation. Here again there is much to be learnt from an anthropological approach since, as Jahoda pointed out, anthropological analysis has often been informed by an historical perspective, often lacking in psychological research.

CONCLUSION

In this chapter a number of separate theoretical approaches have been presented. Although they are separate, there are clearly many points of contact and overlap between them. For instance, dominant interpersonal behaviour and dominance feeling as a primary emotional response may be more prevalent when behaviour settings are penetrated further or when settings provide their occupants with greater responsibility. Individuals may experience more friendliness and may feel more supported if the links that constitute a meso-system are working well. Groups may experience powerlessness if an exo-system or the macro-system are operating without regard for the effects of their decisions upon the inhabitants of local communities. Nevertheless, it has to be admitted that despite these evident connections between the different theoretical schools of thought, the development of a unified theory for community psychology remains a task for the future. At least some of the ideas from this chapter, along with those to be presented in the following three chapters, should prove to be of value for such a task.

3 Psychological Problems in the Community

If the theoretical ideas presented in the previous chapter are to be helpful in the endeavour of community psychology, they must find their application in explaining what we already know about psychological problems in the community, and in suggesting hypotheses and applications so that our understanding and ability to respond may be enhanced. Hence, this chapter will consider some of the major lines of research that have examined the incidence and prevalence of psychological problems in the general population, and their relationship with factors such as gender, social class, and area of residence. It will look at the stress-vulnerability model of psychological disorder and at marital disruption and unemployment as two specific sources of stress. A major theme throughout the chapter, continuing a line of thought started in Chapter 2, will be the question of causation: are we witnessing social causation, social selection, or reciprocal influence?

Most of the theoretical ideas in Chapter 2 have come from psychologists in the USA, where community psychology as a discipline is much further advanced than elsewhere. In contrast, most of the research upon which this chapter draws has been done in Britain. This is no accident since, thanks largely to support by the Medical Research Council and the Economic and Social Research Council, some of the best work in social and epidemiological psychiatry and in certain areas of applied psychology has been carried out in Britain. The work of Brown and Harris and their colleagues on the stress-vulnerability model of depression in the community, and the work of Warr and his team in Sheffield on the psychological effects of unemployment, are leading examples.

POPULATION SURVEYS OF MENTAL HEALTH

Before describing some examples of population surveys, some terms should be defined. The terms *incidence* and *prevalence* are basic to epidemiology but are easily confused. Incidence, sometimes called 'inception rate', is the number of *new cases* of a particular phenomenon that arise in a specified population during a specified period of time. It is usually expressed as a rate per thousand or sometimes per hundred thousand of the population. To have any meaning it is vital that the population and the time period (often one year) to which it refers are specified. Prevalence refers to the total number of *active cases* present in a specified population. If it refers only to those cases active at a particular point in time (say on the day on which a survey was carried out) then it is termed 'point prevalence'. If it refers to all those cases active at any time during a specified period (often a year) then it is termed 'period prevalence' and the period of time to which it refers must be stated (Goldberg and Huxley, 1980; Hartnoll, Daviaud, Lewis and Mitcheson, 1985).

The source of information for estimating incidence or prevalence should also be specified. For example if the source consists of the records of treatment agencies, then the resulting figures are estimates of 'treated incidence' or 'treated prevalence' and are likely to be underestimates of true incidence or prevalence in the population at risk.

Although these terms originated in the study of the spread of infectious diseases they are nevertheless useful in the context of many forms of disability or problematic behaviour, as Hartnoll *et al.* (1985) made clear in their very useful manual for assessing the nature and extent of problematic drug use in a community (the methods they propose will be considered in greater detail in Chapter 6). They are also of value in focusing attention upon, and more clearly conceptualising, efforts at prevention. As we shall see in Chapter 8, primary prevention may be thought of as aiming to reduce overall prevalence by means of reducing the rate at which new cases arise (i.e. by reducing incidence). Secondary prevention, on the other hand, may be thought of as aiming to reduce prevalence by identifying and treating cases at a relatively early stage, hence reducing the duration of an illness or problematic form of behaviour.

One illustrative population survey of psychiatric disorder will be described in some detail. As well as illustrating something of the methods used in this kind of epidemiology, this example also makes two points that are fundamental to the argument of this chapter. The first is simply this: that forms of psychological distress or difficulty most fully documented and described by those who work in specialist settings such as hospitals or child guidance centres, turn out to be very highly prevalent when the trouble is taken to ask relevant questions of those in the community at large. The second is that rates of distress are not random in the community but are patterned by demographic and social groupings. The most straightforward patterns to detect are variations in rates according to socio-economic status, gender, employment versus unemployment, and marital status.

The most comprehensive, recent British survey of adult psychiatric problems in a community sample was carried out by Bebbington and his colleagues in the Camberwell area of South London, when 800 adults (excluding those of age 65 or above) were interviewed by agency interviewers using a shortened version of the Present State Examination (PSE), a standardised interview for making psychiatric diagnoses at various, defined levels of confidence. Most had been selected at random from the electoral register, but because the electoral register has some deficiencies as a sampling frame due to underenumeration, a certain number of interviews were added to correct for this. A further 212 who were selected refused interviews or were not available at this stage. At the second stage a fuller interview (including the full version of the PSE) was carried out with 310 members of the original sample. Second interviews were sought with all those whose PSE results at the first interview suggested a psychiatric disorder of at least 'threshold level' plus a random sample (approximately one in three) of the remainder. Another 44 refused interview or were not available at this stage. These longer interviews were carried out by research unit staff (Bebbington, Hurry, Tennant, Sturt and Wing, 1981).

The PSE method produces a one-month prevalence estimate for psychiatric disorder, which in this survey turned out to be 14.9 per cent for women and 6.1 per cent for men. Bebbington *et al.* pointed out that these figures coincide well with those produced by most recent community surveys of adult psychiatric disorders carried out in industrialised countries. Despite differences in survey instruments used, these have tended to produce prevalence estimates within the range 4–8 per cent for men and 8–15 per cent for women. Most of the disorders detected in the Camberwell survey were relatively mild and nearly all the diagnoses were of depression (most frequent) or anxiety. Excluding those 'cases' defined as being at 'threshold level' (level 5) and including only those at levels 6–8 yields a much stricter estimate of prevalence (2.2 per cent for men and 4.9 per cent for women). However, Bebbington *et al.* summarised the evidence that including level 5 gives the greatest correspondence with global, clinical ratings of 'disorder' and is most likely to correspond with judgements used in hospital out-patient settings.

Although the numbers of 'cases' produced by a study of even this size and level of sophistication are small (only 14 men and 39 women with level 5–8 disorders were interviewed at the second stage), tests were made of a series of hypotheses derived from the general theory that a substantial proportion of the common psychiatric disorders found in a community sample, 'can be regarded as symptomatic distress reactions to a combination of adverse environmental forces, the severity of the reaction being proportional to the balance of adverse and protective factors that have accumulated over a period of time' (p. 561). Of the social and demographic factors examined, employment outside the home versus unemployment was the one that produced the strongest relationship with disorder (prevalence figures of 5.5 per cent and 8.7

per cent for employed men and women respectively versus 13.6 per cent and 25.4 per cent for unemployed men and women). Secondly, a significant inter-action effect was found involving marital status and gender. Whereas the prevalence for married men was lower than that for men who were unmar-ried—either never married or separated, divorced or widowed—(2.6 per cent versus 13.8 per cent) the opposite was the case for women (18.4 per cent versus 9.5 per cent). Amongst different sub-groups that could be created on the basis of these variables, the highest prevalences were found amongst married, non-employed women (41.4 per cent) and non-married, non-employed men (36.0 per cent) and the lowest amongst married, employed men (4.4 per cent).

Regarding social class differences, 20 of 25 population studies reviewed by Dohrenwend and Dohrenwend (1969, cited by Bebbington *et al.*), reported higher rates of psychiatric disorder in the lowest status groups and more recent studies have found the same, including some British studies (Brown and Harris, 1978; Cochrane and Stopes-Roe, 1980). Bebbington *et al.* (1981) did not find a significant difference in prevalence between middle-class and working-class interviewees although they did find a trend in the expected direction (3.8 per cent middle class versus 9.1 per cent working class for men and 11.1 per cent versus 17.5 per cent for women) which would be highly sig-nificant and important if repeated with larger numbers, and they also found a much increased prevalence (24.3 per cent) which was statistically significant, amongst men in the very lowest socio-economic status groups (categories 34–36 in the Goldthorpe and Hope, 1974, scheme of prestige rankings of occupations).

A study by Cochrane and Stopes-Roe (1980) used a different sampling method and a different means for identifying psychological disorder, but found some similar results to those of Bebbington *et al.* (1981). Cochrane and Stopes-Roe trained interviewers employed by a survey research company who then interviewed a total of 232 adults in a number of English cities. They used the *random-walk* technique for drawing a sample. This method, which involves selecting a street at random, calling at every home on one side of the street until an interview is obtained, missing a specified number of addresses before another call is made, and continuing in this way following strict rules for moving from one street to another, is a relatively inexpensive way of pro-ducing a sample which is fairly representative of the general population. Unlike Bebbington *et al.*, their aim was not to decide which interviewees could be counted as 'cases' and to find out what variables were associated with caseness, but rather to assess all respondents on a scale known to be sound as a measure of 'mild, undifferentiated psychopathology' (the Langner 22-item scale, used in the famous Midtown Manhattan Study of Mental Health in New York—Srole, Langner, Michael, Kirkpatrick, Opler and Rennie, 1978) and to see what socio-demographic variables were associated with scores on this scale.

Like Bebbington *et al.*, they achieved moderately high correlations between psychopathology and socio-demographic factors (multiple correlations of 0.43 for women and 0.42 for men). Once again the strongest association was with employment status, the unemployed having very significantly higher scores. The inverse association with socio-economic status that has been found in most community surveys was also found by Cochrane and Stopes-Roe, and in this case the results were statistically significant.

The gender difference found by Bebbington *et al.* and many other survey researchers was again found by Cochrane and Stopes-Roe, with women having significantly higher Langner scale scores. Marital status was not associated with psychopathology, neither was the interaction effect between gender and marital status found by Bebbington *et al.*, recorded in this study. According to Williams (1984) who has reviewed work on sex differences and mental illness, Cochrane and Stopes-Roe's finding on this point is more in line with the general run of results than is Bebbington *et al*'s. She found little support for the theory, advanced by Gove (1972), that rates of mental illness amongst the married were higher for women, but amongst the unmarried were higher for men. She found stronger evidence for a *main*, rather than *interaction*, effect of gender, with higher rates for women irrespective of marital status.

THE PATHWAYS TO CARE

A community orientation in the mental health field has been encouraged by the evidence, accumulating from studies such as these, that large numbers of individuals with psychological disorder are not known to specialist agencies. This point has been well made by Goldberg and Huxley (1980) who described a *filter model* of the 'pathways' to specialist psychiatric care. Since, in the UK at least, the pathway to psychiatry almost always involves the general medical practitioner, successful referral for specialist help requires that the patient pass through each of three filters (see Figure 2). The first necessitates that the individual with a psychiatric disorder does in fact consult his or her GP. Because most people consult their GPs some time in the course of any one year, and because individuals with psychiatric complaints consult more frequently than others, this is a relatively easy filter to pass through. The remaining filters are much less permeable, however. To pass through the second requires that the GP recognises the existence of a psychiatric difficulty, and the third requires that the GP decides upon specialist referral rather than upon treating the problem within general practice. Combining their estimates of the proportions of people filtered out at the different stages, Goldberg and Huxley estimated that around 1 in 15 of all individuals in a community with problems that would be detected by surveys such as Bebbington *et al*'s. (1981) in fact reach the specialist psychiatric level of care. Whether people are always better served by more specialised, professional treatment services (Spector,

	The community	Primary medical care		Specialist psychiatric services	
	Level 1	Level 2	Level 3	Level 4	Level 5
	Morbidity in random community samples	Total psychiatric morbidity, primary care	Conspicuous psychiatric morbidity	Total psychiatric patients	Psychiatric in-patients only
One-year period prevalence, median estimates	250 →	230 →	140 →	17 →	6 (per 1000 at risk per year)
		First filter	Second filter	Third filter	Fourth filter
Characteristics of the four filters		Illness behaviour	Detection of disorder	Referral to psychiatrists	Admission to psychiatric beds
Key individual		The patient	Primary care physician	Primary care physician	Psychiatrist
Factors operating on key individual		Severity and type of symptoms; Psycho-social stress; Learned patterns of illness behaviour	Interview techniques; Personality factors; Training and attitudes	Confidence in own ability to manage; Availability and quality of psychiatric services; Attitudes towards psychiatrists	Availability of beds; Availability of adequate community psychiatric services
Other factors		Attitudes of relatives; Availability of medical services; Ability to pay for treatment	Presenting symptom pattern; Socio-demographic characteristics of patient	Symptom pattern of patient; Attitudes of patient and family	Symptom pattern of patient, risk to self or others; Attitudes of patient and family; Delay in social worker arriving

Figure 2. The pathway to psychiatric care (from Goldberg and Huxley, 1980, *Mental Illness in the Community: The Pathway to Psychiatric Care*, reproduced by permission of Tavistock Publications)

1984) is not the point here, although it is highly relevant to the subjects of later chapters (especially Chapter 10).

The point here is rather that the numbers using specialist services provide a gross underestimate of the total amount of similar distress in the community as a whole, and that the routes to specialist treatment are complex and uncertain even in a country with a comprehensive and well-used system of primary health care. Although the details may be different in countries such as the USA where some people at least have more direct access to specialist services, or with the development, as seen in the UK in recent years, of community mental health centres with easier access (see Chapter 11), the overall picture is unlikely to be very different.

The same model can be used with other kinds of psychological difficulty. The present author, for example, has estimated, on the basis of existing research findings, that within a typical UK health district of a quarter of a million people the number of adults who are consuming alcohol in excess of medically recommended levels is likely to be in the region of 20 000, and the number experiencing some degree of social, medical or psychological problem related to their drinking approximately 7500. Of this number, around 1250 are likely to have been identified by a treatment or helping agency of any kind (including general practices, social service and probation departments, and voluntary agencies) and only approximately 125 will have received treatment for an alcohol problem within the specialist mental health services (Orford, 1987a). Again, although the details may have chanced in recent years with the setting up in many areas of community alcohol teams, which appear to improve access considerably for this client group (Stockwell, 1988), the overall conclusion that the majority of people in need are unlikely to be known to specialist services, or even to non-specialist agencies, probably remains unchanged.

THE GEOGRAPHICAL DISTRIBUTION OF DISTRESS

Although the foregoing work in epidemiological psychiatry has established rates of problems for a community or population, and for sub-groups, and some of the details of the routes to care, the basic unit of analysis remains the individual, and the conception of a problem remains as a form of distress or disorder located firmly at the individual level. An approach within psychiatric epidemiology which begins to consider higher system levels is that based upon geographical district. This approach has sometimes been termed the 'ecological' approach (Cochrane, 1983) although this use of the word is rather different from the more general sense in which the word is used in Chapter 2 and elsewhere in this book. From the classic work of Faris and Dunham (1939) on rates of treated schizophrenia in different districts in Chicago, onwards, it has been found that a variety of psychological problems, including treated mental illness, have higher incidence and prevalence rates in the poorer areas of cities in comparison with better-off areas. Studies in Bristol, Edinburgh and Croydon provide British illustrations of this approach. Although such findings raise as many questions as they answer concerning aetiology, they are of undoubted importance in establishing the needs of communities and in planning services.

In the first of these three studies, Morgan, Pocock and Pottle (1975) calculated the annual incidence rate of *deliberate self-harm* (largely drug overdoses) in the 28 electoral wards in the City of Bristol for a two-year period. Incidentally, they chose the term 'deliberate self-harm' because the alternatives—such as 'attempted suicide' and 'parasuicide'—imply a unitary reason for all such acts, or imply a resemblance to suicide. After correcting incidence rates to allow for the fact that certain wards contained higher proportions of social groups most at risk (particularly young women), Morgan, Pocock and Pottle found that rates in wards with the highest incidence exceeded those in wards with the lowest incidence by factors of as much as nine (women) and six (men).

Using the most recent census then available to obtain socio-demographic indices and rankings for the different wards, they were able to show that significant rank-order correlations existed between incidence rate and overcrowding (percentage of households living at a density of more than 1.5 persons per room), the proportion of residents born outside the UK, the proportion of households not having exclusive use of all domestic amenities, and the percentage of households not having a car. The correlation with overcrowding was high (0.76). The three wards with the highest rates were all inner-city wards, two of them areas of sub-standard housing, overcrowding and poor amenities, the third being part of the city's bedsitter land with a high proportion of rented accommodation. The two wards with the lowest rates were each situated on the outskirts of the city and both had above average proportions of owner-occupied households.

It is very important, in considering the results of studies such as these, to be careful not to make the assumption that *individuals* who harmed themselves are more likely than others to have had those same characteristics that define high-risk *areas*. So common is this mistake of referring to community characteristics as if they were characteristics of individuals, that it has been given a name: the *ecological fallacy* (Cochrane, 1983). The Morgan, Pocock and Pottle study in Bristol provides a good case in point: although wards with higher proportions of immigrants to the UK tended to be those with the higher self-harm incidence rates, an interview sub-study of nearly 400 individuals who had harmed themselves found the number of immigrants to be very little higher than that in the city as a whole. In the case of overcrowding, on the other hand, *individuals* who harmed themselves were found to be five times more likely to live in overcrowded accommodation than was true for the city as a whole.

Unlike the Bristol study which was based on attendance at accident and emergency departments throughout the city, the Edinburgh study (Holding, Buglass, Duffy and Kreitman, 1977) was based on the register maintained since 1968 at the Regional Poisoning Treatment Centre at Edinburgh Royal Infirmary to which almost all hospital-admitted self-poisoning patients were admitted. It should be noted that Holding *et al.* estimated, on the basis of previous research, that around 30 per cent of episodes of what they preferred to call 'parasuicide' that were known to medical agencies, were treated in general practice and were not referred to hospitals, and were thus undetected by studies such as those carried out in Bristol and Edinburgh.

Some of the Edinburgh findings for individual characteristics were the same as those found in Bristol. For example, rates were generally higher for women than for men and were higher for younger adults than for older. Interestingly enough the two alternative hypotheses about the link between gender, marital status and psychological difficulties (see above) each received some support from the Edinburgh data. For those aged 15–34 years rates were higher for women than for men irrespective of marital status, thus providing support for the *gender main effect* hypothesis (Williams, 1984). For those aged 35 years or more, however, there was support for Gove's (1972) *gender marital status interaction effect* hypothesis, with the highest rates being found amongst single men and married women.

Holding *et al.* reported that it was a consistent finding that parasuicide was more prevalent in lower socio-economic status groups. Their data certainly supported this expectation with a rate of male admissions for those in the Registrar General's occupational category V (manual, unskilled) being no less than 14 times as great as that for categories I and II (professional, managerial and higher clerical). The Bristol data, for men and women combined, showed a more modest difference in the same direction (the rate for group V being approximately twice that for groups I and II). Findings for overcrowding were similar to those for Bristol although by the mid-1970s rates for those individuals overcrowded and those not had converged and were no longer different.

What is particularly important for present purposes, however, is confirmation from the Edinburgh study that large differences exist between different districts. In Edinburgh there was a sixfold difference between the highest and lowest ranking wards. Though one of the three wards with the highest rates was in the centre of the city—an area containing much hostel and night shelter accommodation—unlike Bristol the other two were on the edge of the city, containing large inter-war housing estates noted for a wide diversity of social problems. The ward with the lowest rate was predominantly a middle-class, owner-occupier district.

The third study of this kind which will be mentioned here by way of illustration of this general approach is a study of referrals to a child guidance clinic, plus children who came before the courts, in one outer London borough during a five-year period in the early 1960s (Gath, Cooper, Gattoni and Rockett, 1977). The borough chosen, Croydon, was ideal because of its socially mixed population and its single, centrally located child guidance clinic. Rates of referral for child guidance varied amongst the 20 electoral wards in the borough by a factor of three from highest to lowest. The pattern across the wards was much the same for court appearances, although in this case the ratio of rates for the highest and lowest ranking was as much as 14. The highest rates of clinic referrals and court appearances were found in the densely populated inner wards of the borough, together with one outlying housing estate where many families from the decaying parts of the borough had been rehoused. Across electoral wards rates of both child guidance referrals and court appearances correlated positively with proportions of inhabitants in occupational categories IV and V (manual, semi-skilled and unskilled), and with proportions of households renting from the local authority, and both correlated negatively with proportions of persons in occupational categories I and II and with percentages of persons in owner-occupied homes. Correlations with density of population (percentage of persons in households living more than one to a room) were positive, but only became statistically significant when a more detailed analysis was carried out which involved breaking electoral wards down into smaller units—enumeration districts containing approximately 400 households each.

SOCIAL CAUSATION OR SOCIAL SELECTION?

Not only must we be aware of the ecological fallacy in interpreting such findings as these, but we are also faced with a choice in deciding in what direction we believe causality to be operating. As with Faris and Dunham's (1939) original work on mental illness in Chicago, there are two major competing explanations: *social causation* and *social selection*. Broadly speaking these alternatives correspond to two explanations that are always available whenever individual phenomena (mental illness, self-poisoning, addiction, delinquency, mortality and morbidity rates, etc.) are found to be correlated with social or cultural factors (wards of a city, poverty, immigration, social class, etc.). Either the social or the cultural factor has *caused* the individual-level phenomenon (social causation) or else the individual phenomenon (or a tendency or proneness for it) is responsible for differences in the social or cultural factor (social selection). Faris and Dunham originally assumed that the poverty and disorganisation found in the inner city areas in Chicago were responsible for producing the higher rate of schizophrenia, and only later did Dunham admit that it was equally plausible that people with schizophrenia tended to become poor and disorganised (Cochrane, 1983).

The same two explanations have created much unresolved controversy over the years when it comes to explaining the repeated finding that rates of mental illness and psychological distress are highest in the lowest socio-economic status groups. The social selection hypothesis has taken a variety of different forms. One is that individuals who develop psychiatric problems drift downwards in social status as a result—hence the expression *social drift* which is the term by which these hypotheses are frequently known. Evidence in support includes the finding that the distribution of social status for fathers of the mentally ill is much more normal than is the case for the mentally ill themselves, suggesting downward social mobility compared with the previous generation. It also includes the finding that occupational status is often lower than educational achievement would have predicted. A second variant of the social selection hypothesis is that drift has occurred, not just within a single generation but across several generations. A third variety says that, since the proportion of individuals categorised as belonging to the lowest socio-economic status groups has declined in recent decades in the most industrialised countries, then individuals who develop psychological difficulties need not have drifted downwards in status but rather have tended to *remain* in lower status groups whilst others have risen.

Although there has been a move towards greater support for social selection, overall results are inconsistent and the controversy continues. For example, Link, Dohrenwend and Skodol (1986) showed that, consistent with the social drift hypothesis, the first occupations of individuals treated for schizophrenia in an area of New York were equal in status to those of community controls but that the most recent occupations of the former group were significantly lower in status. In support of social causation, however, they showed that a significantly greater proportion of the first occupations of people with schizophrenia had what they called 'noisome characteristics': that is they were characterised by conditions of noise, heat, cold, fumes or physical hazards. In the survey carried out by Cochrane and Stopes-Roe (1980), referred to earlier, the fact that the relationship between psychopathology and downward versus upward social mobility (own occupational status, or that of husband in the case of married women, compared to father's status) was *not* statistically significant suggested to these researchers that social causation rather than social selection was more likely to be operating in their sample.

Of course in terms of ideas of transactional causality introduced in the previous chapter, it is not likely to be useful to think of social causation and social selection as being opposed theories, one of which will ultimately be proved correct to the exclusion of the other. As we shall discover repeatedly, it is usually the case when considering the relationship between variables at different levels (individual person and social environment in this instance) of a causal model, that the relationship between these variables is found to be *reciprocal*. The relationship between two factors A and B may be best depicted, not in terms of one or other of the rival causal hypotheses (A → B or B → A) but rather as a relationship of mutual influence (A ↔ B). In terms of statistical procedures for causal modelling, more complex causal models containing more than two variables are said to be *non-recursive* if they contain reciprocal relationships depicted with double-headed arrows in this way. This distinguishes them from *recursive* models where the causal influence operating between any pair of variables is depicted as unidirectional and all the arrows in a diagrammatic representation of the model have single heads (Asher, 1983).

In the case of social class and mental health and illness, Allen and Britt (1983) have performed a useful task in spelling out some of the ways in which a non-recursive model might work (see Figure 3). In their model the relationship between social class and psychological disorder is mediated by stressful life events. However, the relationship between life events and disorder is seen as reciprocal: not only is the existence of stress thought to increase the probability of disorder, but the existence of disorder is also thought to increase the likelihood of occurrence of certain kinds of stressful life event. Social class position is seen as acting in at least two ways: it affects the likelihood of stress, but also affects the speed with which the feedback between disorder and stressful life events occurs and how large an impact each has upon the other. A relatively privileged class position is thought to dampen the life events—disorder feedback loop. Stressful life events may also act back upon social class position: losing a good job and having to take one of lower status is just one of the more obvious ways in which this link may occur. The model is made still more complicated by the introduction of the idea of *resources*—personal, social and economic—the relative absence of which confers vulnerability.

The details of their causal scheme are less important for our purposes than is the general argument that relationships between variables in a model need not be thought of as unidirectional as implied by the simple social causation or social drift hypotheses. When more facts are in, clearer support may be obtained for one of these theories than for the other, or stronger support for one in the case of some types of psychological problem rather than others, but allowing for the possibility of reciprocal influence increases the range of possibilities very considerably.

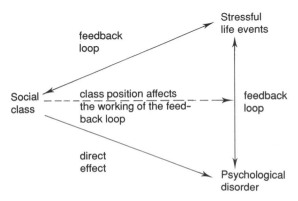

Figure 3. A feedback model of social class and psychological disorder (based on Allen and Britt, 1983)

QUALITY OF LIFE

The studies of parasuicide and of child guidance referrals and juvenile delinquency, discussed earlier, and others like them, have drawn attention to
qualities of the social environment as possible determinants of individual distress and difficulty. A rather different approach to the same subject is one that
has come to be referred to as *quality of life* (QOL). The QOL movement represents, like community psychology itself, a broadening out of concepts about
psychological health and distress from an individualistic, symptom-oriented
approach to include a broader range of factors including properties of
neighbourhoods and communities. Much of the work on QOL, including the
pioneering work of Lehman (1983) has focused upon the quality of life for
people with disabilities or with long-term needs for rehabilitation or care.

Lehman's own work was carried out with a random sample of all adults
with a history of psychiatric hospitalisation who were living in large (at least
40 beds) licensed board-and-care homes in Los Angeles County in the USA.
The median length of stay in the homes was between two and three years. A
study of the quality of life of such a sample is of course particularly relevant
to the debate about community care since this kind of arrangement has been
much criticised for providing a poor substitute for proper care in the community. It could be argued that in some respects living in such residential
accommodation may compare unfavourably with life in a large institution:
the latter may, for example, have given residents more opportunity to walk
around their immediate environment in safety.

Each participant in this study was asked about his or her life satisfaction
in each of eight areas: living situation, family relations, social relations,
leisure activities, work or unemployment, finances, personal safety, and
health. The choice of these areas was based partly on previous work with users
of psychiatric services, and partly upon the growing body of work on QOL
and social indicators in the general population. This latter work, which began
with studies of community samples in the USA (e.g. Andrews and Withey,
1976) has been extended to the European Community and other countries
(e.g. Andrews and Inglehart, 1979). In Lehman's work each of the eight areas
was assessed by a number of seven-point rating scales which ran from 1 = 'ter-
rible' to 7 = 'delighted'. Although at least half of the residents said that they
were at least 'mostly satisfied' in most life areas, there were three life areas
in which more than half were dissatisfied: finances, unemployment (the large
majority were unemployed), and personal safety. A comparison with Andrews
and Withey's US national data showed this group to be significantly less
satisfied than the general population in almost all QOL areas (Lehman, Ward
and Linn, 1982).

Lehman went on to use these data to test some aspects of the QOL model
shown in Figure 4 (taken from Lehman, 1983, p. 369). In particular he was
interested in whether *objective* indicators are correlated with *subjective*, and

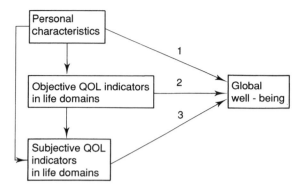

Figure 4. A model of quality of life (reproduced by permission from Lehman, 1983, *Arch. Gen. Psychiat.*, **40**, 369–373. Copyright 1983 American Medical Association)

which provides the better prediction of overall life satisfaction or sense of well-being—a question that has interested many people who have researched in this and related areas. Residents' feelings of global well-being were asked about in three slightly different ways (a single seven-point rating scale, a multiple-item scale of positive well-being, and a series of semantic differential ratings), and results were very similar whichever criteria were employed. A hierarchical regression analysis strategy was used: personal characteristic variables were tested alone at the first stage; objective QOL indicators were added at the second stage; and finally subjective indicators were included at the third. Overall, personal characteristics such as marital status, educational level and psychiatric diagnosis explained relatively little of the variance in global well-being (4–7 per cent), objective indicators accounted for rather more (14–23 per cent), and subjective indicators clearly the most (48–58 per cent) (Lehman, 1983). This pattern of results was consistent with that from similar analyses of general population data (Andrews and Withey, 1976; Campbell, Converse and Rodgers, 1976). Note that it is also in line with Bronfenbrenner's (1979) assumption that it is the *perception* of the environment that is most important, not its objective characteristics (see Chapter 2).

Although correlations between objective and subjective indicators were generally low and often insignificant, there were a number of significant correlations. For example, frequency of contact with family significantly correlated with satisfaction with family relations; social contacts within the board-and-care home (but not contact outside) were significantly correlated with satisfaction with social relations; hours worked per week and total pay per week were both significantly correlated with work satisfaction for those in work; having been the victim of crime in the last year was significantly negatively correlated with satisfaction with personal safety; and use of health care was significantly negatively correlated with satisfaction with health (Lehman, Ward and Linn, 1982). In general, it was Lehman's belief that both objective and subjective factors are important and need to be taken account of in planning better community services.

In particular three objective QOL indicators and four subjective QOL indicators provided the most consistent prediction of perceived global well-being: (a) *not* being a victim of crime during the past year; (b) *lower* total medical care used during the past year; (c) the frequency of intimate social relations in the past year; (d) health satisfaction; (e) satisfaction with leisure time; (f) satisfaction with social relations; and (g) satisfaction with finances. These results suggested to Lehman that future programmes for this group should aim for the following:

> (1) To improve patients' safety in and around board-and-care homes; (2) to ensure that their utilization of health services is appropriate and to make available alternative services that meet their nonmedical QOL needs; (3) to enhance their social skills and opportunities for establishing more satisfying relationships, especially within the board-and-care homes; (4) to identify the types of daily activities, whether leisure- or work-related that they find most satisfying; and (5) to improve their financial resources such as through more realistic work opportunities or more generous entitlement programmes. (Lehman, 1983, pp. 372–373)

This conclusion, that both objective features of the neighbourhood environment and the individual's own subjective experience (two sets of factors which are themselves related although very imperfectly), need to be taken into account in providing a satisfactory model of quality of life, provides us with yet another example of one of the main themes of this book. Like social support and power, two other central concepts for community psychology, which will be examined in detail in the following two chapters, quality of life is at the same time both environmental and personal.

THE STRESS-VULNERABILITY MODEL

Another illustration of the same point is provided by work on the stress-vulnerability model of psychological disorder. The role of social class, stress and vulnerability to one particular type of psychological disorder, namely depression, has been closely examined by Brown and his colleagues in a series of studies amongst women in two contrasting areas of Britain. These studies, although continuing to be based upon the individual 'psychopathology' tradition, have done much to stimulate awareness of social factors, including the nature of community life in the contrasting parts of Britain in which they took place. The areas in which these surveys were carried out were Camberwell in South London, which contains a largely working-class, inner-city area, and an adjacent inner-suburban area, and the Islands of North Uist and Lewis in the Outer Hebrides off the North-West coast of Scotland. In contrast to the London area, the survey areas on these islands represented a rural environment where a traditional way of life had been retained by some of the residents. The greater part of this rural population still relied upon the working of smallholdings, known as crofts. Many crofts were very small however, and earnings needed to be supplemented with other types of work, such as fishing, weaving, tourism and work in the oil industry away from the islands. Another characteristic of the islands, in contrast to the London area, was the strong influence of the Presbyterian church: of women who took part in the survey in the Hebrides 63 per cent were church attenders, compared with only 14 per cent in Camberwell.

Over 800 women took part and depression was assessed by means of the Present State Examination (PSE). The one-year period prevalence for depression was found to be significantly greater in Camberwell (15.1 per cent) than on the islands (11.0 per cent), and the rate for North Uist, the more traditional of the two islands (8.4 per cent) was lower than on Lewis (12.9 per cent) (Brown and Prudo, 1981). That social factors are heavily involved one way or other is shown by the analyses that were carried out within the two samples. In Camberwell depression was class-related (class being judged by the occupation of the, usually male, head of household—on the Hope–Goldthorpe scale) with a higher rate of depression among working class women (22 per cent) than amongst middle-class women (7 per cent) (Brown and Harris, 1978). In the Hebrides on the other hand, depression was not related to occupational status but was strongly related to what Brown and Prudo (1981) called *integration* into a traditional way of life. Two factors were involved in their definition of integration: (a) type of dwelling/involvement in crofting and (b) churchgoing. Rates of depression varied from 3 per cent for churchgoers involved in crofting full or part-time to 43 per cent for non-churchgoing women living in council housing.

In the earlier work in Camberwell, Brown and Harris (1978) developed a model of the social origins of depression in women which involved stressful *provoking agents* (severe life events and major long-standing difficulties) and a number of *vulnerability factors* which appeared to make women more susceptible to depression when provoking agents existed. Provoking agents and vulnerability factors explained the class difference in depression in Camberwell. Working-class women had more severe events or major difficulties (57 per cent versus 39 per cent for middle-class women). They were also more vulnerable, having more than their share of four factors which were significantly associated with depression only in the presence of provoking agents. The four factors were: having three or more children at home under the age of 14; not having an intimate, confiding relationship with husband or boyfriend; having lost her mother before age 11; and lacking employment outside the home (this last factor was only important when a woman lacked a confiding relationship with husband or boyfriend).

The presence or absence of stressful provoking agents helped explain both the difference in prevalence of depression in Camberwell compared to the Hebrides, and the different rates amongst women who were more or less integrated into the traditional way of life on Lewis (these data were not available for North Uist). On Lewis 31 per cent of women had had at least one severe event or had had a major difficulty in the year before interview, compared with 48 per cent in Camberwell. Churchgoing women in full or part-time crofting had the lowest rate of provoking agents (15 per cent), considerably lower in fact than middle-class women in Camberwell (39 per cent). Non-churchgoing women living in council housing on Lewis had the highest rate (53 per cent), a rate very similar to that of working-class women in Camberwell (57 per cent). Severe health-related events differed little between women in different circumstances, but there were large differences in terms of household and socio-sexual events. Events and difficulties cited by Brown and Prudo (1981) as being typical of those occurring amongst the least integrated women on Lewis were: having an illegitimate child; a daughter leaving her husband; a husband starting work on the oil rigs off the island; a best friend moving away; and a son drinking heavily. Events and difficulties involving either economic issues, or 'delinquencies' were virtually absent amongst women involved in full or part-time crofting. As in Camberwell, the experience of a severe event or difficulty in the year before interview was much more frequent amongst women with an onset of depression in the year than amongst other women (81 per cent versus 25 per cent).

Two of the factors that appeared to confer vulnerability to depression amongst women who experienced provoking agents in Camberwell appeared to play a similar role on Lewis—lack of a confiding relationship with husband or boyfriend, and the presence of three or more children under 14 at home.

There have been a number of direct attempts to replicate Brown *et al*'s work. These include Campbell, Cope and Teasdale's (1983) examination of the onset of affective disorder amongst working-class women in Oxford, Murphy's (1982) study of the development of depression in older adults, and Costello's (1982) replication of Brown's work in Calgary in Canada. Almost directly comparable are other studies of the stress-vulnerability model such as Solomon and Bromet's (1982) study of the onset of affective disorder amongst mothers with young children living within 10 miles of the notorious accident at the Three Mile Island nuclear power station in Pennsylvania (they were compared with a control group of mothers who lived elsewhere and who therefore did not experience this life stress which involved evacuation for many and the threat of it for others).

Each of these studies confirmed a higher rate of onset of affective disorder or depression specifically amongst those who experienced stressful life events. In the case of older adults, continuing poor physical health was additionally important (Murphy, 1982). The general stress-vulnerability model was confirmed: some individuals were more vulnerable in the face of stressful events although the precise details of Brown *et al*'s. model, in terms of the vulnerability factors involved, were not confirmed. The vulnerability factor that did emerge, however, in all these studies was lack of intimacy or a confiding relationship. It seems that the general model may be along the right lines, but that some of the specifics may vary from area to area. Certain vulnerability factors found to be important by Brown *et al.* in an urban area in London may not be important in non-urban areas (Solomon and Bromet, 1982) or in urban areas, such as Oxford, where housing for example may be more satisfactory (Campbell, Cope and Teasdale, 1983). Costello (1982) also questioned Brown's conclusion that stress was *causative* of depression onset since he found a stronger stress-depression link for those stressful events and difficulties which might possibly have been affected by an onset of depression (e.g. marital separation).

THE STRESS OF MARITAL DISRUPTION

Bloom, Asher and White (1978) focused upon one stressful life event in particular. They chose marital disruption (separation or divorce) because of its high frequency (affecting more than 2 million adults per year in the USA) and because of the convincing evidence that such events can be highly stressful. They pointed to consistently higher rates of divorced or separated marital status amongst psychiatric patients than amongst the general population (ratios of admission rates for divorced and separated persons to those for married persons varying from 7:1 to 22:1 for men and from 3:1 to 8:1 for women). They also cited the Midtown Manhattan survey (Srole *et al.*, 1978) as an example of a community survey of mental health which had found a substantially higher rate of psychiatric impairment amongst the separated and divorced (approximately 40 per cent compared with 20 per cent for the married). Bloom, Asher and White also cited evidence that motor vehicle accidents, alcohol problems, days of restricted activity due to ill-health, doctor visits, rates of suicide and homicide, and incidence figures for a number of major physical conditions, were all higher amongst the divorced and separated particularly within a period of six months immediately following separation.

Bloom, Asher and White outlined four logically possible causal hypotheses to explain the link between marital disruption and psychological disorder. The first, a selection hypothesis, supposes that there is an increased rate of separation amongst individuals with disorder or proneness to disorder which existed prior to marriage. The second suggests that the marital role offers protection against disorder and that this protection is lost when a person experiences marital separation. The third and fourth are stress hypotheses, the third supposing that the stress associated with disorder causes an increased probability of separation, and the fourth, which is the one that Bloom, Asher and White believed was best supported by the weight of existing evidence, suggesting that separation is itself stressful and causes an increased rate of disorder. They reviewed the results of a number of interview studies which testified to the complex set of losses which can be associated with marital separation. These included economic, affectional and community losses, as well as psychological losses involving the self-concept. These same studies suggested that stress might be greater for those who have been longer married, who have children, who were less active in taking the decision to separate, who have fewer alternative contacts, and who have been more recently separated.

THE STRESS OF UNEMPLOYMENT

Unemployment and its effects provides an excellent example of the macro-level system and its influence upon the lives of individuals. Overall rates of unemployment are affected by factors, way beyond the control of individuals or their micro-systems, such as international recession, labour shortages during and after major war, and whether or not a country has, like Sweden, a national policy of work for all (M. Jahoda, 1979; Banks and Ullah, 1988; Brenner and Starrin, 1988). Certain groups are more likely to experience joblessness at times of overall high unemployment. For example, young blacks in Britain have been at higher risk of joblessness during the late 1970s and 1980s (Banks and Ullah, 1988). Women too still constitute a kind of 'reserve army', entering the labour market at times of high employment but withdrawing from it, often partially or temporarily, when jobs are less available (Banks and Ullah, 1988). According to the novel and important thesis developed by Warner (1985), the mentally ill have constituted a similar 'reserve army', being welcome in the labour market at times of worker shortage and excluded from it when jobs are scarce.

There is now a considerable body of convincing evidence that unemployment causes psychological distress amongst those individuals who experience it. Cross-sectional studies showing higher rates of disorder and distress amongst the currently unemployed raise the kinds of interpretive problems concerning causation which we have met in other contexts. But as well as studies of this kind, there have been a number of longitudinal investigations which show that levels of mental health fall and rise as employment is lost and regained. The series of studies conducted at the Social and Applied Psychology Unit in Sheffield, England, have produced what is probably the largest data base on this subject in the world (Dooley and Catalano, 1988). Summarising the results of these studies, Warr, Jackson and Banks (1988) state:

> significant main effects of employment status have consistently been identified. Unemployed people experience higher levels of depression, anxiety, and general distress, together with lower self-esteem and confidence. From studies examining changes in status over time, unemployment is seen to be causally implicated in the creation of these differences. (p. 64)

Of this series of studies the one reported by Banks and Ullah (1988) in their book *Youth Unemployment in the 1980s: Its Psychological Effects* may be picked out for special mention because it focused upon unemployed 16-year-old school leavers. The study involved two interviews, one approximately a year after the sample had left school and the second a further year later. As a result of this and other studies of youth unemployment, Banks and Ullah concluded: 'It would seem therefore that there is now very strong evidence pointing to unemployment as a major factor in psychological impairment in this age group' (p. 69).

Other investigations that have examined the effects of unemployment longitudinally include studies of the effects of the closure of industrial plants in the USA (Kasl, Gore and Cobb, 1975) and of a shipyard in Denmark (Iversen and Sabroe, 1988).

Research on the effects of unemployment has also shown, however, that the effects are not uniform. For example, there is some evidence that middle-aged men experience increasing distress as a period of unemployment lengthens whilst the level of distress stabilises much sooner for younger people (Warr, Jackson and Banks, 1988). Young blacks become pessimistic about their chances of obtaining work sooner than young whites, but the latter become equally pessimistic after some months of continual unemployment (Banks and Ullah, 1988). Those with certain kinds of social support available to them experience significantly less distress (Bolton and Oatley, 1987; Banks and Ullah, 1988; and see Chapter 4). Warr (1987) has put forward a nine-category model of the psychological functions of employment, and has used these to attempt to explain the effects upon individuals of unemployment and some of the differential effects upon different sub-groups. The nine functions are:

> (1) opportunity for control, (2) opportunity for skill use, (3) externally generated goals, (4) variety, (5) environmental clarity, (6) availability of money, (7) physical security, (8) opportunity for interpersonal contact, and (9) valued social position. (Warr, Jackson and Banks, 1988, p. 62)

The adverse effects of unemployment may continue to accumulate for middle-aged people because of lack of alternative sources for numbers 6–9. Some unemployed teenagers may be able to use parents and peers to compensate in these respects.

In Britain the psychologist who has sustained the longest interest in the psychology of unemployment, spanning the recession years of the 1930s and the more recent years of high unemployment in the 1970s and 80s, is undoubtedly Marie Jahoda (1979, 1988). She has consistently argued for the importance of the latent functions of work for people:

> Whether one likes or hates one's job, it structures time for the day, the week, the years; it broadens the social horizon beyond family and friends; it enforces participation in collective purposes; it defines one's social status; it demands reality-oriented activities ... the enforced categories of experience provided by employment

meet fairly enduring human needs for time structure, activity, social contacts, participation in collective purpose, and knowing where one stands in society. (1988, pp. 17–18)

This macro-level variable of unemployment rate thus seems to affect individuals profoundly. Banks and Ullah (1988) calculated that the rate of psychiatric 'caseness' amongst the teenagers they studied was 2.7 times higher amongst the unemployed than amongst the employed. Platt and Kreitman (1985, cited by M. Jahoda, 1988), whose work on parasuicide in Edinburgh was cited earlier in this chapter, estimated that parasuicide occurred nine times more often amongst the unemployed than amongst the employed. Nevertheless, Jahoda is insistent that social phenomena should not be reduced solely to the individual level. As she provocatively put it: 'To state psychiatric conclusions individualises an issue that is essentially a social one. ... The cure lies not in individual therapy but in the creation of jobs' (p. 21).

INEQUALITIES IN PHYSICAL HEALTH

It is not only in the field of mental health that social correlates of disorder exist. The clearest collection of evidence for Britain in the case of physical illness is the Black Report, the report of a working group set up by the government under the chairmanship of Sir Douglas Black to look into the question of Inequalities in Health. The group reported in 1980 but the report was not properly published and circulated, and after much furore and public debate a version edited by Townsend and Davidson (1982) was published two years later.

Examining available figures from the 1970s for mortality and morbidity, the report revealed major differences in mortality rates for the sexes (higher rates for men than for women in all occupational classes) and for different regions (higher rates in Wales, the North of England and the East Midlands). The bulk of the evidence they presented, however, bears on the relationship between ill-health and occupational class. Overall mortality rates were found to be inversely related to occupational status for both sexes and all ages. The differences were particularly marked for the perinatal and neonatal period, in childhood, and amongst young to middle-aged adults. This inverse relationship held for almost all individual illnesses and conditions (diabetes and heart disease being examples of the very few conditions showing an opposite pattern). The relationship with class was found to be particularly strong in the case of accidents, infectious and parasitic diseases, and bronchitis and pneumonia among infants and children, and for similar illnesses plus gastric disorders in adults. For example, boys in class V (from families where the breadwinner had an unskilled manual occupation) had a ten times greater chance of dying from fire, falls or drowning than those from class I (professional and higher managerial occupations). For deaths caused to youthful pedestrians by motor vehicles the corresponding ratio was more than seven. Among adult males the ratio for pneumonia was nearly three and for bronchitis five.

Figures for morbidity are less easily available, but they exist in the findings of general surveys such as the General Household Survey (GHS), surveys carried out for specific research purposes, and medical consultation rates. These sources confirmed the overall and widespread inverse relationship with occupational status, particularly in the case of chronic sickness. For example in 1976 the GHS found a regular gradient across occupational class groups for rates of 'limiting long-standing illness' with a rate in the unskilled manual group three times that found amongst professionals and senior managers.

Correlations like these, between socio-economic status and morbidity and mortality, have been found regularly and in many countries, both 'developed' and 'developing' (D. Williams, 1990). The Black Report offered three alternative, broad explanations for this pervasive link between physical illness and occupational status. Social causation, or the materialist or structuralist explanation as the authors termed it, emphasises poverty and associated sociostructural factors in the distribution of health and well-being. They pointed out that, although standards of living have greatly improved this century and the major killer diseases of the last century have been all but eradicated, inequalities in the distribution of income and other resources continue, and changes, such as the introduction of new types of industrial process, continually introduce new hazards which bear unequally upon people in different positions in the occupational hierarchy. Furthermore, poverty can be thought of in relative terms (a point developed more fully by Townsend, 1979): the definition of poverty is not absolute but changes as expectations and norms change. Not to be able to afford a telephone, a private means of transport, a holiday, or moderately expensive Christmas presents for children or grandchildren, now puts a person at a disadvantage in society, where once it would not have done so.

The authors of the report conceded, however, that there was also evidence that might support one or other of the two main rival explanations. The first of these is familiar to us, namely social selection: people who are ill or prone to illness have drifted into lower occupational status groups or have tended to be left behind in lower status groups as others have risen. The second alternative to materialist or structuralist explanations is an example of a *third variable* explanation, a familiar phenomenon in social theory. If a link is found between two variables (illness and status in this case), the first may cause the second (selection) or the second the first (social causation). Alternatively a third variable (usually unmeasured and therefore uncertain) may be the real cause of the first variable (illness) but may be linked to the second (status) hence explaining the apparent link between them. In this case the suggested third variable is *health-related behaviour*. As the authors of the report point out:

Such explanations, when applied to modern industrial societies, often focus on the individual as a unit of analysis emphasising unthinking, reckless or irresponsible behaviour or incautious life-style as the moving determinant of poor health status. ... What is implied is that people harm themselves or their children by the excessive consumption of harmful commodities, refined foods, tobacco and alcohol, or by lack of exercise, or by their under-utilisation of preventive health care, vaccination, antenatal surveillance or contraception. (Townsend and Davidson, 1982, p. 118)

At the time of writing the present book, this kind of person-blaming explanation appears to be much favoured by the UK government. It is, however, possible to see behaviour which is conducive to good or bad health in less individualistic terms, embedded more within styles of life that are associated with and reinforced by class divisions in society. If this is so then they are surely amongst the most important aspects of the macro-level social system with which community psychology must come to terms.

4 Social Resources I
Social Support

With this chapter and the next we turn to examine in detail two resources which, it will be argued, are central to human development and well-being. These are *social support* and *power*. As was pointed out in Chapter 2, they correspond to the two major dimensions of social behaviour identified by the interpersonal behaviour theorists. Their importance for community psychology lies in the fact that each stands at the interface between the individual and the social systems of which he or she is a part.

As we shall see, social support—the subject of this chapter—has largely been thought of as an individual-level variable; something that an individual person possesses and which can be assessed by putting certain well-chosen questions to that particular person. In fact some have argued that levels of social support have more to do with an individual's own idiosyncratic ways of perceiving his or her social world, or perhaps with the person's social skills or competence On the other hand, the questions used to assess this construct refer to various aspects of support received *from* other people. Hence the assumption has usually been that social support assesses an aspect of a particular person's external social world or social community. Others have preferred to conceive of social support as a characteristic of networks or communities and not of individuals at all. Hence all shades of interpretation have existed, from the most individualistic to the sociological. For the moment, however, the important point to note is that social support is an attractive contender for a central place in community psychology because it appears to have strong potential for helping us understand the links between individuals and their communities.

Not surprisingly, therefore, social support is a subject that has intrigued an unusually wide range of disciplines (Boyce, Kay and Uitti, 1988). In sociology, the relatively recent popularity of the term 'social support' and intensified interest in the subject reflect a continuation of a long-held interest in social integration within communities (R. Turner, 1981). In psychology, interest in social support is relatively new and for many psychologists its fascination lies in its links with more traditional areas of interest. One of these is the study of *roles* and *role behaviour*. Kahn and Antonucci (1980) took a lifespan approach to social support and were therefore particularly interested in how the need for social support, and its availability, changes over the life course. These are closely related to the roles that people adopt at different times in their lives. They made the identical point about the concept of role linking the individual to the social world as was made about social support above. They referred to:

> the unique quality of the role concept as a link between the social and individual levels. Communities, organisations, groups, and extended families are all structures of roles, and the life of the individual can also be conceptualised in terms of the roles that he or she holds and enacts. (p. 261)

Hirsch (1981), who also favoured a life-course perspective, placed the subject of social support even closer to an interest in individual psychology by relating it to the concept of *personal identity*. Indeed in his opinion the two notions of social support and identity were inseparable:

> Each of the various life spheres—family, friends, vocational, moral/ethical, leisure, sexual and so on—has its own sets of possible identities ... social identities are recognised and supported by being embedded in relationships. (p. 161)

As a final illustration of this point that social support links the social and the individual, reference can be made to the work of Andrews and Withey (1976), whose research on individual life satisfaction is amongst the best known on that topic. They concluded that most people view the satisfactoriness of their social relationships as being one of the most important determinants of their overall feelings of life satisfaction.

THE STRUCTURE OF SOCIAL SUPPORT

In the assessment of social support two broad and distinct approaches exist. The most commonly adopted approach has been the *functional*, focusing on aspects of the quality of a person's relationships or the ability of those relationships to serve certain important support functions. The nature of these functions will be considered shortly. The alternative *structural* approach, which focuses on certain aspects of the structure of *networks* of relationships will be examined first.

A useful introduction to the structural or network approach is provided by Tolsdorf's (1976) admirably clear account of his comparison of the social networks of 10 psychiatric patients (all with diagnoses of 'schizophrenia') and 10 medical patients. The network variables which he included are shown in Table 4. *Size* refers simply to the number of people listed by the 'focal person' as

Table 4. Social network variables (based on Tolsdorf, 1976)

Structure	Content	Function
Size	Relationship density	Functional indegree
Adjacency density	Multiplex relationships	Functional outdegree
	Kinship members	Asymmetric relationships
	Kinship linkages	Functional people
		Adjacency density of functional people
		Relationship density of functional people

being included in his or her social network according to some stated criterion: in this case it was necessary that the focal person and the person in question knew each other by name, that they had an ongoing personal relationship, and that they had some contact at least once a year. *Adjacency density* is a measure of the extent to which the focal person's network is interconnected. It refers to the number of dyadic relationships that exist between people in the focal person's network, as a proportion of the number of such relationships that are possible given the size of the network. In a network containing n people there are $n(n-1)/2$ possible relationships. Hence, if x is the actual number of relationships amongst these people, the formula for computing adjacency density is:

$$\frac{2x}{n(n-1)}$$

The second column of Tolsdorf's table refers to *content*. By this he meant the nature of the relationship between the focal person and a member of his or her network. He considered 12 broad content areas: primary kin, secondary kin, primary friend, secondary friend, economic, recreational, political, religious, sexual, fraternal, mutual aid, and service. *Multiplex relationships* were those that contained more than one content area, and Tolsdorf assumed that such relationships were more powerful and more important to the focal person. He also thought it important to assess how many of the person's network linkages were with *kinship members*, and how many of all the linkages in the network were accounted for by kin. These variables could be expressed as absolute numbers or as proportions of the whole. *Relationship density* was the average number of content areas per relationship for the focal person, and was therefore an attempt to assess the intensity of the focal person's relationships.

Tolsdorf was also interested in the functions that relationships might serve for the focal person, and in the third column of his table are listed a number of measures that are confined to that part of the network which included only those people who served three specific functions (support, advice and feed-back) for the focal person. These functions will not be defined more closely here since the functional approach to social support will be considered in more detail later. Tolsdorf's measures included the number and proportion of people who served these functions for the focal person (*functional people*), as well as the adjacency density and relationship density of the network confined to such people. He was also interested in whether there was an imbalance in the functions which people in the network served for the focal person, and those served for others *by* the focal person (*functional indegree* and *outdegree* respectively). These were based on the total number of functions served and could be expressed as absolute numbers or as averages per relationship. Finally, *asymmetric relationships* refers to the number or percentage of the focal person's relationships which displayed some imbalance between functions received and given by the focal person.

Tolsdorf's paper provides a useful introduction to the network approach because his methods and measures were comparatively straightforward. This approach can be taken much further and can become much more complex. Larger networks can be considered if we include links or ties beyond those people with whom the focal person has a direct relationship (hence tapping part of Bronfenbrenner's exo-system). Other measures of the characteristics of a network then become possible, such as *reachability* (the average number of ties required to link any two network members), and the existence of *cliques* (portions of networks in which all members are tied directly, that is portions where there is a density of 1.0) and *clusters* (portions of networks with high density, but defined by less stringent criteria than cliques) (Hall and Wellman, 1985).

Tolsdorf's approach produced positive results in his small-scale comparison of two groups. The medical group had a higher relationship density, more multiplex relationships and greater functional outdegree, whilst the psychiatric group had a higher proportion of kinship members and linkages, more functional in degree, and a higher proportion of asymmetric relationships.

A useful extension of the idea of personal networks of socially supportive individuals is the notion of *convoys over the life-course* introduced by Kahn and Antonucci (1980). They conceived of the focal person (P) surrounded by a 'convoy' of supportive others who travel with P through his or her life-course, with members leaving the convoy and others joining it as time goes on. One hypothetical example is shown in Figure 5. The convoy is depicted in terms of three concentric circles around P. Closest to the centre of the diagram are depicted those relationships which are most important to P, which are potentially the most supportive, and which are least dependent upon current role positions. These are thus likely to be the most stable relationships and those that would be accompanied by the greatest sense of loss if they were to cease for any reason. Furthest from the centre of the diagram are those relationships that are most directly tied to current roles (e.g.

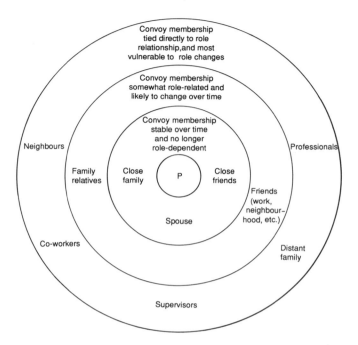

Figure 5. Hypothetical example of a convoy of socially supportive others (from Kahn and Antonucci, 1980, reproduced by permission of Academic Press)

as neighbours or co-workers) and which are thus most vulnerable to role changes. The convoy idea adds the all-important dimension of change over time and also serves to link the topic of social support with that of role. It shares with network approaches the aim of building up a picture of the network of direct relationships experienced by one focal person.

Conducting a network analysis around a single person as the focus has been by far the commonest practice but it is by no means the only way to proceed. Indeed Hall and Wellman (1985) have mounted a vigorous argument for the importance of examining the structures of whole networks in the study of social support and health. They believe that the focus on individuals destroys much valuable information about social structure; for example, the importance of mutual ties to third persons for understanding dyadic relationships, and the existence of clusters and cliques. They conceive of social support as a variety of social resources that flow through ties and nets, and they do not see the links and ties themselves as constituting social support. They also believe that a focus on individual, supportive links for individuals runs the risk of neglecting the importance of non-supportive ties in a network. Furthermore, an analysis of wider social structures enables social support to be seen within the power, influence and communication channels of a network. They conclude:

> The focus on intimacy or support and the use of network concepts in a conventional individualistic manner both reinforce a tendency to seek solutions for health problems by changing individuals ... A broader structuralist approach, however, expands the scope of investigation toward an understanding of why stress and attendant health problems develop in various social contexts ... . (p. 38)

Structural measures alone may be insufficient to capture the quality of socially supportive relationships, however (Cohen and Wills, 1985; Kahn and Antonucci, 1980), and many have recommended a combined structural and functional approach that examines properties of social networks and at the same time the content and functions of the relationships contained within them (e.g. Leavy, 1983; Mitchell and Moos, 1984). Tolsdorf's (1976) study is one of the few to have achieved this.

THE FUNCTIONS OF SOCIAL SUPPORT

A great deal of work has taken a purely functional approach, and Table 5 summarises some of the main functions which have been subsumed under the heading of Social Support. The component of support which is the most straightforward to define, and about which there is most agreement, is *instrumental support*. Other terms for the same thing are 'aid', 'tangible support', and 'material support'. It refers to the provision of goods and services that help to solve practical problems (Jacobson, 1986) and it can include:

> a wide range of activities such as providing assistance with household chores, taking care of children, lending or donating money, running errands, providing transportation, helping with practical tasks (e.g. carpentry, plumbing, moving), looking after a household when the owner is away, and providing material goods such as furniture, tools, or books. Providing help in time of physical injury or illness ... is a particularly important form of instrumental support ... . (Wills, 1985)

Wills suggests that this type of support may be particularly relevant for people on low incomes, and Minkler (1985) suggests that it may be particularly important for older people.

Central to most conceptions of social support, but less tangible than the

---

Table 5. The main functions of social support

Material, tangible, or instrumental support or aid
Emotional, expressive, or affect support, or caring
Esteem, affirmation, or value support, or acknowledgement
Informational, advice, or cognitive support, or guidance
Companionship support, or positive social interaction

---

material or instrumental support described above, is a type of support referred to as *emotional*, 'emotionally sustaining', 'affect', or 'expressive'. For example, Tolsdorf (1976) refers to assistance in the form of, 'encouragement, personal warmth, love, or emotional support' (p. 410). Leavy (1983) refers to support which involves, 'caring, trust, and empathy' (p. 4). Jacobson (1986) writes of behaviour that, 'fosters feelings of comfort and leads an individual to believe that he or she is admired, respected, and loved, and that others are available to provide caring and security' (p. 252).

There is disagreement, however, about whether this area of support should be treated as a single thing or whether it should be broken down into a number of component parts. For example, Cobb's (1976) view of social support as information has influenced a number of later writers and researchers on this topic (e.g. Turner, 1981). Cobb conceived of three separate types of supportive information: that which led the recipient to believe that he or she was cared for and loved; that leading the person to believe that he or she was esteemed and valued; and information leading to the belief that the person belonged to a network of communication and mutual obligation in which others could be counted on. At least the first two of these three types of support, and possibly the third also, appear to be contained within the single 'emotional' support category preferred by others. Another influential way of conceiving of this area has been Kahn and Antonucci's (1980) Three As: affect, affirmation and aid. By affective support they mean, 'expressions of liking, admiration, respect, or love', and by affirmation, 'expressions of agreement or acknowledgement of the appropriateness or rightness of some act or statement of another person' (p. 267).

Thus Kahn and Antonucci wish to make a distinction between affect or emotional support and affirmation or acknowledgement. The latter would appear to correspond to Cobb's 'being esteemed and valued'. There is an absence of agreement, however, about whether emotional support and esteem support are separable. For example Cohen and Wills (1985) use the term 'esteem support' but do not include affect or emotional support in their list and appear to equate esteem support with it:

> Esteem support is information that a person is esteemed and accepted. ... Self-esteem is enhanced by communicating to persons that they are valued for their own worth and experiences and are accepted despite any difficulties or personal faults. This type of support has also been referred to as emotional support, expressive support, self-esteem support, ventilation, and close support. (p. 313)

Elsewhere, Wills (1985) makes it doubly clear that he is equating esteem support with the general category of emotional or expressive support used by others. Esteem support, he says, is, 'having someone available with whom one can talk about problems; this supportive function has variously been termed esteem support, emotional support, ventilation, or a confidant relationship' (p. 67). To confuse things still further Wortman and Conway (1985) include, 'information that a person is esteemed' under the first of the social support functions that they believe have been identified as being conceptually distinct (they call this first one, 'the expression of positive affect'), but also include as *separate* functions both, 'expressing agreement with or acknowledging the appropriateness of a person's beliefs, interpretations, or feelings', and 'encouraging the open expression or ventilation of feelings and beliefs' (p. 289).

There is also difference of opinion as to whether Cobb's third category of supportive information—belonging to a network of communication and mutual obligation—should be treated independently. Wortman and Conway (1985) believed it should and Wills (1985) included a category which he called 'status support' equating it with 'social regulation, social integration, or embeddedness in social roles' (p. 69). Most of those who have taken a functional approach to social support have not included anything of this kind as a separate category, however.

There is a greater measure of agreement about the category of cognitive or *informational support* although not everyone sees this category as central to the notion of social support, and it is frequently omitted altogether. Some, such as House (1981, cited by Leavy, 1983) have divided it into two:

> Informational support which means giving information or teaching a skill which can provide a solution to a problem; and appraisal support which involves information that helps one in evaluating personal performance .... (Leavy, p. 4)

Others refer simply to a single category of informational support including the giving of information, advice and guidance (e.g. Wills, 1985). Wills suggests that esteem and information support tend to derive from the same sources and are in practice highly correlated.

Finally, some include *social companionship* under the heading of social support. For example, Cohen and Wills (1985) stated: 'Social companionship is spending time with others in leisure and recreational activities. This may reduce stress by fulfilling a need for affiliation and contact with others, by helping to distract persons from worry about problems, or by facilitating positive affective moods' (p. 313). The study by Parry and Shapiro (1986), which will be referred to again later, is one in which the number of a person's social contacts was included in the measurement of social support, although in this case it was combined with the number of confidants and time spent with them in an overall measure of 'expressive social support'. In a factor analysis of social support items, Barrera and Ainlay (1983) found some evidence for a factor which they termed 'positive social interaction'. This included such components as 'joking and kidding', 'talking about interests', and 'engaging in diversionary activities'. However, of the four factors which emerged from their analysis this was the most difficult to interpret. The others—directive guidance, non-directive support, and tangible assistance—appear to correspond well with others' informational, emotional and material support.

Despite this quite good consensus that social support consists of at least three or four distinct components, it remains true that only a small number of studies of social support have used multidimensional support measures (Kessler and McLeod, 1985).

SOURCES OF SUPPORT

A question which has naturally intrigued students of social support is whether several, less intense relationships can provide the same degree of support provided by a single, very close relationship (Cohen and Wills, 1985). There is certainly consistent evidence that being married is, overall, associated with lower rates of morbidity and mortality and more positive feelings of well-being (Berkman, 1985; Bloom, Asher and White, 1978; Schulz and Rau, 1985). The evidence that disruption of marriage by separation or death is itself one of the greatest stresses for people who experience it and is followed by an increased incidence of psychological disorder (Bloom, Asher and White, 1978) was presented in the previous chapter. Not, of course, that all marriages are supporting, or that all marital relationships are necessarily confiding ones (Brown and Harris, 1978; Morgan, Patrick and Charlton, 1984). Availability does not necessarily imply adequacy. Nevertheless, marital satisfaction is closely associated with reports of mutual understanding, communication and emotional gratification between marital partners, and the correspondence between these qualities and those that have been used more generally to define emotional social support is obviously a close one (Wills, 1985).

Hence it is unsurprising that a number of studies have used the existence of a single, intimate, confiding relationship as their sole measure of social support, or that studies that have used such measures have been included by reviewers as studies of social support even though their authors did not use this term. Leavy (1983) reviewed a number of studies, including the original one by Brown and Harris (1978), which consistently found the presence of such a relationship to be associated with reduced rates of depression. Other studies of rates of depression amongst women, not included in Leavy's review, have found the same thing. These include Costello's (1982) study in Alberta, Canada, and that by Campbell, Cope and Teasdale (1983) in Oxford, England, both of which were discussed in Chapter 3.

Leavy was able to find few studies which included a prospective design and very few that had focused upon types of distress or disorder other than depression. There are other studies which have done both, however, using concepts and measures closely related to social support. One such study was an investigation of the outcome of alcohol problems amongst 100 married men in the year after they first consulted a psychiatric out-patient department in London (Orford Oppenheimer, Egert, Hensman and Guthrie, 1976). Marital cohesion, which was a multicomponent measure which could be construed as a detailed measure of intimacy, confiding, or social support was found to be predictive of a good outcome. Another would be work on the pre-diction of outcome in schizophrenia carried out within the *expressed emotion* (EE) tradition established by Wing and Brown and their colleagues in London (e.g. Brown, Birley and Wing, 1972). Ratings of EE, found to be predictive of relapse, are based upon interviews with close relatives and in particular upon counts of the number of critical remarks made by a relative about the psychiatric patient. In many ways this is the antithesis of esteem support, and indeed studies of the family interactional behaviour of high and low EE fami-lies confirm that high EE is associated with unsupportive behaviour (Strachan, Leff, Goldstein, Doane and Burtt, 1986).

Despite all the emphasis that there has been upon support derived from the single, closest relationship and the supposition by some that this is all that really counts, there is evidence that a wider circle of support-givers makes a difference and that in many circumstances the support they provide is crucial. Henderson, Byrne, Duncan-Jones, Scott and Adcock (1980) found that the existence and perceived adequacy of more diffuse relationships ('social inte-gration' as they called it) made an additional contribution to scoring low on scales of psychological symptoms, although 'attachment' (the closest relation-ship) was the more important contributor. The study by Miller and Ingham (1976) was another which found that the existence of a friendship network made an independent contribution to freedom from psychological symptoms, although the presence of an intimate confidant was the more important. In a general population study of married men in Saskatchewan, Canada, Syrotuik and D'Arcy (1984) examined the hypothesis that 'community support' might compensate for 'spouse support' when the latter was low. They were unable to find any evidence for the kind of direct, compensatory effect that they were looking for, but did find a specific, compensatory effect for those men who were under job strain of particular kinds (all the men were employed in this study).

SPECIAL NEEDS FOR SUPPORT

Many writers on social support go further than this, however, and argue that parts of the wider network of more distant kin, friends and acquaintances can be of crucial importance. They make the point that this may depend upon the exact nature of the stress that a person is facing. They wish to see more spe-cific research carried out into the links between *specific* stressors and sources of useful support in meeting them (Cohen and Wills, 1985; Wethington and Kessler, 1986). A good example is the provision of social support for women following mastectomy, a topic reviewed by Lindsey, Norbeck, Carrieri and Perry (1981). They concluded that much support comes from friends and from other women who have had a mastectomy, although they emphasised that the husband's or partner's reactions and behaviour are very important for the women's adjustment.

Other groups of people with special needs for social support were considered in the chapters of the book on *Social Support and Health* edited by Cohen and Syme (1985). For example, the special needs for support of older people were considered by Minkler (1985). In this general context, she reviewed the specific research on the health consequences of bereavement, retirement and relocation either in community or residential settings. Although there are some negative findings, the evidence is strong that bereavement has consequences for the elderly in terms of both morbidity and mortality. In the case of retirement and relocation, however, the evidence is more mixed and her overall conclusion was that these events in and of themselves need have no adverse consequences. Nevertheless, the impact of each of these events, including bereavement, depends crucially upon the circumstances and context in which they occur. The availability and adequacy of social support, both emotional and instrumental, is one aspect of context. For older people autonomy and a sense of control, towards which good social support may contribute, appear in addition to be of central importance (see the following chapter for a further discussion of personal power and control).

The needs of people adapting and recovering from physical illness were examined by Wortman and Conway (1985). They pointed out that although this group may have particularly strong needs for support they may also experience special difficulties in having those needs met. Indeed a degree of rejection by other people is often reported which may possibly be attributable to other people's embarrassment, aversion to illness, frustration at lack of progress, and even an element of blame towards the ill person for not making greater efforts to recover. There is some evidence that those with the worst prognosis, or who are coping least well, and who therefore have the greatest needs for social support, are exactly those who are least likely to receive it.

Another group with special needs for social support, until recently relatively neglected, are those, mainly women, who live with and care for or are immediately affected by individual family members with psychiatric disorders, addictions, long-standing physical illnesses, or disabilities (Orford, 1987b). Many of these people are major providers of emotional and/or instrumental support themselves. Their own needs for support are considerable but easy to overlook. One of the few studies to use the concept of social support explicitly in relation to this group was that of Fiore, Coppel, Becker and Cox (1986). Their study was of 68 middle-aged or older carers of spouses with a diagnosis of Alzheimer's Disease, most of whom were living at home. There is now greater recognition of the fact that such carers face much stress and a difficult coping task (Gilhooly 1987; Matson, 1991). Those who were more satisfied with the social support they received had lower scores on scales of psychiatric symptoms in general and depression in particular. Frequency of contact with members of the social network, and the amount of help that was asked of network members, were unrelated to these scales, however. Satisfaction with emotional support was the component of satisfaction most strongly associated with freedom from depression, but satisfaction with cognitive guidance (i.e. informational support) was the component most strongly related to freedom from psychiatric symptoms in general. Another highly stressed group of carers are parents of psychiatric patients with a diagnosis of schizophrenia (Birchwood and Smith, 1987). The concept of social support has been little used with this group, but one finding was that mothers whose children had illnesses of longer duration had the smaller social networks (the same finding did not apply to fathers) (Anderson, Hogarty, Bayer and Needleman, 1984).

Other groups with special needs for social support include the unemployed (see Chapter 3), children whose parents are separating (see Chapter 8) and the victims of disasters (see Chapter 11).

It is worth pointing out here that many of the specific groups just discussed are examples of people experiencing stress of an on-going or chronic nature, whereas most of the research on stress, social support and illness or health has focused upon discrete *life events*. Living with a disability, disabling illness, or long-standing drinking or drug problem or psychiatric disorder, whether as the disabled or ill person or as a close relative or carer, principally involves *chronic* strain, although rates of negative life events are also likely to be higher than normal in many of these groups. It has been pointed out a number of times that chronic strains have been relatively neglected in the social support work although they may have the greater consequences for health and illness (e.g. Mitchell and Moos, 1984; Kessler and McLeod, 1985).

Social support for those who are professionally engaged in human service work, teachers for example (Russell, Altmaier and Van Velzen, 1987), is another area that is receiving increasing attention since the demands on such personnel, which are likely to have risen in recent years as a consequence of greater strain on public resources, are being increasingly recognised and concepts such as *burnout* are focusing attention upon the adverse consequences of stress in these groups (Cherniss, 1980a). Support for staff within human service organisations will be considered in more detail in Chapter 9.

MATCHING SUPPORT WITH EXPECTATIONS, TASKS AND DEVELOPMENTAL NEEDS

A distinction which is seen as vitally important by many, whatever the particular needs being served, is that between the *availability* of social support and its *adequacy* as perceived by the recipient (e.g. Cohen and Wills, 1985). Henderson and his colleagues have developed an Interview Schedule for Social Interaction in their work in Australia. The ISSI assesses both availability and perceived adequacy of social support, the latter showing a generally stronger relationship with mental health in their general population study (Henderson *et al.*, 1980). Leavy (1983) suggested that what might be important was the fit between people's expectations and their actual experiences of support and that future work might fruitfully assess the extent to which the structure and content of social support diverged from an individual's ideal. Boyce (1985) considered a crucial factor to be whether the perception of a source of social support was perceived to be reliable or permanent. In particular he considered children as an age-related sub-group of the population who have obvious, special needs for social support. He drew a parallel between attachment theory in child psychology and the use of such terms as attachment or emotional support in the work on social support, which has largely been carried out with adults. He argued for the importance for child health of *stability* of close attachments. His own specific theory was that the stability of day-to-day family routine was crucial, and that where this was disrupted, as for example in some families where a parent has a serious alcohol problem (Bennett, Wolin and Reiss, 1988), then child health was particularly likely to suffer.

More recently Boyce and colleagues have adopted the necessary, but relatively unusual, step of studying intensively and qualitatively the perceptions of their support held by a small number of individuals—in this case five unmarried adolescent mothers in the year following the delivery of their firstborn children. They found that all five used some concept of *reliability* or permanence to differentiate amongst their sources of social support. Acceptance (versus rejection) was an important feature for some of the young women, as was the accessibility of support (Boyce, Kay and Uitti, 1988).

Others have drawn attention to the importance of the *timing* of social support in relation to a stressful event and have suggested that support from different sources may be valuable at different times. For example Mitchell and Moos (1984) suggested that family members may be most important during a crisis, for example immediately following a bereavement, but that a wider circle of supportive others may be more important as time goes on. Others have suggested that particular functions served by social support may be relatively important at different times. For example Wortman and Conway (1985) suggested that in adapting and recovering from physical illness informational support may be more important shortly after a diagnosis has been made, whilst instrumental or tangible support may become more important later if symptoms persist and become chronic. The relevance of support needs to be judged in relation to the particular 'tasks' facing the adjusting or recovering patient. Jacobson (1986) has proposed a more general theory about the matching of support functions to the nature and process of stressful events. He follows Weiss (1976) in distinguishing between three types of stressful situation—*crisis, transition* (a period of change that involves a shift in a person's assumptive world), and *deficit state* (a situation of chronically excessive demands)—and in recognising that these may occur in a temporal sequence. Jacobson suggests that emotional support is most appropriate in a crisis, informational or cognitive support during a period of transition, and instrumental or material support for a deficit state. He stresses the importance of the right kind of social support being given and received under the right circumstances and at the right time.

A theory linking the source and the function of social support was proposed by Lin, Woelfel and Light (1985). Their proposal, based on a variety of *social resources theory*, was that different sources could provide the most helpful social support depending upon whether the task at hand was 'expressive' or 'instrumental'. For the former, support would be most helpful if provided by 'strong' ties (particularly those with partners) and ties that were 'homophilous' (i.e. ties with people who were similar in terms of characteristics such as age, gender, occupation, education, and marital status). On the other hand:

> For successful instrumental actions, use of numerous and widely diverse social resources is desirable. Access to resources other than one's own is more likely to occur through weak rather than strong ties and heterophilous rather than homophilous ties. (p. 249)

It will of course be difficult to test some of these more specific theories about interactions between types of stress or task, sources and functions of social support, and the timing of their application, and so far there appear to have been no very clear-cut conclusions reached about the differential value of support under different circumstances (Leavy, 1983). One such theory which has received at least partial support, however, is Hammer's (1983) theory that small, dense social networks would be best for dealing with crises whilst diffuse networks would be preferable for coping with transitions. In a study which is much quoted in the social support literature, Hirsch (1981) showed that network density (see Tolsdorf, 1976, and pp. 61–63 above) was *positively* related to symptoms and negative mood and *negatively* to self-esteem amongst two groups of women: 20 recently widowed younger women and 14 mature women who had recently returned to studying full-time. These correlations, which were not statistically significant, became so when network density was calculated solely for that part of the network relating to the boundary between the nuclear family (mainly children for the women in this study) and friends. The explanation for this counter-intuitive finding may lie in the fact that the less dense this family-friends boundary the more likely it was that women would have 'multidimensional' rather than 'unidimensional' friendships (a distinction very similar to Tolsdorf's (1976) between multiplex and uniplex). Hirsch suggested that it may have been important for women facing the need for life transitions following early widowhood or return to college to forge new friendships and relationships that did not depend entirely upon their roles as mothers:

> In this manner, low-density, multidimensional social networks could serve as the cornerstone for a successful coping strategy. This strategy was designed to cultivate relationships outside the family sphere in order to develop a repertoire of satisfying social roles. (p. 159)

With its focus on the family-friendship boundary, this study thus provides us, in addition, with an illustration of Bronfenbrenner's (1979) point about the importance of what he termed the meso-level social system (see Chapter 2).

Bronfenbrenner predicted that the close integration of different micro-level social systems (for example those of home and school) would be good for the development of young children, but he recognised that the opposite might be the case, as apparently in Hirsch's study, for older people making transitions to new roles and looking for a measure of independence. Hirsch's results certainly debunk the assumption that densely knit networks are necessarily related to greater support and better health under all circumstances. It has also been pointed out that strong ties, as opposed to more diffuse, extended networks may restrict access to new information and exert greater pressure for conformity (Hammer, 1983; Hall and Wellman, 1985).

This discussion is closely related to that found in sociology concerning the nature of communities in modern, industrialised societies. In that literature there has been much debate as to whether the former, tightly-knit communities, with distinct boundaries, have been lost in favour of more sparsely knit, loosely bounded networks which may be better for acquiring new information and resources but less well equipped for solidarity and the exercise of internal social control. In one of the few studies that bears directly on this question—a survey of 845 adults in a predominantly British-Canadian inner-city suburb of Toronto—Wellman found the predominating social network to correspond not to a 'community lost' or a 'community saved' pattern, but rather to what he termed a 'community liberated' pattern including both kin and non-kin and extending beyond the local area (Wellman and Leighton, 1979).

Mitchell and Moos (1984) and Cohen and Wills (1985) are amongst those who have argued for much more sophisticated research in the area of social support. Amongst other things they look for research based upon much more precise theorising about the function of support and its timing in relation to people's needs for support, plus a thorough assessment of support deriving from a variety of sources including both family and work sources as well as others. Cohen and Wills also called for a combination of quantitative and qualitative research on the subject. Apart from Boyce, Kay and Uitti's (1988) study, the latter has certainly been conspicuous by its absence (see Chapter 6 for a discussion of qualitative research in community psychology).

WHAT IS THE LINK BETWEEN SOCIAL SUPPORT AND HEALTH?

Despite all these unresolved complexities regarding the conceptualisation of social support, the evidence for its link with health is generally considered to be strong. In the case of mental health or freedom from symptoms of psychiatric disorder or psychological distress a number of reviewers find the evidence convincing. For example, Aneshensel and Frerichs (1982) referred to, 'a fairly consistent pattern of results ... demonstrating ... a negative relationship for support with psychiatric impairment (p. 363). Leavy (1983) concluded: 'Altogether these studies produced remarkably consistent findings, although the definitions of support and psychopathology, and the means to measure them, vary greatly' (p. 7). Kessler and McLeod (1985) referred to 'compelling evidence that support is significantly associated with well-being and the absence of psychological distress in normal population samples' (p. 219). Munroe and Steiner (1986) wrote, 'The breadth and consistency of the research and the beneficial effects of social support are impressive. ... Either through direct protective effects, or by buffering the adverse consequences of life stress, social support is associated with a decreased likelihood of developing disorder' (p. 29). And it is not just in the area of mental health that evidence for an association between social support and health is strong. In particular, reviewers are convinced by the evidence for an association between lack of social support and *mortality* with the evidence for physical morbidity being less consistent (Berkman, 1985; Cohen and Wills, 1985).

In an effort to understand how social support might be related to health and well-being, one of the questions that has been asked more often than almost any other is whether social support has a *main effect* or a *stress-buffering effect*. The main (or 'direct') effects model supposes that social support has an effect independently of level of stress: it can, 'promote good health, both in the absence and in the presence of stressful life events' (Ullah, Banks and Warr, 1985). The alternative stress-buffering model, on the other hand, suggests that social support works by diminishing the potentially harmful influence of stress: where no stress exists, social support has no effect.

To test these models it is of course necessary to have variation (at least two levels) of stress, and of social support, and some measure of health or ill-health. The pattern of results expected from the two theories is shown in diagrammatic and simplified form in Figure 6, which is taken from Cohen and Wills' 1985 review. The main effects model would predict the pattern shown in Figure 6A whilst the stress-buffering theory would predict the pattern shown in Figure 6B. The two theories are not mutually exclusive; both effects may be operating (Berkman, 1985; Ullah, Banks and Warr, 1985).

Conclusions have differed about whether the evidence supports the stress-buffering model of social support or not. For example, Wethington and Kessler (1986) referred to the buffering effect as 'clearly documented', and they themselves found that the event × support interaction term added significantly to the prediction of psychological distress, over and above the main effects of life events and perceived support, in their analysis of results from over 1000 married adults in the USA. On the other hand, Kasl and Wells (1985) concluded that, 'On balance the results favour an absence of detectable buffer effects. ... Among the studies that have found a buffer effect, a clear cut strong effect is rather rare ... mostly, the results are weak and often further compromised by inadequate data analysis strategies' (p. 179). More balanced conclusions are reached by authors such as Aneshensel and Frerichs (1982), Leavy (1983) and Parry and Shapiro (1986). They independently concluded that some studies have been supportive of the stress-buffering theory,

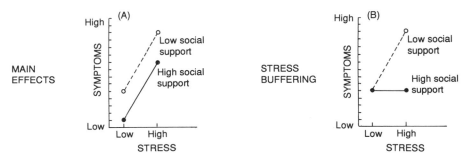

Figure 6. Predictions from the main effects (A) and stress-buffering (B) models of social support (reproduced by permission from Cohen and Wills, 1985. Copyright 1985 by the American Psychological Association)

others have found mixed results, and still others have found main effects only. All three of these reviewers were of the opinion that the results depended upon methodological issues including the choice of measures of social support and other key variables, and the way in which results had been analysed.

Amongst those studies which have produced mixed results, was the one discussed in Chapter 3, of young unemployed people in Britain, carried out by the Sheffield group. With five separate indices of social support and two measures of whether the young people were thought to be under particular stress because of unemployment (a scale of commitment to being employed, and a scale of perceived pressure from others to obtain a job), they were able to make 10 separate tests of whether there were main or interaction effects in the prediction of psychological distress (assessed using the General Health Questionnaire, and short versions of Zung's depression and anxiety scales). Of these only two produced the significant interaction effects predicted by the buffering model. There was a significant interaction between having someone to turn to for help with money and perceived pressure from others to get a job: those without this kind of support and with greater perceived pressure having the highest distress scores. Having someone to turn to for cheering up when feeling low interacted significantly with employment commitment: those with high commitment and low support having the highest distress scores (Ullah, Banks and Warr, 1985).

Mixed findings were also produced by Syrotuik and D'Arcy (1984) in their study of nearly 500 employed, married men living in the province of Saskatchewan, Canada, to which reference has already been made above. They discovered a significant interaction between one of their two measures of social support (support from spouse) and one of their three measures of job strains (job pressures) in the prediction of GHQ scores. Those men with high job pressure and low spousal support had particularly high GHQ scores. It will be recalled that Syrotuik and D'Arcy were particularly interested in the possible compensatory effects of community support under conditions in which spousal support was low. In their study they found some evidence for a *compensatory buffering effect* of high community support on the relationship between low job opportunities and GHQ scores. For those men with low opportunities *and* low spousal support, level of community support appeared to be particularly important in determining average GHQ scores.

Yet another study that produced mixed results was Turner, Grindstaff and Phillips' (1990) of the outcome of 250 teenage pregnancies in Ontario, Canada. Two measures of outcome were employed in the study: the baby's birth weight (corrected for gestational age) and the mother's depressive symptomatology assessed at interview about four weeks after delivery. Of three measures of social support during pregnancy, support from the mother's parental family turned out to be more important than support from friends or from the baby's father. For those mothers from lower socio-economic status families there was support for the main effects model: support was positively correlated with birth weight and negatively with mother's depression both for high-stressed and low-stressed mothers (stress was measured by a life events inventory plus an index of financial hardship). For those from higher status families, on the other hand, there was support for buffering in the form of a negative correlation of family support with mother's depression for high-stressed mothers only.

Can some sense be made of these very mixed results? Both Cohen and Wills (1985) and Kessler and McLeod (1985) believed that it could. The logic of their interpretation is, as previously discussed, that social support will be effective in so far as it is *matched* to the particular needs for support which exist. Cohen and Wills argued that, although there had been relatively little research that had looked at the specific needs of people for support to cope with specific stresses, general stress buffering would be expected whenever social support measures tapped either esteem support (more usually called emotional support—see above) or informational support, since these are the two forms of social support that are most generally useful in coping with stress. In their review, Cohen and Wills found consistent evidence for buffering under those conditions, and when they excluded studies that they believed to be weak methodologically Kessler and McLeod also found strong evidence for the buffering effect of emotional support. On the other hand, both these reviews concluded that structural, social network measures, although they produced main effects, gave no evidence that embeddedness in a social network was helpful in buffering stress.

In general, Cohen and Wills' conclusion was that:

> data are consistent with the proposal that specific support functions are responsive to stressful events, whereas social network integration operates to maintain feelings of stability and well-being irrespective of stress level. We conclude that social integration and functional support represent different processes through which social resources may influence well-being. (p. 349)

SOCIAL SUPPORT, STRESS AND HEALTH AS A FURTHER EXAMPLE OF COMPLEX, RECIPROCAL CAUSATION

Both the main and stress-buffering theories of social support require us to make the assumption that social support and stress are independent of one another, and that both are causally antecedent to health or ill-health, symptoms or distress. That these three sets of variables (support, stress, and health or disorder) are confounded—conceptually, methodologically and empirically—has been most convincingly argued by Thoits (1982) and by Munroe and Steiner (1986).

First, there is likely to be a mutual influence upon one another of social support and health or well-being. For example, Turner (1981), in an earlier, longitudinal study of new Canadian mothers, found that psychological well-being at time 1 was as strongly predictive of social support at time 2 as was support at time 1 of well-being at time 2. This is the cross-lagged panel analysis approach to causal interpretation: if social support is cause and psychological well-being effect, then time 1 support–time 2 well-being should be the stronger of the two cross-correlations. (A useful discussion of cross-lagged panel analysis, path analysis, and other statistical techniques for assisting in making causal inferences in the study of social support is provided by Dooley, 1985.) As Syrotuik and D'Arcy (1984) put it:

> while social support has implications for psychological well-being, the reverse is also true with one's psychological condition affecting the availability and utilisation of support. The conceptualisation of this relationship as spiral rather than strictly linear would therefore appear to be more appropriate. (p. 235)

The further likelihood that social support and stressful life events and circumstances are not independent is considered by a number of writers on the topic of social support. Many stressful life events involve loss of social support almost by definition: marital disruption, bereavement, loss of work, and moving home for example (e.g. Cohen and Wills, 1985; Ullah, Banks and Warr, 1985). Support and stress are usually found to be correlated in random samples of the normal population; high stress and low support tending to occur together (Parry and Shapiro, 1986). In the context of their work on unemployment, Atkinson, Liem and Liem (1986) have pointed out that work on unemployment stress in the 1930s, and their own more recent work on the subject, found that the stress of unemployment could have profound effects upon family support, sometimes diminishing it and sometimes enhancing it. They concluded:

> Stress and support processes ... need to be reconceptualised from a mechanistic model, where stressors and supports are viewed as stable factors which produce main or interactive effects on health, to a more dynamic model which would consider these factors to be mutually determinative and responsive to a range of conditions. (p. 319)

Figure 7, which is adapted from one presented by Munroe and Steiner, contrasts the simple assumptions of the main and stress-buffering theories with the greater complexity that is likely to exist in reality. When this picture is coupled with an awareness that relationships may not be linear, but may in some instances be curvilinear (Kahn and Antonucci, 1980) or may involve step or threshold functions (Mitchell and Moos, 1984) we see how very complicated the subject can become.

One community study which succeeded in overcoming some (but not all) of these problems was that carried out by Aneshensel and Frerichs (1982). They interviewed over 700 Los Angeles residents four times over a period of 12 months. In fact their paper is a particularly instructive one on this issue both because of the number of separate interviews and because they used an approach to causal modelling using latent variables which has been used more and more frequently in this kind of multivariable quantitative research in recent years. They found that social support (measured in three separate ways) had quite a strong total inverse effect on depression (measured in four slightly different ways). This was not only true at one moment in time (for example the correlation of social support and depression at time 1), but it was also the case that social support at time 1 had an influence on depression at later time points, including the fourth, although it was concluded that this influence was mostly indirect via depression at time 1.

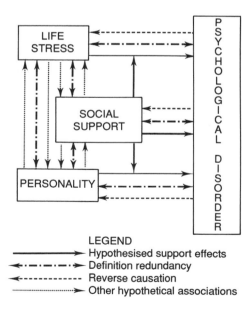

Figure 7. Possible complex interactions between social and personal factors and psychological disorder (reproduced by permission from Munroe and Steiner, 1986. Copyright 1986 by the American Psychological Association)

IS SOCIAL SUPPORT MERELY A REFLECTION OF PERSONALITY

One of the main reasons why the subject of social support is of such significance for community psychology is that it provides a bridge between a psychology dominated by an interest in individual, personal or intra-psychic factors and a psychology which places at least as much emphasis upon social context or environment. Nevertheless, as has already been noted, social support has largely been treated by psychologists as an individual variable. It has mostly been what individuals have said about the social network that surrounds them as individual focal people that has been studied rather than (as Hall and Wellman, 1985, would have wished) the study of social networks themselves.

This has inevitably left the door open for a possible reinterpretation of social support, as assessed in most of the work referred to in this chapter, in terms of individual perception or personality. A particularly strong personality orientation was taken by Kobasa, Maddi, Puccetti and Zola (1985) who studied the correlation of three 'resistance resources' with severity of illness symptoms (both physical and mental) amongst business executives with a high level of exposure to stressful events. They also examined the ability of the same resistance resources to predict illness symptoms a year later. The resources concerned were: social support at work, exercise and 'personality hardiness'. The authors of this report describe the latter as 'a personality style consisting of the inter-related orientations of commitment (vs alienation), control (vs powerlessness), and challenge (vs threat)'. Of the three resistance resources, personality hardiness was most strongly related to symptom severity, both concurrently and predictively, and social support was comparatively unimportant although significant. Hardiness and social support were moderately correlated (0.23). The important point to be made here is the interpretation that Kobasa *et al.* placed upon these findings:

> It may be that the important place given to social support in previous conceptualisations of stress resistance is based on the undetected overlap of this admittedly heterogeneous construct with such personality constructs as hardiness. (p. 532)

In his study comparing psychiatric and medical patients Tolsdorf (1976) also commented on an apparent difference of outlook by patients in the two groups. Most of the medical patients had a positive 'network orientation': 'a set of beliefs or expectations ... that it is safe, advisable, and in some cases necessary to confide in the social network and draw on it for advice, support, and feedback'. All the psychiatric patients, on the other hand, had a negative orientation: 'a set of expectations or beliefs that it is inadvisable, impossible, useless or potentially dangerous to draw on network resources' (p. 413). Having noted this difference, however, Tolsdorf was not inclined to relegate social support to the level of a reflection of, or proxy for personality, but rather saw the two in dynamic relationship to one another:

> The adoption of a network approach requires the simultaneous consideration of two interlocking systems: one on the individual level and one on the interpersonal level. It is the rich complexity of interaction between these two systems that provides the data for network analysis. For instance, an individual's expectations and beliefs help determine his behavior, but they in turn are partially determined by the characteristics of the network. Conversely, an individual's network is shaped and maintained by his use of it and by his attitude toward it. Thus the individual and the network are in constant interaction, both influencing and being influenced by the other. (p. 416)

A very similar point of view was expressed by Leavy (1983). He pointed out that social support should refer not only to the structure and content of helping relationships available in the environment, but also to the processes by which people make use of these. An understanding of the complexity of these matters was not well served by traditional cause-and-effect thinking. He saw the same danger that is being highlighted here:

> we must attend to the prospect that social support will be conceptualised as one more 'person' variable related to disorder. Social support is an issue at the heart of community psychology ... it is an environmental factor which interacts with an individual to provide strength, confidence, and a sense of belonging. Rather than seeing support from an individual/deficit perspective ... and designing studies to fit that vision, future investigators should focus on how families, organisations, and whole communities provide a spectrum of supporting resources to individuals. (p. 18)

OR IS IT PART OF A WIDER CONTEXT?

Others have echoed this view that social support should be seen, not in a narrower person-centred way, but in a wider social context (e.g. Minkler, 1985; Ganster and Victor, 1988). For example Hammer (1983) has taken those who have researched and written on social support to task for forgetting the large amount of epidemiological findings that show social status to be related to measures of ill-health (see Chapter 3). Some of the research which she reviewed shows positive relationships between social status and *amount* of social support, and some shows the *patterning* of social support to be different in different occupational groups—white-collar workers having larger networks of people who are seen less often in comparison with blue-collar workers, for example. Leavy (1983) raised the possibility that social support, whatever its level or pattern, might have different effects in reducing stress or in lowering ratings of illness or distress depending upon factors such as socio-economic status. For example, in one longitudinal study of the effects of unemployment, duration of unemployment showed a very different pattern of correlations with social support depending on occupational group. Amongst white-collar workers longer periods of unemployment were associated with lower marital and family support but higher support from outside the family. For blue-collar workers a longer duration of unemployment was associated with a reduction in network size and frequency of contact with network members (Atkinson, Liem and Liem, 1986).

What little work there has been on the issue of social support and ethnic group or immigrant status lends support to the reasonable expectation that major differences lie in this direction also. Leavy (1983) referred to research suggesting that a lack of neighbourhood attachments had an effect on symptomatology over and above the effect of close, emotional attachments for ethnic minorities in the USA (Chinese-Americans and Southern and Eastern European-Americans in these studies) but not for other groups. In a study of the social networks of physically disabled people living in the London borough of Lambeth, Morgan, Patrick and Charlton (1984) found that people born outside the UK were significantly more likely to have 'locally based kin networks' of the kind which have traditionally formed an important feature of working class communities in Britain (see Young and Willmott, 1957, for one of the best descriptions of life in one such London community in the 1950s). They were less likely than the UK-born to have networks of one or other of the two further types identified by Morgan, Patrick and Charlton: 'dispersed kin networks' and 'friend networks'.

Gender differences in psychological health and well-being were discussed in Chapter 3 and it is not surprising to find strong suggestions of gender differences in social support too. Reviewing the evidence Leavy (1983) concluded that both young and older women have more intimate, confiding and stable network ties than men of the same age, and additionally that the evidence points to the relative importance of work support for men and of family support for women. Wills (1985) concluded from his review that women obtain more benefit from the 'close support' derived from relationships that are intimate and confiding, whereas men derive relatively more benefit from marital and diffuse network relationships where there are shared activities and interests.

EXTENDING THE CONCEPT OF SOCIAL SUPPORT

How widely should the concept of social support be applied? There are those, amongst whom Gottlieb (e.g. 1985) has been particularly prominent, who would wish to connect the more narrowly defined work on social support with wider issues and who would embrace within the concept of social support such things as self-help groups, hostel or halfway house provision, or professionally-provided support for people following surgery. Others, such as Kiesler (1985), believe that to extend the idea of social support so far is to cloud the issues surrounding the subject and that this may actually do a disservice by impeding progress towards understanding and strengthening informal support. The present author's own view is that, on the contrary, it may be unnecessarily restricting to confine the term 'social support' to certain predetermined forms, such as support provided by a marital partner or a network of close friends, and to ignore the fact that at least some of the forms of support shown in Table 5 may be provided at least in part by work supervisors, teachers, health professionals and a host of other people who have special role relationships with the recipients of support (a number of instances will be discussed in later chapters). In a later chapter on self-help and non-professional help (Chapter 10) we shall see that, in any case, the distinctions between formal and informal, professional and non-professional are blurred and often unhelpful in understanding people's needs and how they may best be met.

5 Social Resources II Power and Control

In this chapter we turn to the second of the social resources which are believed to be necessary for the well-being of people-in-context. This is the resource of powerfulness and a feeling of control. The chapter will begin by considering some of the social psychological theories of power and will then proceed to consider leadership and participation in decision-making in organisations, particularly human service organisations. The chapter will conclude by looking at powerlessness—the obverse of power—both as an individual and a collective attribute.

THE SOCIAL PSYCHOLOGY OF POWER

INEQUALITY

Inequalities in power, both between individuals and between groups, are so ubiquitous that it has appeared to many that such inequalities are an inevitable characteristic of all social systems (e.g. Ng, 1980). As Ng notes in his review of the social psychology of power, power inequalities have been recurring features in studies of relationships in micro-level systems—for example between partners and between parents and children in families and in studies of small group interaction. Power inequalities are even more starkly obvious in larger groups or organisations, such as schools or workplaces, in which people spend very large proportions of their time. In organisations, power inequalities are formalised, or depersonalised, by the creation of positions and titles which almost always indicate some degree of hierarchical structure. Such a structure increases the reliability with which power can be wielded—for example power-holders may be absent for periods of time without fear of their positions being usurped. It also increases the flexibility with which power can be used—those at the top of the organisation can, for example, wield power over many via a hierarchy of intermediaries, middle managers or lieutenants (Ng, 1980). Even organisations such as political parties that may have come into being in order to redress previously existing inequalities, themselves develop a hierarchical structure and a means of controlling their membership (Wrong, 1979).

On a macro-system level, also, 'one can take as a universal fact, at least among modern industrial societies, that the distribution of power in society is unequal' (Ng, 1980, p. 191). The sociological literature on social stratification by class is large and contains a number of leading theories on the sources of class stratification (Ng, 1980; Ragan and Wales, 1980). Since Karl Marx and Max Weber, the classical theorists on stratification, the argument has raged over the source of class inequality. Does it lie in the different *roles* that classes play in the production of wealth (particularly owning the means of production versus selling one's labour), in differences in income and other material *resources*, in differences in *prestige*, status or reputation (a view associated with Weber), in the *functional value* of having different classes for performing the necessary different roles in society and for keeping order (the theory of Davis and Moore, 1945, cited by Ragan and Wales, 1980), or in the relative dominance of certain interest groups in society which are in *conflict* with others (a view particularly associated with Dahrendorf, 1968, cited by Wrong, 1979)? Others, such as Lenski (1966, cited by Ragan and Wales, 1980) have attempted to produce a synthesis of these various theories.

Although power inequalities in terms of social class groups have received most attention in the literature on stratification, a more complete view for the purposes of community psychology must consider social stratification in terms of multiple hierarchies of power inequality (Ragan and Wales, 1980). In addition to class, the main forms of inequality of which we need to be aware are those based upon gender, race, age and disability. Ragan and Wales' (1980) discussion of age stratification raises a number of issues that apply to each of the other sources of stratification. They point out that older people (an indefinite category which can start as low as 50 years and as high as 75 years depending upon the purpose to which the categorisation is being put) are relatively deprived in terms of two of the resources most valued in an industrialised society—work and income. Hence older people are likely to be relatively deprived of power both on account of having fewer material resources and in terms of loss of status or prestige. This latter aspect of *role valorisation* (Wolfensberger and Thomas, 1983; see also Chapter 11) has particular application to considering the power position of the disabled as well as older people in society. The fact, pointed out by Ragan and Wales, that older people may be relatively advantaged in some ways (for example in free use of time), and that there is great variability in the degree to which older people retain resources such as wealth and prestige, should not obscure the basic fact of age stratification and the relatively deprived position of those in the older strata. Furthermore, the idea of multiple hierarchies draws attention to the likelihood of sub-groups who are particularly powerless, for example older members of minority ethnic groups, or older women of lower social class. In summary, Ragan and Wales state:

> In spite of some limitations in the conceptualisation of age strata, there are real advantages to an age stratification analysis. One can go beyond the conventional gerontological approach of studying the individual's adjustment to becoming old in a given social system, and focus rather on the characteristics of the system itself that impinge on the status of the aged. (1980, p. 394)

THE NATURE AND BASES OF POWER

Let us look more closely at the psychology of power. In so doing this discussion draws heavily upon the books by Wrong (1979) and Ng (1980). To begin with, most definitions of power are couched in terms of the ability of one person in an interaction to influence events in a direction preferred by the self but not by the other. For example, Weber defined *Macht*, which is usually translated into English as 'power', as 'The probability that one actor within a social relationship will be in a position to carry out his [sic] own will despite resistance' (1947, p. 152, cited by Ng, 1980) and Dahl defined power in these terms: 'A has power over B to the extent that he [sic] can get B to do something that B would not otherwise do' (1957, pp. 202–203, cited by Ng, 1980).

Wrong follows Jouvenel (1958) in distinguishing between three variable attributes of all power relations: *extensity, comprehensiveness* and *intensity*. Extensity refers to the number of people over whom an individual has power: the power of major political leaders is very extensive, that of a parent the opposite. Comprehensiveness refers to the variety of other peoples' actions—or the number of 'scopes' as they are sometimes called—over which a person has power: parents have very comprehensive power over young children, as do the staff of 'total institutions' over the inmates. Intensity refers to the degree of influence one person has over another within any one 'scope': this corresponds to the degree of dominance which A has over B within a certain sphere of B's action. Mostly individuals' powers are severely limited along at least one of these dimensions; only under totalitarian political regimes or in large total institutions do individuals wield power that is extensive, comprehensive *and* intensive. It should not be assumed either that power relations are always unequal. Wrong uses the term *intercurcive power* to refer to a relationship in which A's power over B in certain scopes is balanced by that of B over A in others. The traditional, role-segregated marriage might be said to correspond to this balanced arrangement. On the other hand it is usually the case that one partner (normally the husband) has power in areas that carry the greater prestige or where control is exercised over the more valued resources. Alternatively, one partner may be found to exercise 'meta-power', that is the power to decide which partner has power in which area (Safilios-Rothschild, 1970).

What makes inequality and power possible? On what basis does A have power over B? It has always been recognised that there are a variety of bases to power, and this has led to many terminological disputes. For example: Is *force* a form of power or does it represent a breakdown of power? Is influence through *persuasion* a form of power, or should it be excluded on the grounds that persuasion by rational argument implies power equality rather than inequality? The scheme shown in Figure 8 is a slightly amended version of the one suggested by Wrong (1979). He preferred to define power broadly to cover any intended influence, and to subsume under the term 'power' the various forms shown. Some of the terms Wrong used speak for themselves, but others require a word of explanation. For example, *manipulation*. Wrong reserves this term for any intended influence where B was unaware of A's intentions, or in some cases even of A's existence. Included here would be propaganda, some forms of advertising, and even the setting of prices in a market economy.

Authority in Wrong's scheme implies a relationship in which A directs and B follows, or A commands and B obeys. This relationship may be based upon the threat of violence or punishment (*coercive* authority); the offer of rewards for compliance (*induced* authority, which can range from egalitarian exchange to grossly unequal exploitation, and which as a form of power can be very extensive); norms of the wider society, community or organisation within which A and B are embedded, and which give A the right to issue directives and B the obligation to conform (*legitimate* authority, which can be very comprehensive and intensive, and which because of the shared norms between A and B which it implies, is likely to be more reliable and efficient than other forms of authority); A's greater competence or expertise in a particular area (*competent* authority: the doctor–patient relationship is a classic example summed up by the expression 'doctor's orders'—by its very nature this form of power is unlikely to be very extensive); and the desire of B to please or serve A because of love, admiration, friendship, B's submissiveness, or A's charisma (*personal* authority). In an earlier, and often quoted work, French and Raven (1960) referred to these five bases of power as: 'punishment', 'reward', 'legitimate', 'expert' and 'referent' power respectively.

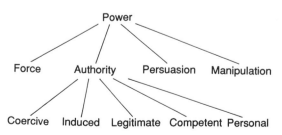

Figure 8. The principal forms of power (based on Wrong, 1979)

As Wrong was at pains to point out, this typology should certainly not be thought of as static. The system contains a number of interesting combinations, transformations and paradoxes. For example, power-holders who wield the most comprehensive and intensive power, such as parents of young children, are often able to draw upon a number of or even all of these forms of power. Indeed they may use different forms sequentially (e.g. personal authority, followed by persuasion, legitimate authority, coercion and even force if necessary), however paradoxical it may seem to know that the possibility of punishment or force lies behind a relationship of legitimate or personal authority. Those whose power is extensive but not necessarily comprehensive and intensive, usually try and extend the basis of their power to include legitimate and personal authority (Machiavelli advised that a successful prince should be both feared and loved), and if they use very different forms of power with different subjects (for example force with some and personal authority with others) they often attempt to keep the respective subjects apart and in ignorance of how the others are being treated. There is a further paradox inherent in the nature of legitimate authority according to Wrong, since compliance is felt at one and the same time to be both voluntary and mandatory. There is a constant tendency for one form of power to metamorphose into another. For example, if persuasion is repeatedly effective it is likely to become competent or legitimate authority. Induced authority becomes coercion if B becomes so reliant upon A's inducements that their absence or withdrawal is perceived as punishment. The competent authority of the professional may drift into legitimate or even coercive authority, particularly when it is supported by a collective organisation of experts and legally recognised by the State. In the case of personal authority, if A and B associate too intimately together, even this type of authority may degenerate into inducement or coercion.

An important question for community psychology is whether power must always be manifest in terms of an action on A's part which is influential on events involving A and B, as many definitions of power suggest, or whether it can under some circumstances be *latent* or potential. One of the trends in studying political power, and the same has been the case in studies of power in the family, has been to equate power with influence upon observable decision-making. In an influential paper entitled, *The Two Faces of Power*, Bachrach and Baratz (1962, cited by Wrong, 1979) criticised this behavioural, decision-making view of power. Central amongst their criticisms was the point that the latter ignored the more 'hidden' but equally important aspect of power in which people worked, not to influence open decisions, but rather to keep important decisions from being discussed, to preserve the status quo by keeping issues off the agenda:

When a person or group—consciously or unconsciously—creates or reinforces barriers to the public airing of policy conflicts, that person or group, according to the authors, has power. It is not even necessary for the person or group to participate in decision-making, since the occasion of decision-making never arises in the first place. To distinguish this face of power from the power of winning a decision, the authors coined the term 'nondecision-making' power. (Ng, 1980, p. 107)

Other terms that capture a similar idea to non decision-making power have been 'ecological control' and 'environmental power' involving manipulation of the environment or others' perceptions of the environment, as opposed to 'interactive power' involving direct communication and interaction between two parties.

Even this two-dimensional view of power has been criticised, most influentially by Lukes (1974, cited by Wrong, 1979). There are at least two grounds for this criticism. One is that even the two-dimensional view of power continues to focus too much on the actions of individuals—either actions to influence decisions or actions to prevent decisions being taken. Secondly, the two-dimensional view ignores the maintenance of power relations by the more profound and subtle process of shaping peoples' very desires and attitudes. To understand how power operates within a community, it is necessary, according to this view, to include a further dimension which consists of the taken-for-granted operation of social forces and group and institutional practices:

> No strings need to be pulled but the outcome is still that *some* people passively enjoy advantage and privilege because of 'the way things work', and because those ways are not challenged. Power derives more from the routine application of effectively unchallenged assumptions than from the manifest dominance of one group over others in open conflict. A major source of power for dominant groups is simply the routine operation of social institutions. (Ng, 1980, p. 14, original emphasis)

This third face of community power is of course still further 'hidden' than the second. As Ng aptly points out, most people whose lives are adversely affected by the operation of power at this level, 'are unable to relate their personal problems to public issues. Because of this they are not being able to define their "real" interests in terms of the social structure' (1980, pp. 112–113).

The most hidden, third dimension of power has been well recognised by those who have written of the need for advocacy for people with disabilities or mental health problems (see Chapter 11). Writing about special educational needs, Barton (1986) states that it is, ' "well-meaning", individual intentions, constrained by organisational and structural demands' (p. 276) that are most likely to create dependency and leave unrecognised the rights of those with learning difficulties. Similarly, writing about advocacy for psychiatric patients, Bloom and Asher (1982) made the point that it is when the aims of those in authority appear well-meaning that resistance is least likely to be invoked and rights may be most at risk. To put it another way the assumption that well-meaning professionals and administrators can make decisions on behalf of client groups fails to recognise that there may be conflicts of interests involved (Barton, 1986).

Most writers on the subject of power, such as Wrong (1979) and Ng (1980), follow Dahrendorf (1959, cited by Wrong, 1979) in distinguishing between two views of power in society, *consensus* and *conflict*. The consensus view, particularly associated with the work of Talcott Parsons, assumes that power differentiation is functional and that those who wield power largely do so benignly so as to enable society and its institutions to function smoothly, to socialise members into their workings, and to bring about changes that are for everyone's benefit (Ng, 1980). This is the well-meaning face of power. Its uglier face was emphasised particularly in the writings of C. Wright Mills who saw society as being in a constant state of conflict between groups. Power was seen as being wielded by currently dominant groups *over* others, rather than, as in the consensus view, being wielded *in order to* achieve generally valued ends (Ng, 1980). One variety of conflict theory sees power in society as very likely to become concentrated in the hands of a relatively small *Power Elite* (the title of Mills' 1956 book, cited by Wrong, 1979).

The consensus, or 'power in order to', perspective stresses the good that the relatively powerful can do to improve everyone's lot (and therefore perhaps to increase the total amount of power that exists in society—a controversial notion). It emphasises legitimate authority as a source of power, and is perhaps the best suited to understanding stability and equilibrium. The conflict, or 'power over', perspective, on the other hand, emphasises the uneven distribution of power in society, stresses coercion and force as sources of power, and is probably best equipped to deal with change (Wrong, 1979). It is generally in the interests of the relatively powerful to emphasise legitimation and the benign uses of power, whilst the relatively powerless are much more likely to call attention to power differentials, the coercive nature of power, and its abuses (Ng, 1980).

Most writers on the subject now accept that power has both aspects. Wrong (1979), for example, argued that the basis of power is nearly always mixed, and that legitimate authority and coercion often go hand in hand, or else one is in the process of being transformed into the other. Ng (1979) followed Duverger (1966, cited by Ng, 1980) in concluding that power is always ambivalent: 'Power in its organised form, such as the political state, is inherently ambivalent because it always contains an element of antagonism or conflict, as well as an element of integrational harmony' (Ng, 1980, p. 85). Like the god Janus, the true image of power is two-faced, and the divisive and integrating aspects of power are inseparable. Although power ensures a particular social order and integrates people into groups and institutions, it leads to conflict, firstly in the struggle to attain or share power between individuals or groups, and secondly as a result of the antagonism that develops between those who then hold power and those who are subjected to it (Ng, 1980).

POWER IN ORGANISATIONS

Nowhere is the nature of power, in its various forms and with its different faces, more apparent than in organisations. Not surprisingly, power and the related topics of leadership and influence, decision-making and autonomy, have received a great deal of attention within organisational psychology. Some of these issues will be discussed in Chapter 9 where organisations and organisational change are discussed. In the following section of this chapter some of the work that specifically looks at the issue of power in organisations will be examined. The focus will be principally upon human service organisations specialising in the mental health area.

LEADERSHIP IN ORGANISATIONS

Katz and Kahn (1978) define leadership as 'influential increment': in other words leaders can exert influence over and above sheer mechanical compliance with the routine directives of the organisation. They recognised that the basis of such influence in organisations, as elsewhere, lies in one or more of the types of authority or power outlined by French and Raven (1960) and Wrong (1979) and referred to above: induced or reward, coercive or punishment, legitimate, competent or expert, and personal or referent. In a theoretical article, Manz and Gioia (1983) also discussed the inter-relationships between power, control and influence in an organisation. They defined power as the ability or *potential* of an individual or sub-unit to influence other individuals or sub-units. They argued that this is closely related to the idea of *dependence*, and that an important basis of power is the dependence of one individual or sub-unit upon others for access to information, persons or resources, with the added proviso that this powerful source cannot be substituted by another. Control is the process of actually influencing others based upon the use of authority or power of one or more of the Wrong or French and Raven types.

Manz and Gioia argued that the relationship between controller and controlled will much depend upon the type of power upon which control is based. Coercive or punishment power is likely to lead to alienated involvement on the part of the controlled individual or sub-unit, whereas the use of induced or reward power might be expected to elicit a calculative involvement, and personal or referent power is more likely to lead to commitment. Katz and Kahn (1978) similarly expressed the view that the use of personal and expert types of power is likely to have fewer unintended side-effects within an organisation. They also suggested that use of these types of power might add to the total amount of influence that is felt within the organisation. They subscribed to the view that power in an organisation is not of fixed quantity such that more for one means less for another, but is an 'expandable pie' with more or less influence being exerted in toto depending upon the way it is exerted.

A number of more detailed models of leadership in organisations have been developed. These have been reviewed by Yetton (1984). Early trait theories looked for the personal characteristics of individuals that made for good leadership. Although there was some agreement that higher intelligence, self-confidence, need for job success, and initiative made for effective leadership, there was a great deal of inconsistency in the findings, and trait models gave way to behavioural theories which tended to support the view that a participative style of decision-making with an emphasis on both *task direction* and psychological *supportiveness* was generally the most effective. However, such models ignored the possibility that the best leadership style might depend upon the nature of the job, and the few longitudinal studies that were carried out suggested that leadership style might be responsive to the performance level of subordinates rather than simply being a cause of it as the behavioural models had assumed.

This led to *contingency models* of which Yetton reviewed a number. All such models assume that the most effective leadership style depends upon the circumstances that pertain within an organisation. Some of these are trait-contingency models which assume that leaders with particular traits are differentially effective under different circumstances. Perhaps the best known of these is the one put forward and tested by Fiedler in a lengthy programme of research involving experiments and field studies in a variety of government and industrial settings (1967, cited by Katz and Kahn, 1978, and by Yetton, 1984). This model assumed that the preferred level of supportiveness shown by a leader would depend upon three characteristics of the organisational setting.

1. Whether the job task was structured or unstructured.
2. Whether the leader's position of power in the organisation was strong or weak.
3. Whether the relationship between leader and members was good or only moderate to poor.

Two levels of each of these three contingent variables creates eight possible sets of circumstances (often referred to as 'octants'). Yetton found that there had been strong support from a number of studies, especially regarding two of these octants. When high task structure and strong position power were combined with good leader—member relations, correlations between leader supportiveness and group performance were negative, indicating that controlling, active, structuring leadership rather than supportiveness might be best under these circumstances. However, where high task structure and strong position power were combined with only moderate to poor leader—member relations, correlations were positive, suggesting that under these circumstances permissive, or passive, considerate leadership was more effective.

Whereas Fiedler's model and others like it assume that leaders with

Table 6. Different leadership styles (reproduced by permission from Yetton, 1984)

1. You solve the problem or make the decision yourself, using information available to you at the time.
2. You obtain the necessary information from your subordinates, then decide the solution to the problem yourself. You may or may not tell your subordinates what the problem is in getting the information from them. The role played by your subordinates in making the decision is clearly one of providing the necessary information to you, rather than generating or evaluating alternative solutions.
3. You share the problem with the relevant *subordinates individually*, getting their ideas and suggestions without bringing them together as a group. Then *you* make the decision, which may or may not reflect your subordinates' influence.
4. You share the problem with your subordinates *as a group*, obtaining their collective ideas and suggestions. Then you make the decision, which may or may not reflect your subordinates' influence.
5. You share the problem with your subordinates as a group. Together you generate and evaluate alternatives and attempt to reach agreement (consensus) on a solution. Your role is much like that of chairman. You do not try to influence the group to adopt 'your' solution, and you are willing to accept and implement any solution which has the support of the entire group.

different traits are better for different circumstances, other contingency models assume that leaders can modify their styles depending upon the situation. The Vroom–Yetton model is one such. It proposes five styles of leadership (see Table 6, taken from Yetton, 1984, p. 24) and a decision-tree that enables the best choice of style to be made according to seven rules. Between them these rules aim to guarantee the two necessary characteristics of good decisions, three of the rules protecting the *quality* of the decision itself and the remaining four its *acceptance* by subordinates. Yetton reported that a tendency had been found for managers to behave in the ways suggested by this model, except that they do not behave as extremely participatively or autocratically as the model suggests would be appropriate under some circumstances. He also noted that most managers avoid a participatory style in circumstances where there exists strong conflict amongst subordinates even when the model suggests that this would be appropriate.

PARTICIPATION IN DECISION-MAKING

Contingency models notwithstanding, Katz and Kahn (1978) clearly believed that there was evidence for a general law of participation:

> Perhaps the most persistent and thoroughly demonstrated difference between successful and unsuccessful leadership ... has to do with the distribution or sharing of the leadership function. By and large, those organisations in which influential acts are widely shared are most effective. (p. 571)

They believed that this was partly for reasons to do with the increased motivation and commitment that individual members displayed when involved in decision-making: because such involvement itself gratifies the need for participation and autonomy, a more democratic organisation has a built-in reward system. Furthermore, wide sharing of leadership functions can be more effective because better decisions are made if the amount of information that is used is maximised: for example, disasters can usually be foreseen by someone in the organisation.

Although there have been many studies showing correlations between participation in decision-making at work and job satisfaction, Jackson's (1983) study of nurses, clerical workers and technicians working in an out-patient department of a university hospital in the USA is one of the few to have manipulated participation within a longitudinal design. New regulations required that regular and frequent staff meetings be held in each of the special clinics in the department, and as a step in that direction half the units (chosen randomly) were immediately asked to hold two or more meetings a month from then on. Other units continued to meet once a month or less often. Standard measures of job satisfaction and of a number of variables, such as role conflict, thought to mediate between participation and satisfaction, were taken three months and six months later. Role conflict, role ambiguity and emotional strain were all less in the units with more frequent meetings, and perceived influence was greater. Job satisfaction was also greater but here the difference between intervention and control conditions was only of borderline statistical significance. Jackson was also interested in the possible processes whereby increased participation might have an effect. A path analysis based on the intercorrelation of variables at three and six months suggested the effects shown in Figure 9. These were (1) there had been a direct effect of participation in reducing role conflict and ambiguity and in increasing perceived influence; (2) that perceived influence was directly related to job satisfaction; and (3) decreased role conflict and ambiguity were related to increased job satisfaction via a reduction in emotional stress. She pointed out that the generalisability of her findings might be limited by the fact that all the workers studied were women working in small hospital units, and that the participation in decision-making involved was of a particular kind, namely (a) informal rather than formal, (b) involuntary rather than voluntary, (c) direct, rather than indirect via representatives, and (d) very partial, involving merely an increase in frequency of staff meetings.

One relatively simple way of studying the degree to which influence is shared throughout an organisation is the *control graph* method used by Tannenbaum (1974, cited by Katz and Kahn, 1978). Each person is asked to rate on a simple five-point scale (little or none, some, quite a bit, a great deal, a very great deal) how much influence s/he thinks different groups (e.g. manager, supervisors, workers) have within the organisation. Results are averaged and plotted on a graph; results from different groups of members can be

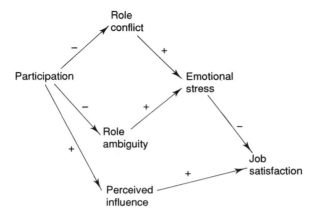

Figure 9. Causal pathways suggested by the results of Jackson's (1983) study of participation in decision-making

amalgamated or kept separate depending upon the analysis. The steepness of the resulting curve indicates the extent to which influence is shared: a very steep curve indicates that higher status members are perceived to have much more influence than those of lower status whereas a flatter curve indicates greater sharing of influence. Tannenbaum's studies of a wide variety of organisations, including military, voluntary, business, labour, municipal agencies, and colleges, as well as a five-nation study of large and small factories, showed that some degree of slope to such control graphs is almost universal. As predicted, the curve was flattest in the case of voluntary organisations and in those countries (Yugoslavia and the Israeli kibbutzim) where the philosophy was to involve the rank and file in making policy decisions. There was evidence for the 'expandable pie' idea of power in organisations from the finding that there was in total more felt influence in organisations in some countries (particularly the USA) than in others (Italy and Austria).

CLIENT AUTONOMY IN HUMAN SERVICE ORGANISATIONS

In human service organisations the question of member influence or involvement in decision-making has generally been divided into two sub-questions: (1) how influential are different levels of *staff* in the organisation? and (2) to what extent are *clients* involved in decision-making? In reality, of course, these questions are connected and it would probably be more fruitful if they were considered together, using the same concepts and measures.

Because of the dependency of clients on account of their youth, poverty, illness or disability, and because of the expert power (and other sources of power in many cases) of staff, human service organisations are just as prone to authoritarian forms of decision-making as are other types of organisation. Where service is provided on a residential basis there is the further danger of creating what Goffman (1961) called a *total institution*. In hospitals for the mentally ill or mentally handicapped, for example, and in prisons (as well as in such institutions as army barracks, ships and monasteries), almost all aspects of life are conducted in the same place and under the same authority. Normally, in modern Western society at least, people conduct different aspects of their lives—for example sleeping, playing and working—in different places, with different people, and under different authorities.

The subjugation of individuality to authoritarian rule and routine was an important element in Goffman's picture of the total institution. The stereotype serves as a warning of what can so easily happen given an institutional framework, but does not provide an adequate description of all institutions. Considerable progress has been made in describing the variety which exists within health and social care residential institutions, and no doubt similar variety exists within educational establishments, and even within closed penal institutions.

One of the most relevant studies is that carried out by Apte (1968) who developed a hostel-hospital practice profile (HHPP) designed to assess two separate aspects of involvement of residents in decision-making (although it is clear from the results obtained that these two aspects were highly correlated). The first—restrictive versus permissive practices—concerned such matters as control of residents' physical movement, of their food and drink intake, over privacy, personal belongings, and social relationships. The second—responsibility expectations—covered responsibility for the residents' personal property, for starting his/her own day, for personal appearance, medical care, and participation in hospital or hostel management. On average, hostels were less institutional than the mental hospitals, the former having between one half and two-thirds the number of restrictive practices found on the average hospital ward. However, considerable variation was found in both types of facility and there was overlap between them. Some of the hostels, whilst being small in size, and designed to provide a link between the large institution and the community, nevertheless retained a number of institutional practices. Hostel staff were particularly likely to maintain control over activities such as smoking, watching television and daytime resting on the bed, and also over social relationships such as visitors and mixing with the opposite sex, the latter being only very infrequently encouraged. Similarly with responsibility expectations, hostels varied from one which expected responsibility from its residents in 19 out of 21 areas, to one that expected responsibility in only 8. The question about participation in the operation of management of the hostel showed that only 4 of 25 hostels fostered this kind of responsibility. The overlap between practices in hostels and those of hospital wards was such that the notion of continuity from institution to halfway house to community was sometimes contravened. In one instance the hostel had more institutional practices than the hospital rehabilitation ward from which most of its residents came.

An increase in decision-making responsibility in such settings may have important outcomes for people who are vulnerable to distress or illness. In one study of a convalescent home, carers were trained to encourage one group of older adult residents to take responsibility for determining what their rooms should look like, where and when they would go out, and with whom they wanted to spend time. A comparison group were encouraged to feel that the staff would care for them and would try to satisfy their needs. Not only did the former group become more active and alert and engaged in a wider variety of activities, but an analysis of their medical records also showed greater improvements in health during the six months follow-up period and a reduced death rate during the following 18 months (Rodin, 1983, cited by Newton, 1988).

Otto and Orford (1978) have also described variation in the degree of involvement in decision-making of residents of small hostels for people with drinking problems. They produced a scale of decisions varying from those in which hostel residents were frequently involved (for example, deciding when was an appropriate time to get up in the morning, and deciding to initiate leisure-time events for the resident group), to those at the other extreme in which residents were rarely if ever involved (for example, decisions involving finances, and purchases of major items of furniture or equipment). Particularly discriminating were items to do with the selection or discharge of fellow residents. Several of the hostels were like larger institutions in reserving such decisions for staff alone. In others, residents were involved in these crucial decisions. Rarely, however, were they the sole decision-makers, and in several their real decision-making power was limited to ratifying previously made staff decisions. Control over membership is a central feature of the concept of home and may be crucial to an understanding of privacy. Hence this is an important aspect of an organisation's functioning to know about: how is the input and output of individual members managed and decided upon? In many institutions, not only are the pupils, residents, or inmates not consulted, but neither are those members of staff who are most closely in touch with them (the teachers, nurses, prison officers, etc.), nor sometimes the staff in charge of the day-to-day running of the place (the matron, the warden, etc.). For example, in their study of residential institutions for the physically handicapped and the young chronic sick, Miller and Gwynne (1972) described the adverse effects upon the climate of the home when local social service or hospital authority policy reduced the control which members of a unit had over their own intake.

As we discover time and again (see Chapter 9 for further examples), the events and processes that are found to be of importance in human service organisations turn out to be of relevance to almost all organisations whatever their type and purpose. Amongst the questions that Katz and Kahn (1978) suggested should be asked to discover whether an organisation is truly democratic are the following:

How are decisions made about expanding or contracting the organisation? About altering the organisation's structure? About changes in the nature of the product? About the organisation's location, its relationship with the environment or its use of resources? Who has the use of a veto? How are selection, tenure and dismissal determined, especially for key executive positions?

Amongst the scales included in Moos' (1974) instruments for assessing client and staff perceptions of the climate or atmosphere in hospital wards and community programmes such as halfway houses (see Chapter 2) was one termed *staff control*. This, which in Moos' scheme is one of the system maintenance and system change dimensions, assesses the necessity for staff to restrict residents by means of rules, schedules and regulations and other measures taken to keep residents under effective control. In his research Moos regularly found that residents perceived a higher level of staff control than did staff themselves: an illustration of the general law that the powerless are generally more sensitive to power differentials than the powerful.

Amongst important questions are: How flexible is the use of different behaviour settings in the organisation? How many settings are closed to members? How freely can members move in and out of the buildings and grounds? How flexible is the time schedule? Institutional life can be *normalised* as much as possible by allowing flexible use of kitchen and laundry equipment for example, and the use of recreational objects such as television and the record player. Residential institutions usually deprive adult inmates of the opportunity to take part in *complete activity cycles*. In this respect the relationship between the institution and the client is similar to that between an hotel and its guests. Instead of taking part in the complete cycle of shopping for food, preparing it, eating it, clearing away and washing up after it, the residents may simply be required to eat what others have purchased and prepared. Miller and Gwynne (1972) provided some telling examples of how institutions, in this case for the physically disabled, could stifle a resident's initiative in the use of objects—in one instance, for example, making it impossible for a young man to use the record player he had brought with him to the home on the grounds that there was nowhere that he could play it. Barker's (1968, 1978) approach to understanding the rules governing entry to and conduct in behaviour settings offers a potentially rich, although hitherto largely neglected, way of understanding these important aspects of human service residential establishments.

STAFF AUTONOMY

However, staff autonomy in human service organisations is crucial also. Those staff who have the closest dealings with the organisation's users or clients may be deprived of a large measure of decision-making power, not only over intake of new clients, but even over their day-to-day interactions. Indeed it is this variable of staff autonomy which J. Tizard, Sinclair and Clarke (1975) considered to be one of the strongest influences upon the quality of staff-client interaction in an institutional setting. The firmest evidence for this hypothesis is contained in a chapter of their book written by B. Tizard. It concerns residential nurseries run by voluntary societies. She observed 13 such units all of which had been modernised to provide 'family group' care. Groups of six children each had their own suite of rooms and their own nurses. Despite this effort at 'de-institutionalising', marked differences existed in the degree to which nurses truly had control over their own work practices. Nurseries were divided by the research team into three categories on the basis of the amount of *unit autonomy*. The first group, it was felt, were in effect run centrally by the matron:

> Decisions were made on an entirely routine basis or else referred to the matron. Each day was strictly timetabled, the matron would make frequent inspections of each group, and freedom of the nurse and child was very limited. The children were moved through the day 'en bloc'. ... The nurse had little more autonomy than the children, e.g. she would have to ask permission to take the children for a walk or to turn on the television set. As in hospital each grade of staff wore a special uniform, and had separate living quarters, and the nurse's behaviour when off duty was governed by quite strict rules. (p. 106)

At the other extreme was a group of nurseries which more closely approximated a normal family setting:

> the staff were responsible for shopping, cooking, making excursions with the children and arranging their own day. The children could move freely about the house and garden and the staff rarely referred a decision to the matron. The nurse-in-charge did not wear uniform, and her off-duty time was not subject to rules. Her role, in fact, approximated more closely to that of a foster-mother. Since she could plan her own day and was not under constant surveillance she could treat the children more flexibly. (p. 107)

A third group of nurseries was intermediate in terms of staff independence. As predicted, the more autonomous staff were observed to spend more time talking to children, and more time playing, reading and giving information to the children. Furthermore, children in units with more autonomous staff had higher scores on a test of verbal comprehension. The difficulty of teasing out what is important in complex social situations such as those that exist in institutions is illustrated by Tizard's findings. Autonomy was correlated with having a relatively favourable staff-to-child ratio and hence we cannot be certain that autonomy was the crucial variable.

Nevertheless the autonomy hypothesis fits a great deal of informal observation and comment that has been made about institutional organisation, and Tizard made a convincing case for its importance. Her team observed what they interpreted to be a strong influence of staff hierarchy. When two staff were present at once one was always 'in charge'. Having someone else present and in charge appeared to have an inhibiting effect on a nurse's behaviour toward children: she would function in a, 'notably restricted way, talking much less and using less "informative" talk than the nurse in charge' (p. 117). If this is a general effect, it would explain the differences between autonomous and less autonomous units, as staff in the latter type of unit would be much less likely to feel 'dominant' (Mehrabian and Russell, 1974—see Chapter 2) and would be much more likely to feel that someone else was in charge whether that person was present or not.

Control over the use of space, time and other resources is a vital aspect of the power and control system operating within any organisation, as Tellis-Nayak and Tellis-Nayak (1984) showed in their ethnographic study based upon observations and interviews of doctors and nurses in four hospitals in Midwest USA. Their report is particularly interesting since it describes some of the everyday micro-processes whereby hierarchical differences between staff of different disciplines may be maintained and reinforced. The relationship between doctors and nurses is, of course, usually confounded, as it was in this study, by the fact that the majority of doctors are men and the large majority of nurses women.

In accordance with the higher status of doctors, differences were found in the use of space as a privilege and time as a resource. Physicians, whether resident or attending, had private offices, whilst nurses did not. Physicians had separate lounges whilst nurses either had lounges that were less spacious, less well decorated and furnished, and without the same degree of services such as food and television, or else they had none at all. There were differences in the assignment of conference rooms, car parking privileges, access to exclusive recreational dining facilities, and invitations to and seating arrangements at formal ceremonies. Physicians' territories were usually guarded by a nurse or secretary and were rarely invaded by others, whilst patients and doctors did not deem it improper to invade the nurses' station without notice or regard for activities in progress. Physicians had much more control over their own time. Nurses on the other hand were required either to punch time cards or to sign in and there were specific sanctions in operation governing their late arrival or early departure. Doctors were not expected to be kept waiting whereas nurses could be.

Again consistent with a marked difference in status, it was noted that doctors frequently addressed nurses by their first names, moved into close proximity to a nurse within her 'personal space' and showed friendly support and comfort by touching a nurse. The reverse of these behaviours, from nurse to doctor, was rarely observed. Humour, a sensitive index of dominance, was often initiated by physicians but rarely by nurses, and then usually in the company of long-standing acquaintances. In a dialogue of any kind doctors often monopolised, interrupted, contradicted, corrected and even reprimanded, whereas nurses were much more self-effacing. If they were required to correct a physician they tended to resort to circumlocution and indirect cues.

Although Tellis-Nayak and Tellis-Nayak agree that gender, as well as racial, differences carry over into the professional relationship between doctors and nurses in a hospital setting, their observations and relationships between male doctors and male nurses supported their view that these ways of relating existed independently of such factors as gender and race.

Whether these power differences between doctors and nurses, of which there were so many signs in the everyday life of the hospitals, are seen as benign or reprehensible is of course a matter of interpretation. To use one of the concepts introduced earlier in this chapter, it depends upon whether the greater power of the doctors is seen as power that is wielded *over* the nurses or as power used *in order to* bring about desired outcomes for the general good. Indeed the very word 'power', with its negative connotations, is only likely to be used if the interpretation is along the former lines. If the latter, more positive interpretation is made then the doctors' power is much more likely to be referred to as 'leadership'.

POWERLESSNESS

POWERLESSNESS AT THE INDIVIDUAL LEVEL

The topic of powerlessness is of particular relevance for community psychology since it is the relative *absence* of power, or feelings of power, amongst individuals or groups with high rates of psychological distress that is likely to be more apparent to those who work with a community psychology approach than will be the relatively advantaged position of those who wield power. Indeed it is a paradox that the dark side of power is so well appreciated (power 'corrupts', 'is abused', etc.) whilst the possibility that lack of power may be undesirable and unhealthy for those who experience it is less well articulated (Ng, 1980).

Ng points to the rich variety of overlapping concepts used by psychologists to describe individual feelings of control versus lack of control over events. These include McDougall's *self assertion*, Maslow's *dominance-feeling*, White's *competence*, de Charms' *personal causation*, Rotter's internal versus external *locus of control*, Seligman's *learned helplessness*, and Bandura's *self-efficacy*.

A number of points can be made about these various psychological terms. The first is, as Ng notes, that they are all basically power terms. Each of these influential concepts has served, in its own way, to identify feelings of personal power as a central component of the human psyche. Furthermore, most have linked feelings of power with psychological health, and feelings of lack of power with mental ill-health or psychological distress. In addition, although these concepts are firmly located at the level of individual feelings or perceptions, inherent in several of them are at least potential links with formulations at other levels. One such potential link is towards a more generalised dispositional or personality level. For example, Maslow's dominance-feeling has an explicit link with generalised self-esteem, and Rotter's internal versus external locus of control has often been treated as a dispositional rather than context-specific attribute. More important for present purposes, however, is the link that can be made with environmental events or circumstances. For example, the theory of learned helplessness is that this is a state brought about by an individual's experience of the environment—specifically the experience that the avoidance of aversive events is outside the individual's control. In locus of control theory, powerful other people, and complicated events, are two of the external factors to which those with a relatively external locus of control are said to attribute control. There are obvious parallels here with the kinds of settings in which Mehrabian and Russell (1974, see Chapter 2) predicted people would experience low dominance feelings. Most of the other theories are less explicit about links with the environment, but it is difficult to conceive that an adequate account of personal power versus powerlessness could do other than take into account both its personal and environmental determinants.

As an example let us consider Rosenfield's (1989) model for explaining the effects of women's employment on anxiety and depression. This account gives a central place to personal feelings of control or power but sees their determinants as lying within the structure of family roles, the labour market and societal norms. Previous theory had suggested that sex differences in anxiety and depression were due to inequalities in power between the sexes in the family, and that going out to work would equalise women's and men's power resources (although this would only fully be the case if earned incomes were similar) and hence would equalise rates of psychological distress. Results have given only inconsistent support to this prediction. By analysing results from three existing survey data sets in the USA, Rosenfield was able to show that the addition of a further variable—role overload or demands—helped explain much of the inconsistency. Thus the advantages of outside employment and earned income, in terms of reduced rates of anxiety or depression, were not so apparent for women who had children at home, or who described domestic or outside employment as creating greater demands upon them. This, incidentally, is a good example of the combined operation of a number of Bronfenbrenner's (1979) systems levels. The micro-level is represented by the sharing of tasks and the relative incomes of husbands and wives; the meso-level by the relationship between the demands of outside employment and family life; and the macro-level by prevailing norms about the distribution of labour in the home and legislation regarding women's and men's incomes. The exo-level could also be said to be present, if not explicitly in Rosenfield's paper, in terms of local decisions and negotiations about pay and conditions, to which most individuals would not be a party but by which their lives would be much affected.

COLLECTIVE POWER AND POWERLESSNESS

One of the great attractions of the concept of power for community psychology is that it can be thought of as both an individual and a collective quality. Much of the social psychological theorising about power has dealt with it at the individual level or at the level of the dyad (the power of person A over person B). The third dimension of power, as discussed earlier, deals with power as something embedded within a complex set of structural relationships between people within organisations or institutions or society as a whole (Ng, 1980). This is the taken-for-granted or hidden form of collective power. A different type of collective power occurs when a formerly relatively powerless group takes social action in order to improve its power position. This requires collective awareness of a common cause, and the development of group solidarity, and these conditions may be hard to develop. Whatever the form of collective power, or its manner of development, the flexibility with which collective power resources can be put into effect (the 'liquidity' of power to borrow an economic term) and its overall strength are, arguably, much greater than is usually the case for individual power (Wrong, 1979).

The inter-relationship between power at the level of individual behaviour and at the level of institutional structure is also to be seen in the circumplex models of the interpersonal behaviour theorists whose work was discussed in Chapter 2. Dominant behaviours (shown, appropriately, at the top of all such models) can be considered as an aspect of one individual's behaviour at one particular moment in time, but may also be thought of as indicative of a position in a set of structural power relationships. This same crucial point can be made with respect to power's opposite—submission or powerlessness.

Although models of personal control or power recognise some of the environmental determinants, they do not deal with collective power or its absence. One recent attempt to couple personal and collective control in the context of health promotion is that of Peterson and Stunkard (1989). They considered the evidence that feelings of control are linked to positive health. They recognised the point made by Rosenfield (1989) in her study of women's mental health, namely that, 'it [personal control] resides in the transaction between the person and the world; it is neither just a disposition nor just a characteristic of the environment' (Peterson and Stunkard, p. 820). They go on to make the further point that control may itself be used at a collective level:

> A major strength of the concept of personal control is the possibility of using it at the social as well as the individual level of analysis. It may be possible to characterize groups as well as individuals as more or less efficacious with respect to a given goal. ... We propose that this sense of *collective control* can result not only in greater accomplishment on the part of the group, but by analogy to the findings on personal control, can also lead to higher morale, greater perseverance in the face of failure, greater tolerance of interruption and turnover, and better physical health. (pp. 821–822)

They continue to suggest that one way of promoting health would be to identify organisations and groups, such as schools, work sites or neighbourhoods, where a sense of collectivity or common identity exists, and where this might be used to enhance group or collective feelings of power, control or mastery.

Powerlessness at a collective level has been embodied in sociological theory for a long time in concepts such as *alienation* and *anomie*. Deflem (1989) has considered the concept of anomie and some of the, often imprecise, ways in which the concept has been used in mental health research. He points out that the term has been defined slightly differently by different sociologists but that it always refers to conditions at a collective, societal level. The most influential definitions of anomie have probably been those of Durkheim, for example in his book on suicide (1897/1952, cited by Deflem, 1989), and that of Merton (1938, cited by Deflem, 1989). Durkheim considered that a major function of society was to regulate and control its members' desires which would otherwise be unrestrained and unlimited. In this capacity society had the role of a superior authority or moral power, and it was at times of abrupt transitions, when society proved incapable of exercising this function, that a collective state of anomie resulted. A high rate of suicides was one index of this collective state.

Merton was interested in rates of social deviance which he linked with a collective state of demoralisation or anomie in society. For Merton this came about when there was a dissociation between goals which society defined as being valued and important (financial success in American culture for example) and the means of striving towards those goals which society prescribes (working hard, saving, and keeping within the law, for example). Anomie would result, for example, if in society as a whole, or in certain social groups within society, the goals were well-defined but the institutionalised means to achieve them were not well-defined or emphasised.

Deflem believes that these seminal ideas have been misrepresented in much mental health research and he illustrates this with reference to Srole's survey work on mental health in the general population in the USA (e.g. Srole *et al.* 1978) and Jilek's study of depression in Salish Indian communities on the

Pacific coast of South West Canada and North West USA (e.g. Jilek, 1974, cited by Deflem, 1989). Srole used the term 'anomia', in a number of senses, for example to refer to an individual state of mind which included a perception that community leaders were detached from and indifferent to the individual's needs, that the social order was unpredictable, that life was meaningless, or that his or her network of personal relationships was no longer predictable or supportive. Although it was of value to demonstrate, as Srole and his colleagues did in more than one study, that socio-economic status was inversely related to anomia (although Deflem suggests that this finding may not apply universally) and that both low status and high anomia were related to mental ill-health, the use of the concept of anomia at an individual level was certainly not what Durkheim and Merton had in mind, and the concept as used by Srole *et al.* is really a ragbag of components related to perceptions of society and community, social support, and personal feelings.

Jilek was interested in accounting for the change that seemed to have occurred in Salish society from a time when 'spirit sickness'—an illness-like but time-limited and situation-specific state associated with ceremonial occasions—was a regular occurrence. In modern Salish society spirit sickness appeared to have been replaced by a high rate of 'anomic depression'. Jilek examined individual case histories to discover the socio-dynamic and psycho-dynamic patterns of depression, and concluded that they were reactions to alienation from aboriginal culture under Westernising influence. In particular the syndrome derived from experiences of anomie, relative deprivation, and cultural identity confusion. This is in fact a very interesting attempt to relate conditions of society to individual distress. Nonetheless, Deflem takes Jilek to task for not defining anomie precisely and for attempting to make direct links between properties of society and the experiences of individuals. The latter is a form of psychological reductionism, of which Durkheim, who saw rates of suicide as an attribute of *society*, would not have approved. It is of course just this kind of linking which is likely to be of interest to those with a community psychology approach. Deflem appears to be guilty of the same rigidity on this question as some anthropologists whom G. Jahoda (1982, see Chapter 2) criticises for ignoring the individual level altogether.

It is after all by 'revealing the ways in which personal troubles are connected with public issues' (Ng, 1980, p. 61) that a start can be made to mobilise social action to change environmental conditions that help induce powerlessness. If mental ill-health and psychological distress have much to do with the maldistribution of power, as Joffe and Albee (1981) suggest, and which is the position that Jilek would certainly support in the case of Salish Indians, then not to recognise this link is to run the risk of continuing to take a purely individualistic approach. Joffe and Albee suggest that symptoms of psychological ill-health are often attributed, even when the issue of powerlessness is recognised, to faulty perceptions which are then the target of therapeutic change. They think that in order to prevent psychological disturbance, 'we should not alleviate feelings of powerlessness by altering perceptions but by altering reality' (p. 323). Most of us are caught up in a system that tends to put blame for psychological difficulties on defects of the individual victims themselves (Ryan, 1971). As Joffe and Albee state: 'The problem of powerlessness is exacerbated by the victims, in fact, blaming themselves, as they accept society's assessment of their plight' (p. 323).

A NEED FOR AUTONOMY

Moscovici's (1976, cited by Ng, 1980) work concerning the influence of 'active minorities' has been highly influential in social psychology. His suggestion was that social influence and social power were not the same thing and that even apparently powerless minorities could be influential if they consistently advocated on behalf of their cause in a persuasive fashion. Ng considered Moscovici's uncoupling of influence and power to be naïve, and considered that minority influence must be based at least upon some degree of legitimate authority of the charismatic type. Persuasion would in any case qualify as a form of power according to Wrong's scheme. Moscovici's work does, however, give hope to minorities and calls into question the assumption that minorities are bound to comply with powerful majorities.

Wrong (1979) considered the circumstances under which relatively powerless groups become mobilised for social action. The necessary conditions that he identified were: an awareness by members of their collective identity as a group and common commitment to a goal, interest or set of values; perception by members that shared goals, interests and values were in conflict with those of other groups or established power holders; perception by members of the relevance of action to promote or consolidate their shared interests and values; and some social organisations specifically designed to promote the goals, interests and values that are perceived to be in competition or conflict with those of others. These conditions are more likely to pertain amongst certain groups in society: particularly ethnic and religious communities which may have clear identity and common cause, a strong value system, and much contact amongst members, and relatively higher status urban dwellers who may have wider contacts and good communications, more time, and higher levels of information, education and skill favourable to political awareness and organisation (Wrong, 1979).

But perhaps people, or some people, have a need to be powerless or to submit to authority—a question considered at length by Wrong (1979). Like the reverse question, whether people have an inherent power drive, which Wrong also considered in his book, this is probably an unanswerable question. What Wrong did point out, however, is that all the forms of power relationship which he outlined (see Figure 8, above), with the exception of force and manipulation, require some complementary motivation for compliance on the part of the subordinate parties. A similar point is inherent in the social exchange theories of power, reviewed by Ng (1979), which suppose that B's *dependence* upon A is the complement of A's power over B. These same theories, however, assume that the relationship between A and B will survive until such time as one or other party exits from the relationship. The basis for leaving a relationship is assumed to be a comparison with alternative relationships, which suggests to the individual that a more profitable exchange can be had elsewhere. Although Ng criticised social exchange theories for being so naïve as to assume that the relatively powerless have alternatives to which they can escape when they wish, it does at least suggest that a general motive for remaining in a relationship in which one is relatively powerless is to obtain valued 'resources' which the relatively powerful can provide. As Wrong put it:

> one may doubt that submission in itself is generally desired and experienced as gratifying. Is it not, rather, accepted as the price that is seen as having to be paid for protection, material security, and an orderly world. (Wrong, 1979, p. 120)

Indeed his view was that authority, however benign, is always irksome, and that, 'aspirations to autonomy, self-determination and freedom ... are frustrated even when authority is genuinely maternalistic in its regard for the subject' (Wrong, p. 118). This explains why competent authority is often the preferred form, since it is severely restricted in scope and can survive only so long as the less competent recognises the more competent person's greater expertise. However, even this form of authority runs the risk of creating over-dependency—for a discussion of the risks of creating dependence through certain professional approaches to the assessment and management of people with learning disabilities and others who may be in a dependent role, see Wolfensberger and Thomas, 1983; Barton, 1986; and Chapter 11. Thus, there may be no universal drive to submit to authority. Indeed there may be a widespread need to assert autonomy and to *resist* being the subject of power.

6 Research Methods

The way in which knowledge is advanced is fundamental to a discipline. As a branch of psychology, community psychology draws upon the wide range of research methods that are used in the parent discipline. Because of its distinctive approach, however, community psychology finds more use for some methods than others, and is likely to make particular use of certain research approaches that have recently been imported into psychology from other fields. In particular, the ecological focus on person-in-context, with an appreciation of the complexities involved, renders inappropriate some of the traditional, relatively highly controlled, research designs.

It is sometimes thought it is only via the traditional, rigorous research approaches that psychology can be truly 'scientific'. This is certainly not the case. In fact such a view represents a misunderstanding of the very nature of science. It is certainly not good science to slavishly apply certain methods when they are inappropriate to the phenomena being studied. What the best research paradigms are for community psychology is not yet entirely clear, but in this chapter some of the more promising approaches will be considered. In a single chapter it will not, of course, be possible to look at all the research methods that have been used to good effect, or which could be, in community psychology. Instead the chapter will focus on a few chosen methods: methods for estimating the extent of a problem within a community and the needs of individuals affected; quasi-experimental designs; case studies; qualitative research approaches; and programme evaluation.

INCIDENCE, PREVALENCE AND NEEDS ASSESSMENT

Community surveys represent the tried and tested epidemiological method for estimating the incidence and prevalence of psychological problems within a given population. A number of such surveys were reviewed in Chapter 3 (e.g. Bebbington *et al.*, 1981; Cochrane and Stopes-Roe, 1980).

Methods of obtaining representative samples of the whole population within a particular age span, for example by household—using the electoral register—or via schools, are not foolproof and there is always a certain refusal or non-response rate. However, they have the overwhelming advantage of enabling an approach to be made to an estimate of the true incidence or prevalence of a particular type of individual-level disorder, problem or difficulty in the community. They provide the most direct estimates in the case of relatively commonplace causes of distress such as depression or anxiety, excessive alcohol consumption, and emotional and behavioural problems in children. They may be less useful with difficulties that are less common, associated with much stigma, or when those people with the problem concerned are particularly likely to be missed out. Certain types of problematic drug use, for example, may be particularly difficult to estimate by community survey. Surveys of drug use amongst school pupils, for example, face the problem that problem drug users are more likely than others to be absent from school when the survey is conducted.

In their manual, Hartnoll *et al.* (1985) described various alternative ways in which the incidence and prevalence of a problem such as drug misuse may be gauged They described three alternative types of information source. These are (a) *agency surveys*, (b) *fieldwork* with drug users and (c) use of *indirect indicators*.

Agency surveys may take the form of preliminary surveys of staff to estimate the proportion of their cases believed to have a particular type of problem. Alternatively, current case records may be examined in greater detail, or a prospective investigation can be carried out to examine treatment incidence for a particular agency (Hartnoll *et al.*, 1985). Any study using agency or other official records has to contend with the obvious fact that records are not normally kept for the purpose of estimating incidence or prevalence and are likely to have major shortcomings. It is also important to distinguish between events and individuals. Not every new referral to an agency constitutes a new case. The work of Holding *et al.* (1977) on rates of parasuicide in Edinburgh (see Chapter 3) provides a good example. They had the advantage of being able to use the register maintained at the regional poisoning treatment centre which had been specifically designed to monitor trends in parasuicide. They reported trends for (a) all admissions within a year, (b) all persons admitted within the year (a smaller number because some people were admitted more than once during the year) and (c) all persons admitted for the first time ever during that year with no previous history of parasuicide (a still smaller number since some people admitted during the year were not being admitted for the first time).

A much more complete picture can be obtained, and a more satisfactory estimate of *treated prevalence* achieved, by conducting multiagency surveys, involving an enquiry of all the helping agencies which serve a particular catchment area and which are thought to come into contact with people with the kind of problem or difficulty that is of interest. Double counting is obviously even more of a potential problem with a multiagency survey, and some means has to be found of identifying individuals who are in contact with more than one agency. Although names are the most obvious ways of identifying individuals, and of eliminating double counting, it may not be possible or indeed desirable to record names, and a small number of characteristics such as date of birth, sex, initials or street, can be used as alternative means of identification (Hartnoll *et al.*, 1985).

Multiagency surveys can form the basis for *case registers* if the information obtained in the initial survey is then continually updated. The resulting register may then serve as a powerful tool, not only for estimating incidence and prevalence, but also for establishing trends over time, for planning, monitoring and evaluating service provision, and for conducting more detailed investigations of the needs of individuals on the register, their families and their helpers. A good example of psychiatric case registers was the Camberwell register which began with a census of all residents of the district of Camberwell in South London who were in contact with psychiatric services on 31 December 1964 (Wing and Hailey, 1972). Although this and other such registers served valuable functions in their time, general psychiatric registers are no longer felt to repay the considerable cost involved in maintaining them.

One of the great assets of a register is that it is based on a geographical area, not just upon one or a limited number of agencies. Not only does this enable use to be made of local data from the most recent national census for comparative purposes, but it is also in keeping with two of the central tenets of community psychology and community mental health. One is the principle that problems presented by individual people should be seen in their social and community contexts, and the possible contribution of social and environmental factors explored. A second is that services should be planned *proactively*, on the basis of what is known of the needs of people within an area, rather than reactively on the basis of the needs of those who have followed the uncertain and difficult pathway to a particular agency (see Chapter 3 on the Pathways to Care). The geographical area basis of a register creates one of its most difficult problems, however. Many residents will receive relevant treatment outside the area concerned and these contacts must be included if the register is to be at all comprehensive. Furthermore, a limitation from the community perspective is that many geographical areas that are convenient for administrative purposes (the old London borough of Camberwell is an example) do not correspond to communities in any other sense (Wing and Hailey, 1972). However, the advantages of having a near-total picture of need within an area are such that registers continue to enjoy popularity in those cases where *administrative prevalence* (or 'agency', or 'treated' prevalence) is presumed to be near to *true prevalence*. Such is the case, for example, for handicaps arising from learning disabilities (e.g. Cubbon, 1984, 1985) and, although to a lesser extent, for parasuicide (or 'deliberate self-harm') (Holding *et al.*, 1977). Questions of confidentiality arise with all methods for estimating incidence, prevalence and need, although it is important to emphasise that, strictly speaking, it is only registers which require that names and addresses be obtained. In the case of registers strict rules have to be drawn up to regulate who has access to individual information including names and addresses, who has access to information excluding names and addresses, and who has access to grouped data only.

In the case of a phenomenon such as drug use, agency surveys may be misleading on their own. Surveys of individuals who are identified, for example as problem drug users, because they are clients of a helping agency, or who have been arrested for drug-related offences, can provide a lot of information about the nature and course of such problems, but can provide only a very limited idea of the scale of the problem in the community. In the case of problems that carry a deviant status in the population at large, and/or where individuals are quite likely to know others in the same position, as is the case with certain types of problematic drug use, then it is possible to spread the net much more widely by asking one interviewee or respondent to provide an introduction to others. This is the technique often referred to as *snowballing*. It was put to particularly good use, for example, by Biernacki (1986), in his study of opiate addicts who had ceased their addiction but who had not been in treatment. An extension of such fieldwork is provided by the group of techniques known as *participant observation*. The precise details of the method, and in particular the degree to which the investigator participates (the method requires at least some participation but complete participating is generally held to be incompatible with the objectivity required), vary from investigation to investigation. However, the aim of all studies using this method is to collect detailed information about the behaviour, use and needs of members of the group, from their perspective, by participating in the daily lives of the individuals concerned. These methods clearly have affinities with the methods of cultural anthropologists. Such methods are not usually directed at estimates of incidence and prevalence, although they may produce a much fuller picture of the prevalence of a phenomenon within a single community than can be obtained by any other means. A very good example was Plant's (1975) participant observation study of drug-taking in a single English provincial town.

In those instances where administrative and true prevalence are thought to be widely divergent, as is the case with drug problems, a number of indirect techniques, some quite ingenious, can be resorted to. Various *multiplier techniques* constitute one such. For example, the number of regular opiate users in a part of London was estimated by multiplying the annual number of deaths of drug addicts occurring in that area by 50 and 100 to obtain reasonable lower and upper estimates, based on studies which suggested an annual mortality rate for opiate addicts of between 1 and 2 per cent (Hartnoll *et al.*, 1985). Similarly, notifications of addicts to the Home Office are thought to constitute some basis for estimating total numbers using a multiplier of as much as 5, or even according to some estimates as much as 10.

A further method of indirect estimation is known as the 'capture-recapture' or *indicator dilution technique*. The method, which originated from efforts to determine the number of fish in a lake or animals in a forest, is based on the following logic. If two independent random samples of all the fish in a lake, or all the drug misusers in an area, are taken, and if the overlap between the samples can be determined, then the total number of fish in the lake or misusers in the area can be determined by the formula:

$$N = \frac{n1 \times n2}{x}$$

where N equals the prevalence figure which is being sought, $n1$ and $n2$ are the numbers obtained in the two samples, and x is the overlapping number appearing in both samples. This can be done with fish because it may be relatively straightforward to draw out a sample, tag each fish that is caught, return them to the lake, and later on take a second sample which is virtually independent of the first. This is obviously not so simple with drug misusers. It may be possible to obtain two separate lists—for example lists from two different agencies, or from one treatment agency and from a court, or from the same agency at two different times—but it is unlikely that these will be truly independent. There is also, as with multiagency surveys, the problem of determining overlap between the two samples. In the case of multiagency surveys this was important in order to eliminate double-counting, whereas in the case of the indicator dilution technique it is of course the overlap that is of particular interest. Although there are obvious problems with this method, obtaining several different estimates of prevalence using varieties of this method can help provide a much better estimate of the scale of a problem within an area, and hence of the need for services, when little other information is available (Hartnoll *et al.*, 1975).

Another method of obtaining a rough idea of the extent to which treated prevalence falls short of true prevalence is the use of *nomination techniques*. These may be useful when those individuals with particular needs are likely to know others in a similar position. Those in contact with agencies can then be asked to describe friends with similar problems or needs and to provide a small amount of information about them including whether they were in touch with treatment or helping agencies themselves.

All the methods so far described are aimed at counting numbers; and indeed this is likely to be the first and possibly the most important step in estimating the needs for services of a particular kind within a certain geographical area. Incidence or prevalence may not in themselves provide sufficient information about needs, however, particularly when individual needs may vary greatly within any one category of people in need. Such is the case, for example, for people with psychiatric problems who need health and social care over a longish period of time. Awareness of this fact has led to the development of various forms of *needs assessment*.

A good example of needs assessment is a project carried out by McAusland and Patel (1987) in Exeter, a city of approximately 100 000 people in South

West England. Their focus was the development of services for people in the city with severe long-term mental health problems. Their aims were to find out:

1. How many people there were in the city with such difficulties.
2. What life was like for them and what difficulties were experienced by them and by those who supported them.
3. How professional and other community resources were used by them, and what steps were already being taken to develop services in the future.

There were two phases to the project. The first was an agency survey involving approximately 60 agencies or teams providing some help for people in this category. The second involved interviews with a one in ten sample of people identified at the first phase. An interesting aspect of this form of needs assessment is the involvement of agency staff in conducting the interviews. In the Exeter project two of the needs-assessment project officers were joined by nine mental health workers of different disciplines who worked in the city with people with long-term needs. In other needs-assessment projects, service managers have been included in such data-gathering exercises, thus giving them invaluable experience of talking in depth to some of the users of the services for which they are responsible. This involvement of agency staff in collecting data is an element of the *action research* process which will be described in Chapter 9.

McAusland and Patel found 340 individuals who were in contact with one or more agencies and for whom there existed a substantial amount of information and evidence of long-term psychiatric disability. They comment that: 'Typically individuals have contact with a variety of psychiatric and other services—either simultaneously or sequentially—and the pattern of overlap is complicated and frequently changing' (p. 10). They also identified smaller groups of individuals for whom less information was available or who had had recent contact with services but were now out of touch with them. Their report goes on to provide much detailed information about needs, as stated by agency staff and by service users themselves. Needs were discussed under the following headings: accommodation; crisis help; employment; personal finances; social and leisure activities; family contact and support; physical health and medication. Amongst other conclusions was the highlighting of three areas which appeared to be receiving insufficient attention. One was employment. Despite an extremely low level of employment of any kind amongst this group of people, this was a topic which appeared to have low priority in the workloads of mental health agencies and professionals. Similarly with personal finances, although income levels and amounts of personal possessions were found to be generally very low, and a low income was often stated as a reason for not being involved in more social and leisure activities, this was not a principal concern of the professionals involved. Finally, despite the fact that nearly half the service users had regular contact with family members who lived nearby and who provided regular support of some kind, the amount of supportive work with families was found to be little.

QUASI-EXPERIMENTAL DESIGNS

We turn now to a different area of community psychology research—methods for testing the effectiveness of an intervention. The randomised controlled trial holds pride of place as the best research design (or rather designs in the plural since there are many variations) for testing the outcome efficacy of a psychological intervention. Indeed in many quarters it is still believed to be the only satisfactory design for such research, besides which all others are flawed. This is a troublesome position for the community researcher who is likely to believe that such designs are impossible to achieve in his or her field and, furthermore, that results of research using such designs are surprisingly often irrelevant to his or her needs. To someone in this predicament the ideas of Campbell and his colleagues, and particularly the notion of quasi-experimental research design, bring a great sense of understanding and liberation (Campbell and Stanley, 1963; Cook and Campbell, 1979).

The sense of liberation comes from the fundamental insight of the quasi-experimental design school that all research designs have strengths and weaknesses, and that the aim should be to achieve the best match between the research design, the research question, and the circumstances under which the research is carried out, so as to maximise strengths and minimise weaknesses. According to Campbell and Stanley, a strong design is one that goes a long way towards minimising threats to two types of experimental validity, internal and external:

> *Internal validity* is the basic minimum without which any experiment is uninterpretable: did in fact the experimental treatments make a difference in this specific experimental instance? *External validity* asks the question of *generalizability* ... to what populations, settings, treatment variables, and measurement variables, can this effect be generalized? (Campbell and Stanley, 1963, p. 5, their emphases)

The power and popularity of the randomised controlled trial are due to its great potential for minimising common threats to internal validity. In particular it minimises biases resulting from differential selection of participants for different groups (since the participants, usually but not always individual people, are randomly assigned to groups), and faulty interpretations due to change having been caused by the passage of time (maturation effects) or uncontrolled events which have occurred during the course of the experiment (history effects). The assumption is that the only difference in the experience of members of different groups during the course of the experiment is the extent to which they receive the relevant intervention: in the simplest two-group design, one group receives the intervention in full and the other none of it. The reader is referred to Cook and Campbell's (1979) book for a more complete list of threats to internal validity.

Nevertheless randomised controlled trials are often not ethical, or are not feasible, or are simply not the best designs under the circumstances. Although they often pose the fewest threats to internal validity, it is an oversimplification to assume that such a design automatically eliminates such threats. Perhaps the commonest impediment to carrying out such a design is the need to ensure that one group receives the treatment, and that the other does not (or that groups receive the stipulated type or amount of treatment), and that these differences are not compensated for or augmented in some way that is irrelevant to the research question. In the case of psychological treatments, and particularly in the case of social and community interventions, this degree of control may be impossible.

It is on grounds of external validity, however, that the randomised controlled trial may be found particularly wanting. Sources of threat to external validity (Campbell and Stanley, 1963) may largely be summed up by the single question: To what extent are the arrangements of the experiment representative of those arrangements found commonly elsewhere, and to what extent can the results of the former be generalised to the latter? In an effort to obtain the necessary control for a randomised controlled trial, it may be necessary to select participants, employ assessment techniques, or design interventions, which are too unlike those pertaining elsewhere for the results, however internally valid, to be of much use in generalising to the kinds of samples, interventions or settings most commonly found in practice. In other words, the arrangements lack 'ecological validity'. Which is why alternatives to the randomised controlled trial are so important to those whose work has a community orientation.

Some of the principal forms of quasi-experimental design discussed by Campbell and Stanley (1963) and by Cook and Campbell (1979) are shown schematically in Table 7. One of the most powerful of these designs is the *regression discontinuity design*. It will be discussed at some length here because of its potential usefulness, and because it is still relatively little known.

The strength of the regression discontinuity design lies in the fact that, in common with the randomised controlled trial, it includes a control group and the rule for assigning individuals to interventions or to control is *known* and *strict*. However, whereas in the case of the randomised controlled trial this known and strict procedure is one of randomisation, in the case of regression discontinuity assignment is carried out according to an individual's position above or below a cut-off point on some continuously distributed variable. This pre-intervention assignment variable is very likely to be a variable that reflects degree of need (Trochim, 1984). For example, in the educational field, which is where ideas on quasi-experiments originated and where much of the work using the regression discontinuity design has been carried out, assignment might be according to some variable—such as reading age—indicative of need for the remedial programme that is being evaluated. In a study of alcohol use amongst patients admitted to the medical wards of the general hospital in Exeter in South West England (Daniels, Somers, Orford and

Table 7. Principal forms of quasi-experimental research design (based on Cook and Campbell, 1979)

1. Pre-test, post-test with comparison group:
   i.e. Intervention Group: O_1 X O_2
        Comparison Group: O_1 O_2
   (where O_1 = assessment on occasion 1
        O_2 = assessment on occasion 2
        X = the intervention)
2. Regression discontinuity:
   i.e. The same as above but the comparison group, instead of being chosen for as close as possible equivalence to the intervention group, is deliberately chosen to be distinct from the intervention group but in a known way
3. Cohort design:
   If the intervention and comparison groups are assessed at different times, i.e. they are different cohorts (e.g. two classes of pupils from successive years), this becomes a cohort design
   i.e. Intervention Group: O_1 X O_2
        Comparison Group: O_1 O_2
4. Simple interrupted time series:
   i.e. Intervention Group: O_1 O_2 O_3 O_4 O_5 X O_6 O_7 O_8 O_9 O_{10}
5. Time series with comparison group:
   i.e. Intervention Group: O_1 O_2 O_3 O_4 O_5 X O_6 O_7 O_8 O_9 O_{10}
        Comparison Group: O_1 O_2 O_3 O_4 O_5 O_6 O_7 O_8 O_9 O_{10}
6. Pre-test, post-test, with comparison variable:
   i.e. The comparison is made not with a non-intervention group, but with a variable that is not expected to change as a result of the intervention (e.g. accidents early in the day versus at pub closing times, as a result of the introduction of the breathalyser in the UK)
   i.e. Intervention Group: $O_{1.1}$ X $O_{1.2}$
                            $O_{2.1}$ $O_{2.2}$
   (where $O_{1.1}$ = assessment of variable 1 on occasion 1
        and $O_{2.1}$ = assessment of variable 2 on occasion 1, etc.)
7. Removed (and repeated) intervention designs:
   i.e. The influence of the intervention is further examined by deliberately removing it (shown by $\bar{X}$ below). This design can be further extended by repeating the intervention later
   i.e. Intervention Group: O_1 X O_2 $\bar{X}$ O_3
        Comparison Group: O_1 O_2 O_3
   or Intervention Group: O_1 X O_2 $\bar{X}$ O_3 X O_4
        Comparison Group: O_1 O_2 O_3 O_4
8. Time series (with or without comparison groups) with comparison variable, or removed and repeated interventions:
   i.e. Time series design can be combined with designs 6 or 7

Kirby, 1991) advice to reduce alcohol consumption plus a self-help book were given only to those patients who scored above a certain threshold on a composite score of alcohol intake and alcohol-related problems.

Such a design is likely to be particularly useful in community settings for two reasons. First, unlike the randomised controlled trial, it is compatible with the goal of allocating scarce resources to those that need them most (Trochim, 1984). Secondly, it is therefore likely that agreement could be obtained for an experiment using a regression discontinuity design in many circumstances in which a randomised controlled trial would be unethical or impossible. Indeed decisions about the allocation of services are often made in this way in the normal course of events, particularly in education, thus offering *natural experiments*, the results of which can be analysed according to regression discontinuity principles.

As the name of the design suggests, analysis is in terms of regression and the plotting of regression lines that best describe the relationship between outcome and the pre-intervention assignment variable. The principle of the analysis is to compare the regression line that best fits the data for the group receiving the intervention with the *expected* regression line based upon a projection of the best fit regression line produced for the non-intervention group. In other words, what is being compared is what actually happened for the intervention group with the best estimate of what would have happened for them in the absence of intervention.

Figure 10 shows a number of hypothetical results. The examples given show, respectively: (a) *no effect* since the regression line for the intervention group does not depart from what would be expected on the basis of a projection of the non-intervention group regression line; (b) a *positive effect* of the intervention, reflected in a significant difference between the points of intersection of the two regression lines on the vertical axis drawn through the cut-off point on the pre-intervention variable; (c) a *negative effect*, opposite in direction to that expected; and (d) a significant *interaction effect* suggesting that, although those who received the intervention who were nearest to the pre-intervention assessment cut-off point did not benefit, those with highest pre-intervention scores may have benefited most (this is reflected in a difference in the slopes of the regression lines).

Table 7 shows a number of alternative quasi-experimental designs which can be used when it is neither possible to assign to intervention and no-intervention on the basis of randomisation nor, as in regression discontinuity, on the basis of a known rule. One of these is the *non-equivalent comparison group* design. Provided it is possible to test the comparison group before and after intervention, in the same way as is done for the intervention group, then there are some definite advantages of including a comparison group in an experimental design even though the groups are not exactly equivalent. They should, however, be chosen to be as similar as possible. In contrast with a simple design that lacks any kind of comparison or control group, the non-

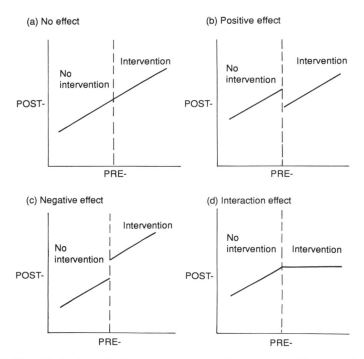

Figure 10. Hypothetical results from experiments using regression discontinuity design NB In these illustrations the aim of the intervention was to *reduce* scores on the measure used pre- and post-

equivalent comparison group design has the advantage of minimising some of the major threats to interval validity, such as maturation, history and the effects of assessment (Campbell and Stanley, 1963). It is particularly useful in community research when the impact of an intervention upon a whole area, town or community is being assessed and where it may be possible to find a comparison that is similar but has not been subject to the intervention.

Another generally very useful design is an *interrupted time-series*. This design uses change over time as the basis for interpreting the effects of an intervention, and it requires multiple tests or assessments both before and after the intervention is introduced. This design is not unlike regression discontinuity except that the basis for assigning intervention is time rather than a decision rule about who receives which intervention. In community research the intervention is delivered to a whole system or setting—a school, a mental health centre, neighbourhood or community—but interrupted time series is, in essence, identical to single-case experimental design which is used in clinical psychology with individuals instead of larger entities.

A good illustration of the use of a quasi-experimental design which combined an interrupted time-series with the use of a non-equivalent comparison group was a test of a new crisis intervention scheme set up as part of the community mental health service in a particular health zone in Illinois, USA (Delaney, Seidman and Willis, 1978). The scheme commenced on 1 January 1970 and consisted of a team of two staff responding to mental health crises within 24 hours wherever they occurred (home, hospital, jail, bar, etc.). The aims were to commence assessment and diagnosis at an early stage, to prevent life crises developing into psychiatric disorder, to get necessary treatment underway, and as far as possible to prevent hospitalisation.

To test whether the last of these aims was being achieved, admissions to state psychiatric hospitals from the zone in which the scheme was operating were plotted for each three-month period from two years prior to the scheme starting to two years after the start. This plot is shown by the circles in Figure 11, taken from Delaney, Seidman and Willis (1978, p. 41). On its own this corresponds to an interrupted time-series design. Like regression discontinuity data, these can be analysed to see if there is a change in level at the point of 'discontinuity' or 'interruption' (i.e. when the intervention commenced) and to discover if the slope of the curve following the intervention has changed in comparison with the previous slope. Visual inspection of this plot—which in the case of quasi-experimental designs is often sufficient to make a fairly confident interpretation—certainly suggests in this case that admissions came down sharply during the first year of the scheme's operation so that in the second year hospital admissions were running at a consistently lower rate than they had done for at least two years previously. Statistically, the *increase* in admissions for the first quarter after the scheme started was significant. This appears to have been a temporary increase, however, and the change in slope following the commencement of the scheme was also statistically significant.

The squares in Figure 11 represent data from a similar zone in the same area of Illinois. It is the addition of these data that makes the design also an example of the use of a non-equivalent comparison group. Clearly there was no possibility of random assignment in this experiment, but the conclusion that the operation of the new crisis intervention scheme was really of influence in reducing hospital admissions was very much strengthened by taking the additional trouble of collecting data from a similar area that had not started such a scheme. As a comparison an area was sought that was within the same zone, and hence subject to the same policies and leadership regarding mental health, and which was broadly similar in other ways. For example, both experimental and comparison areas contained large state universities, had no major industries, and were primarily agricultural. Statistically, there was no significant change in either the level of admissions or the slope of the plot of admissions over time in the comparison area.

Examples of the use of non-equivalent comparison groups in research in Britain include attempts to assess whether the Samaritans had been influential in lowering the suicide rate. Both Bagley (1968) and Jennings, Barraclough and Moss (1978) carefully chose comparison towns without Samaritan

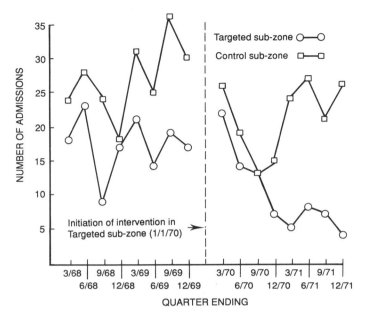

Figure 11. Use of time-series analysis with comparison group, showing the effect of introducing a crisis intervention service (reproduced from Delaney, Seidman and Willis, 1978, by permission of Plenum Publishing Corp.)

branches to compare with Samaritan towns. In Bagley's analysis the first 15 county boroughs to have Samaritan branches were individually matched with comparison towns in two separate ways: according to 'ecological similarity' (using two dimensions: social class, and population change 1931–51) and according to three variables predictive of suicide rate (percentage of the population aged 65 or over, number of females per thousand males, and a social class index). Bagley found that the suicide rate in the Samaritan towns had fallen by 6 per cent since the opening of the branches, whilst over the same period that of the comparison towns had risen by 20 per cent or 7 per cent, using the first and second matching methods respectively. In both cases the differences were statistically significant. Using slightly different methods for choosing comparison towns, Jennings, Barraclough and Moss found no significant differences in suicide rates. They did point out that they were solely concerned with the effect of the Samaritans on the suicide rate, and that the value of the Samaritans' contribution in relieving distress in other ways was not in question.

PROGRAMME EVALUATION

One of the most frequently occurring community psychology research tasks is the evaluation of a human service programme, whether this be educational, in the health or social care field, or in the socio-legal sphere (for example a programme offering an alternative, community treatment in place of a custodial sentence). This is so common a task, particularly in the USA where agencies are often required to devote at least a certain percentage of their budgets to evaluation, that whole journals and many books have now been devoted to the subject of programme evaluation. The reader is particularly referred to the books by Rossi and Freeman (1986) and by Posovac and Carey (1985).

There are, needless to say, many different ways of going about evaluating a service, programme or project, and there is often confusion about what exactly is meant by the term 'evaluation'. One useful distinction is between *formative* and *summative* evaluation. The latter aims to arrive at some summary statement about the effectiveness of the programme in achieving its aims. Most of the examples given in the previous section of this chapter could be classed as partial attempts at summative evaluation: To what extent were the projects concerned successful in reducing heavy drinking, or reducing psychiatric hospital admissions, or lowering the suicide rate? Evaluation may have such a purpose but it certainly need not. Formative evaluation does not attempt to reach a summary statement about outcome, but rather seeks to aid the development of the programme by discovering ways in which the programme is operating that make it more or less likely that it will achieve its aims. The emphasis is upon process rather than outcome. Formative or process evaluation is no less valid than outcome or summative evaluation; indeed summative evaluation may be premature or wholly inappropriate if the programme concerned is not yet fully functioning or is thought to be operating in such a way that its aims could not be fully achieved.

Hence evaluation may serve a number of different functions. These include:

1. To clarify what the aims of the programme are. It is surprising how often aims are left unclear. Often there are too many aims and priorities are uncertain. For example, those who run a small therapeutic hostel may find it difficult to decide whether the priority lies with a relatively small number of people who have longer-term needs for a home, or with a larger number of people who will stay for shorter periods and use the hostel as a halfway house. Goal analysis often reveals that aims have never been formulated or have been lost sight of, or that they are couched in overgrand terms or in terms of what the service does rather than what outcomes are expected (Pancer and Westhues, 1989).

2. To find out whether the programme is reaching its intended users or clients. Programmes often fail to achieve their initial aims because their intended clients are difficult to reach or to help. What often occurs is a 'drift' towards clients who are 'easier' in some way. For example, a community mental health team finds itself working with a majority of clients whose problems are less severe and shorter-term than those it was intended

to work with; or an alcohol detoxification programme that set out to de-criminalise drunkenness by working with excessive drinkers referred by the police, finds itself working with people without offence records who are referred by their doctors; or a TV programme intended for educationally underprivileged children turns out to be watched more by middle-class families.

3. To find out how the programme is functioning in practice. What are its procedures? How much time is spent on different activities? What is thought to be working particularly well? What are the gaps, and what is thought not to be working? Ideally, data should be collected from a variety of sources: logs and time sheets, observations, analysis of records and documents, and information from users, staff and management via questionnaires and interviews.

4. Outcome or summative evaluation using experimental or quasi-experimental design.

5. Cost-effectiveness analysis. This requires an examination of outcomes against the costs of running the programme. Costs are likely to come under many different headings, some obvious and some hidden. They may not be at all easy to calculate and the advice of a health economist is strongly recommended.

A good example of a programme evaluation which has attempted at least categories 2, 3 and 4 was an evaluation of the innovative Exeter Home Detoxification Project (Stockwell, 1989; Stockwell, Bolt, Milner, Pugh and Young, 1990). The aim of this project was to provide detoxification safely at home instead of in hospital for individuals who were dependent upon alcohol. In terms of Cook and Campbell's nomenclature the outcome or summative aspect of this evaluation used an after-only with comparison groups type of quasi-experimental design. The first 36 people who took part, and as many of their close relatives as were available, were interviewed after the acute phase of detoxification was completed. Background information and detailed records of the detoxification process itself were collected by the community psychiatric nurses who visited each client at home, daily on average, for the first six days. In order to check that the service was being provided for people who were as severely dependent upon alcohol as those who would otherwise be detoxified in hospital, a comparison was made with the results of a hospital detoxification programme from another area. Both projects used a standard scale of severity of alcohol dependence and the results were equivalent.

In terms of safety and completion rates, comparisons were made with the hospital group mentioned above, and also with a group hospitalised for detox-ification in the Exeter area within the 12 months prior to the start of the home detoxification project. Very similar proportions failed to complete (8 out of 41 in the home detoxification group). Only one person developed a serious complication—a withdrawal fit—and again the same was true of the hospital sample. Other milder withdrawal symptoms, as well as medication prescribed, were both at a lower level in the home group than in the hospital comparison.

Home detoxification clients and their relatives were asked to state what they liked most and what they liked least about the programme, and were in addition asked to rate how satisfied they were with a number of specified components of the programme. Both methods revealed quite clearly that the support received from community psychiatric nurses was the element most valued by both detoxification clients and their relatives. It is interesting to note that the daily breathalyser check on the client's breath alcohol level was also highly valued by both whilst a carefully prepared information sheet about detoxification was significantly less valued.

One of the best examples of programme evaluation—indeed one of the best examples of the scientist-practitioner model in community psychology in general—is the series of action cum research projects carried out by Fairweather and his colleagues into the rehabilitation of people with long-term needs for mental health services. His work started with the experiment in creating social change on one ward of a psychiatric hospital (Fairweather, 1964) which was referred to in Chapter 2. This was highly successful in so far as careful assessment showed that patients' behaviour and attitudes were markedly more positive than those of comparison patients on a traditional ward. Yet follow-up showed that this powerful change to hospital practice made comparatively little difference to outcomes for patients once they had left the hospital. The next step in this programme of work was to set up a post-hospital residence, known as the 'lodge', where ex-patients were trained to take over administration of the residence, to live together as an autonomous unit, and to run a joint office-cleaning business (Fairweather, Sanders, Maynard and Cressler, 1969). Residence and work programmes like these have started up in many places since, but they were innovative then. What further marks this work as an excellent piece of community psychology, is the thoroughness with which it was evaluated. As in the hospital ward study which preceded it, patients were randomly assigned to the programme or to standard after-care. The comparison showed that the lodge group faired much better in terms of time working whilst staying at the lodge and amount of time remaining out of hospital. On the other hand, the numbers of ex-patients returning to the hospital at any time were little different and most lodge residents were unable to obtain employment once they left the lodge (Rappaport, 1977).

Nor was that all. The final stage in this exemplary programme of work was a systematic attempt to *disseminate* the positive findings of the lodge experiment throughout the USA. Over 250 mental hospitals were contacted and were offered, on a random basis, either a brochure describing the lodge and its results, or a workshop on the subject, or help in setting up a demonstration project (Fairweather, Sanders and Tornatsky, 1974, cited by Rappaport, 1977). The level of person contacted was also systematically varied—from hospital superintendent to head of nursing. Brochures, workshops and demonstrations were taken up by 70 per cent, 80 per cent and 25 per cent respectively, but nearly half of those who were helped to set up a demonstration project finally agreed to adopt a full replication of the project as opposed to less than 20 per cent of those receiving workshops or brochures. The level of person contacted made no difference. Of particular importance seemed to be commitment to action and change on the part of a group of mental health workers in the hospital, plus early involvement in joint tasks.

CASE STUDIES

Just as quasi-experimental methods are of particular relevance to community psychology, so too are all those research methods that can be subsumed under the title 'case studies'. Particularly useful discussions of this term and the ways in which it might be applied in psychology, are provided by D'Aunno, Klein and Susskind (1985) and by Bromley (1986). The former have written about the case study as one amongst a number of approaches that are particularly relevant to the study of community phenomena, and the latter has written about the case-study method as a general approach in applied psychology.

On the very first page of his book, Bromley describes a psychological case study as, 'an account of the person in a situation'. This immediately inspires anyone with an interest in community psychology to read further, since persons-in-situations is at the heart of community psychology, as Chapter 2 of the present book has attempted to explain. Case studies, Bromley continues, may take many different forms. Usually they concern a relatively short, self-contained episode or segment of life that is critical or formative. A life history is a special example looking at a series of such episodes but inevitably less closely. Case studies are usually descriptive but also provide a causal analysis which attempts to explain. They may involve one or more individual person, group, organisation, or community, but all involve, 'singular, naturally occurring events in the real world ... not experimentally contrived events or simulations' (Bromley, p. 2). The aim of the method is to

> investigate and illuminate the complex system. ... An adequate explanation for a person's behaviour in a given situation is one which contains enough empirical evidence, marshalled by a sufficiently cogent and comprehensive argument, to convince competent investigators that they understand something that previously puzzled them. (Bromley, 1986, pp. 22, 37)

Amongst distinctive characteristics of the case-study method according to D'Aunno, Klein and Susskind are the small number of units involved (whether individuals, groups or communities); the fact that they nearly always concern a span of time, whether prospectively or retrospectively; and the fact that they are about events taking place *in vivo*. Another characteristic that renders the case study particularly relevant for our purposes is the fact that it has often been used in the course of applied work of a problem-solving nature, rather than as pure research. The same could be said of *action research*. The latter is as much a method of organisational change as of research *per se* and it will therefore be discussed in Chapter 9, although it could equally well be included in this chapter. D'Aunno, Klein and Susskind divide case study approaches into three groups: those conducted within a personal service framework in which information is gained in the course of helping a client or client micro-system; those where the object of study is a more complex system such as an organisation or a community and where information is gained in the course of providing consultation, training or action research; and those conducted outside a framework of help- or service-providing.

Bromley points out that although a great many people are engaged in applied work, very few are engaged in developing the science of individual cases. He suggests that this may be because a great deal of patience and hard work is required to carry out a convincing case study, and because in practice the case study has acquired a bad name in psychology because most have been rather unconvincing. He criticises most published case histories in psychology and social work for being overbrief, oversimplified, often being based upon a single source of information and for containing assertions of doubtful validity, unchecked statements and unspoken assumptions. He stresses the need for dispassionate objectivity and believes there may be a danger of conflict between the investigator role and that of advocate. This is an interesting point in view of the importance of advocacy within community psychology (see Chapter 11) and on this point the view of D'Aunno, Klein and Susskind is somewhat different. Although they share the view that self-reports may often be inaccurate, and that multiple sources of data are preferable for case studies, they believe a positive feature of case studies is the very emphasis that is usually placed upon the experiences of those most directly involved in the phenomena concerned, and a greatly reduced distance between researcher and researched in comparison with more traditional approaches.

According to Bromley the basic rules for carrying out a good case study are the following:

1. The need to report truthfully and accurately: each fact needs to be established by rational argument, not by rhetoric or special pleading.
2. The aims and objectives should be explicitly and unambiguously stated.
3. The report should contain an assessment of how well these were achieved, for example acknowledging when information was not available.
4. Time is needed to explore and to cross-check information, to look for consistencies and inconsistencies, to conduct a friendly interrogation of participants in order to reduce accidental errors, omissions or misrepresentations; and if matters of deep emotional significance are being dealt with, someone trained to handle these should be involved.

5. It must deal with the 'ecological context', the situational part of the total 'person-in-situation' as well as the personal or individual component.
6. The report should be written in good, plain language in a direct, objective way, with regard for a high standard of evidence and argument.

An example of a case study cited by D'Aunno, Klein and Susskind is of particular interest since the subject was home–kindergarten relationships—an important example of a meso-level system, to use Bronfenbrenner's (1979) terminology. The aim was to study the impact of school entry on the family. Forty-five mothers and nine fathers from 46 families participated. The method consisted of weekly group interviews over a period spanning the new entry of children to kindergarten. Each group consisted of six to ten parents and two researchers, one acting as a non-participant observer and the other as a leader who facilitated group discussion. Data included verbatim records of group discussions, and observer notes and ratings on the sequence of topics, initiators and participants for each topic area, group tension level and degree of involvement at intervals of approximately five to ten minutes throughout each meeting (Klein and Ross, 1960, cited by D'Aunno, Klein and Susskind, 1985). Results were used to construct a model of the sequence of parental responding over the first few weeks of school, and to make suggestions about the prevention of school adjustment problems by helping families deal with the stress induced by role transition in ways that would strengthen school–home collaboration.

A second example involves a small voluntary (non-statutory) organisation serving people with alcohol problems in one county in Southern England. The organisation operated from 1975 until 1987, and the present author was asked to conduct a study of the circumstances responsible for its closure. The final report was based upon interviews with 14 key informants and an analysis of minutes of the executive committee, which had been well kept throughout (Orford, 1988). From these data it was possible to extract a number of leading themes which together constituted a theory to explain the demise of this one particular small organisation. Two of the main elements consisted of tensions that had existed within the organisation from its beginnings. One was a difference of opinion between those who favoured a supportive role for the organisation (mainly the 'professional' members of the committee) and those who favoured a more active counselling role. The second was a tension between a desire to take on a number of tasks and the need to limit activities on account of scarce financial resources. Elements that entered the picture later on included conflict with statutory organisations who were developing their own services for the same client group in the same area, and increasing frustration at lack of funding coming from a particular source of which the organisation had long been hopeful. The final year was characterised by an increasing downward spiral of frustration and hopelessness, and an element of scapegoating of the main paid employee who showed clear signs of despair and exhaustion. This combination of long-term tensions and more recent negatively spiralling events may be characteristic of many organisations in decline.

The case-study method is an example of the *ideographic approach* which studies individual units (people, organisations, communities), not simply by comparing their standing to other units on certain measures, but rather in individual terms and using internal descriptions and analyses. However, Bromley, D'Aunno, Klein and Susskind, and Mitchell all argue strongly that by conducting a series of case studies and by comparing and contrasting them, theory can be built, prototypical and unusual cases described in detail, and general understanding advanced. Exactly the same kind of reasoning is advanced in support of action research as a scientific method (see Chapter 9). The strength of the case-study method lies in its contribution to careful, detailed description of phenomena plus its inductive approach to the accumulation of knowledge (D'Aunno, Klein and Susskind, 1985). As Bromley put it, the case-study method is not

> concerned exclusively with particular, unique individuals. ... Individual cases can be described and interpreted only in terms of a general conceptual framework. ... The essential scientific value of a case study lies in its conceptual structure. ... Case studies which fail to develop such a conceptual structure fail in their prime scientific and professional purpose. (pp. 6, 295)

QUALITATIVE RESEARCH

Because qualitative research has been less well known and less often used than quantitative approaches in psychology in the past, and because of its particular relevance to community psychology, it will be dealt with at some length here. Case studies are very often qualitative in nature and much of what was said in the previous section applies here too.

The relevance of qualitative approaches for community psychology lies in the particular strengths of qualitative work which are complementary to those of quantitative research. The first of these strengths is the focus on the insider's view. As Wiseman (1978) puts it in her excellent, short account of the type of qualitative research which she practices: 'I am trying to make sense out of the social world of the people I am studying. I am attempting to reconstruct *their* view of the world' (p. 119, her emphasis). In his discussions of grounded theory analysis, one variety of qualitative analysis, Turner also sets great store by the fact that the results are couched in the language of those who occupy the settings in which the data were collected (B. Turner, 1981; Martin and Turner, 1986). Hence the results are accessible to the participants who can then scrutinise and comment upon them.

A second, and perhaps the most important advantage is that qualitative research aims to capture the complexity of social phenomena in the concepts and theories that it generates, and to take fully into account the ways in which these phenomena are expressed in a specific context or a particular location. Thus qualitative approaches are particularly suitable for studying social interaction and perception within complex behaviour settings such as schools, community residential units or families (Corrie and Zaklukiewicz, 1978). Their strength lies in the development of *substantive theory*, that is theory that is applicable to a circumscribed topic or problem area (e.g. a theory of how husbands or wives cope with having an elderly, confused partner) rather than grand or *formal theory* (e.g. a general theory of how people cope with stress) (B. Turner, 1981; Strauss, 1987).

Qualitative research is therefore ideally suited as a method for *induction* (the discovery and development of theory) rather than *deduction* (the testing of hypotheses derived from previously established theory) (Corrie and Zaklukiewicz, 1978; Martin and Turner, 1986). Wiseman likens the process, very aptly, to, 'a detective story that starts out with no suspects' (1978, p. 113). Part of the process of doing qualitative research, according to most writers on the subject, is the making of links with existing theory, but this should be done only at a relatively late stage in the process when much of the work of analysis is already complete and the major concepts that have emerged are already in place (B. Turner, 1981; Strauss, 1987).

How is qualitative research carried out? Space permits only a relatively brief answer to this question here. In any case there exists a wide variety of types of qualitative research (Good and Watts, 1989). The discussion here will concentrate on *grounded theory* analysis and related forms of qualitative research. For more detail the reader is referred to the chapters by Wiseman (1978) and by Corrie and Zaklukiewicz (1978), papers by B. Turner (1981, 1983) and by Martin and Turner (1986) and the book by Strauss (1987). There would probably be general agreement about the main steps involved in the qualitative research process and these are shown in Figure 12.

Most of these authors stress the desirability of having more than one source of data: semi-structured or unstructured interviews, participant observation, non-participant observation, case material, records or other documents. In practice it is unusual to find a study based on several sources of data, although a combination of semi-structured interviews and observations has often been used in settings such as production companies (one of the examples given by B. Turner, 1983 is a case in point) or in hospitals (where much of the research discussed by Strauss, 1987, has been based). Much qualitative research employs interviews alone (e.g. Wiseman, 1978) and B. Turner (1983) provides an example of an analysis based on documents alone, in this case reports of government enquiries following major accidents (such as the Aberfan disaster when a coal tip engulfed a school in South Wales).

Where interviews are employed, some qualitative researchers prefer to use the complete transcripts of tape-recorded interviews for their analysis, whilst others prefer to work directly from tape-recordings, and yet others prefer to

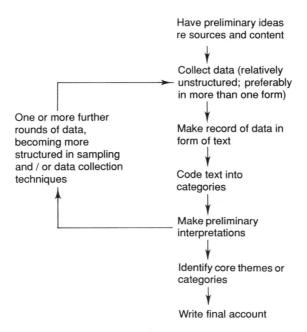

Figure 12. The qualitative research process

work from detailed notes written up very soon after the interview or period of observation (Corrie and Zaklukiewicz, 1978). The present author uses the latter method. Although much information must inevitably be lost in the process, the taking of brief notes at the time followed by the writing of full notes afterwards (which must be done within 24 hours), including some direct quotations, provides more than enough data with great detail. Strauss (1987) also argues that tape-recordings are unnecessary unless the analysis is to be concerned with the precise details of verbal or non-verbal behaviour.

The particular questions asked or observations made are, of course, guided by preliminary ideas about what is of interest, but in the early stages of the research the enquiry should be made in as open-ended a fashion as possible. This is not only to obtain the widest possible range of answers to the original questions, but also to allow for the raising of new questions that had not originally been thought of. This relative lack of structure at the beginning is one of the aspects of qualitative research that makes those brought up in the tradition of quantitative research—and that includes most of us—feel uneasy. It is, however, an essential ingredient if the theoretical account that is produced is to be firmly based or grounded in the actual data collected (hence the term 'grounded theory' coined by Glaser and Strauss, 1967, cited by Strauss, 1987). The other aspect of the process which is very unfamiliar to those who are not used to it, is the way in which the analysis commences straight away and the way in which later stages of data collection are informed by the early stages of the analysis. A 'constant interplay of data gathering and analysis is at the heart of qualitative research. ... In no other approach is the inter-relatedness of all portions of the research act quite so obvious' (Wiseman, 1978, p. 113).

The process of analysing qualitative data is a rigorous and time-consuming one. It is certainly quite wrong to think that it lacks the discipline of quantitative research or, as students sometimes think at first, that it is an easy option. Different researchers set about the process of analysis in different ways, but they all engage in the process of reading and re-reading the 'large amounts of data, which accumulate in non-standard and unpredictable formats' (Martin and Turner, 1986, p. 144) and which can appear overwhelming to the novice. They then all involve a fine-grained system of coding in the search for useful categories or concepts. Some prefer to do this paragraph by paragraph of the transcript, record or document (B. Turner, 1981). Others prefer to code smaller units of one or two sentences (Wiseman, 1978; Orford, Rigby, Tod, Miller, Bennett and Velleman, 1991), whilst Strauss (1987) illustrates in his book the way in which concepts may be developed and elaborated by examining separately several key words within a single sentence. Some prefer to create a separate card or file for each emerging category. Some prefer to make annotations in the margins, some find it useful to use a computer text analysis program such as ETHNOGRAPH or TEXTBASE ALPHA and yet others are wedded to the time-honoured method of scissors and paste. For some the process of coding becomes quite mechanical: after the initial development of the coding frame which may consist of as many as 15–20 topic codes with 10–15 sub-topic codes within each of the former, Wiseman employs a coder to code the rest of her data. For Strauss, on the other hand, the process never becomes mechanical: he advocates that a process of active thinking about and interpreting the data should continue throughout, aided by discussions with team members and colleagues and the holding of *seminars* with interested parties, experts and collaborators. These meetings generate further ideas about the interpretation of the data. Neither, in his view, should personal experience be neglected. For example, in analysing material from his studies of hospitals and their social organisation, he would not hesitate to use the fact that most members of a seminar group discussing the data had themselves been in hospital at some time, and that amongst the group of graduate students attending the seminar were one or two who had worked as hospital nurses.

A prominent feature of the grounded theory analysis process as described by Strauss (1987) is the use of *memo-writing*. Memos should be written regularly, accumulated, sorted periodically, and some of them should be incorporated in modified form into the final report. If there are team members or colleagues to whom memos can be passed, they can serve as a means of promoting further discussion. The memos illustrated by Strauss in his book each consist of half a page or more expressing ideas that are emerging about the analysis. Memos may be of different types. A memo may announce a new category, discuss the distinction between two or more categories, open new issues or questions, discuss the use of a particular word in detail, speculate on the link between the present data and results from other research, or simply remind the researcher not to forget to explore a particular question.

Whatever the exact process of analysis preferred by a particular researcher, one thing that is agreed upon is that analysis does not wait until all the data are in. This enables preliminary analysis to affect the conduct of further stages of data collection. Wiseman (1978) suggests collecting an initial wave of data (say 10 interviews or observations), conducting a preliminary analysis of these initial data, and then embarking on a second wave of data collection which can now be more focused upon the issues that have emerged from the analysis so far. There may be several rounds of data collection in a single project, and she stresses that the last round should not be conducted until the draft report of the project has been prepared. The process of drafting the report alerts the researcher to areas where the data have been inadequate, contradictory, confusing or absent, and these deficiencies can be put right in the last wave of interviews or observations.

The final stage of analysis consists of the development of a small number of core themes or categories which enable the material to be unified in terms of a clear theoretical statement or conceptual framework. Hence, although the categories, concepts and themes are derived directly from the data, the data do not simply 'speak for themselves' (as Strauss, 1987, says, this is sometimes disappointing to those who expect the final report to consist entirely of illustrative material): there is a progressive focusing as the research goes on and the final result is an account at a higher level of abstraction than the accounts given by individual participants or those contained in individual observational records.

The structure of the final account or framework may be provided in a number of possible ways (Wiseman, 1978). One is in terms of a time sequence or *career*. A good example is the research of Biernacki (1986) who interviewed 100 ex-drug addicts all of whom had quit drug use without the help of treatment. His final account in the book *Pathways from Heroin Addiction* was largely in terms of a sequence of stages through which most addicts passed in the process of becoming ex-addicts. The stages that Biernacki identified were: resolving to change drug use; breaking away; staying abstinent; and becoming and being ordinary. Personal identity was the key concept at the final stage of becoming and being ordinary, and identities that were taken up were divided into three major categories: new, emergent identities; reversions to old identities; and extensions of previous identities.

Another type of structure to a final account or framework is that of *a typology*. An example is taken from work by the present author and colleagues in the UK and Mexico on the subject of how families cope with having an alcohol or other drug problem (Orford, Natera, Casco, Nava and Ollinger, 1990; Orford *et al.*, 1991). The data consisted of detailed records of semi-structured interviews held with relatives (mainly partners or parents) plus, in Mexico, records of family meetings attended by between two and seven family members. Part of the theoretical framework which is emerging from analyses of these data consists of an eightfold typology of family coping actions (Emotional, Tolerant, Avoiding, Inaction, Controlling, Confronting, Supporting the User, Independent). A preliminary typology was derived from early work and later work has added many further examples of coping actions to help define these categories. In addition their meanings were extended by discovering conflicts and contradictions for family members (for example the difficulty of distinguishing Tolerant and Supportive actions) as well as types of action which did not neatly fit into any one category. Examples of the latter were praying and encouraging the problem user to take an oath in church to give up drinking or drug use—actions which were more common amongst the Mexican families.

Another account using a typological approach was that developed by Dobash and Dobash (1987) in the course of their work on marital violence in Scotland. They asked wives to describe a number of incidents in which their husbands had been violent towards them: the first such incident that had occurred, the worst, the most recent, and a typical incident. They developed a typology of the immediate precipitants of violent incidents: arguments over the wife's domestic duties; over the husband's possessiveness; and over money matters. The overall theme of their conceptual framework, supported by analysis of historical material, was in terms of patriarchal power and the ways in which norms of wifely obedience and deference to husbands still pertained.

A qualitative interview study of leadership exercised by supervisors and managers of three British construction firms engaged on three different, and comparatively large, construction projects (Bryman, Bresmen, Beardsworth and Keil, 1988) led to a detailed contingency model of leadership appropriate to this particular setting. Leadership style had to vary depending upon the likely response of the person being dealt with: knowledge of individual subordinates as well as personal judgement were required in deciding what approach to take with a particular person. In addition a different leadership style (on the whole more blunt and firm) was thought to be necessary with sub-contracted workers than with the company's own workers (with whom there needed to be a greater emphasis on encouragement and motivation), and a much more directive, hard line approach was thought necessary when working under greater time pressure.

A further type of framework is illustrated by Wiseman's (1970) own work on the lives of homeless men in a US West Coast city. Her major theme was that of an itinerant life which was, nevertheless, confined to passing through a limited number of cheap and available residences—some cheap commercial establishments, others part of the legal justice system, others run by religious orders, and others part of the health or social welfare services. The analogy she drew was with stops on a loop line of a transport system. Hence the title of her book, *Stations of the Lost*. This conceptualisation of circular movement, implying impermanence but entrapment and lack of forward progress, is a powerful one and it had a real influence on the field at the time.

Part II

PRACTICE

7 Sharing Psychology with Workers in Human Services

This chapter is about sharing psychological ways of understanding and responding to human problems with those whose jobs directly concern people and their problems. Those who are in the 'people business' include health visitors, teachers, doctors, nurses, police and clergy, to name but a few. The work done by these modern armies of human service workers, is, in large part, psychological. Furthermore, as Chapter 3 has already documented, the prevalence of psychological problems amongst both children and adults is high, far higher than a level that would allow everyone in need to receive specialist psychological help. Hence, it is the teachers, nurses, social workers, lawyers, and many others, who deal with much the greater proportion of psychological distress and difficulty. Yet psychology was unlikely to have been the main priority in their training, nor is understanding and responding to psychological difficulty likely to be the first priority in the organisations for which they work.

It is for this reason that finding ways of sharing psychological formulations and interventions with workers in human services has become one of the main preoccupations of community psychology. From the community psychology perspective, what goes on between nurses and their patients in the general hospital, between police and the victims of family violence, or between teachers and their more troublesome pupils, is of greater significance for the psychological health of a community than the relatively small number of individual treatments that can be delivered by psychological specialists. The latter must, to use Miller's (1969) famous phrase, 'Give psychology away' to the nurses, police and teachers who are, in effect, the real psychological practitioners.

Not that this has been totally uncontroversial within psychology, however. Some have argued that to share psychological wisdom and expertise too widely is to dilute its impact, to lose control of the quality of psychological work, and in the process to jeopardise the emergent growth of psychology itself as a profession. Such a view is hardly tenable if one adopts the philosophy of community psychology espoused in Chapter 1. Community psychology is concerned with psychological health within human collectives—towns, neighbourhoods, communities—and hence with the systems and settings that comprise them and the interactional patterns of power and social support that operate within them. What goes on within its doctors' surgeries or its schools, or what goes on in the homes of ordinary people when health visitors or police officers call, is the very essence of its concern. It is central to the psychological well-being of the community, not peripheral to it. Any attempt to plan for improvements in the psychological health of a district or locality must consider how psychology is to be shared with those who are in the best position to use it in the course of their work with people. Indeed, even the expression 'giving psychology away' has an unwelcome ring to it, since it implies that expert power resides with the psychological specialist within whose gift it is to offer to others, or to withhold, knowledge which only he or she possesses. It sounds too patronising. Those whose work is with people, in whatever capacity, nearly always possess a rich fund of psychological expertise, and it is by tapping this source, freeing it up from some of the constraints that prevent its use, and perhaps by adding a little extra specialist knowledge, that improvements can be made.

Finally, by way of introduction, it may be pointed out that the topic of this chapter occupies a key place in applied psychology because it provides a bridge between traditional, individually-oriented psychology on the one hand, and community psychology with its emphasis upon people within their wider settings on the other. Practitioners brought up to practise in a more 'clinical' way can feel relatively comfortable acting as sharers of psychology whilst they

Table 8. Illustrations of the range of psychological consultation and education activities (based on Koch, 1986)

Training other professionals who work with children in methods of behavioural assessment and behavioural therapy

Advising and training teachers, care staff, and police trainees in their work with adolescents

Providing consultation to a local authority community home on matters such as evaluation and the handling of violent incidents

Helping mental handicap staff cope with challenges and changes to their roles so as to maximise the use of their knowledge and skills

Providing mental health consultation services to general practitioners and health visitors who treat problems of anxiety, depression and alcohol problems

Supporting landlords and landladies, and training staff, who work with people with long-standing psychiatric difficulties to de-emphasise illness and to emphasise self-responsibility

Supporting carers, and training and supporting volunteers, in the case of services for the elderly

---

might feel relatively uncomfortable moving into wholly new fields such as pre-vention, organisational change, advocacy, or self-help. Similarly at the agency level, the development of consultation services may be one route whereby a service that is constrained, by reason of tradition, demand, or management expectations, to deliver a service almost wholly directed towards individual clients who are already displaying psychological problems, may nevertheless develop more of a community orientation.

Much of what has been written about ways of sharing psychology has appeared under the title 'consultation'. This term does not fully cover the range of sharing activities which the present author has in mind (see Table 8), and it probably fits better in a country such as the USA with its greater market economy emphasis in human services than in a country such as Britain with its tradition of a comprehensive, state health service. Nonetheless, it is in the field of psychological consultation that many of the leading ideas about sharing psychology have been developed, and it is to these ideas that we should now turn.

CONSULTATION: WHAT IT IS AND WHAT IT ISN'T

There have been many definitions of consultation (see for example Ketterer, 1981, p. 127, or A. Brown, 1984, p. 3). Most of them contain the following common elements:

> Consultation is the process whereby an individual (the consultee) who has responsibility for providing a service to others (the clients) voluntarily con-sults another person (the consultant) who is believed to possess some special expertise which will help the consultee provide a better service to his or her clients.

Hence consultation always refers to a triadic arrangement, the three parties involved being *consultant, consultee* and *client*. For example, the triad might be an educational or school psychologist (consultant), a school teacher (con-sultee), and a pupil (the client). Alternatively, the threesome might consist of a mental health professional, a general medical practitioner, and a patient. Each may be represented by more than one person: the consultants may be a group (e.g. a family therapy team); help may be sought by a group of consultees (e.g. an agency or work team); and help may be sought over the provision of services for a number of clients or indeed for the whole of a con-sultee's clientele (e.g. over how to handle clients with particular types of pro-blem, over class management in general, or over the operation of a particular programme). Since the range of human services is so great, and the types of personnel who provide them so many, the possibilities for consultation are clearly very varied indeed.

In an effort to define consultation more precisely, most writers on the subject have been at pains to distinguish between a consultation relationship and other types of relationship with which it might be confused. One of these writers was Caplan (1970), who wrote one of the first, and still one of the most influential books on the subject, and who originated the whole branch of the subject known as 'mental health consultation'. He wished to make it quite clear that consultation did not include supervision or education or any other similar process in which two people had a superordinate-subordinate relationship in which the subordinate party was not totally free to seek out the other party, to continue or discontinue the relationship, or to set the agenda. The notion of the consultant-consultee relationship being a 'coordinate' one with no built-in hierarchical authority tension, and with no compulsion on either side—the consultant is not responsible for the consultee's work, nor is the consultee obliged to respond to the consultant's ideas or influence—is fundamental to Caplan's idea of consultation and most others have followed him in this. He expected that the consultant and consultee would usually be members of different professions and that they would normally work in different institutions, hence preserving their independence and fostering the kind of coordinate relationship that he had in mind. The relationship should be egalitarian in the sense that the consultant has expertise that the consultee wants, but the consultee as 'customer' is in charge.

It should be pointed out, however, that not all writers on the subject would delineate consultation in this way. For example A. Brown (1984), writing about consultation in social work, extends the idea of consultation to include elements of *supervision*, both during training and in later practice, and considers that a great deal of consultation, certainly in British social work agencies, occurs *within* the agency and is not completely independent of the hierarchical relationships that exist there. His point is that good supervision includes consultation and that it would therefore be unhelpful to exclude it. From the point of view of community psychology the touchstone is the sharing of specialist knowledge and expertise more widely with groups of people who are more in touch with the community from which clients come and/or in touch with larger numbers of clients than can be the case for the consultant or the professional group which he or she represents. By this token, the kind of consultation-as-part-of-supervision within an agency, of which Brown writes, is itself of rather less interest although the process may be similar and it may provide a model on which to base consultation activities with others outside the profession.

Caplan was equally clear that consultation should not be confused with therapy for the consultee. The two goals of consultation were, 'to help the consultee improve his [sic] handling or understanding of the current work difficulty and through this to increase his capacity to master future problems of a similar type' (1970, p. 29). Hence the focus was on work difficulties and Caplan stated that the consultant should not allow the discussion of personal and private material. The aim was to improve the consultee's job performance and not his or her sense of well-being. However, because the two were linked, the consultation process might have a secondary effect upon the consultee's well-being, but this would be purely secondary and not the aim of the process. Again others have followed Caplan's lead here.

Another distinction, made for example by Gallessich (1982), is that between consultation and *advocacy*. Although the consultant's help may have been sought because the consultee lacked experience or understanding of a particular client group, the consultant is not there to advocate on behalf of a client or a client group: 'In consultation, any adversarial elements are minimised or eliminated' (Gallessich, 1982, p. 14). Advocacy will be considered in more detail in Chapter 11.

TYPES OF CONSULTATION

Nevertheless, within this coordinate, non-therapeutic and non-adversarial process, there exist many possibilities for different kinds of action. A number of complex typologies of consultation exist, containing up to 100 separate types (Dustin and Blocher, 1984). One of the simplest and best-known, however, is Caplan's. Caplan (1970) distinguished between the following four types of consultation:

1. Client-centred case consultation
   The focus in this type of consultation is the client's problem and how the consultee can best assess and treat it. A variety of practices may actually occur. At one extreme is the traditional type of medical consultation where the focus is clearly upon the client case and where the consultant, who may well meet the client, with or without the consultee being present, provides the consultee with an expert opinion and recommendations. A rather different type of client-centred case consultation is *behavioural consultation*. For example a consultant knowledgeable in the principles and methods of behaviour modification may collaborate with a consultee in developing a treatment programme for a client, and in the course of this collaboration they may meet with the client together (Dustin and Blocher, 1984).
2. Consultee-centred case consultation
   Here the focus is upon the nature of the consultee's difficulty in working with a client or clients, and in trying to remedy this difficulty so that the consultee can work more effectively with this client(s) and with future clients. This is probably what most writers on the subject have had in mind when they have discussed consultation, and it is the type that most closely corresponds to what is meant by *mental health consultation*
3. Programme-centred administrative consultation
   With administrative consultation, or what others have called programme

consultation (Gallessich, 1982) or process consultation (Dustin and Blocher, 1984), the focus shifts away from the effective functioning of the consultee with individual clients towards the effective planning or execution of a programme for multiple clients. In parallel with type 1, the consultant's goal is to recommend a course of action, and a hoped-for side-effect is that the consultees will learn something that they could use in dealing with future problems of a similar type. As in type 1 the consultant may meet the clients or potential clients and be actively involved, either with or without the consultee, in data-gathering and assessment. Methods used may include needs assessment (see Chapter 6) and action research (Chapter 9).

4. Consultee-centred administrative consultation

As in type 2, the primary concern here is with elucidating and remedying the consultees' difficulties and shortcomings that interfere with their effective programme planning and execution. But here the focus is on the group, team, agency or organisation, and the aim is the improvement of functioning of the group or system. Difficulties are as likely to lie in group properties such as leadership, authority and communication patterns, roles and their clarity and complementarity, and issues of power and autonomy, as in individual consultee factors such as knowledge, skills, self-confidence and objectivity. Hence, this type of consultation is likely to draw heavily on the kind of material about organisations which is discussed in other chapters (particularly Chapters 5 and 9).

Although no one would now suppose that these are four discrete types of consultation process, or even that they exhaust the possibilities, they do serve to draw attention to the diversity of interventions covered by the term 'consultation'. In particular they draw attention to a number of distinctions or dimensions in terms of which different varieties of consultation may be described: for example (a) the degree of contact between consultant and client(s); (b) the relative focus on recommending a course of action for a specific problem versus helping the consultee overcome difficulties of his or her own; and (c) the degree to which the consultee is concerned about service to individual clients or the administration of a service programme or system. In much the same way as appreciation has grown of the importance of the social context in which clients live and work (much of Chapter 3 of this volume was on this theme), so awareness has grown of the importance of the setting in which consultees work. Hence, more recent descriptions of consultation place greater emphasis on the inter-relationships between consultees and the systems within which they work, and make less of a clear distinction between forms of consultation focused on individual consultees and those based on teams or agencies (e.g. Gallessich, 1982).

It has also been pointed out that the distinction between consultation and education is often not as clear cut as Caplan supposed. For example,

Ketterer's (1981) book addresses a field that has come to be known in the USA as *consultation and education*. Although the two concepts are distinguished clearly by Ketterer, it is evident that the two are often practised together. Gallessich (1982) included education and training, often provided in the form of *staff development*, *in-service training*, or *human resource development*, as one of six models for the practice of consultation. Of the other five—clinical, mental health, programme, and organisational consultation correspond reasonably well with Caplan's types 1, 2, 3 and 4. The remaining model is the behavioural model which is also picked out by Dustin and Blocher (1984) as one of the two most clearly delineated models of consultation—the other being Caplan's mental health model.

CAPLAN'S MENTAL HEALTH CONSULTATION

The strength of Caplan's mental health model of consultation lies principally in the formulation and methods which he described for carrying out consultee-centred case consultation. He stated that consultees' difficulties usually lay in one or more of four areas: knowledge, skill, self-confidence and objectivity. Either they lacked knowledge about the type of problem presented by the client(s), lacked skill in making use of such knowledge, lacked the self-confidence necessary to use knowledge and skills, or were unable to make objective perceptions and judgements due to the interference of subjective, emotional factors. Caplan's prediction was that in mental health work difficulties with objectivity would be the largest category. Indeed he implied that the other types of consultee difficulty which he saw—those based upon lack of information, skill, or self-confidence—were matters for the training, supervision and support systems of the consultee's profession or organisation, and that it might endanger the consultation relationship, as well as being unduly costly, for the consultant to get too much involved in attempting to correct these deficits. He did acknowledge, however, that the same mental health consultant might, in another role, provide didactic seminars—preferably for supervisors rather than those in closest and most regular contact with clients, since providing education for the former would have more of a lasting widespread influence—or act as a resource person for supervisory groups within an organisation. Even in Caplan's work, then, we see a blurring of the distinction between the roles of consultant and educator: as has already been noted, others have found that the two activities are not clearly distinct but rather are complementary and often overlapping (e.g. Ketterer, 1981). As we shall see, others employ concepts in consultation work which imply that the distinctions Caplan made between information, skill, self-confidence and objectivity are not always so clearcut either (e.g. Spratley, 1987).

Caplan considered that most cases of lack of objectivity in consultees fell into five overlapping categories: (a) direct personal involvement, (b) simple identification, (c) transference, (d) characterological distortions and, (e) theme interference. As examples of the first four of these he cited: (a) a middle-aged woman school counsellor who was emotionally overinvolved with young adolescent boys whose parents were divorced; (b) a young nurse who over-identified with the anger towards her parents expressed by an adolescent girl who came from the same part of the world as she did; (c) a teacher who found very troublesome a pupil whom she considered to be in the 'pampered' younger sister role in her family; and (d) a teacher who appeared to be preoc-cupied with sexual matters and saw instances of 'harmful sexual behaviour' in a number of pupils.

Caplan reserved special attention, however, for that cause of lack of objec-tivity which he termed *theme interference*. He believed it to be a common occurrence that otherwise effective workers would from time to time become relatively ineffective in working with a client because unresolved present or past personal problems had become displaced onto task situations. More spe-cifically he believed that a consultee's objectivity in assessing and handling a client case was interfered with by the intrusion of a 'theme' or fixed, irrational belief of the kind, 'Whenever A, B follows'. For example Gallessich (1982) gives the example of a teacher who believed that a badly behaved pupil from a bad home would inevitably turn out badly: this belief was making it particu-larly difficult for this teacher to work objectively with a particular pupil who was defined in the teacher's mind as 'a bad girl from a bad background'. Caplan described two procedures for helping consultees gain greater objec-tivity in such cases. The first, which was the less preferred because although it might help in the individual case it left the prejudiced belief intact, was to 'unlink' the perception of the particular client (the girl pupil in this case) from the theme by helping the consultee to see that the theme did not apply in this case (i.e. that the pupil was not in fact 'bad' or did not come from a 'bad background'). The preferred solution was *theme reduction*, achieved by helping the consultee appreciate that although the client was indeed an example (i.e. in this case the pupil did indeed have some elements of 'badness' in her behaviour, and did indeed come from a family with some 'bad' fea-tures), nevertheless this need not inevitably lead to the presumed and feared outcome. In the case cited by Gallessich, the consultant helped the consultee, through discussion, to see that the pupil concerned had many positive charac-teristics and was capable of achievement and maturity despite the negative aspects of her previous behaviour and family background.

Caplan's mental health model of consultation has often been criticised (Gallessich, 1982). Some have questioned the overriding importance of lack of objectivity. In one of the few studies to test this, daily logs were kept over a 14-week period by school-psychology graduate students who served as consultants with teachers from 10 primary schools. These suggested that 38 per cent of consultations were related to lack of knowledge, 27 per cent to lack of skill, 27 per cent to lack of confidence, and only 7 per cent to lack of objectivity (Gutkin, 1981, cited by Dustin and Blocher, 1984).

The validity of the concept of theme interference has also been questioned, and others have doubted the ability of a consultant to reduce the interference in a short time. Furthermore, the 'pyramidal' spread-of-effects concept, which supposes that what the consultee learns from a specific case generalises to future clients, has sometimes been said to be unsupported. One of the main criticisms, however, has focused on the assumption that the relationship between consultant and consultee is egalitarian or coordinate. To many this has seemed inconsistent with certain features of Caplan's approach; for example the subtle and largely covert analysis of a consultee's difficulty, the emphasis on diagnosing the causes of the consultee's lack of objectivity, and the working out of a plan by the consultant to correct the consultee's difficulty without the latter being aware that his or her objectivity has been questioned.

Caplan's view was that it was so essential to preserve the equal partnership of consultant and consultee that the full truth of the latter's lack of objectivity or other difficulty needed to be kept from him or her; hence the flavour of subtlety and mild deception which comes across from much of his writings about the consultation process. For instance, in the extended example which he gave of consultee-centred case consultation in his book (1970, Chapter 9) he commented on the transcription of a consultation session between a consultant (not himself) and a public health nurse who was concerned about a male client with advanced cancer and his family. The nurse was particularly concerned with what she saw as the negative and unhelpful attitudes and behaviour of the man's wife and young adult children. The consultant appears to have come to the conclusion that the nurse was not acknowledging to herself or to the family that the patient would shortly die. Because this lack of acknowledgement of death was not something that would be expected of a professional in her position, the consultant tackled the difficulty indirectly by focusing discussion on the patient's wife and *her* ability to recognise and to face up to the patient's impending death. Caplan considered this case to be an example either of personal involvement, with the nurse having become too involved with a favourite patient to be able to acknowledge his likely death, or an example of theme interference, the theme being, 'All people who care for a dying man will be blamed when he dies, because they did not succeed in saving him'.

SOME RECENT MODIFICATIONS AND DEVELOPMENTS

There have been numerous attempts to modify Caplan's methods to overcome these perceived shortcomings or to adapt them for specific purposes. One such, described by Spratley (1987), is an approach to consultation for consultees concerned with their clients' alcohol-related problems. Alcohol-related problems are examples of client problems very frequently faced by workers of many different professions, yet most have received little training or experience in dealing with them, and perceived difficulties in handling this group of clients are likely to be very common. Indeed previous research by Spratley and his colleagues had shown that these difficulties were very widespread amongst community workers such as probation officers, social workers, community nurses, and general medical practitioners (Shaw, Cartwright, Spratley and Harwin, 1978; Cartwright, 1980). It was very common for these workers to suffer from some combination of all of the common consultee shortcomings identified by Caplan (1970), plus others. Workers often felt that they lacked the necessary information and skills to recognise and respond to drinking problems: hence they experienced anxiety about *role adequacy* as Shaw *et al.* termed it. Even if they felt they possessed the necessary knowledge and skill, they often lacked self-confidence in dealing with problem drinkers. Although Caplan's terms, 'lack of objectivity' and 'theme interference', are not ones used by these authors, it is clear that many of the workers whose attitudes they studied were unable to take an objective view of working with this client group, since they often held overly pessimistic attitudes about possibilities of positive client change. It was as if their ability to work effectively with people with drinking problems was interfered with by the general theme: 'If a person is in the category alcoholic or problem drinker, then the chances of change are small'.

Shaw *et al.* discovered other impediments to working effectively with this client group which had not been so clearly foreseen by Caplan, or which at least he had not incorporated into his theory of consultee-centred case consultation. For one thing many workers, particularly social workers, scored low on what Shaw *et al.* termed *role legitimacy*: they often felt that they did not have the right to ask their clients for information about drinking, and sometimes thought it was not part of their job to work with alcohol problems. It was often not possible to isolate the workers' own difficulties from the shortcomings of the setting in which they worked—another example of the principle of personal and environmental interaction. It was often found that a worker's managers were not in full support of work with this client group, or alternatively that personal support and supervision were not easily available. These types of work setting factors were termed *lack of role support* by Shaw *et al.* (1978) and *situational constraints* by Lightfoot and Orford (1986).

Not surprisingly these factors (summarised in Table 9) led many community workers to experience low *therapeutic commitment* to working with problem drinkers. Hence, although Spratley's (1987) approach is clearly in the mental health case consultation tradition, with the consultant meeting with the consultee to discuss the consultee's work with an individual client who is not present, his assessment is more broadly based than Caplan's. In order to attempt to increase a consultee's sense of role security and feeling of therapeutic commitment in working with a current client with a drinking problem (and perhaps with others in the future), he enquires about characteristics of the client, of the worker (knowledge, skills, concepts, attitudes, etc.), their relationship, and the setting in which the consultee works. It is also clear that

Table 9. Components of therapeutic attitude for working with people with drinking problems (based on Cartwright, 1980)

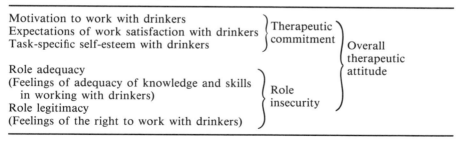

Motivation to work with drinkers		
Expectations of work satisfaction with drinkers	Therapeutic commitment	
Task-specific self-esteem with drinkers		Overall therapeutic attitude
Role adequacy		
(Feelings of adequacy of knowledge and skills in working with drinkers)	Role insecurity	
Role legitimacy		
(Feelings of the right to work with drinkers)		

Spratley's method is not consultee-centred in pure form. It also includes elements of client-centred case consultation, and even explicit elements of training in understanding and responding to people with drinking problems. For example, although he does not expect to meet the client, he does like to have written information about the client beforehand, and much of what he says implies that he and the consultee are together formulating a plan of action for working with the particular client. Nevertheless, he is clearly at pains to avoid the elements of fault-finding and deception which some have sensed in Caplan's work. Spratley stresses the need for complete openness with the consultee, advocates the use of the consultee's language whenever possible, and states it as an ideal that a report of a consultation should be sent to the consultee afterwards.

Clement's (1987) account of an experiment carried out in Salford in Northern England is of particular interest, since it is an attempt to evaluate a project that set out to provide a consultation service to general medical practitioners, social workers, probation officers, health visitors and district nurses. Like Spratley's work, the topic of consultation was clients with alcohol-related problems, and the conceptual background, like his, was concerned with the low role security and therapeutic commitment of many such workers in dealing with alcohol problems. A community alcohol team (CAT) consisting of two psychiatric nurses and a social worker was set up with special funding, and two research workers were appointed to help evaluate the scheme.

One of the most interesting aspects of Clement's account of the project concerns the compromises that had to be made in the methods used. The original intention had been to offer a pure form of case consultation. To the team's credit they put much effort into discussing their proposals face-to-face with groups of members of the target professions and distributing explanatory leaflets and posters. As a result they discovered that their proposals were unacceptable to the majority of their intended consultees, and the team found that they had to compromise by offering joint client assessments plus short-term intervention if required, during and after which the consultee would continue to see the client with the team's support. General medical practitioners found themselves unable to accept even this compromise and insisted on a more traditional arrangement whereby they referred clients to the team for treatment. In fact, even when general medical practitioner cases were excluded from analysis, only 26 per cent of all client assessments were carried out jointly in the two years of the evaluation.

Nevertheless, the result was a thorough and well-evaluated project carried out in a large urban community with a population of about 1 million inhabitants, and which in the end involved a combination of direct client work, consultation and education, which was adapted to the expressed needs of the workers-cum-consultees themselves. A quasi-experimental, comparison group design was used. One group of workers was chosen—not at random but in a way designed to make the groups as equivalent as possible—to receive a series of one-day alcohol education events in addition to receiving the client/consultation service. A second group received the client/consultation service alone, and a third group was offered no service at all. There was evidence that a meaningful degree of consultation occurred in just under half of those cases referred by workers other than general medical practitioners, and that therapeutic commitment rose over the two years, particularly for those who received education as well as the client/consultation service. Feelings of role support increased in the group offered a service compared to the no-service comparison group, and the former identified a larger number of problem drinkers on their caseloads in the second year of the project. Although GPs did not take advantage of the consultation aspects of the service, those offered the service were positive about the rapidity of the team's response to their patients, and they also reported experiencing a much greater degree of support in dealing with patients with alcohol problems than did controls.

Clement also has some interesting things to say about the need for agency or management support, and this confirms what others have suggested. The professional group that took most advantage of consultation was probationer officers and this was the group that reported the highest level of support from their own agency in working with clients with alcohol problems. Community psychiatric nurses did not report management support internal to their own profession but this was compensated for by external agency support in the form of demands placed upon them by referrals from other agents such as GPs, and they also responded quite well to the project. Social workers, health visitors and district nurses were without either internal or external agency support and responded least well. This led Clement to argue that the problem often lay more with the 'therapeutically uncommitted agency' than with the 'therapeutically uncommitted agent'.

Whereas the Spratley–Clement model is a mixed one, with Caplan's influence still very apparent, others have gone still further in developing a model of consultation which is consultee-centred, not in Caplan's sense of focusing on the consultee's shortcomings and how to change them, but in the sense that the consultee's own language and framework are accepted by the consultant. The latter avoids the temptation, 'to redefine the material in the consultant's own terms and conceptual framework' (A. Brown, 1984, p. 44). Brown also has some very useful advice to give about the need for both consultant and consultee to be very clear, right from the start when contact between them is first made, about the goals of consultation and the methods to be used. Indeed they should have an explicit contract or agreement. Because the social work context in which Brown was working is normally one in which workers are operating, not as fully independent practitioners, but rather as members of teams with line management arrangements, he also has much to say about the need to be clear at the outset concerning the role of supervisors or line managers, even to the point of including them in an early, contact-making meeting. For one thing there exists the possibility of siding with a consultee in conflicts with a supervisor hence reinforcing a split between worker and supervisor and perhaps undermining the latter's position. Such advice could clearly be generalised to other work settings where a consultee must respond to other influences, such as that of a manager, besides that of a consultant. Consultee, supervisor or manager, and consultant form another example of a meso-system (Bronfenbrenner, 1979).

As well as containing a great deal of such sensible advice for the would-be consultant, Brown's approach differs from some others because he defines consultation broadly to include a number of types of work which others might exclude. For example, he writes about *participant consultancy* which may involve joint work with a client (as in Clement's, 1987, Salford project) or *live consultancy* in which the consultant observes the consultee working directly. He refers also to *periodic on-site consultancy* in which, as the term implies, the consultant periodically visits the consultee at his/her place of work. He includes consultation with groups or teams of two or more consultees together (in which case the relationship between the consultees is likely to become a central issue itself), and *community work consultancy* where the consultant may be in the role of conflict mediator between groups. He also discusses peer consultancy in which two workers take it in turns to be in the role of consultant and to help the other with their needs, as well as consultancy given by an internal agency-appointed 'official' consultant (which carries special problems in terms of relationships), as well as consultancy given by a person who is also the consultee's supervisor.

As already discussed, the latter is explicitly excluded by some writers on consultancy on the grounds that this confuses roles and compromises the important principle that the consultee should be completely free to accept or reject the consultant's help or advice. While recognising these difficulties,

Brown believes that if a supervisor uses his or her authority sensitively this may enable the supervisor-consultant to make more demands of a supervisee-consultee, and therefore to have more influence than a consultant who lacks this authority. The consultant, as envisaged by Caplan and others, uses his or her expert or competent authority, but our discussion of power and influence in Chapter 5 suggested that the different sources of power are not always so distinct as the typologies of power sources suggest, and that one form of power can easily metamorphose into another. On the other hand, a supervisor may draw upon a broader base of influence—including legitimate, personal, induced and even coercive authority—and, more important still, the supervisor's power is likely to be more comprehensive and intensive. It is therefore a reasonable, although at present untested, assumption that a consultee whose consultant is also his or her supervisor will experience less autonomy and feelings of dominance than would a consultee who has access to the consultant who is not in a supervisory role.

EVALUATING CONSULTATION

Many writers on consultation have bemoaned the lack of critical evaluation of consultancy work. For example, Dustin and Blocher (1984), who drew together the results of a number of reviews of the field at that time, were particularly harsh. They felt the term 'consultation' was being used too widely, without definition, and that most of the evaluative studies that had been carried out had failed to use an appropriate experimental or quasi-experimental design. They found that consultation was often being carried out without any clearly laid down formulation of the intervention and its rationale, and without sufficient description of what actually takes place when something called 'consultation' is provided. The latter is a particularly good point. There can be little doubt that the field would be well served by some good, detailed descriptions of what actually goes on in the name of consultation.

Dustin and Blocher's final conclusion was:

> at the present time there is simply not a sufficient body of credible empirical research upon which to assess the overall effectiveness or ineffectiveness of consultation as a model for the delivery of psychological services. (1984, p. 777)

A more favourable conclusion was reached by Medway and Updyke (1985) as a result of their review of the better controlled studies of consultation that had been carried out up until that time. They used the procedure known as *meta-analysis*. This method for aggregating the results of a number of studies had come into popularity by that time as a result of its use in a number of influential analyses of the results of psychological therapies (Smith and Glass, 1977; Shapiro and Shapiro, 1982). It is superior to a simple system of categorising studies into those that find a significant effect of an intervention and those that do not, because it is based on the calculation of an 'effect size' whenever a measured outcome is reported for both an intervention and a comparison or control group. An effect size (ES) is essentially the difference between the mean outcome scores from intervention and comparison groups divided by the standard deviation of the comparison group scores. Meta-analysis thus uses much more information than a simple categorisation of studies, and further analyses can be carried out to see whether average ES varies with important characteristics of the studies such as the consultation model employed, or whether outcomes are being assessed for consultees or for clients. We shall meet another important example of meta-analysis in Chapter 10 when we consider the role of untrained personnel in psychological treatment.

Medway and Updyke located 54 studies for which one or more ESs could be calculated. The majority of these studies concerned consultation carried out in schools and other educational settings. It should be pointed out, however, that so few studies with follow-ups were located that they were excluded from the meta-analysis, which was therefore based entirely upon outcomes measured within a short period following the intervention. The average ES was found to be $+0.47$ or $+0.71$ depending upon the exact method of calculation (the latter figure was obtained if ESs from a single study were averaged before calculating an overall average from all studies). These figures can be interpreted to mean that the average consultation participant was better off after consultation than 68 per cent or 76 per cent of non-consultation comparisons.

Further analyses indicated stronger effects when measures were taken from consultants (average ES = $+0.62$) or from consultees (average ES = $+0.55$) than when measures were taken from clients (average ES = $+0.39$). This depended, however, upon the type of consultation employed. Models of consultation were divided into three categories: mental health, behavioural and organisational development. The three types were equally effective overall. But, whereas behavioural and organisational development types of consultation appeared to be equally effective for consultees and clients, mental health consultation stood out as having a higher ES when measures were taken from consultees than when taken from clients (average ESs = $+0.68$ and $+0.28$ respectively). As Medway and Updyke state, this result is in keeping with the philosophy of mental health consultation which focuses on the relationship between the consultant and the consultee and which puts a priority upon changes in consultees' attitudes and behaviour.

Medway and Updyke's conclusion was as follows:

> over the last 30 years consultation has taken its place along with psychotherapy as the two primary means of assessing the mental health needs of individuals, groups, and organisations and for mobilising resources to meet those needs ... we find clear

statistical support for consultation as a service to consultees and clients. Even though many of these studies still are not of the highest quality, it does seem that consultation can now be given a less qualified endorsement than it has in the previous outcome reviews. (pp. 489, 502)

SHARING PSYCHOLOGY: THE FUTURE

This chapter has focused upon the theory and practice of psychological consultation because it is in that field that a specific body of ideas and experience has accumulated. But in reality the sharing of psychology between those who are trained as psychologists or in one of the mental health professions, and those who use psychology constantly in the course of their work with people, is going on all the time in a hundred and one different ways. Many of these ways are informal and not easily embraced within the concept of consultation which implies a more deliberate and formal process. What the work on consultation does give us, however, is a framework within which to consider the best ways in which psychological knowledge can be more widely shared. As was stated at the beginning of this chapter, the need for good psychology is so great and so widespread that there can surely be little doubt that it must be shared. One of the reasons why it has been less widely shared in the past is that no framework has existed to guide the process of sharing. Hence, professionals with psychological expertise to share have felt uneasy about so doing, as if sharing was not a legitimate part of their professional roles. The ideas presented in this chapter may not, in time, turn out to be the most useful for guiding the sharing process. They do, nonetheless, represent a useful starting point—a stimulus to further theorising, practice and evaluation.

We may confidently expect rapid and wide-scale developments of sharing in the years to come. Gallessich (1982) pointed out that the consultation role may develop more strongly over time both within the career of an individual professional and within the history of a particular profession. As a professional discipline develops, consultation may emerge as an occasional or only vaguely defined extension of the professional role. With time such activities may become more frequent, the need may be felt to borrow relevant theory from other fields in order to practise consultation more effectively, and greater success may be achieved in beginning to penetrate the organisations in which consultees work. This may be a frustrating and disappointing stage, however, as professional training rarely prepares trainees for the role of consultant, much consultation work is atheoretical, and progress may be held up by complex organisational dynamics and resistances in the form of adherence to traditional ways. Ketterer (1981) provided considerable evidence that consultation and education (C and E) in the mental health field had not moved beyond this stage. He described C and E's marginal status in the mental health field, its lack of theory, the absence of special training, and the existence of organisational and other constraints. Surveys of the activities of community mental health centre staff in the USA in the 1970s showed only between 4 per cent and 6 per cent of staff time devoted to this type of work. In one study half of the staff carrying out C and E activities had received some relevant formal training, but in half the cases this amounted to only a single session. In another study none of those carrying out this type of work had received special professional training for these roles.

Gallessich foresaw the third stage in which a branch of professional knowledge and practice develops, specifically devoted to consultation, drawing extensively on relevant knowledge from other fields. This could lead to loosening of identification with the basic discipline and even the development of training for graduates whose primary identification is with the role of consultant. Ketterer (1981) also discussed the emergence of specialist C and E staff as opposed to generalists who carry out such activities as an extension of their role in providing direct services to clients. One suspects that the development of specialist consultants is not something of which Caplan would have approved. He explicitly stated that mental health consultation was, 'a method of communication between a mental health specialist and other professionals. It does not denote a new profession—merely a special way in which existing professionals may operate' (1970, p. 30). Many would still endorse his view that a solid background and continued practice in the area about which the consultant is being consulted is a prerequisite for effective consultancy work.

8 Prevention

If one of the limitations of past practice in applied psychology has been a failure to share psychological knowledge widely, another has undoubtedly been an overconcentration upon existing disorder to the virtual exclusion of attempts to prevent disorder ever occurring in the first place.

An interest in prevention is one of the hallmarks of community psychology which was identified in Chapter 1. Indeed some writers, such as Cowen (1980), have considered community psychology's emphasis upon prevention to be its principal defining feature. Like case consultation, discussed in the previous chapter, the prevention of disorders which would otherwise have occurred in individuals represents a useful bridge between an individually-oriented, disorder-focused psychology, on the one hand, and a more radical psychology concerned with macro-level systems and collective action, on the other hand.

In this chapter some examples of preventive psychology will be described and discussed. Before doing so, however, it is necessary to provide a framework for thinking about prevention. There are at least the following two reasons why examples should be prefaced with some scene-setting remarks. First, there is the fact that the field of preventive psychology is a wide and disparate one which is potentially confusing: a framework is necessary to bring some order to the area. The second reason lies in the resistance to prevention which those who argue for its importance often meet; hence a need to be on sure ground when arguing the case for prevention.

A FRAMEWORK FOR PREVENTIVE PSYCHOLOGY

The typology which is still most frequently referred to is the one put forward by Caplan in 1964 in the context of preventive psychiatry He separated preventive activities into those which he termed *primary*, *secondary* and *tertiary*, as follows:

> programs for reducing (1) the incidence of mental disorders of all types in a com-
> munity (primary prevention), (2) the duration of a significant number of those

disorders which do occur (secondary prevention), and (3) the impairment which may result from disorders (tertiary prevention). (pp. 16–17)

Although the limitations of this terminology have often been pointed out—Swift (1980) refers to Caplan's typology as 'battle-weary' for example—it has a number of distinct advantages which should not be lost sight of. Principal amongst these is the continuity which this scheme provides between prevention and treatment. The two are not to be seen as totally distinct but should rather be viewed as parts of a wide spectrum of activities the purpose of which is to reduce the incidence and prevalence of disorder, and the extent of disability or handicap resulting from disorder.

Primary prevention seeks to reduce incidence (see Chapter 3 for a definition of terms) by preventing new cases of a disorder developing. Thus, the recipients of primary prevention are people who are completely free of the disorder at the time; although, as we shall see later, they may be people who are thought to be at particularly high risk for developing the disorder. *Secondary* prevention aims to detect disorder, or incipient disorder, early on, and to provide effective treatment at an early stage in the development of the disorder. It differs from most treatment because early cases are actively sought out—the 'seeking' rather than 'waiting' mode of work referred to in Chapter 1—and because treatment is likely to be less intensive than would be the case if the disorder had progressed further. In epidemiological terms the effects of successful secondary prevention are to reduce the prevalence of a disorder. Because it is aimed at people who already are showing signs of the disorder to some degree, it cannot reduce incidence, but if it successfully nips progressive conditions in the bud then its effect will be to shorten the duration of disorder and hence the overall prevalence within the community. The intention of *tertiary* prevention is to prevent the disabilities and handicaps which may be associated with a disorder. Although it may not have been possible to prevent a new case of a disorder from occurring, or to shorten its duration by applying successful treatment early on, it may nevertheless be possible to prevent disorder from producing disability, or to prevent disability from producing handicap (an effect upon normal development or life adjustment). The idea that a disorder need not necessarily produce disability, and that a disability need not necessarily result in handicap, is central to the notion of tertiary prevention (Yule, 1980).

Thus, Caplan's framework enables us to see the continuity that exists between what is commonly thought of as 'prevention' and what is normally termed 'treatment'. What is peculiar to prevention is its future orientation. It aims to prevent something happening which has not yet occurred: the onset of a disorder in the case of primary prevention, the continuation and worsening of a disorder in the case of secondary prevention, and disability and handicap in the case of tertiary prevention. Awareness of this continuity is important for one of the central arguments of this book, namely that a community emphasis in psychology is complementary and not contradictory, to prevailing approaches which have stressed individual treatment. Taking on board prevention is simply to extend a range of activities to more adequately cover the spectrum of possibilities for reducing disorder and its consequences.

The second major advantage of Caplan's categorisation is that it draws attention to this range of possibilities, whilst at the same time offering a way of being somewhat more precise when talking about prevention. There are a number of other ways of drawing attention to similarities and contrasts within the field of prevention, and some of these are shown in Table 10.

Another useful typology, put forward by Bloom (1968) and clearly described again by Heller *et al.* (1984), contrasts *community-wide* prevention, *milestone-type* prevention and *high-risk* type prevention. In the first, all of the residents of a community receive the preventive intervention, whether it be a public education campaign, a modification of a public service provision such as fluoridation of the water supply to prevent dental caries, or a development project in a particular community. The target community may be large (a whole country at one extreme) or small (a local community or a neighbourhood), but in either case it is intended that individuals should receive the intervention irrespective of their current circumstances or of their individual risks of developing a particular disorder. The British government's 1987 AIDS campaign, for example, involved leafleting every home irrespective of whether families were thought to contain individuals at a particular stage of the life-cycle, or individuals particularly at risk of infection because of their sexual or drug-using practices.

Milestone- or life transition-type prevention, on the other hand, is directed

Table 10. Some alternative approaches to prevention

Caplan		
Primary (To reduce incidence: target individuals without disorder)	Secondary (To reduce prevalence by reducing duration)	Tertiary (To reduce disability or handicap)
Bloom–Heller		
Community-wide (Targeted at all in a community)	Milestone (All those passing a life milestone)	High-risk (Those thought to be at risk)
Public health		
Host (e.g. individual vulnerability)	Agent (e.g. availability and supply, stress levels)	Environment (Ecology or circumstances)
Bronfenbrenner		
Micro-level (e.g. family or workplace)	Meso-level (e.g. home, peers and home–peer relationships)	Macro-level (e.g. prevailing attitudes, laws or opportunities)

at people who are currently at a particular milestone in their lives. Such developmental periods, which include entry to school for the first time, change of school, leaving home for the first time, first year of marriage, birth of the first child, retirement, and death of a spouse, are thought to carry particular risks and to be critical for future development. However, it is the *life-stage*, through which everyone or at least large sections of the population pass as a matter of course, that is the identified risk-making factor in planning this type of prevention, rather than risk associated with particular individuals.

High-risk type prevention, by contrast, does focus on populations of *individuals* who are thought to be vulnerable or at 'high risk'. Examples include the children of parents who have alcohol, drug or psychiatric problems, children who are bereaved at an early age, children or adults with disabilities or chronic illnesses and their families, individuals who are about to experience major surgery, and survivors of natural or person-made disasters including earthquakes, floods, aeroplane or ferry disasters, and war (Heller *et al.*, 1984).

By definition, all secondary and tertiary prevention is of high-risk type since people are excluded if they show no signs of the development of a disorder or condition. Elements of the milestone approach may be included, however. For example, a group intervention with physically disabled young adults still living at home, and with their parents, was designed specifically to address the problems that such young people might face in leaving home and becoming independent (Mitchell, 1986). This was therefore an example of milestone-type tertiary prevention aimed at a group of disabled people thought to be at high risk for development of certain handicaps arising from their disabilities.

Primary prevention programmes may be of any one of the three Bloom–Heller types. It is important to be clear that prevention aimed at high-risk groups qualifies clearly as primary prevention, provided the individuals taking part are not currently showing any signs of developing the disorder for which they are thought to be at risk.

Preventive projects also differ in the level at which they attempt to tackle the problem. In the language of public health, disorders can be prevented by intervening at the level of the *host*, the *agent*, or the *environment*. In the case of infectious diseases these correspond, respectively, to the person infected, the infectious agent (virus, etc.) and the environmental medium through which the infection is transmitted (a 'vehicle' if the carrier of the agent is inanimate, and a 'vector' if the carrier is animate) (Robertson, 1986). Again these are useful concepts because they draw our attention to a range of possibilities. It should certainly not be assumed, although it often is, that interventions designed to prevent psychological problems need always be directed at individuals—the hosts or potential hosts.

Although it is helpful in suggesting alternative approaches, the host-agent-environment analogy may be less valuable for thinking about preventive psychology than a more psychologically oriented set of concepts such as

Bronfenbrenner's (1979) scheme of micro-, meso-, exo- and macro-systems which was introduced in Chapter 2 as a framework of general applicability in community psychology. A number of recent writers on the subject of prevention in psychology have used concepts such as these in drawing attention to the need to consider forms of prevention which are not merely targeted at individuals or at micro-level social systems.

Amongst such writers are Catalano and Dooley (1980) who pointed out how the mental health establishment in the USA (in the form of the influential President's Commission on Mental Health, 1978) favoured *micro-level* prevention of a *reactive* type, that is strengthening individuals in reacting to stresses that originate in micro social systems such as the family. They themselves argued that attention should be paid to prevention of a quite different order, namely *proactive macro-level* prevention, for example the reduction of stress caused by unanticipated economic changes. This would require social and political action to influence governmental and commercial decision-making to help bring about, amongst other things, stability of employment and income. The likely causal role of unemployment in psychological disorder was considered in Chapter 3.

Discussing prevention in mental health, Plaut (1980) asked whether, in view of the evidence that rates of mental disorders are related to social class and to other measures of economic and social disadvantage, prevention projects should aim to bring about income redistribution, or to reduce poverty, racism or sexism. He questioned an approach solely directed at individuals:

> Suggesting to people that they can take responsibility for their own health (physical and mental) is consistent with current trends for consumer activism and less dependence on medical and other professional specialists. However, there is some danger that emphasis on individual responsibility may lead to a disregard of societal and institutional factors that often have major effects on people. Ryan (1971) has pointed out the essentially conservative nature of this approach—that is, 'blaming the victim'. (p. 200)

C. Swift (1980) also commented that the traditional approach has been to fit the person to the environment, but that there is increasing recognition that prevention must go beyond projects that focus on strengthening the host to those that involve systems change. Amongst the targets she had in mind were noise, overcrowding, economic fluctuation, cultural and linguistic alienation, social isolation, racism and sexism.

Developments in accident and crime prevention are particularly instructive (Levine and Perkins, 1987). Each had, until quite recently, been dominated by an individualistic approach which located cause in, respectively, the individual who had an accident and the individual perpetrator of a crime. Approaches to these topics now include those that address the behaviour settings in which accidents or crimes occur as well as prevailing attitudes that make crimes easier to commit (Nietzel and Himelein, 1986) or accidents more likely to occur.

Another way of looking at this is to use the ecological analogy: we are talking about individuals, their environments, and the interactions between person and environment. Writing about the prevention of stress-related disorders in Sweden, Levi (1981) stated:

> It would be more efficient to regard the individual, the group, and the environment as *components in a system* in which each is affected by the others in many ways. ... Thus, the administration of disease prevention and health promotion may involve ensuring that the environment is free of noxious substances, counteracting destructive living habits, teaching the population good eating habits, making sure that the workplace environment promotes health and well-being instead of impairing them, and ensuring that housing and leisure time are enriching and favour good health. (p. 15, his emphasis)

An instructive example of prevention on several levels is provided by M. Swift and Weirich (1987). They set out, according to their account, to provide a secondary prevention programme for pre-school children who were displaying maladaptive behaviour in kindergarten. This individually-oriented approach developed into a much broader and more complex programme that included working with the children's mothers, their teachers, a specialist local librarian, the organisation of the school itself and in particular the school administrators, as well as the network of relationships amongst these various participants. Neither were they able to neglect policy-makers with influence on the local school system. Thus, this is a good illustration of the workings of Bronfenbrenner's (1979) micro-, meso- and exo-systems in action.

Similarly, writing about attempts to reduce environmental problems, such as littering, underuse of public transport, and overuse of expensive forms of energy by modifying the behaviour of individuals, Geller (1986) writes

> the behavior change strategies applied so far to environmental problems have been criticised by many psychologists on the grounds that the research has been too reductionistic, too individualistic, too disciplinary, too insular, and critically negligent of an ecological or systems perspective. (p. 373)

To correct these faults, Geller recommends that an ecological, systems-level approach to the prevention of environmental problems should: (a) select targets for intervention only after careful analysis of the likely social, economic and environmental effects of the intervention including impacts on individuals and environments that were not directly aimed at; (b) analyse reciprocal relationships between behaviour and environment; (c) involve 'indigenous delivery agents' including family members and peers and other community members; (d) include in the analysis of outcome both micro-level and macro-level changes; and (e) employ long-term intervention and withdrawal phases.

With possibilities for primary, secondary and tertiary prevention, interventions of community-wide, milestone and high-risk types, and efforts at prevention that aim at one or more of a number of levels ranging from the micro to the macro, the scheme for understanding preventive psychology shown in Table 10, is already becoming complex. Further complexities are added when we consider the all-important question of the aims and goals of prevention. It is at this point that some of the otherwise valuable concepts derived from the fields of physical disease and public health—the reduction of incidence or prevalence of disease or of associated disability for example—begin to fail us. Many recent writers on the subject of prevention in mental health and behavioural medicine have recognised a number of differences which make the direct application of such concepts difficult (e.g. C. Swift 1980; Heller *et al.*, 1984; Levine and Perkins, 1987). One of these is the apparent multifactorial aetiology of many of the health and social difficulties which have a large psychological component and which are proving most difficult to prevent —such as heart disease, alcohol abuse, delinquency and depression. With all of these problems it is difficult to identify single factors which are necessary, let alone sufficient, causes for particular problems, or even to identify factors which explain very much of the variation in risk. A second difficulty is the length of time that would need to elapse before the effects of prevention upon an end-state such as diagnosed psychiatric disorder or criminal conviction could be judged.

These two factors in combination—the one making it unlikely that primary prevention targeted at particular identified causes would have more than minimal effect upon distant outcomes and the other making it extremely difficult to detect such outcomes when they do exist—have led to a reappraisal of some formerly held, overly optimistic ideas about psychological prevention. The prevention of schizophrenia is a good example: optimism about high-risk type primary preventive interventions to reduce rates of schizophrenia have given way to more realistic ideas about the short-term benefits of various kinds—not just a reduction in risk for schizophrenia—that may result from providing help to offspring of parents with the disorder (Goodman, 1984a)

At the same time, the movement to reconceptualise health in positive rather than negative terms has been growing. This has been partly a response to increasing recognition that problems that affect people's lives are by no means confined to those that result in psychiatric diagnosis, conviction, or other official recognition or detection (see Chapter 3 for a summary of some of the evidence on this point). The change towards a positive conception of health has also come about in response to the evidence that the building of positive habits, attributes, or states of mind—such as regular exercise, a balanced diet, non-smoking, sensible drinking, social competence, and positive self-esteem— may reduce, not just one specific negative outcome or end-state, but a *variety* of negative outcomes across the board, as well as having positive effects on quality of life generally.

The distinction is between disease prevention, which aims to prevent identifiable disorders such as depression or alcohol abuse, or prevention of certain high-frequency outcomes associated with such disorders (e.g. suicide, road accidents, or liver cirrhosis), and health promotion (see C. Swift, 1980). WHO Europe (1984) advocates health promotion in the following terms:

> It has come to represent a unifying concept for those who recognise the need for *change* in the ways *and* conditions of living, in order to promote health. ... This perspective is derived from a conception of 'health' as the extent to which an individual or group is able, on the one hand, to realise aspirations and satisfy needs; and, on the other hand, to change or cope with the environment. Health is, therefore, seen as a positive concept emphasising social and personal resources, as well as physical capacities. It *involves the population as a whole in the context of their everyday life, rather than focusing on people at risk for specific diseases.* (their emphases)

Health promotion and disease prevention are probably complementary rather than conflicting, however, and it may be premature to abandon a disorder prevention approach altogether. Newton (1988) has put forward a cogent argument in favour of retaining a disorder prevention approach in the case of psychological disorders such as depression and schizophrenia. She argues that the complex, multifactorial aetiology of such conditions should not stop us building up, through research, more detailed models of causation specific to individual conditions, and using these to mount prevention programmes tailored to impinge upon causal factors.

BARRIERS TO PREVENTION

Before turning to an examination of some specific examples of prevention projects, it is important to consider some of the barriers or difficulties that are likely to be met by anyone embarking upon preventive activity whatever the precise nature of the project and its aims. Not only will an appreciation of these difficulties help to explain why more preventive work has not been undertaken, but it may also serve to arm the would-be preventer in facing some of the resistance that he or she is likely to meet along the way.

Some of the obstacles derive from the priorities and practices of the relevant professions and their training establishments, as well as those of the organisations for which professionals work after training (see Chapter 1). Such impediments can be overcome in time. Indeed there are signs of a strong movement in the direction of prevention. Community psychology is an important component of that movement, and this book hopefully a small part of it. Less easy to deal with are some of the conceptual and ethical dilemmas involved and these require continued thought and research. Most of these dilemmas arise from the central defining feature of prevention: its future orientation. This creates problems for all kinds of prevention, but particularly for high-risk/primary disease prevention and for secondary prevention. Both of these strategies involve selecting individuals who are thought to be at particular risk for future harm: future onset of disorder in the first case, and future continuation and worsening of an already existing or incipient disorder in the second case. The particular problem that arises is the danger of overprediction, particularly when the base rate for the disorder concerned is low in the general population. This inevitably leads to the making of a large number of positive errors: the selection of individuals who receive the preventive intervention because they are thought to be at high risk, but who in fact would never have developed the disorder in question. This would matter little if the costs of selection and intervention in those cases were few. However, such strategies have been criticised on the grounds that selection for intervention because of supposed high risk may be positively harmful because of the processes of labelling and stigmatisation which are set in train as a result.

For example, in the case of secondary prevention, the Primary Mental Health Project conducted in Rochester, New York, by Cowen and his colleagues (e.g. Cowen, Pederson, Babigian, Izzo and Trost, 1973) is an often quoted illustration. About a third of first-year primary grade children in one school were tagged as having 'incipient problems' on the basis of classroom observations, psychological tests, and interviews with their mothers. Providing extra help for these children on a one-to-one or small-group basis, using 'paraprofessionals' including homemakers and college students, produced significantly better results on a variety of measures including those of school achievement and self-reported freedom from anxiety, compared to control schools. It was the results of the follow-up study, however, that led commentators such as Levine and Perkins (1987) to question the overall advisability of this strategy. Not only did the experimental intervention *not* reduce the numbers of children who received psychiatric treatment in community clinics in the subsequent 11–13 years (although it appears to have brought treatment forward: children from the experimental school who received treatment did so on average at 12.6 years of age compared with 14.9 years in control schools) but only 19 per cent of all those children labelled earlier as having incipient problems received psychiatric treatment during that period. In this sense, no fewer than 81 per cent were 'false positives'. Levine and Perkins point out that this project has evolved over a period of 30 years, and has continually adapted to developments in the field of prevention. Most recently it has developed a positive health promotion aspect including training in social competency, with a high-risk/primary prevention component focusing upon children of parents who had experienced separation and divorce (Pedro-Carroll and Cowen, 1985—see below for a description of this work).

The same dilemmas apply to most high-risk/primary prevention activities, particularly where these are underpinned by a disease prevention theory that assumes, for example, that children of parents with a particular disorder are themselves at high risk for the same disorder later in life. Problems related to the excessive consumption of alcohol constitute a good example. Having had a parent with an alcohol problem is one of the best predictors of later alcohol problems in the offspring but it is not a strong predictor (Orford and Velleman, 1990). Any attempt to prevent alcohol problems, using the high-risk strategy of selecting individuals solely on the grounds of their having had a parent with an alcohol problem would have to address the inevitable problem of many false positives and the dangers of producing harmful effects as a result of unwarranted labelling.

Community-wide and milestone-type prevention strategies are free of problems inherent in selection and labelling. One of the major difficulties, however, is that of financial cost, because the numbers of people who it is intended should receive a preventive intervention are likely to be very large in relation to the number of harmful outcomes which may be prevented. Furthermore, particularly with large-scale, community-wide interventions that use the media or other methods that do not involve face-to-face contact (as well as many of those that do), it is often found that those who it is thought might benefit most turn out to be those who are least likely to have received the intervention (Heller *et al.*, 1984). Some of the television components of the Head Start projects (see below) were examples of this: relatively well-off families took more advantage of the educational programmes than did under-privileged families for whom the programmes were principally intended.

Also community-wide and milestone-type preventive approaches may not be entirely immune to the charge of unwittingly producing some harmful effects for some people. Concern has been expressed, for example, about the possibility of inducing feelings of guilt amongst pregnant women as a result of albeit sound advice about smoking, drinking and nutrition: guilt that is likely to be particularly felt if the birth results in a less than perfect infant (McCluskey-Fawcett, Meck and Harris, 1986).

Knowing some of the properties of systems, such as interdependence of parts and multifinality (see Chapter 2), we should expect a variety of effects of a preventive intervention, some of them of kinds and in places that were unintended and unwanted. Numerous examples could be given. One example, provided by Robertson (1986), concerns the provision of driving tuition in secondary schools. The intended effect was a reduction in subsequent accidents. According to Robertson, the effect of such schemes in the USA was harmful overall: an unintended effect was that those school pupils who had taken such courses received licences to drive earlier, thus increasing the numbers of very young, and hence particularly vulnerable, drivers on the roads.

Child sexual abuse prevention programmes have also been questioned on the grounds that outcomes, intended and unintended, are unknown. Repucci (1987) argued that such programmes have swept the USA in the last few years despite the absence of a consistent definition of what constitutes sexual abuse and any evidence that the interventions are effective either in reducing it or helping children cope with it when it occurs. Programmes have largely been evaluated simply in terms of pre-post changes in knowledge; for example about what constitutes appropriate and inappropriate touching by an adult, and that sexual abuse can occur within a family. With only a single exception (Swan, Press and Briggs, 1985), Repucci could find no programme that had assessed the possible negative reactions or effects: in the Swan, Press and Briggs study only 5 per cent of parents said that their children had shown adverse reactions from the programme such as loss of sleep or appetite, nightmares or fears. In general Repucci finds the emphasis upon knowledge in these programmes to be simplistic, and states that they often neglect the developmental levels of the children involved as well as social and cultural differences.

Finally, there is a wider and more fundamental concern which has to be faced whenever prevention is thought about or attempted. Because, by its very nature, prevention is a planned, proactive activity, designed to prevent future harm, rather than something that is sought out by individuals because of present discomfort or distress, its potential for abuse is considerable. It would be only too easy for it to be imposed on an unknowing public, without due consultation, by experts who assume they know what is good for people. Or worse, psychological prevention could be used by a political regime in the interests of social control or political repression (Heller *et al.*, 1984). Hence, although it may be a source of frustration to the experts—the continued successful activities of the few who are still opposed to the fluoridation of public water supply in some parts of the USA and elsewhere for example (Frazier and Horowitz, 1986)—public scepticism and resistance are at least indications that preventive interventions cannot be imposed without informed public debate.

That these various difficulties and obstacles in the way of prevention are being seriously voiced and thought about by the leading exponents of prevention in community psychology should be seen as a strength. Although there is a danger of a double standard operating, with preventive activities being required to meet higher ethical and proven efficacy standards than treatment, it is to the credit of the prevention field that these dilemmas are being addressed. All applied psychology involves facing ethical and conceptual difficulties; it is simply impossible to hide them in the case of prevention. It would certainly be no solution to return to an exclusively reactive and individualistic, treatment-of-existing-disorder approach to the application of psychological knowledge. Prevention of various kinds must find an important place alongside traditional therapeutic activities.

EXAMPLE: SCHOOL TRANSITION

One of the normal life transitions that has been identified as being stressful and as sometimes having a harmful effect upon development is the transition from primary or elementary school to secondary school. The stresses may include adjusting to a larger building, to having a larger number of different teachers, to having to move around more during the day, to having to master a personal locker and to manage belongings, to having more homework and greater academic pressure, having to undress in front of others for sports, being approached to smoke or drink, mixing with a larger and more diverse group of peers, and being teased or ridiculed by others. These were the very stressors which were the target of a life transition or milestone-type prevention programme carried out by the local community mental health centre in one small community in the Eastern part of the USA (Elias, Gara, Ubriaco, Rothbaum, Clabby and Schuyler, 1986).

As well as providing a good illustration of the milestone- or life transition-type of primary prevention, this project also offers a good example of the use of a quasi-experimental design for evaluating the outcome. The locality concerned had four elementary schools and one 'middle' school, to which all pupils transferred at around age 11. Using an adaptation of Spivack and Shure's interpersonal cognitive problem-solving (ICPS) approach (see below), all children in the last year at two of the elementary schools received social problem-solving training throughout the year, covering two phases of training—instructional and application. Pupils in the other two schools commenced training only halfway through the school year and received only the instructional phase. Both groups were compared with pupils in the same four schools who had reached this identical transition point a year earlier: they had received the same assessments but no ICPS training.

The training was provided by class teachers in the last year of elementary school. They were supported by two consultants—students in clinical and school psychology whose role was, 'to work with teachers to ensure their understanding of coming lessons, model appropriate teaching in the classroom as new teaching skills were being introduced, and monitor and provide feedback to teachers about performance' (Elias *et al.*, 1986, p. 265). The consultants themselves were supervised by a team consisting of an 'educator-clinician' from the community mental health centre, a member of staff of the university psychology department, and one of the elementary school principals. The instructional phase consisted of 20 lessons focusing in turn on a number of ICPS component skills. In the application phase these skills were applied to conflicts between individual pupils or between larger groups, as well as problems which children were encouraged to discuss with the group who helped solve their problems.

Results were assessed in terms of a standard scale of Middle School Stressors given to participants early in their first year in the new school. Elias *et al.* reported a significant difference for the scale as a whole and in terms of many of the individual items in favour of those who received both phases of training in comparison with those who received the instructional phase only. This was particularly the case for stresses to do with adjusting to academic requirements, the logistics of adjusting to a larger school (lockers, finding your way around, etc.) and coping with peer pressure. They also reported that both conditions were associated with a lower level of self-reported stress compared to the previous year's cohort who had received no training.

A more modest intervention, to help primary school-aged children transferring to a larger school following a forced closure of their local school, was reported by Jason (1980). This consisted of a two-day orientation programme that occurred one week before the beginning of attendance at the new school. It involved tours of the new school, peer-led discussion groups, and information about school rules and regulations. Despite the brevity of this project children who took part were subsequently significantly higher than control children in terms of self-esteem related to peer relationships, knowledge of school rules, and teacher conduct ratings.

EXAMPLE: PREPARATION FOR SURGERY

A different kind of life stress, experienced by most people at some time or another in their lives, is the stress involved in preparing for, undergoing, and recovering from surgery. Preventive work in this area is relatively long-established compared to some of the prevention methods considered in this chapter, and relatively little controversy surrounds it. There are probably a number of reasons for this. For one thing this type of prevention does not require the identification or tagging of people who are thought to be at special risk or who are not otherwise undergoing certain routine procedures. Also, like Jason's (1980) intervention for primary school pupils, prevention in this context consists of relatively simple and inexpensive additions to already established routine. Furthermore, there is evidence that children and adults undergoing surgery often experience considerable stress at the time, but also that some experience the effects of stress for some time afterwards, and that symptoms of stress during the immediate recovery from operations can even include psychiatric symptoms including hallucinations and delusions (Heller *et al.*, 1984). Finally, the results of a number of studies of preventive preparation for surgery have been highly positive.

Demonstrations of the value of preparation for an impending operation include work reported by Egbert, Battit, Welch and Bartlett (1964, cited by Heller *et al.*, 1984) with adults, and by Cassell (1965, cited by Heller *et al.*), and Skipper and Leonard (1968, cited by Justice, 1982), with children. In the Egbert *et al.* study, patients received instruction concerning post-operative pain during a routine visit by the anaesthetist the night before the operation. They were given information about the likely severity and duration of pain and were instructed in simple relaxation exercises. They were also encouraged to request medication if they should need it. Compared to patients who received only the routine visit, those who received this further instruction subsequently used *less medication* and were discharged earlier.

Cassell (1965) made use of puppet theatre to prepare children between the ages of 3 and 11 for cardiac catheterisation. The procedure was acted out in puppet play with the child patient taking the role first of the 'child' and then of the 'doctor'. Compared to a control group, children who received this anticipatory help showed less emotional upset during the catheterisation procedure and later expressed a greater willingness to return to the hospital for further treatment. There was no difference, however, in levels of general emotional disturbance post-operatively.

The Skipper and Leonard (1968) study is of particular interest because it demonstrates the successful impact upon children of an intervention that took place with their mothers. Once again these results could be seen as confirmation of the importance of Bronfenbrenner's (1979) meso-system. At the time of the child's admission to hospital and at several other times before and after the operation, a special nurse met for about five minutes with the child's mother—at admission the child was present also although the focus of interaction was the mother. An attempt was made to portray an accurate picture of the reality of the situation—what would occur and when—and to create an atmosphere that would facilitate communication so that mothers would feel free to verbalise any fears and anxieties and to ask questions. Results showed a variety of positive effects. The children's blood pressures and pulse rates, recorded at admission, pre-operatively, post-operatively and at discharge, showed significant differences, especially at discharge, and a follow-up questionnaire completed by mothers showed fewer ill-effects from the operation and speedier recovery in the case of those whose mothers took part, a lower frequency of excessive crying, disturbed sleep, or unusual fear of doctors, nurses and hospitals, and less stress experienced by mothers both during and after the operation.

EXAMPLE: CHILDREN OF DIVORCED PARENTS

Unlike transfer from primary to secondary school or undergoing surgery, parental divorce or separation is not something that occurs for almost everyone. It does, however, occur for very large numbers of children and there is convincing evidence that children of divorced parents, as a group, are at risk, at least within the first few years of their parents' separation (e.g. Hetherington, 1979; Kurdek, 1981). Although the children of divorced parents may be at higher risk as a group, of course not all such children will display the kinds of problems that are the targets of prevention programmes for children of divorced or separated parents, and research has been devoted to examining the possible factors that may mediate between parental divorce and childhood or adolescent adjustment. These include the presence of stresses and life changes associated with divorce, including the degree of parental conflict surrounding divorce, and the degree to which the child is drawn into that conflict, as well as parental remarriage and the tasks of adapting to a new family system (Farber, Felner and Primavera, 1985). In their own research Farber, Felner and Primavera examined some of the factors mediating adjustment amongst a group of 17–23-year-old college students who had experienced parental separation or divorce sometime after age 12. Adjustment, which was assessed by means of questionnaire scales of anxiety, depression, hostility and self-esteem, was most consistently related to the degree of organisational conflict and change that was reported to have been associated with the divorce, the degree to which the young person had coped by introjecting blame, and the physical distance that now separated the student from home (the greater the distance the poorer the adjustment)

A number of projects have been described, the aims of which are to increase the level of adjustment of children of divorce. One of these is the Children of Divorce Intervention Program (CODIP) reported first by Pedro-Carroll and Cowen (1985) with a replication study reported by Pedro-Carroll, Cowen, Hightower and Guare (1986).

Ten or eleven one-hour group meetings for 9–11-year-old children whose parents had divorced were held in each of a number of schools in Rochester, New York. Children were recruited by sending letters to parents, followed by holding group meetings for interested parents and by phoning some parents of children who had been identified by their teachers as possible participants. The groups were held in the children's own schools, and each group contained between six and nine boys and girls. Pedro-Carroll et al. (1986) described the essence of this group approach as follows:

(a) an emphasis on support throughout; (b) establishing a climate in which important feelings could be examined, dealt with safely, and misconceptions clarified; (c) training situationally relevant skills (e.g. feeling expression, interpersonal problem solving, communication, and anger control skills); and (d) enhancing esteem. (p. 287)

The revised version of the programme described in the 1986 report included the use of films portraying divorce-related issues, techniques for expressing feeling such as creative writing, poetry and a group newsletter, and an exercise, spoken highly of in the report, in which children took turns at being members of a 'panel of experts' on separation and divorce, answering questions from other group members (e.g. Is it true that kids cause their parents' divorce?).

Twelve volunteers—described as 'Five school mental health professionals, one clinical psychologist, two school administrators, two teachers, one research associate, and one experienced paraprofessional', co-led the groups. In the month leading up to the start of the programme, group leaders received training to increase their understanding of the effects of divorce on family and children and to acquire programme and group skills.

In their first study of this programme, Pedro-Carroll and Cowen (1985) compared the results for 40 children who were assigned to the programme at random and 32 children assigned to a delayed-intervention control group

(they later received a condensed version of the same programme). In the replication study Pedro-Carroll *et al.* (1986) adopted a quasi-experimental design
strategy of comparing the results for 54 children of divorced parents with a
demographically matched comparison group of 78 children from intact families who were attending the same school classes. In both studies results were
assessed in terms of pre-post changes on child, parent and teacher questionnaires and ratings. A limitation of these studies is that the outcome measures
were taken only at two weeks after the intervention ended and no later follow-
up is reported. Nevertheless, both studies showed convincing changes for
those children who had partaken in the groups in comparison to the control
and comparison children. Improvements were significantly greater for
teachers' ratings of problem behaviours and competences, parents' ratings of
their children's adjustment, and the children's own ratings of their levels of
anxiety. The authors report that participants described the group experience
very positively.

It should be noted that efforts at prevention with children of divorced
parents are just the kinds of interventions which make Caplan's (1964) distinction between primary and secondary prevention difficult to sustain. Unless the
threshold for defining this order of distress is placed at a high enough level,
it is likely that participants in such programmes will be a mixture of those
who are already experiencing difficulties (for whom prevention is therefore
secondary in Caplan's terms) and those who are not experiencing such
difficulties, but who are thought to be at high risk (primary prevention)
(Newton, 1988).

EXAMPLE: INTERPERSONAL COGNITIVE PROBLEM-SOLVING TRAINING

One line of preventive work which has become very popular in recent years,
and which illustrates many of the general points made in this chapter so far,
has involved the attempted enhancement of health or competence in young
children through programmes of interpersonal problem-solving training. The
rationale for this approach is that adjustment is in large measure a result of
how well children deal with interpersonal conflicts and other difficult situations, and that how such situations are dealt with depends upon whether
a child uses a number of very general mental strategies for solving such
problems. This approach was pioneered by Spivack and Shure and their
colleagues at a mental health centre serving an inner-city population in Philadelphia. Their initial observations were that the better adjusted primary
school children were more likely to use certain basic *interpersonal cognitive
problem-solving (ICPS)* skills of which the following appeared to be central:

Alternative thinking: the ability to develop alternative solutions to
    problems.

Consequential thinking: the ability to anticipate accurately the consequences of one's own actions upon others.

Means-ends thinking: the ability to develop a course of action to meet a goal, and to modify the plan at different steps.

On the basis of these observations this group mounted a series of preventive interventions with pre-school children (Spivack and Shure, 1974, cited by Durlak, 1983; Shure and Spivack 1979, 1982). The training, which involved short daily lessons lasting in some cases for a term and in other cases for as long as a year or two, consisted of 40 or more 'game' activities, designed to teach the components of ICPS as well as certain prerequisite skills such as listening to and observing others, identifying common emotions, and learning that others have feelings and motives in problem situations.

The results were extremely encouraging. Groups of children who received such a programme were shown to have acquired more of the problem-solving skills than control children and six months after the intervention there were sizeable differences in rates of satisfactory adjustment amongst those initially rated as maladjusted (73 per cent of those who received training versus 35 per cent of controls). It appeared that the programme was of influence across a broad range of types of maladjustment—impulsive children were reported to become more tolerant of frustration and inhibited children were reported to become more outgoing. Amongst other important findings were the following: (a) mothers were found to be just as effective as trainers as pre-school teachers; (b) positive effects generalised from the training setting to other classroom settings, and from home to school when mothers were the trainers; (c) the ability to generate alternative solutions to problems emerged as one of the most important component skills; and (d) a particularly important skill for both teachers and mothers was what Shure and Spivack called 'dialoguing', that is when a child was faced with an acute interpersonal problem, the trainer would encourage the child to talk through how he or she was thinking about the problem, what his or her feelings were, what he or she could do, what would be likely to happen, and which alternatives might be more effective.

The use of such a general skills enhancement approach was so promising and the initial results so encouraging, that the approach has been widely adopted. The work has been extended to age groups other than pre-schoolers and there has been at least one report of using this approach with adults (Dixon et al., 1979, cited by Durlak, 1983). But most extensions have been to 6–10-year-olds, and here the results have been less uniformly positive. Work by a group in Connecticut (Allen et al., 1976) and by the Rochester Primary Mental Health project group (Weissberg et al., 1981) is amongst work that has been reported in detail. Positive results have not been reported for all groups of children. For example, the Rochester group found improvements with suburban school children but not with inner-city children. In the latter schools some teachers even reported that generating alternative solutions to problems produced a large number of aggressive alternatives with negative effects on classroom discipline. It has been more difficult to demonstrate generalisation of effects beyond the specific classroom setting in which teaching took place, there have been few follow-up studies, and relationships with later adjustment have not been so clearly established. Nevertheless, a summary of the results that have been achieved shows that the short-term effects have mostly been an increase in problem-solving skills and an improvement in teacher ratings (Durlak, 1983).

Those who have summarised the findings of work using this approach make a number of general points and raise a number of pertinent questions. They ask, for instance, whether individual life problems and tasks do not call for a range of skills and abilities, some of which are specific to those problems and tasks, and hence whether it is not unrealistic to expect a general training programme concentrating on one set of skills to have widespread and positive effects on later adjustment (Durlak, 1983; Levine and Perkins, 1987). From his detailed review, Durlak (1983) concluded that there is stronger positive evidence for social problem-solving preventive strategies which focus on the prevention of more specific unwanted outcomes (drug abuse, unwanted pregnancy, unemployment and marital conflict, for example) rather than a general skill-enhancement approach. He favoured an alternative problem-solving approach, that of D'Zurilla and Goldfried (1971) which focuses upon the abilities demanded of an individual in a particular situation. Levine and Perkins (1987) also comment that the individual competence-building approach, because maladjustment is seen to reside in individual skill deficits, may be criticised for falling into the trap of 'blaming the victim' (Ryan, 1971).

Durlak also pointed to the lack of clearly documented evidence that problem-solving is causally related to mental health:

> To be successful, preventive programs must first demonstrate that some important negative outcome has indeed been prevented, and then that the effects are relatively long-lasting. Whereas some programs have achieved the former goal, none has effectively met the latter criterion. (Durlak, 1983, p. 45)

With this argument we have come full circle. Proponents of primary prevention are in a bind. The *specific* disease-prevention approach has been criticised, as has already been noted, but *general* health- or competence-enhancement approaches are likely to run into criticism unless they can show a reduction in longer-term harm of some specific kinds. In their review, Weissberg and Allen (1986) argued that it is difficult for social problem-solving outcome studies to capture more than a small part of the many possible mediators of positive adjustment that training offers. These include an increased belief that problems can be solved, a common language in which to communicate about problems to peers and adults, opportunities to observe and to practise solutions, and to improve impulse control. They concluded that, although there are many unresolved problems of implementation and evaluation, 'The approach shows promise for benefiting large numbers of children' (p. 168). More cautiously, Heller *et al.* (1984) concluded that, 'the value of social problem-solving training as a prevention strategy remains an open question' (pp. 201–202), and Levine and Perkins (1987) state: 'The empirical literature on competence building, while encouraging overall, has nevertheless left us with a complicated picture' (pp. 215–216).

EXAMPLE: EARLY LIFE ENRICHMENT

Some of the best-known primary prevention projects using the high-risk strategy have involved making special provision for pre-school children in deprived areas. The best documented programmes of this kind, from the USA, are the Milwaukee Project and the numerous projects that were sponsored under the Head Start programme. The former project took place in a single area in one city and had the specific target of preventing childhood learning difficulties of the kind that could be ascribed to an educationally impoverished early environment rather than to specific organic deficit ('mild mental retardation' as the authors of the reports of this project describe it, for example Heber, 1978). The Head Start programme, in contrast, when it started in the mid-1960s embraced several thousand individual projects covering more than half a million children. Funded by the US government, it was part of the War on Poverty programme set up in the Kennedy era. Its goals were comparatively broad. They included improving physical health, emotional, social and cognitive development, self-esteem, and adults' expectations for the children (Levine and Perkins, 1987).

The Milwaukee project was confined to families in which the mothers had low IQs (75 or less). Because of its broader aims, Head Start families were not restricted to the same extent, but all were from poverty-stricken backgrounds, and, like families in the Milwaukee project, all were black.

The success of these two schemes can probably be attributed to the fact that they incorporated a number of sound ecological principles. Each assumed that intervention at the individual level and at Bronfenbrenner's (1979) micro- and meso-system levels would be necessary to bring about definite and lasting improvement and both involved parents as full participants. As well as pre-school education for the children, the Milwaukee project included job-training, home management and remedial education for the mothers. Parental involvement was mandatory in the Head Start projects: many parents took classes in child-care, others took jobs as teacher assistants, cooks or playground supervisors, and in at least one of the better documented individual projects (Berrueta-Clement, Schweinhart, Barnett, Epstein and Weikart, 1984, cited by Levine and Perkins, 1987) weekly home visits with the mothers were included which may have helped mothers become more familiar with, and knowledgeable and discriminating about, schools and education. In this way many of these projects may have influenced children not only directly, but also via their families (the micro-system) and via the kinds of child–family–school links (the meso-system) which form one of the central components of Bronfenbrenner's (1979) theory of positive child development.

Another principle which was incorporated into Head Start only after the first round of projects, which took place over two months during one summer, was that significant change of this kind takes time. The next round of Head Start projects lasted a full year.

Initial results of Head Start projects, and in particular the Westinghouse Report (Cicirelli, Cooper and Granger, 1969, cited by Lloyd and Bettencourt, 1986) were disappointing. They suggested that although there were IQ gains for the children immediately following participation, differences in comparison with children who did not take part disappeared within a few years of entering primary school. The Milwaukee project, on the other hand, perhaps because of its focus on families where mothers were of low IQ, coupled with its intensive training programme for mothers and children, produced large and statistically significant differences in IQ between participant and control children. At age 10 there was still a difference of 20 IQ points between the groups, and no children from the experimental group (compared with 60 per cent of control children) obtained IQs below 85.

Changes in IQ were not central to the aims of the Head Start programme, however, and the Westinghouse report was controversial. Later reports of individual projects (e.g. Berrueta-Clement *et al.*, 1984) and of the results from several projects combined (e.g. Darlington, Royce, Snipper, Murray and Lazar, 1980) have been much more encouraging. Berrueta-Clement *et al.* report on 58 and 65 children randomly assigned to one project and to a control group respectively, who have since been followed-up to age 19. The former group in comparison to controls: (a) were less often ever classified as 'mentally retarded' (15 per cent versus 35 per cent); (b) had higher grade-point averages and more favourable attitudes towards school at the secondary educational stage; (c) more often graduated from high school (67 per cent versus 49 per cent); (d) were more likely to be working by age 19 and had higher median earnings; (e) had less often been arrested as a juvenile or adult (31 per cent versus 51 per cent); (f) and in the case of the female members of the groups reported fewer pregnancies or births by age 19 (17 per cent versus 28 per cent). These results of one project are supported by the findings of Darlington *et al.*'s (1980) follow-up of children who took part in 11 separate projects that involved approximately 3000 children. They found that fewer project children had spent time in special classes (24 per cent versus 45 per cent) and fewer had stayed down in a class.

It appears that in many areas Head Start survived initial adverse reports and a change in political climate because of its popularity, not least with parents. It is now judged by many to have produced lasting benefits for many children. Current explanations are couched, not so much in terms of the early 'plasticity' of intelligence, but rather in terms of cognitive and social factors including higher aspirations and motivation and increased sense of control, as well as a better 'fit' between child and school leading to positive experiences early in a child's school career (Levine and Perkins, 1987).

What is not so clear, because of the wide variety of educational and developmental philosophies and methods involved in the different projects, is what precisely it is about a pre-school project which is of benefit. In their review, Lloyd and Bettencourt (1986) conclude that projects are more successful if they involve structured programmes including intensive instruction in specific skills. Berrueta-Clement *et al.* (1984), on the other hand, believed the evidence to be insufficient to support one approach rather than another, but concluded that what matters is that the project has a definite, consistent philosophy and that it be implemented consistently and be well supervised.

Levine and Perkins (1987) conclude of Head Start that it 'stands as a significant landmark in the development of programs in the prevention of psychosocial problems' (p. 226).

EXAMPLE: LIFESTYLE AND THE PREVENTION OF HEART DISEASE

An area of preventive psychology which has emerged strongly in the last two decades and which is now firmly established is concerned with the prevention of morbidity and mortality associated with physical disease. As evidence has accumulated that aspects of lifestyle, such as diet, tobacco and alcohol consumption, and exercise, are major determinants of physical health and illness, so the opportunities for prevention through modifying lifestyle have begun to be realised. Two different approaches have been adopted. The first is a disease-prevention approach which is particularly exemplified by programmes aimed at the prevention of coronary heart disease (CHD). Even with this strategy, however, the approach is broadly based since CHD covers a number of specific diseases or disorders and the immediate aim of most projects has been to reduce risk factors across a number of facets of behaviour. These projects can hardly be criticised for taking a narrow approach. A second general strategy aims at the modification of one form of behaviour which is known to affect the incidence of a number of different diseases. The reduction of tobacco smoking provides the best example.

A number of large-scale CHD-prevention projects have been reported or are ongoing. Of these the Stanford Heart Disease Prevention Program in California and the North Karelia Project in Finland are probably the best known. Others include the Minnesota Heart Health Program (Blackburn, Luepker, Kline *et al.*, 1982) and the Pawtucket Heart Health Project (Lasater, Abrams, Artz *et al.*, 1982), both in the USA, and the Heartbeat Wales Project in the UK (1985).

The Three Community Study was completed by the Stanford group in the 1970s (Farquhar, Maccoby, Wood *et al.*, 1977; Farquhar, Fortmann,

Maccoby *et al.*, 1982). The study took place in three small Northern Californian communities with a total population of 43 000. Like the other major projects of this type it provides a good example of use of a quasi-experimental design in a community setting where random assignment to groups would have been both inappropriate and impossible (see Chapter 6). One community received an extended mass media campaign over the two years of the study. This included radio and television programmes and spot announcements, newspaper articles, posters on hoardings and buses, and direct mailings to households. The campaign aimed to increase awareness of cardiovascular risks and to provide knowledge about how to make changes in behaviour such as smoking, diet and exercise. A second community received a similar mass media campaign but supplemented by intensive face-to-face instruction for a sub-sample of individuals at highest risk. The third community served as a no-treatment comparison group. A random selection of people in each community were surveyed and their cardiovascular risk status determined before the campaign began, during it, and at yearly intervals for three years of follow-up.

Knowledge about risk factors increased in the two campaign communities. Actual risk, calculated on the basis of combining a number of risk factors, also decreased by 20 per cent or more in these communities particularly in the media plus face-to-face community which experienced a 28 per cent reduction in overall risk score. The greatest changes occurred in smoking, diet and blood pressure. Knowledge gains and risk reductions were maintained throughout the follow-up period. The difference in favour of the media plus face-to-face community compared with the media only community was greatest in the first year but was not significant thereafter.

Maccoby and Alexander (1979) believed that the success of the three-community study may have been due to the use of a relatively long-term campaign and the care with which it was planned. Care was taken to formulate specific objectives for each component of the campaign at every stage, to target components at defined audience segments, to create clear and salient messages by careful pre-testing, and to use the media creatively to reach the intended audience sufficiently frequently. Solomon and Maccoby (1982) have described in detail the way in which use of a communication-behaviour change approach to this kind of preventive work dictates that a programme with vague, overall objectives and a blind shotgun approach to achieving change is not good enough. Careful analysis of the problem, targets for intervention, their current position regarding the behaviours concerned, the appropriateness of the media or other channels of communication, and the specific design of the messages are mandatory. For example, as they point out, pregnant smokers are likely to be quite different in their motivation from middle-aged male smokers, and teenage smokers are different again. A number of models of change suppose a hierarchy or series of stages of change, and the Stanford group argue for the importance of prior information about the position of segments of the population in terms of such a hierarchy. The model described by Farquhar, Fortmann, Maccoby *et al.* (1982) consists of the following six stages:

Stage:	*Campaign Should:*
1. Becoming aware	Gain attention
2. Increasing knowledge	Provide information
3. Increasing motivation	Provide incentives
4. Learning skills	Provide training
5. Taking action	Model action
6. Maintaining change	Provide support

The media may be particularly appropriate in gaining the public's attention over a health issue at stage 1, but other channels may be more appropriate for segments of the population who have already moved beyond this stage. They also stressed the great importance of formative research in this process. Not only is this essential in the preliminary stages of problem analysis, and later in pre-testing and modifying components of a campaign, but without it, they argued, it is sometimes impossible to interpret the reasons for an unsuccessful outcome or even sometimes of a successful one.

Employing these principles, the Stanford group went on to conduct an even more ambitious project, known as the Five-City Project, which began in the late 1970s and continued throughout most of the 1980s. The two campaign communities and three comparisons totalled 350 000 in population and the project was designed to run for a total of six years. The age range was extended from 35–59 to 12–74. A criticism of the three-communities study was that actual effects on morbidity and mortality were not monitored (Heller *et al.*, 1984), but such monitoring is included in the Five-City Project. It was estimated that a greater than 20 per cent reduction in overall cardiovascular risk could be achieved if average changes of the following sizes were to occur in individual risk factors: (a) a 9 per cent reduction in the proportion of smokers; (b) a 2 per cent average reduction in weight; (c) a 7 per cent reduction in systolic blood pressure; and (d) a 4 per cent reduction in blood cholesterol.

With an even longer campaign than the one employed in their previous project, the Stanford group now aimed to involve the communities more directly and as a consequence to lay the foundations for health-promotion activities which would continue long after the formal campaign had ended. As an example of activities that might serve this end, they cited the joint establishment with the County Health department of anti-smoking classes in the communities, with the Stanford team helping with training, curriculum development, evaluation, and curriculum revision (Farquhar, Fortmann, Maccoby *et al.* 1982).

Community involvement was even more apparent in the case of the North

Karelia project which began in 1972 following a local petition calling for action to do something about the abnormally high rate of CHD in that area of Finland (Puska, 1982). North Karelia was a large and mainly rural area with 180 000 inhabitants. According to Puska, it was realised early on that the high level of risk in this community was a consequence of general lifestyle, and was not limited to small sections of the community, and that this lifestyle was in turn closely linked with local culture, social organisation, and even the physical environment. The aim was to involve the whole community, and to this end the project was located within the system of local services (at the County Health Department). Project staff travelled throughout the area establishing close contacts with community leaders including politicians, local doctors, representatives of the food industry, and local mass media personnel. The project appears to have caught the imagination of the community. Puska stated that: 'The project goals were associated with the pride and provincial identity of the population. People were urged to participate, not necessarily for their own benefit, but "for North Karelia"' (p. 1142).

The project ran for five years in the first instance. Its elements included mass health communication, organisation of individual and group services, training of local health personnel, and environmental modification. Specific rather than general advice was given (for example to switch from fatty milk to low-fat milk rather than simply to reduce fat consumption), and the message often emphasised that families or work groups should attempt changes jointly. Support from local nurses and doctors was encouraged and a network of local lay leaders was trained. In terms of environmental change, smoking restrictions were introduced in various places and large quantities of anti-smoking signs were distributed. Cooperation was established with local dairies, the local sausage factory, and local shopkeepers, in order to promote the production and sale of low-fat products. Thus this Finnish project went somewhat further than the Stanford group had done in correcting what some have seen as a bias in this kind of work towards the focus on individual-level risk factors and a relative neglect of environmental and community-level risks for heart disease (Heller et al., 1984).

Again a quasi-experimental design was adopted and a similar County in Eastern Finland was chosen as comparison. Although the comparison County showed a downward trend in CHD risk over the five-year period, risk reduction was greater in North Karelia. The overall net risk reduction for men (after adjusting for the reduction in the comparison County) was 17.4 per cent. Contributing to this was a 4.1 per cent decrease in serum cholesterol, reductions of 3.6 per cent and 2.8 per cent in systolic and diastolic blood pressure respectively, and a 9.8 per cent reduction in the average number of cigarettes smoked per day. The corresponding overall risk reduction for women was 11.5 per cent (Puska, Salonen, Nissinen et al., 1983).

Ten years after the start of the project it was found that reductions in cholesterol and blood pressure had been maintained and overall reductions in smoking had become greater still (28 per cent for men and 14 per cent for women). That the project did in fact save lives was shown by an analysis of age-standardised CHD mortality amongst men for the years 1974 – 1979 (the project commenced in 1972). This reduction was 22 per cent for North Karelia, 12 per cent for the comparison County, and 11 per cent for the rest of Finland (Salonen, Puska, Kottke, Tuomilehto and Nissinen, 1983). One indication of the cost-effectiveness of the project was obtained from analysing pension disability payments, which in Finland are recorded by County and by disease in a national central register. Until the start of the project, trends had been similar in North Karelia and the comparison County. Rates for CHD-related disabilities started to diverge in 1974 and by 1977 North Karelia had approximately a 10 per cent lower payment rate for such disabilities. This amounted to savings of approximately $4m, or more than five times the $0.7m spent on the project (Puska, 1982).

Finally, Puska (1982) described the successful diffusion of components of the North Karelia project to other parts of Finland. Finnish national television had carried a major risk-reduction programme based on the project, and many of the health-promotion materials and health service strategies developed on the project had become available throughout the country. In general, Puska stated: 'The North Karelia project has become popular as a practical and positive example that health promotion and control of modern chronic disease epidemics is feasible' (p. 1146). The importance of disseminating experiences and results, and the value of work that is evaluated and widely reported, in setting examples for other areas to follow, is a general theme in community psychology and one which receives mention in a number of other places in this book.

9 Understanding and Changing Organisations

Work with a large variety of different types of organisation comes within the purview of community psychology. This includes schools requiring help with internal communication, voluntary organisations seeking help with evaluation or advice on management structures, multidisciplinary teams in the health and social services asking for help in team building or in planning a halfway house or group home, or factories wishing to develop health policies or stress-management programmes for their staff. The aim of this chapter is to introduce some ideas from organisational psychology which may be helpful as a basis for understanding such a diversity of organisations. Multidisciplinary teams will be taken as particular examples.

TYPES OF ORGANISATION

A useful place at which to start to try to make sense of this diversity is with some of the ideas generated by organisational psychologists in the form of typologies of organisations. Although typologies should never be taken too literally or seriously, since the 'types' to which they refer are almost always 'pure' types which scarcely exist in practice (most real world instances are hybrids or variants of one sort or another), typologies often serve to draw attention to key issues and to important sources of variation. There have in fact been numerous typologies of organisations, and the one that will be used here is the one put forward by Kilmann (1983) in an effort to bring together a number of themes that were common to a number of other typologies.

The four types of organisation that make up Kilmann's typology are shown in Table 11. The four types differ one from another in terms of two major dimensions: *technical* versus *social*, and *open* versus *closed*. The requirement for efficiency in organisations inevitably leads to a tendency towards 'bureaucratic' or 'mechanical' practices, particularly as organisations grow in size.

Table 11. A typology of organisations (based on Kilmann, 1983)

Closed-technical		Open-technical	
Values:	Efficiency, bureaucracy	Values:	Adaptability, resource acquisition, marketing
Power:	Coercive, induced, legitimate	Power:	Competent
Closed-social		Open-social	
Values:	Commitment, communication, participation	Values:	Responsiveness, relevance
Power:	Personal	Power:	Competent, personal

Hence many organisations in which people work or which people use as residents or customers, have features of the *closed-technical* system and it is important to be aware of some of their effects.

In pure form this type of organisation ignores the environment external to it: it operates as if it were a closed rather than an open system. The emphasis is upon internal efficiency with relatively little concern about where its resources (which may be in the form of people, materials, or both) are coming from or where its products (which again may be in the form of people, goods, or both) are going to or how well they are received by the outside world. This may not be harmful so long as the external environment is stable and predictable, but it is not functional if external conditions and demands are changing (or 'turbulent' to use an organisational psychology term).

The other major shortcoming of the closed-technical system according to Kilmann's view is that it ignores the personal and social side. It relies on rules and regulations. No account is taken of the informal, social system which operates in all organisations whatever their official or formal purpose, and individuality tends to be submerged within the role that is assigned to a person. Authority is likely to be concentrated at the highest levels and most individuals in the organisation are likely to have only a very limited sense of participation or control over what goes on (see Chapter 5 for a discussion of power differentials and participation in organisations). In larger organisations of this type, roles may be highly specialised with little overlap or 'blurring' of roles between individuals who are trained for or assigned different tasks (Katz and Kahn, 1978). It also assumes that members are primarily motivated by economic and security concerns and that they have a preference for order, detail and logical arrangements (Kilmann, 1983). Hence there is likely to be a better match or 'fit' between the styles and preferences of some individuals and the requirements for being a member or user of an organisation of this type.

In contrast, organisations that conform to the *closed-social* type have a relatively informal, almost family-like atmosphere and the influence of the personal characteristics of members is important and the organisation changes as individual members come and go. This is quite different to a purely technical system which tends to suppress the expression of individual personality and which operates through individuals fulfilling the requirements of certain depersonalised roles.

The notion of trying to humanise the more technical or mechanical work organisations and of recognising the informal, social processes operating in reality in even the most technical of organisations, was part of the *socio-technical systems* approach developed at the Tavistock Institute in London, and of the general Human Relations Movement. Impressive work was carried out, for example, in the British coal industry in restoring to small groups of miners the autonomy in their work which they had lost with the introduction of mechanical cutters, and in the Indian textile industry by introducing small-group working (Trist and Bamforth, 1951; Trist, Higgen, Murray and Pollock, 1963; Rice, 1958—cited by de Board, 1978).

Whether technical, socio-technical or social, closed systems in Kilmann's typology pay little attention to external relations and hence, particularly if the external environment is changing, they risk neglecting adaptability, responsiveness, relevance to society, and their own long-term survival. In closed-social systems, the development and maintenance of the group itself becomes an important goal, sometimes the overriding one. Sometimes this is appropriate, but in work settings it is rarely so.

The open types of organisation in Kilmann's typology are aware of and responsive to the world beyond the organisation. The *open-technical* type has a technical core but is concerned also with its adaptiveness. The *open-social* type of organisation couples these adaptive features of the open system with the internal, social, human resources maintenance strengths of those organisations that are more 'social' than 'technical'.

Another way of looking at this question of variation between organisations is to consider the principal functions carried out within organisations. These are shown in Table 12 which is taken from Katz and Kahn (1978, Table 4-2, p. 84). They refer to these as the sub-systems of organisations, although only in larger organisations will they be carried out by different groups of specialists whose jobs do not overlap. Whether carried out by the same or different members, different functions will be stronger or even dominant in different organisations. The production function is dominant in Kilmann's closed-technical organisations, the maintenance function in closed-social systems, and the adaptive function in open systems, for example. Katz and Kahn's point, however, is that organisations need to attend to all of these functions one way or another.

The idea must be resisted that there is one perfect type of organisation suitable for all contingencies. Contingency models have had an important place in organisational psychology. They have in common the central idea that the best arrangement—the best type of leadership (see Chapter 5) or the best type

Table 12. The necessary sub-systems and functions of organisations (reproduced by permission from Katz and Kahn, 1978)

Sub-system structure	Function	Dynamic	Mechanisms
1. Production: primary processes	Task accomplishment: energy transformation within organisation	Proficiency	Division of labour: setting up of job specification and standards
2. Maintenance of working structure	Mediating between task demands and human needs to keep structure in operation	Maintenance of steady state	Formalisation of activities into standard legitimised procedures: setting up of system rewards; socialisation of new members
3. Boundary systems (a) Production-supportive: procurement of materials and manpower and product disposal	Transactional exchanges at system boundaries	Specifically focused manipulation of organisational environment	Acquiring control of sources of supply; creation of image
(b) Institutional system	Obtaining social support and legitimation	Societal manipulation and integration	Contributing to community, influencing other social structure
4. Adaptive	Intelligence, research and development; planning	Pressure for change	Making recommendations for change to management
5. Managerial	Resolving conflicts between hierarchical levels	Control	Use of sanctions of authority
	Coordinating and directing functional substructures	Compromise versus integration	Alternative concessions; setting up machinery for adjudication
	Coordinating external requirements and organisational resources and needs	Long-term survival; optimisation, better use of resources, development of increased capabilities	Increasing volume of business; adding functions; controlling environment through absorbing it or changing it; restructuring organisation

of communication system for example—depends upon finding the right match with circumstances. In the case of types of organisation, the best arrangement is likely to depend, at least, upon the nature of the organisation's task, the nature of demands from the external environment, and the personal styles and preferences of the individuals involved. Individual differences should not be forgotten. It is a key tenet of the ecological model introduced in Chapter 2 that satisfaction and effectiveness will be greater if there is a match or 'fit' between individual needs and the demands of the environment or setting. This is as likely to apply to organisations as to any other type of setting. Although at any one time there are likely to be individuals in most organisations who do not 'fit in' in this way, an overall match between the needs and personalities of individual members and the structure of an organisation is likely to come about naturally by a variety of processes. The three main processes are likely to be: (a) *selection-in* (selection of new staff will most likely operate in a way that increases uniformity); (b) *selection-out* (the setting may retain for longer periods those members whose attitudes are in conformity with the prevailing climate); and (c) *attitude change* (it is difficult to maintain a non-conformist position in the face of combined opinion).

MULTIDISCIPLINARY HUMAN SERVICE TEAMS

One form of organisation which illustrates many of the features touched upon in this chapter is the multidisciplinary team operating in the field of health or social service. They are particularly pertinent to a book on community psychology written from a British perspective, since many such teams have sprung up in Britain in recent years as services have devolved from institutions to community settings and as an emphasis has been put upon collaboration between different professions and agencies (Clement, 1989). These have taken the form of Community Mental Health Teams, Community Mental Handicap Teams, Community Alcohol Teams, Community Drug Teams, and Community Elderly Teams, amongst others. In the education service Child Guidance Teams have existed for much longer. These teams are also of special interest since many practitioners wishing to use the principles of community psychology in their work will have had experience of attachment to such teams during their training. Thus they can represent a convenient training ground for understanding and working with organisations.

Because those who work in them have been trained in a variety of different disciplines, and because members usually continue to be managed by line managers within their own disciplines, there is usually a need for negotiation, and often conflict exists about the very aims and goals, philosophy or ideology, of this type of organisation (Mansell, 1986). This itself is an illustration of a phenomenon that is very prevalent within organisations. Many organisations that are large enough to have specialist groups of staff have mixed and competing ideologies. These are often represented by different cadres of staff, and frequently give rise to conflict within the organisation. For example, educational and disciplinary philosophies compete within institutions for young offenders (e.g. Thornton, Curran, Grayson and Holloway, 1984). Furthermore, organisations such as community teams may well have been set up with a number of different purposes in the minds of those who originated the organisation. This may lead to lack of clarity and confusion for those who are then to operate the organisation. For example, Mansell (1986) states that the role of the community mental handicap team in Britain was defined as a mixture of coordinating service delivery provided by others, making potential consumers aware of the range of services, and providing direct services to handicapped people and their families.

Hence the need, often stated, for such organisations to have a clear operational policy. But who finally decides on policy? Is decision-taking over important matters conducted in a bureaucratic-technical or social-democratic fashion? Some teams are more hierarchically organised, with leadership retained by one person in most situations, and with relatively little team discussion or negotiation to set policy or to resolve conflicts or problems. This type of team is sometimes referred to as 'leader-centred', and is distinguished from those that are 'collaborative' (M. Payne, 1982) or 'integrative' (Kane, 1975, cited by Noon, 1988). In the latter there is much joint negotiation and decision-making and leadership passes around members of the team at different times for different purposes.

Contingency is likely to apply to these teams as to all organisations. Noon (1988) suggests two types of condition under which leader-centred patterns are more likely to exist. He uses a framework suggested by Webb and Hobdell (1980, cited by Noon, 1988) which creates a taxonomy of teams by dividing them according to whether the tasks to be undertaken by the team are all rather similar or many and varied (homogeneous versus heterogeneous tasks), and also dividing them according to whether the members all have similar or differing skills and abilities (homogeneous versus heterogeneous skills). Noon suggests that leader-centred team structures are more likely to occur when both tasks and skills are homogeneous: in this case a common philosophy is more likely to exist without much negotiation, and the relative absence of major differences of opinion amongst members allows a hierarchical structure to exist.

The other conditions under which Noon thinks it likely that a leader-centred structure will fit the circumstances is where a number of different professions have a contribution to make, but where these contributions are made at different points in time (for example during a patient's rehabilitation) and where these contributions are coordinated by a central figure, usually a doctor in health-care teams. This type of team would appear to correspond to the heterogeneous tasks/heterogeneous skills type in Webb and Hobdell's (1980) scheme.

The more a team approximates to the homogeneous tasks/heterogeneous skills type, at least where those varied skills derive from varied backgrounds and types of training, the less appropriate a leader-centred structure is likely to be and the more relevant the collaborative or integrative approach, according to Noon. This may be all the more important when teams have been created by inter-agency collaboration, involving members formally employed by different services: for example education and health, health and social services or probation, or a combination of statutory and voluntary organisations (Orford and Stockwell, 1988).

Allocating tasks and deciding upon roles for individuals is a central problem in all organisations, but in multidisciplinary teams it takes on a particular form and can give rise to much debate and disagreement. Because members in such teams are heterogeneous in terms of their background and at least to some extent in terms of philosophy, they usually wish to retain a degree of separate professional identity—as social worker or community nurse for example. On the other hand the tasks to be performed by members of the team are rarely so heterogeneous and clearcut that simple, mutually agreed boundaries can be drawn between the work of one member and another. In practice there is always a measure of role overlap or 'blurring'.

Many see such role overlapping as a strength. For example, Rowbottom and Hey (1978, cited by Furnell, Flett and Clark, 1987) commented about multidisciplinary health teams: 'Members of different professions must be able to work together, and work together flexibly, modifying or exchanging their roles to a significant degree according to the needs of each case.' Indeed it would be hard to imagine that some degree of role blurring could not occur if such teams were examples of organisations that lie towards the social end of the technical-social dimension in Kilmann's (1983) typology, and particularly where they were collaborative/integrative in style (Noon, 1988; M. Payne, 1982). In such teams one would expect much negotiation between members about task assignment with the opportunity for individual abilities, areas of knowledge, interests and values to emerge irrespective of discipline. Nevertheless, members of such teams frequently become anxious if they feel that their roles are blurring too much with those of others and if they feel that their disciplinary identity is in danger of being lost altogether.

LINKS WITH OTHER SYSTEMS AND SUB-SYSTEMS

It is for these reasons, amongst others, that teams can become preoccupied with the internal, social aspects of the organisation. But there are also aspects of their external environments to which multidisciplinary teams must adapt successfully unless they are to suffer some of the disadvantages of a purely closed-social organisation. One of these is the larger organisation, or organisations in the plural, of which the team is a part, and the second consists of other organisations with which the team needs to have working relationships. Taking the first of these, it is important to bear in mind that management and accountability is an essential part of all organisations (Katz and Kahn, 1978) and cannot be ignored. Even in the most autonomous of small organisations, members must find some way of carrying out such management functions as allocating scarce resources and deciding upon priorities. Multidisciplinary teams in human services are scarcely ever fully autonomous, however, and the larger organisation of which a team is a part will require that management functions be carried out in one way or another.

M. Payne (1982) has outlined some of the possibilities. These include the 'link-pin' system in which every level of the organisation is linked to the level immediately superior to it via a team leader; the 'matrix structure' in which teams are drawn together from time to time in order to work on particular tasks; and a system in which teams are free to organise themselves as they choose with inputs and monitoring by management. Each system has advantages and disadvantages for team members and for management.

With regard to management, it may be recalled from Chapter 2 that Barker (1968) found virtually all behaviour settings in Midwest to have identified single or joint leaders. The same point was made by Rowbottom and Billis (1978) in a chapter in the book on the organisation of health services edited by Jaques. As they put it, 'strong elements of hierarchical structure still manifestly and stubbornly abound in most real life organisations, public as well as private' (p. 114). They suggested that one of the reasons for this is that there really are different kinds of work to be done at different levels. They identified the five levels of work shown in Table 13 (Table 7.1, p. 119). They illustrated these with examples taken from action research projects carried out in social service departments. In the health service, independent practitioners such as hospital consultants or general medical practitioners would be assumed to be working at stratum 3 at least, with no managers above them. At most there might exist monitoring and coordinating relationships. In many professional groups the question arises about the stage in professional development at which full independence should be attained. For example, Rowbottom and Bromley (1978) give the example of trainee and newly qualified social workers working in the transitional zone between strata 1 and 2. They are usually thought to require a managerial relationship in the form of supervision. Uncertainty exists, however, about the managerial/supervisory requirements of fully-fledged practitioners capable of stratum 2 work but not yet working at stratum 3.

This is related to the complex issue of 'responsibility' when members of different disciplines work together as in hospitals and community teams. One person may take *prime responsibility* for coordinating the work that is carried out in a particular case. Who takes this responsibility for coordinating may vary from case to case—this is often referred to as the 'key worker' system. This is to be distinguished from the alternative arrangement whereby one particular discipline has overall *primacy* and regularly takes prime responsibility. Whether primacy of one discipline over others is tenable is related to at least

Table 13. Levels of work within human service-providing organisations (reproduced by permission from Rowbottom and Billis, 1978)

Stratum	Description of work	Upper boundary
1.	*Prescribed output*—working toward objectives which can be completely specified (as far as is significant) beforehand, according to defined circumstances which may present themselves	Not expected to make any significant judgements on what output to aim for or under what circumstances to aim for it
2.	*Situational response*—carrying out work where the precise objectives to be pursued have to be judged according to the needs of each specific concrete situation which presents itself	Not expected to make any decisions, i.e. commitments on how future possible situations are to be dealt with
3.	*Systematic service provision*—making systematic provision of services of some given kinds shaped to the needs of a continuous sequence of concrete situations which present themselves	Not expected to make any decisions on the reallocation of resources to meet as yet unmanifested needs (for the given kinds of services) within some given territorial or organisational society
4.	*Comprehensive service provision*—making comprehensive provision of services of some given kinds according to the total and continuing needs for them throughout some given territorial or organisational society	Not expected to make any decisions on the reallocation of resources to meet needs for services of different or new kinds
5.	*Comprehensive field coverage*—making comprehensive provision of services within some general field of need throughout some given territorial or organisational society	Not expected to make any decisions on the reallocation of resources to provide services outside the given field of need

two other factors (Jaques, 1978). One is whether there exists an 'encompassing' profession—one that is agreed to have a deeper or more encompassing view of the practice in the relevant field of work—a claim that is likely to be increasingly questionable in modern health-care systems according to Furnell, Flett and Clark (1987). The second related factor is the degree of professional development of the different disciplines involved, in terms of theory and practice and a professional structure.

It often happens in health service organisations, and indeed in other types of organisation, that a member of one discipline needs to work to some extent under the authority of another, usually encompassing discipline. This can lead to an uncomfortable situation of *multiple subordination*, and it is important to be clear about the nature of the links between the three key people involved: the worker, and the managers of the two disciplines involved. Jaques and colleagues at the Brunel Health Services Organisation Research Unit (1978) discussed in great detail the alternative arrangements that could be made under these circumstances and four of these are shown in Table 14.

Multidisciplinary human service teams, like all other organisations, must maintain relationships with at least some other teams or organisations. Two examples with which the present author is familiar are the relationships between a multidisciplinary team of workers from statutory health and social services working in the field of alcohol-related problems and their relationship with a non-statutory Council on Alcohol working in the same district; and a Community Mental Health Team and its relationship with the staff of the psychiatric in-patient ward to which patients in their area are admitted if they need in-patient care.

Adapting ideas put forward by Davidson (1976, cited by M. Payne, 1982), Payne lists the levels of linking between organisations shown in Figure 13. Simple though this framework is, it certainly helps provide a description of changes that occurred in the relationships between the statutory and non-statutory parts of the alcohol service in the first example. As Figure 13 shows, these moved from a baseline of cooperation, through coordination to federation in the form of a Community Alcohol Team which survived for six years

Table 14. Four ways of allocating responsibilities between managers from two different professional groups (based on Jaques, 1978)

1. *Outposting* of B without attachment or secondment

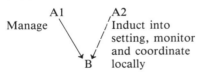

2. *Attachment* of B to work with A2

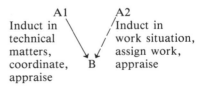

3. *Secondment* of B to work temporarily under A2's management

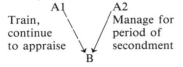

4. *Functional monitoring and coordination* by A1 while B remains under A2's management

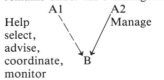

A1—Manager from B's own profession.
A2—Manager from another, often 'encompassing' profession.
B —Human service worker.

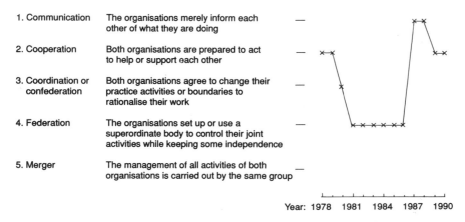

1. Communication	The organisations merely inform each other of what they are doing
2. Cooperation	Both organisations are prepared to act to help or support each other
3. Coordination or confederation	Both organisations agree to change their practice activities or boundaries to rationalise their work
4. Federation	The organisations set up or use a superordinate body to control their joint activities while keeping some independence
5. Merger	The management of all activities of both organisations is carried out by the same group

Year: 1978   1981   1984   1987   1990

Figure 13. Levels of linking between organisations (Payne, 1982), illustrated by links between statutory and non-statutory alcohol problem services (Orford and Stockwell, 1988)

(Orford and Stockwell, 1988). Management of the non-statutory Council on Alcohol remained independent throughout, however, and when circumstances changed the federation broke up. When this occurred, the level of linking between the two parts of the service fell to a point that was probably somewhere below the former baseline level of cooperation, with communication being maintained with some difficulty. Payne discusses how relationships between organisations can be broken off in such a way that useful linking is still maintained.

In the case of the hospital ward and community team example, some minimal degree of coordination was clearly necessary over the admission and discharge of patients to and from hospital. However, there existed many misunderstandings about the nature of each other's work as well as differences of perspective about the nature of psychological disorder. Hence, communication itself was difficult and cooperation often given grudgingly. This appeared to be a case, probably very common, of two organisations assumed to be linking at one level (coordination in this case) but in fact needing to consolidate their relationship at a more fundamental level (communication).

Clement (1989) discusses the role of community teams, such as Community Mental Handicap Teams (CMHTs), in helping to coordinate services delivered by a number of other agencies operating in their areas. Although she speaks highly of the Individual Programme Plan (IPP) system whereby different agencies meet to coordinate a plan for an individual client of the service, Clement makes the point that whilst CMHTs may themselves be at the federation level of linking, the overall service system within which they are operating may still be at the stage of cooperation. This mismatch often means that the CMHT is in no position to coordinate services, having to rely on the goodwill of others in order ever to be in a position to liaise.

Relationships between sub-systems of a single organisation can be looked at in the same way. We have already come across the point (in Chapter 5) that sub-units within organisations may be hierarchically arranged themselves, and one sub-unit may be in a position of control over another (Manz and Gioia, 1983). Much effort often goes into breaking up an organisation into smaller, more manageable groups: classes, houses, and year groups in schools, and wards and small units within hospitals, are examples. Although members then have the experience of being part of a relatively small unit within a larger organisation, the latter may continue to exercise strong influence. As an illustration, Mazis and Canter (1979) found no correlation between unit size and the number of institutional practices in institutions for handicapped children, but when they correlated the number of institutional practices with the overall size of the institution of which a particular unit was a part, they found a substantial positive correlation. Staff adopted the more institutional methods of handling children when they worked in units that were part of larger institutions. Such a finding clearly indicates that factors to do with the organisation of an institution as a whole may override the smallness of size of the units which may comprise it.

Thus, when considering any institutional unit, whether educational, penal or health-care providing, it is important to determine the wider organisational setting within which the unit is embedded. In secondary schools the experience of being part of the whole school may be as important as the experience of being a member of the class. Hospital wards receive constant inputs from the rest of the hospital in terms of staff, policies, food and other supplies. Even in the case of small hostels or halfway houses it is important to establish how truly independent such units are. They may be located close to a larger institution, even within its grounds, and may share staff or catering arrangements. Such dependence on the larger institution may deprive the smaller unit of the advantages of reduced size. Others are almost certain to be part of a larger statutory or voluntary organisation which will impose at least some constraints on selection or treatment policy.

COMMUNICATION AND CLIMATE

As organisations grow in size, which there is a tendency for them to do (see below), communication becomes more complex and more thought has to be given to making sure that communication occurs effectively. It is a simple matter to calculate that the number of two-person relationships (or 'communication channels') in organisations containing 5, 20 and 100 members are, respectively, 10, 190 and 4950. In general, if the number of members is n, the number of two-person relationships is to be found by using the formula: $n(n-1)/2$. It is clear from this that as an organisation grows a point will rapidly be reached at which not all potential communication channels can be 'open'. Some people will simply not be able to communicate at all with some others, and members may feel disappointed that there are other people working in the same organisation that they do not know. By the same token, however, the larger organisation gives members more choice in forming social relationships and a larger organisation may seem less restrictive and intense—the same point was made in relation to social support networks in Chapter 4. When it comes to task performance, of course, such choice is not usually possible and certain lines of communication must remain open, and this raises many questions about which are the most effective communication networks to use in practice (Katz and Kahn, 1978).

Katz and Kahn stressed the importance for any organisation of information and the need to arrange for information to flow adequately. They considered separately communication 'down the line', horizontally, and 'up the line'. The first, from superordinate to subordinate, often concentrates on job instructions, and information about overall philosophy or job rationale can easily be neglected. Feedback about performance is another important 'down the line' type of communication, but there often exists dissatisfaction with this on the grounds that when feedback is negative it is not given early enough. It is often the case that neither subordinates nor superiors like the surveillance aspects of leadership or management. What subordinates usually want is recognition of their merits and to know how to develop their talents more fully. One problem is that downward communications are often too remote and general, and need 'translating'.

Horizontal communication is necessary for task accomplishment in some jobs, but it is also necessary for social and emotional support. It is horizontal communication between peers that occurs most naturally and without effort, and the influence that peers have upon one another can be seen as consonant or dissonant with the goals of management. In extreme cases the collective attitudes of subordinates are so dissonant with the official ideology that a *counter-culture* can be said to exist (see below). Katz and Kahn make the point that a characteristic of all authoritarian regimes is the attempt to minimise horizontal communication which may threaten to undermine the regime's ideological control.

Upward communication within an organisation is often not spontaneous or full, and the needs of subordinates and bosses for this type of communication may not be congruent. Bosses are often told what subordinates think they want to hear and what subordinates want them to know, or they may be bypassed by formal suggestion systems or grievance procedures. M. Payne (1982) made the point that all leaders must deal with the issue of the inevitable distrust that members feel towards those with designated status. Members may feel that leaders might not obtain what the team or organisation wants, or they may feel that a leader might be more loyal to 'management' than to themselves, or even that the designated status might be used against them.

Leaders are very often scapegoated when things go wrong. De Board (1978) goes so far as to say that leaders inevitably disappoint in the end because of the high and unrealistic expectations which members invest in them.

All the facets of an organisation considered in this chapter so far contribute to its climate or atmosphere. Many ways have been suggested for conceptualising and measuring the perceived climate or atmosphere of an organisation or the attitudes of members towards it. Principal amongst these is Moos' scheme of nine or ten dimensions of perceived atmosphere in hospitals and other human service organisations and other settings which was described in Chapter 2.

A piece of research that has been highly influential in educational circles in Britain was that carried out by Rutter and his colleagues on the 'ethos' or climate of 12 inner-city London secondary schools (Rutter, Maughan, Mortimore and Ouston, 1979). By means of detailed interviews with school staff at all levels, pupil questionnaires, and systematic week-long observations of classroom teaching in each school, Rutter *et al.* obtained a large number of measures of school processes. They employed four outcome criteria: school attendance, pupil behaviour, delinquency record, and examination results. These were adjusted for pupils' verbal reasoning scores, the occupational status of the main breadwinner in pupils' homes, and the existence of emotional and conduct problems, using screening methods employed by Rutter and colleagues in previous research.

Many of their school process measures, which they took to be indications of ethos or climate, showed large differences between schools and were correlated significantly with at least one, and often two or three, of their four outcome criteria. For example, it was found that overall more punishments were given than rewards (pupils reported three times as many, and classroom observation suggested twice as many) and the use of rewards was associated with outcome criteria: the percentage of pupils named in assembly for work they had done correlated with the behaviour criterion; the amount of topic-related praise given in lessons (which only occurred three or four times per lesson on average) correlated with both behaviour and delinquency; the amount of pupils' work displayed on the walls correlated with exam results; and prizes for sporting achievements correlated with attendance. The percentage of pupils who had taken special responsibilities such as form captain or homework monitor (which varied from 7 per cent to 50 per cent) correlated with both behaviour and exam results - a finding in line with certain predictions from responsibility theory. Factors to do with staff organisation were also correlated with outcomes. For example, the existence of some check on whether teachers were setting homework (which varied from 10 per cent to 100 per cent) correlated with exam results. The existence of some group planning of the syllabus, as opposed to purely isolated planning, correlated with both attendance and delinquency, and the availability of adequate clerical help correlated with behaviour.

There remained substantial correlations between certain 'ecological' influences and outcome criteria. The work of Gath *et al.* (1977) reviewed in Chapter 3 would lead us to expect at least a connection between area of residence and delinquency. Indeed Rutter *et al.* found the area in which pupils lived (categorised as 'advantageous', 'middling' or 'disadvantageous', according to a previous cluster analysis of areas based on 40 demographic variables) was related to delinquency and exam results. But most important was the academic balance of pupils in the school as measured by the percentage of pupils in the highest verbal reasoning band: this theoretically should have been 25 per cent for all schools but in practice varied from less than 5 per cent to 25 per cent. Multivariate analyses suggested that the school's ethos or climate ceased to be a significant correlate of attendance and delinquency once these ecological influences had been statistically controlled, but that it remained significant in the case of exam results and particularly in the case of pupil behaviour. This last finding is an illustration of what is probably a general principle, namely that the circumstances pertaining in a setting have their strongest influence on outcomes that are *proximal* or 'near at hand', in this case behaviour within the school itself, and that they have less influence upon outcomes that are more *distal* or remote, in this case academic achievement and delinquency.

Although this important work was criticised—as is all substantial work which has implications for theory or policy—on grounds such as small sample size, details of statistical techniques, and possible neglect of other important background variables such as family size, family attitudes towards education and subject attainments (B. Tizard, 1980; Goldstein, 1980), Rutter *et al.*'s work has been influential in helping to overcome the feeling, prevalent in education in the early 1970s, that schools were impotent in the face of poor neighbourhoods, the environment, and the shortcomings of society, and that no one school could be expected to do any better than another (Gillham, 1981). Their more positive conclusions have been supported by the work of Reynolds in eight secondary schools in South Wales who found that schools using 'incorporation' (getting pupils involved, establishing good relationships with pupils, etc.) had a better outcome than those using 'coercion' (negative attitudes, keeping pupils at a distance, etc.), as well as other studies from the USA (Reynolds and Sullivan, 1981).

Reynolds and Sullivan believed that schools which achieved good outcomes were successful in preventing the development of an ethos or climate which was counter-educational. The main thrust of Rutter *et al.*'s findings, also, is the idea that some schools are more successful than others in creating a pro-educational culture. The struggle to develop a positive rehabilitation-oriented climate in 'correctional' establishments for young delinquents, in the face of the forces making for the development of a strong, informal 'counter-culture', is a related theme that has often been referred to in the literature on delinquency and its management (Grygier, 1975).

The way in which staff behaviour may help to create different atmospheres in health-care settings has been demonstrated in a number of studies (e.g. King, Raynes and Tizard, 1971; Shepherd and Richardson, 1979). For example, in their study of hospitals and hostels for mentally handicapped children, King, Raynes and Tizard (1971) developed a 30-item scale to assess the degree to which practices were child-management-oriented or institutionally-oriented. The institutional practices with which they were concerned fell into four areas: *rigidity of routine* (e.g. Do children get up and go to bed the same time at weekends as on weekdays?); *block treatment* of children (e.g. Do children line up for breakfast or wait together as a group before and after bathing?); *depersonalisation* (e.g. Do children keep and use their own clothes and toys or not? Do they have pictures or photos up?); and *social distance* between staff and children (e.g. Do children have access to the kitchen or not? Do staff use a 'conveyor belt' system at bath and toilet times so that one child passes through the hands of several staff members?). They found child-management practices to be much more frequent in the hostels than the hospitals, and they also found more frequent interaction between staff and children as well as more warm and accepting behaviours by staff toward children in the hostels.

Social distance between staff and clients was an important concept in Goffman's (1961) and R. Barton's (1976) analyses of institutions and in the studies of institutional practices carried out by King, Raynes and Tizard and others. Avoidance, or reduced time in contact, is a fairly universal indication of lack of affection and often of prejudiced and stereotyped attitudes. The necessity for a staff member to be involved in other duties outside the unit is one means whereby contact time is kept low.

Use of space within the organisation is another. In fact a very useful concept outlined by Katz and Kahn (1978) is that of *organisational space*. Each member of an organisation will see things from their own position and will be a poorer judge of others' positions the greater the 'distance' that separates them. Sheer geographical separation is just one element: Katz and Kahn referred to different members of an organisation having separate work areas, dining rooms and recreation areas, for example. Other elements that make up organisational space are functional separation (separate tasks lead to separate interests, problems, use of language—all made worse if training has been separate also), and differences in perceived status or prestige (which will tend to dictate both formal and informal channels of communication).

NATURAL PROCESSES OF ORGANISATIONAL CHANGE

Like individual people, organisations do change. If things are going well it is folly to assume that this will remain the case; if things are going badly it is overly pessimistic to presume that they can never get better. The remainder of this chapter will look at a number of examples of changes that have occurred in organisations, both naturally and under the influence of deliberate change efforts.

Both M. Payne (1982) and Katz and Kahn (1978) wrote about the changes that can occur naturally in teams and organisations in the early period of their development. It has seemed to a number of observers of teams that they develop through a series of recognisable stages: (a) coming together as work groups, becoming oriented towards one another, and starting to form into a team; (b) accommodating to one another, including some jostling for position and role; (c) negotiating agreements about how the team should work; and (d) getting on with operating within the team without so much concern about relationships within the group itself. The terms used by Tuckman (1965, cited by M. Payne, 1982) to describe these stages are easily remembered: *forming, storming, norming*, and *performing*. Probably few teams go through precisely these stages in exactly this order, but it is likely that most do move through periods characterised by different tasks and perceived climates.

Katz and Kahn described three stages in the early development of an organisation. At the first stage the organisation is relatively primitive as people with common needs start to cooperate to deal with a common problem. At the second stage this primitive system develops into a more stable organisation. In order to ensure the stability of the structure, rules develop and the basis of an authority structure and a managerial system emerges. At first, they stated, organisations are often under the control of a strong, charismatic personality, but impersonal rules are bound to develop and a tension then exists between the initial spirit of self-determination and spontaneity on the one hand and the need for some degree of uniformity and routinisation on the other hand. At the third stage the structure becomes more elaborate with development of specialised sub-systems for such functions as personnel and support, and research and development.

According to Katz and Kahn most organisations, however much they might wish to remain as they were, then experience pressures to grow and expand. This may be because members wish to use their experience, because their efficiency increases, because of competition from outside, as a solution to conflict within the organisation that may be resolved by separating functions or adding new staff, as an insurance against future disruption or difficulty, to add specialised units to educate the public or for research, or for any one or more of a number of other reasons. Whatever the reasons, organisations may grow by: (a) increasing the size of units within the organisation without major structural change; (b) increasing the number of units that are doing similar work; (c) increased differentiation and specialisation with the creation of new units or sub-systems undertaking specialised functions; or (d) merger with or takeover of other organisations.

Katz and Kahn made the important point that an organisation is much more than a machine (to which organisations have sometimes been compared) since unlike mechanical structures, social structures are essentially contrived, loosely articulated, imperfect and highly vulnerable. There is a high early death rate amongst organisations, and yet organisations can last for centuries independently of the individuals who comprise their membership at any one time. They also have much greater variability than biological systems (to which they have also been compared) since a single organisation can be devised to meet a range of objectives, and it can acquire new functions during its lifetime. Unlike biological systems, they are not held together by a physical structure and hence much of the energy of organisations has to be devoted to control mechanisms for maintaining sufficient cohesion for survival (Katz and Kahn, 1978).

In similar vein, Pettigrew (1975) described typical changes that occur in specialist organisations in their first few months or years. He observed how an initial pioneering phase associated with feelings of optimism was regularly followed by a period of self-doubt. Depending upon whether the response to this phase was adaptive or maladaptive, the result could be the unit's absorption or demise by default, planned demise or absorption, or consolidation and renewal. Both Katz and Kahn (1978) and Pettigrew (1975) referred to the high probability of the death or demise of an organisation after only a few years. One case example of a human service organisation that came to an end 12 years after it came into being was briefly described in Chapter 6 as an example of the case-study type of research. Another is a classic of the organisational literature—an account of one private psychiatric hospital in the USA which opened in September 1950 and closed 10 years later (Stotland and Cobler, 1965).

The lives of these two organisations came to an end for complex reasons and many other organisations go through periods of crisis from which they recover. For example, in his study of the therapeutic community unit at Belmont Hospital (The Henderson Unit) Rapoport (1960) described oscil-

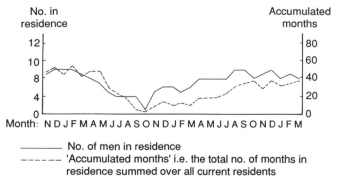

Figure 14. A natural crisis in a small organisation—a residential establishment for men with drinking problems (reproduced by permission from Otto and Orford, 1978)

lations in the atmosphere in the unit which he considered to be endemic to this kind of community which was working with 'difficult' young adults and which as part of its philosophy encouraged much resident involvement in day-to-day decision-making about the running of the unit as well as freedom of expression of emotion as an aid to treatment.

In our study of halfway houses we also observed marked oscillations (Otto and Orford, 1978). The inherent difficulty with this type of small organisation (with places for around 8–10 residents in the case of the two houses we studied in detail) is the difficulty of maintaining resident numbers, and particularly of maintaining a core group of residents who are sufficiently familiar with the ideology of the house to be able to pass this on to newcomers, in the face of uncertain input (not all applicants are suitable) and unpredictable output (there is always a certain probability of relapse and hence of premature termination of stay). Under these circumstances there is the possibility of a downward spiral of confidence in which the house loses its more reliable members (itself a desired outcome in the case of halfway houses), numbers in residence decrease sharply, and it begins to prove difficult to recruit new members. Figure 14 illustrates such a crisis that occurred at one of the houses we studied. Along with this crisis of resident numbers went the familiar scenario of decreasing confidence on the part of staff and management committee and a tendency to blame the staff member in charge for everything that went wrong.

A number of common themes can be discerned in these descriptions of naturally occurring organisational change. One is the constant interplay between the personal contributions of individuals—either as charismatic leaders, or as destructive influences and scapegoats—and the structure and functioning of the organisation itself. These are vivid illustrations of the central theme of individual-in-context which was introduced in Chapter 2 and which runs throughout this book. A second discernible theme is the spiralling of negative events, and the way this process may lead to crisis or disaster if no effective intervention is found along the way. Again, this returns us to a principle about the working of systems which was discussed in Chapter 2. In discussing the impact of environmental change, the point was made there that cause-effect relationships in real world settings are far from straightforward. Although causal sequences may be reconstructed retrospectively, it is usually not possible to predict the outcome at an early stage.

SCHOOLS OF ORGANISATIONAL CHANGE

A consideration of the way in which organisations naturally grow, fluctuate in their fortunes, or go out of existence, leads on to the question of whether deliberate interventions can be made into the lives of organisations in order to effect useful change. There has been a growing need within all branches of applied psychology for a body of theory and knowledge about how best to change organisations. For example, many educational psychologists have attempted to disentangle themselves from a role that is solely that of diagnostician or therapist with individuals in order to take on as part of their role that of someone who can study the school itself and who can act as advisory colleague or action researcher within schools (Gillham, 1981). Similarly, as the harmful effects of large institutions have been recognised and as services have developed into less institutional settings in the community, health service psychologists have been faced with tasks for which their training may not have prepared them: improving hospital wards and designing smaller units in the community such as hostels, halfway houses and group homes. At the same time there has been growing recognition of the importance of the workplace as a setting that may give rise to much stress with consequences for health (Briner and Hockey, 1988) and as a setting for detecting and responding to psychological problems and for providing health promotion (Holroyd, Penzien and Holm, 1986).

A large number of systems or schools of thought exist on the question of organisational change. They include approaches such as *job enrichment*, *employee participation*, and the *quality of working life* (QWL) approach which have been much used in industrial settings and which tend to focus on the design of jobs themselves. The changes that have been brought about under these systems have generally been in the direction of giving workers greater autonomy and decision-making responsibility. They include changes as varied as creating complete sub-assembly teams to replace isolated individuals each doing fragmented tasks in car assembly plants, allowing women workers spraying dolls on a moving belt to set a rate at which the belt moved, and appointing worker directors in large corporations such as British Steel (Guest, 1984).

Systems of organisational change also include Caplan's (1970) *administrative consultation* (see Chapter 7), *action research* (AR), and *organisational development* (OD). Of these OD is perhaps the most general and the best known although it is difficult to summarise because it covers such a broad spectrum of activities. Amongst its unifying principles, however, are the application of psychological theory and methods to organisational change, the use of a 'change agent' (an outside agent who acts as catalyst or facilitator), and an emphasis on integrating both individual and organisational change (Guest, 1984). In practice, it has covered a wide variety of methods varying from those with a greater focus on individual change, such as the T-group method developed at the National Training Laboratories at Bethel in the USA, to those such as AR which place a much clearer emphasis upon changing the organisation itself. T-groups have become less popular as a result of concern about a proportion of participants becoming casualties, and as questions have been raised about the degree to which any results were capable of being transferred back to the workplace (Guest, 1984). In general, the movement has been towards systems of change directed towards an organisation as a whole, or towards part of an organisation, rather than being directed at individuals who work within an organisation. Hence, much of the remainder of this chapter will concentrate on action research which is a leading system of organisational-level intervention.

THE ACTION RESEARCH SCHOOL

The term 'action research' was introduced by Kurt Lewin in the 1940s as a general approach towards solving some of the problems of society which he perceived and was concerned about at that time (e.g. fascism, anti-semitism, poverty, inter-group conflict, and minority issues). Its methods could be used with groups of any size including whole communities or sub-groups within communities (Susman and Evered, 1978; Ketterer, Price and Politser, 1980). In practice, it has been most closely associated with private industry and schools of business administration, and more recently with human service organisations (Ketterer, Price and Politser, 1980).

'Action research' is an apt term because its methods are designed to cope with the tension between the need to solve pressing problems and the need to advance scientific understanding of social systems such as organisations—a tension of which Lewin was very conscious and which is very familiar to most psychologists. Hence one of AR's central principles is that the process should simultaneously advance positive organisational change and the theory and knowledge of organisations. It should serve both practice and science. One of the most frequently quoted definitions of AR is Rapoport's:

> Action research aims to contribute both to the practical concerns of people in an immediate problematic situation and to the goals of social science by joint collaboration within a mutually acceptable ethical framework. (Rapoport 1970, p. 499, cited by Susman and Evered, 1978, p. 587)

In similar vein, Clark (1976) pointed out that:

> Action research sets out both to make scientific discoveries and to solve practical problems. In any particular engagement, the proportions may vary according to circumstances, research or problem solving gaining dominance, but the objective is an optimum mix of the twin goals in one project, or at least, in a series of them. (Clark, 1976, p. 1, cited by Ketterer, Price and Politser 1980, p. 7)

In order to achieve these twin aims, a close collaboration is necessary between practitioners and action researchers/scientists. The latter is not simply an objective, disinterested observer: researcher and client systems are fully interdependent, and the direction of the AR process is influenced by the needs of the clients at all stages. This close collaboration, with the formulation of the problem, the methods used, and the conclusions drawn, all being as much client-led as imposed by the action researcher, is of course likely to be in the interests of practical problem-solving, let alone theory and knowledge building. Hence, in practice, many who use action research may not think of themselves as 'scientists' at all, and there are those who believe that the theory and knowledge-building aims of AR have been little achieved (e.g. D'Aunno, Klein and Susskind, 1985).

The process of AR involves stages of assessment, action and evaluation, and is often depicted as a cyclical process, as shown, for example, in Figure 15, taken from Susman and Evered (1978, p. 588). The diagnosing or assessing stage and the evaluation stage both involve the collection of data about the organisation. This may involve direct observation, the use of questionnaires, in-depth interviewing, and/or the analysis of archival material in the form of records or reports available within the organisation. This breadth itself reflects the multiple origins of AR in psychology, sociology, anthropology, psychoanalysis, and business administration. In keeping with the collaborative philosophy of AR, decisions about which data to collect, as well as the actual collection of the data themselves, are often tasks shared by the action researchers and members of the organisation. Hence the latter have a stake in the data and share in their 'ownership'.

Very often those who have become involved as external agents in organisational change collaborate with their clients in only part of the full AR cycle shown in Figure 15. They may for example take part in helping to assess or

Figure 15. The action research process (reproduced by permission from Susman and Evered, 1978. Copyright 1978 *Administrative Science Quarterly*)

diagnose and in feeding data back to the client system. Susman and Evered 1978) referred to this as *diagnostic* action research. Or they may become involved in a further stage, that of action planning—*participant* action research. Alternatively the outside agent may only be involved in evaluating actions undertaken by the client system and in feeding back evaluative data—*empirical* action research. This latter role is often requested of health service psychologists, for example.

Many are of the opinion, however, that effective organisational change requires not only the completion of the full AR cycle, but also a spiralling process of several cycles, a process that is likely to take a matter of several years rather than weeks or months (Susman and Evered, 1978; Ketterer, Price and Politser, 1980). The full AR process implies some degree of organisational development in the form of new or modified structures or communication and problem-solving procedures in the organisation. This process is begun by creating the infrastructure necessary to conduct the collaborative enterprise of AR itself (Susman and Evered, 1978).

The foregoing discussion has made mention of only two categories of actor in the AR process: the action researchers and the organisational members or 'client system'. AR has been put in a rather wider context, however, by Ottaway (1983) who has produced, on the basis of theoretical writings and previous research, the taxonomy of change agents shown in Table 15.

He argued that all 10 types of change agent are required in every change

Table 15. A taxonomy of change agents (based on Ottaway, 1983)

---

1. Change Generators (least in number and most clearly focused on change)
    (a) Key change agents—they convert an issue into a need for change, are often dominant, charismatic
    (b) Demonstrators—they visibly demonstrate support for change, need to be tolerant of confrontation and hostility
    (c) Patrons—they generate public support through their position or resources
    (d) Defenders—they keep the issue alive, work out the details, and are often more representative of those whose cause is being fought
2. Change Implementors
    (e) External implementors—they are invited in from outside, includes action researchers
    (f) External/internal implementors—they have the task of developing internal implementors
    (g) Internal implementors—they are assigned the task of promoting change within units or groups
3. Change Adopters (most in number and least clearly focused on change)
    (h) Early adopters—they have a high commitment to practice and normalise change, often in-house 'radicals'
    (i) Maintainers—they are primarily committed to maintaining the organisation but adopt change once it occurs
    (j) Users—they underpin and reinforce change by using the organisation's products or services

---

process that occurs in a social system such as an organisation, and that no one person can function in more than one category unless his or her role changes over a long period of time. The three groups of agent—*generators, implementors* and *adopters*—correspond to the much-quoted three steps in the change process originally formulated by Lewin (1952, cited by Ottaway, 1983): *unfreezing, moving* and *refreezing*.

EXAMPLES: AN UNSUCCESSFUL CASE

Examples from the literature on organisational change may serve to make some of these theoretical ideas about change seem more real. We will start with three examples from Gallessich's (1982) book on consultation which he uses to illustrate the organisational approach to consultation or what Caplan (1970) would have called administrative consultation.

The first appears to have been unsuccessful. The client organisation was a 300-bed hospital specialising in chronic diseases and rehabilitation (Nadler, 1977, cited by Gallessich, 1982). The hospital administrator became concerned about difficulties in recruiting nursing staff, high turnover and absenteeism, poor communication, low morale, and 'increasing staff interest in unionisation' (sic). He asked a consultant team in to make a diagnosis to serve as a basis for change. The team met with the executive committee which consisted of the administrator and those who reported directly to him. They then held orientation meetings with each work group, in order to introduce themselves, to describe the goals and data-gathering activities and to answer questions. Data collection took two months and included observing employees in staff meetings, examining hospital records, holding in-depth interviews with a random sample of 100 staff and subsequently observing staff at work, as well as administering a short questionnaire to all employees. During data collection the head of the consultant team met weekly with the hospital administrator to report on progress and obtain assistance in gathering data. Data analysis highlighted confusion about lines of authority: nursing staff felt they lacked direction, whilst members of the executive committee felt that the hospital administrator made most decisions in secret without consulting them.

The consultant team wrote a 26-page report which they discussed at length with the executive committee and wished to circulate to all staff. The committee refused to allow this, but instead scheduled a number of feedback meetings attended on each occasion by 60–100 members of staff. But executive committee members were present at all meetings, there was disappointment that the written report would not be circulated, many staff did not feel free to speak up, and attendance fell off in the later meetings. The consultants later learned that the committee had not followed any of their recommendations. In this case it seems fairly clear, at least in retrospect, that the hospital administrator and committee were not receptive to the kind of diagnosis which the consultants made, and that the consultants had collaborated with them as the 'client system' and had not succeeded in setting up a true collaboration with other staff. Nor had the kind of infrastructure which is necessary for successful action research according to Susman and Evered (1978) been developed. Nor had many of the types of change agent that are necessary for change according to Ottaway (1983) been identified.

EXAMPLES: TWO SUCCESSFUL CASES

A second case, which Gallessich described as an example of OD consultation, lasted in all for four years (thus illustrating the point about the time which such work can sometimes take) and appears to have been much more successful. It concerned a county police department to which a new, progressively oriented chief officer had been appointed three years previously (Boss, 1979, cited by Gallessich, 1982). After two years he had appeared to suddenly change his style, directing that all communication must be filtered through his assistant chief who was to settle as many matters as possible. A lot of anger and tension developed amongst top level staff and the chief officer called in a consultant. The latter attended staff meetings as an observer, held interviews with each of the top administrative staff, and obtained their agreement for a six-day off-site meeting for the purposes of team-building, and solving human relations and department problems. In preparation for this meeting he held in-depth interviews with the seven top administrators, and recorded responses to a number of key questions: these answers were displayed during the retreat meeting without being attributed. The interviews revealed disapproval of the assistant chief's attitudes and management style, feelings of resentment about lack of access to the chief officer and his frequent absences to attend politically related community activities, as well as unhappiness with the stiff and defensive atmosphere in the department, with poor communication and lack of trust. The retreat meeting appears to have been well thought out and well handled. It included various exercises in consensual decision-making, confrontative feedback, and agreement to interpersonal contracts. The meeting was long enough to allow expression of much anger early on, a cooling off period, a period when confrontation was allowed but with ground rules preventing defensiveness and arguments, and a practically oriented problem-solving phase towards the end.

The result seems to have been dramatic: on a 10-point scale the mean level of trust on the first evening was rated at 1.5, but by the end of the meeting this had risen to 9.5. The consultant remained in contact with the department for four years, using a variety of OD interventions. Amongst other things, he assisted in an organisational restructuring and settling of disputes over personnel assignments and space allocations; he led additional off-site retreats; and he trained supervisors in leadership skills. Periodic surveys indicated significant improvements in the effectiveness of all administrators and in the climate of the organisation. These changes were reflected in a marked decrease in employee turnover and even in jail breaks.

The third example of organisational change described by Gallessich took place in a company producing electrical equipment (Stein and Kanter, 1980, cited by Gallessich 1982). The development of new structures played a large part in this successful intervention The company had grown rapidly and market conditions required change. One plant in particular was affected by these changes but was of concern to management since staff were felt to lack the ability to make the necessary adaptations. The personnel manager secured central office funding for a consultant team to develop staff competence and promote adaptability. From the outset the consultant team worked on the theory that staff who are given opportunities and power within an organisation become motivated to develop and use their abilities productively and are likely to support the organisation's goals. At the first stage they held interviews, group discussions and seminars with plant staff at all levels in order to explain their concepts and to bring out doubts and anxieties and to discuss them at length. At this stage they also asked senior managers from inside and outside the plant to form a project advisory group which would provide authority and reward for staff participation, consider implementation, form linkages between the plant and the wider corporation, and disseminate information about the project.

At the second stage data were gathered by means of questionnaires, interviews and observations. Data particularly concerned opportunities and power available to staff of different levels and in different units, and the results were quickly disseminated and discussed in meetings. In the third, 'action planning' stage the consultants formed a steering committee of plant managers and persons from other units, in order to begin to construct a new sub-organisation which would involve representatives of a number of levels, would be independent of the normal line management system, and would be responsible for pilot projects concerned with organisational change. This new structure thus resembled the matrix type of team structure discussed earlier. Members of this new sub-organisation were divided into several pilot groups: the first made recommendations about redesigning the organisation of the assembly line; the second a mechanism for bringing new staff into the organisation more quickly and thoroughly; and the third a more adequate supervisory and training programme. These pilot groups completed their work within six months, their proposals were implemented, and this new structure became a permanent part of the plant.

EXAMPLES: CHANGING SMALL HUMAN SERVICE ORGANISATIONS

Examples of organisational change in small human service organisations are given by Otto and Armstrong (1978) who provided an action research service for a consortium of mostly voluntary organisations providing residential accommodation and day care for people with drinking and drug problems in South London. One of their examples concerned a day centre for drug addicts. Some very useful data already existed in the form of attendance records and these simply required the help of the action research team in collating the information in order for it to be useful in planning and monitoring change. Archival data very often exist in the form of organisational records and these should be made use of where possible. Other information at the day centre, for example daily records of how the staff spent their time, how often addicts 'fixed' on the premises, and how much contact the centre had with local people, groups and projects (something centre staff were keen to increase), was collected by the staff with the help of the AR team. Yet further information, such as users' attitudes towards the centre, were collected by the action research team themselves.

A further example from Otto and Armstrong's report is of particular interest because it directly concerned the wider management context. The project concerned ran a number of small hostel and day centre facilities for problem drinkers. The action research team was asked in to investigate the powers, functions and relationships between trustees, management committee, project coordinator, and staff with a view to improving the project's organisational structure. Data were collected from members at all levels of the organisation, concerning perceived roles, decision-making powers, and rights and responsibilities for passing and receiving information. A picture emerged which confirmed the need for improved organisation. In theory the project coordinator was responsible to the management committee which in turn was responsible to the trustees. In practice, however, there was gross misperception of the role of the management committee. The trustees thought the committee had major decision-making powers. Members of the management committee on the other hand felt they lacked these powers and the project coordinator shared their view. A decision-making 'vacuum' existed between trustees on the one hand and the project coordinator on the other. A work group was set up consisting of two trustees, two management committee members and two staff, plus the project coordinator and the action research team. This work group met nine times before recommending a new improved management structure.

EXAMPLES: BRINGING ABOUT CHANGE WITHIN LARGE PSYCHIATRIC HOSPITALS

In a particularly instructive account for our purposes, Towell and Harries (1979) described a number of changes brought about at Fulbourn Hospital, a psychiatric hospital in Cambridgeshire, England, with the help of a specially appointed 'social research adviser'. For example, one of the Fulbourn projects concerned a long-stay ward which had adopted an 'open door', no staff uniforms policy, and which was designated as suitable for trainee nurses to gain 'rehabilitation experience'. The staff, however, felt 'forgotten' at the back of the hospital, felt that scope for patient improvement was not often realised, and that they were unable to offer the rehabilitation experience that they were supposed to provide. The social research adviser helped the staff devise a simple interview schedule which focused on such matters as how patients passed their time, friendships amongst patients, and feelings patients had about staff and their work. Each member of staff was responsible for carrying out certain interviews and for writing them up and presenting them to the group. All reports were read by all members of staff and discussed at a special meeting. The group reached a consensus that patients were insular, took little initiative, expected to be led by staff, had no idea of 'self-help', saw little treatment function for the nurses, saw little purposeful nurse–patient interaction, and had only negative feelings, if any, towards fellow patients.

Although there were no immediate or dramatic changes, a slow development over a period of 18 months was reported in the direction of a much increased 'counselling approach to care'. The research interview was incorporated into routine care. This itself involved the setting up of a special contact between individual nurse and individual patient, a factor which is mentioned in other projects described by Towell and Harries and by many other writers who have described constructive changes in institutions. At first the social research adviser took a leading role in groups in helping to understand the material gathered in interviews. This role was later taken over by the ward doctor and later still by a senior member of the nursing staff. At this point the social research adviser withdrew. Later on, patients read back interview reports and there were many other signs of reduced staff and patient distance. Towell and Harries were able to quote a number of testimonials from staff, attesting to the value of these changes. More concrete evidence came in the form of number of patients resettled outside the hospital, which increased from two in the first year to eight in the second, to eleven in the third.

Unlike some of our earlier examples, this is more of a 'bottom up' approach with the motivation for change coming in large part from workers who were not particularly highly placed in the organisation, and the work of the action researchers being carried out much more with this group than with the higher echelons (Cope, 1981). Nevertheless, Towell and Harries (1979) stressed the need for some pre-existing motivation for change on the part of at least some key role occupants, as well as the possibility of generating appropriate authoritative sanction for organisational change projects. Cope (1981) considered their work to have been a milestone in the field but pointed out that they were working within a fertile hospital climate that was amenable to and encouraging of change, and that other environmental changes were occurring simultaneously.

Cope described a number of change projects that were attempted, with varying degrees of success, in a different psychiatric hospital setting. One of the more satisfactory in its outcome was a project that sought change in one psychiatric 'mini-hospital'—a unit of five wards serving its own catchment area. Cope's report of this project included, incidentally, a fascinating account of the workings of such an in-patient psychiatric unit with all its problems of lack of direction, difficulties of communication, and bureaucratisation. The entrée was through the interest and request of an assistant nursing officer, and the process began with two action researchers working as nursing assistants. Staff were found to be kind but custodial, there was no leadership for psychological care, which was sadly lacking, there were no psychological goals or objectives, and discipline of patients by staff was arbitrary. Nearly all nursing staff in the unit were then interviewed, and subsequently a questionnaire was drawn up which covered the main areas of concern elicited by the interviews. In general it covered organisational climate, evaluation of patient care, and staff job satisfaction. Cope considered it to have been very important that the draft questionnaire was discussed with a representative group of all grades of nursing staff who rejected some questions, altered the wording of many, and inserted other questions of their own. Staff satisfaction was found to be low. Resources were felt to be inadequate, promotion was difficult, it was not easy to voice disagreements or to solve problems, management was felt to be out of touch and to provide unclear direction, and confidence in medical staff in promoting psychological and social aspects of care was low.

Several feedback meetings were held, first with more senior nursing staff and medical staff, and then at meetings with all ward staff. These produced anxiety and much discussion. Then a feedback meeting of the whole unit was held which Cope considered to have been the start of the process of change. This meeting was very carefully engineered and arranged. It was introduced by the assistant nursing officer who welcomed people and stated support for whatever emerged. The meeting then broke up into groups with subordinates and superordinates in different groups in order to generate issues for subsequent discussion. Following lunch, the meeting divided into different groups which contained both subordinates and superordinates together in order to formulate plans to deal with these issues. A date for a follow-up meeting was decided before the meeting ended. The consequences of this process included the writing of policies and agreement about the frequency of assessments of patients, and regular patient reviews.

The hospital management team asked the researchers to extend the project to management. Essentially the same process, of assessment, feedback and action planning, was followed. In this case, assessment included interviews with all members of the multidisciplinary management team as well as an analysis of the minutes of team meetings. The latter showed that decisions were made in relation to a mere 6 per cent of all discussion items. Many of the decisions that were made were trivial, and many of the more important decisions were referred upwards to the area management team, which resulted in delay, often of several months. Results were fed back to joint meetings of the area and hospital teams as well as to individual groups within the hospital, and as a result the hospital management team produced a document containing proposals to alter team membership, to clearly state objectives and procedures, to clarify the budget position, to create a new clinical committee with a clear role, and to improve communication with the area team. These proposals were agreed by the area team and were adopted.

It is interesting to compare the AR approach to changing hospital settings and systems with the approaches of Holahan and Saegert (1973) and Fairweather (1964) which were described in Chapter 2. The reports of the latter two examples of hospital change concentrated upon physical and social modifications themselves—partitions, furniture, repainting, etc. in the one case and alterations to rules and routines governing meetings, decisions, etc. in the other case—whilst the AR or OD approach of Cope and others concentrated rather upon the social processes that create the climate for change.

SOME RULES FOR SUCCESSFUL CHANGE

Although evaluation of change is an important stage in the ideal AR cycle, many published accounts of organisational change efforts are weak on this stage or omit it altogether. Cope's descriptions are much stronger on assessment and feedback phases, and the all-important phase of evaluation of change is virtually absent except for a section towards the end of his book where he considers general approaches to evaluation. He was in favour of an inductive, case-study approach in which as much data as possible are collected before and after an intervention to enable a picture to emerge and to allow for going back to the data to test leads that emerge. This suggests that he is in favour of the theory-generating role of AR (Susman and Evered, 1978; Ketterer, Price and Politser, 1980). His own experience, and in particular the relative success of the mini-hospital project, at least led Cope to formulate some 'rules of thumb' for bringing about change.

Principal amongst these rules is the need to obtain a useful balance between 'top-down ' and 'bottom-up' approaches. He attached great importance to staff perceiving the need for change, to the involvement of staff in the process of collecting data, and in generating options for solving problems, as well to clarifying what satisfactions there would be for staff for participating in a project. At the same time he stressed the need to obtain the support of as many people as possible and especially of the most powerful and key people in the organisation. In general, like Cherniss (1980b) and most others who have written on the subject, he emphasised the need to understand the psychology of influence and power within organisations (see Chapter 5). Additionally, he believed that one of the effective components of the mini-hospital project was the feedback of data showing the existence of discrepancies between the ideals of staff themselves and what was currently happening in practice. He advocated such a process as an aid to 'unfreezing'. Amongst his other rules of thumb were: 'New relationships may need to be established to provide new patterns of reinforcement or reward', and 'Try as many different approaches as possible: "Light many fires"'.

The emphasis that Cope gave to obtaining support for change at all levels of an organisation is mirrored in the Figg and Ross (1981) account of analysing a school system. Three members of the school psychology service contracted with a particular school that they would carry out a systems analysis (with a focus on the interface between the school and the school psychology service) involving the collection of data from staff and pupils. To assist this process a 'systems team' was set up which consisted of two class teachers, two heads of departments or years, the headteacher and deputy, and the three psychologists. It was this group that designed and analysed a questionnaire for members of staff concerning their views of the school psychology service (it turned out that most had had no contact with it); a checklist for staff to obtain their role titles and role definitions; questions about whom staff would communicate with over any problems they might have (a large number could not answer concerning problems of class management, suggesting that they would in practice not talk to anyone); questions to be circulated by staff to pupils about a number of issues, including whom pupils would go to with various problems; and a staff time record for a single week (which showed, for example, that those teachers with extra responsibilities still did as much teaching as others). Hence, this was a good example of what Susman and Evered (1978) called 'diagnostic action research', and it illustrates well the involvement of staff at different levels. Figg and Ross also made the point that when working within an organisation, such as their school psychology service, which had not traditionally provided much support for organisational change work, it might be necessary first to obtain the support of allies within the organisation from which the action researchers themselves are drawn.

The need for good support for those charged with carrying through innovation and change in work organisations such as hospitals and community-based human service organisations is also the major thrust of the paper by Georgiades and Phillimore (1975). This paper has been influential, at least in health service psychology in Britain, perhaps partly because of its colourful use of the image of the 'hero-innovator':

> the idea that you can produce by training, a knight in shining armour who, loins girded with new technology and beliefs, will assault his organisational fortress and institute changes both in himself and others at a stroke. Such a view is ingenuous. The fact of the matter is that organisations such as schools and hospitals will, like dragons, eat hero-innovators for breakfast.

Their own guidelines for carrying through change were as follows. First, the manager of change should aim to produce a self-motivated team of workers—a 'critical mass'—to prevent their isolation within the organisation. Arrangements should be made for teamwork in small groups or pairs for mutual learning and support, and for frequent group meetings, as well as presentations and demonstrations by outsiders and attendance at professional meetings and courses. Secondly, work should be carried out with members of the organisation who have sufficient authority to carry it through: this means working with individual small groups who have sufficient freedom and discretion to manage their own operations and resources, and it means involving key personnel. This latter involvement needs to be appropriate and realistic, and need not necessarily mean that the highest levels of management be involved. Third, work should be carried out with those parts of the organisation and with those forces within it that are most supportive of change and those that have the will and resources to improve: their advice was to follow the path of least organisational resistance, and to avoid being tempted to work with parts of the organisation that are felt to be most difficult or most resistant to change.

10 Self-Help and Non-Professional Help

A good point at which to start a discussion of this topic is 1979 and the controversy sparked off by Durlak and an article of his which was published in *Psychological Bulletin*. He noted the many positive comments that had been made about the contribution within the mental health field of untrained, or relatively untrained, people including college students, volunteers and parents. He set out to review research that had been carried out up until that time which compared the effectiveness of those helpers who had received formal clinical training in professional psychology, psychiatry, social work or psychiatric nursing (the group he called 'the professionals') and anyone else who had not received such training but who was working as a therapist in the mental health field. This second, and large, group he referred to collectively as the 'paraprofessionals'.

Durlak (1979) found 42 studies which had directly compared the effectiveness of these two groups, and his article largely consisted of a careful tabulation and evaluation of these studies. The quality of each study was evaluated on a 5-point scale (A to E) according to how well the study met 13 methodological criteria. The kinds of mental health problems being dealt with included 'moderate to severe disturbance' amongst psychiatric in-patients and out-patients (19 studies), and specific target problems such as obesity, stuttering, insomnia, test and speech anxiety, and enuresis (13 studies), with small numbers of studies involving academic counselling for college students, and crisis intervention for adults.

Of the 42 studies reviewed Durlak found that 28 showed no significant differences in measurable outcome between those who received professional and those who received paraprofessional help. Of the remainder, 12 found significant differences in favour of the paraprofessionals and in only one was there a clear difference in favour of the professionals, with another study showing professionals to have been more successful than one group of paraprofessionals, but no different from another.

Durlak was careful to point out that many of the studies had some design weaknesses; although he concluded that the quality of research in this area was comparable to that in other areas of outcome research, and his table of the results shows that those favouring paraprofessionals were equally well represented in the better designed studies (those rated A or B) as in the less well designed ones. He also pointed out that the research he had reviewed told little about *why* paraprofessionals sometimes do comparatively well, nor did it have much to say that was useful about their selection and training.

Nevertheless Durlak's conclusion that paraprofessionals achieve outcomes that are equal to or significantly better than those achieved by professionals in mental health, and that the education, training and experience of the latter are not necessary prerequisites for an effective therapist, provoked a strong response from Nietzel and Fisher in an article published in *Psychological Bulletin* in 1981. Their first point was that Durlak had not been sufficiently critical about the design of the studies he reviewed. They felt that it was essential that four design features be met since these were required for internal validity: random assignment, equivalent duration of treatments, essential similarity of treatments, and an absence of obvious confounding by personal-social characteristics of the therapist. In fact the elimination of the more poorly designed studies, either by Durlak's original criteria or by Nietzel and Fisher's alternatives, results in a set of better designed studies in which those appearing to show a superior outcome for the paraprofessionals are just as well represented, if not slightly more so, than in the group of 42 studies as a whole.

Nietzel and Fisher's second main criticism concerned Durlak's definition of 'professional' and 'paraprofessional'. He had attempted to make the distinction objective by only including in the professional group those who had received training in one of four 'core' mental health professions, but nevertheless this resulted in some anomalies. For example, he was roundly criticised by Nietzel and Fisher for including amongst the professionals those who were still in training in one of the core professions albeit at an advanced level.

Durlak's definition also required him to exclude some therapists trained in a professional discipline that seemed thoroughly appropriate: a speech pathologist in the treatment of adult stutterers, and an occupational therapist in the treatment of psychiatric in-patients for example. Nevertheless, the majority of these studies did indeed involve a comparison of the effectiveness of personnel who had had some relevant professional training and those who had not undertaken a professionally recognised, relevant training course. The latter group—the paraprofessionals—largely included college students, community volunteers, adult volunteers, adult women, and psychiatric aides. Some of these groups would have had lengthy on-the-job experience and others had received quite intensive training for the particular project in which they were taking part. Nevertheless, it would be surprising, to say the least, if scarcely any studies had been able to show that those with relevant professional training produced better results. It is this that Durlak purported to show.

Nietzel and Fisher were much more circumspect and cautious in their conclusions, although in a reply Durlak (1981) maintained that their conclusions were very similar to his own. This was not the end of the story, however. Three years later Hattie, Sharpley and Rogers (1984) carried out a meta-analysis of the same studies reviewed by Durlak and his critics. This method of reviewing the results of a large number of studies was described in Chapter 7 when we were considering the success or otherwise of consultation. It is superior to the simple 'box score' method used by Durlak (a simple categorisation of studies into those favouring professionals, paraprofessionals, or neither) because it is based on the calculation of one or more 'effect size' (ES) for each study. It thus uses much more information than the simple procedure used by Durlak (1979) and further analyses can be carried out to see whether average ES varies with important characteristics of the studies such as their methodological adequacy, sample size, or the experience level of the therapists.

The average of the 154 effect sizes that Hattie, Sharpley and Rogers were able to calculate from the 39 studies that they were able to use with this method was 0.34 (with a standard error of 0.10) indicating that overall the results favoured paraprofessionals:

> These data indicate that the average person who received help from the paraprofessional was better off at the end of therapy than 63% of the persons who received help from professionals. ... Altogether there was convincing evidence that, on the whole, paraprofessionals are more effective than (or at least as effective as) professionals. (p. 536)

There was evidence that effect sizes were significantly greater (i.e. paraprofessionals did comparatively well) when paraprofessionals were more experienced (i.e. such personnel as hospital workers, medical students, speech pathologist, public health officer, in comparison with college students and adult volunteers) and when they had received more training (more than 15 hours versus up to 15 hours versus brief orientation only). Whether paraprofessionals were selected or only self-selected appears to have made no difference to the results, and although there was a trend towards a larger effect when a professional assisted a non-professional, supervision or assistance did not prove significant either. The more methodologically adequate studies were in fact more in favour of the paraprofessionals. However, results were most in favour of paraprofessionals when the helper rated the change in the client, were less so when clients rated outcome, and there was no difference between groups when a specific behavioural measure was the criterion. Finally, effect size correlated modestly but significantly with the year in which the study was reported (-0.23) indicating that results of such studies were tending to become somewhat less favourable to paraprofessionals as time went on.

Overall, Hattie, Sharpley and Rogers reached conclusions that were, 'supportive of but not as strong as Durlak's ... and not as pessimistic as Nietzel and Fisher' (p. 540). This seems to the present author to be a fair conclusion. All were agreed that across the whole range of studies then available, paraprofessionals were actually doing better. These results suggest not just a minor shift in the use that professional personnel make of 'paraprofessionals', but a much more fundamental rethinking about the nature of psychological change and the circumstances under which it occurs.

SOCIAL SUPPORT IS WHERE YOU FIND IT

The work of Cowen and his colleagues on informal, interpersonal help-giving by hairdressers and bartenders is another that has captured much attention and which raises many questions. In a series of sub-studies, between 50 to 100 representatives of both of these groups were asked a similar set of questions about the amount and kind of help with problems that they gave to their clients in the course of their everyday work. The results are summarised in an article entitled provocatively, 'Help is where you find it' (Cowen, 1982).

The results concerned only that part of the respondents' work during which their clients raised 'moderate to serious personal problems'. The main results are shown in Table 16. It can be seen that both hairdressers and bartenders spoke with many clients about the latters' problems. Within each group there were some who considered interpersonal helping a normal and important part of the job. On average members of both groups felt more comfortable than uncomfortable in the helping role, and considered that they were more effective than ineffective as helpers. Women were more often called upon to deal with personal problems, used more engaging, task-oriented strategies, and felt more comfortable in the help-giving role.

Cowen was intrigued by what he called the 'ecology' of informal helping. He felt it was important to take account of the opportunities and constraints on helping offered by the physical setting and other circumstances in which potential informal helpers work. The bar and the hairdressing salon are interesting examples of behaviour settings (Barker, 1968, 1978—see Chapter 2). One thing Cowen noted was that afternoon, as opposed to evening, bar staff saw fewer customers, were required to handle twice as many moderate to serious personal problems, handled those problems more patiently and sympathetically, and had fewer negative feelings about them.

A smaller scale replication of Cowen's work with hairdressers and bartenders was later carried out in Exeter, England (Hunt and Orford, 1988). Twenty of each group were interviewed, ten male and ten female in each group. In comparison with Cowen's groups the English respondents estimated that fewer of their contacts with customers involved discussing moderate to

Table 16. The work of hairdressers and bartenders in dealing with customers' personal problems (based on Cowen, 1982)

	Hairdressers ($N = 90$)	Bartenders ($N = 76$)
Average number of customers	55/week	104/session
Proportion raising moderate to serious personal problems	33%	16%
Most frequent problems raised	1. Difficulties with children 2. Physical health 3. Marital problems	1. Jobs 2. Marital problems 3. Financial problems
Most frequently used strategies	1. Offering support and sympathy 2. Trying to be lighthearted 3. Just listening 4. Presenting alternatives 5. Telling the person to 'count their blessings' 6. Sharing personal experiences	1. Just listening 2. Trying to be lighthearted 3. Offering support and sympathy 4. Presenting alternatives 5. Sharing personal experiences 6. Trying not to get involved

serious personal problems (hairdressers estimated 13 per cent, bartenders 6 per cent). However, all but two of the hairdressers reported dealing with such problems at some time during the course of their work, and 50 per cent of the hairdressers and 35 per cent of the bartenders enjoyed dealing with them. The kinds of problems mentioned to the English groups were similar to those found by Cowen, as were the helpers' responses. Women helpers were more likely to talk about alcohol problems, but were less likely to discuss sex problems, and they reported responding more often than male helpers with listening and asking questions. Compared to bartenders, hairdressers listened more, presented alternatives more often, and rated themselves as more often feeling helpless. Bartenders more often discussed alcohol problems, more often told customers to count their blessings, and more often felt bored.

Clearly, and as Cowen freely admitted, there is no evidence from these studies that these kinds of informal 'helping' interactions were indeed helpful in any important way. Also questionable is his conclusion, 'that the problems people raise, in the aggregate, are not unlike those fielded by the mental health establishment' (p. 392). Although it is now better appreciated that the majority of psychological problems never find their way to mental health professionals (Gurin, Veroff and Feld, 1960; Goldberg and Huxley, 1980), those who attend psychiatric out-patient departments have, as might be expected, more severe problems on average than those who do not receive such specialist help (e.g. Hurry, 1989). Nevertheless, Cowen's central point, and it is a crucial one for community psychology generally, was that the majority of potentially helpful interpersonal transactions for people with psychological problems take place outside the formal mental health system. These transactions involve a range of 'human service providers' who may not specifically be trained in mental health—including general medical practitioners, general physicians and nurses, school teachers, clergy and the police—as well as family members, friends and neighbours. They also include an intermediate group of people, such as those included in Cowen's studies, whose jobs give them the opportunity to engage in helping interactions: indeed the very circumstances and settings of their jobs may give them distinct advantages as people with whom psychological problems may be discussed. If we want to understand the processes whereby people are helped, he argued, we must learn more about these types of informal interaction and not confine ourselves to studying those that take place in the formal and professional mental health context.

In Cowen's studies hairdressers and bartenders were asked what they would like to do if they left their present occupation, and whether they would be interested in a consultation programme that might increase their ability to respond to customers' personal problems. Hairdressers as a group were much more positively oriented towards helping. About one-third of alternative occupations mentioned by them were clearly help oriented, and nearly half expressed an interest in a consultation programme. In the English study bartenders were somewhat more enthusiastic about the possibility of consultation, 8 out of 20 expressing keen interest, whilst the view of most hairdressers was that on-the-job experience was the only relevant training.

The 10-week group mental health consultation and training programme which was subsequently offered to 25 of the US group of hairdressers was described by Wiesenfeld and Weiss (1979). The consultants' goals were to aid hairdressers in developing their interpersonal helping skills—so that customers in distress might be able to leave the beauty shop feeling 'a little better, stronger, and more able to cope'—and to provide informational resources for referral to mental health agencies within the community. They neither expected nor wanted hairdressers to become lay psychotherapists. Ten attended the first session and a core group of six of them attended at least seven of the ten meetings. Although it was not possible to evaluate whether changes occurred on the job, in comparison with a group of seven hairdressers who had also been contacted, but who were unable to participate because of time difficulties, those who took part changed from the first to the last session in terms of their responses to a number of hypothetical problems. There was a significant shift from giving specific advice and recommending counting your blessings towards 'reflecting feelings'. The authors of this report, however, expressed some ambivalence about training non-professional workers.

They asked themselves whether it might be unwise to try and alter systems that might already be functioning adequately by introducing, 'well-intentioned, yet misguided professional biases' (p. 791).

STUDENTS AS VOLUNTEER THERAPISTS

For obvious reasons college students represent one of the groups that has been more consistently deployed over the years in a non-professional helping capacity. They are available in large numbers at little or no cost. They are bright and very often enthusiastic about the idea of taking part in a helping project which is often seen as being relevant to their own education and development. One type of programme which was popular in the USA in the 1960s was the kind in which students spent time with psychiatric patients on the 'back wards' of mental hospitals. Such patients were mostly long-staying and were usually neglected in terms of professional treatment services (see Rappaport, Chinsky and Cowen (1971) for a well evaluated example). The *companionship therapy* programme reported by Goodman (1972) and the replication of his work reported by Dicken, Bryson and Kass (1977) will be described in some detail since, unlike most companionship and similar programmes using college students, this work was another that was extremely well planned and executed, described and evaluated.

Goodman's method was to provide a male college student companion for nine months for each of nearly 100 10- or 11-year-old boys drawn from the public school system in Berkeley, California. The aim was to help, 'boys with emotional problems (that is, boys who seemed hostile, depressed, withdrawn, or lacking in self-esteem) who were experiencing serious difficulty in performing school work' (p. 16). An early discovery was that the public school system lacked a routine method for identifying troubled children, and accordingly Goodman gained permission to use a sociometric instrument amongst the children themselves, and a questionnaire sent to parents. All parents received a full description of the project and an invitation to nominate their son to take part. Surprisingly, as many as a quarter of all parents of boys in that age group showed an interest in the programme, although the focus on emotionally disturbed boys was made very clear. In one year 10 per cent and 16 per cent in the next, got as far as filling in an application form. Only those who met the criteria for emotional disturbance were accepted. Boys were then randomly assigned to companionship or no-companionship groups, the control group consisting of those families in the latter group where parents were willing to complete assessments, despite not taking part.

Particular care was taken over communication, selection (they rejected about a third of all students who applied to become companions) and training of the student 'activity counsellors', and over the structuring of the companionship process itself. The organisers of the project communicated their ideas fully to parents and teachers (both were involved in assessment) and made themselves continuously available to answer queries or to sort out problems. Project organisers were also available to companions throughout the project, and on average companions availed themselves of this consultation opportunity for one to two hours in total.

Companionship pairs were free to develop their relationship as they wished, but within carefully laid down boundaries. Clear instructions were given to companions about how to make the initial contact with the family. They were also instructed to see the boys two or three times every week, no more and no less, to keep visits between one and four hours in length, with a total contact time each week of between four and eight hours. This was carefully monitored throughout and attention drawn to any deviations that occurred. On average, pairs met twice a week for three hours on each occasion, with an average total of 141 hours of contact. Companions were required to complete a Visit Report within a few hours following each meeting.

The aim was to facilitate frequent individual contact with an adult who was neither a member of the family (hence rarely using discipline or making customary adult demands) nor a professional. The organisers emphasised to parents that counsellors, 'would not attempt to intervene as professional therapists but rather would build gradual friendships, whose potential therapeutic effects were under study' (p. 16). Companions were told that the intention was to establish one-to-one relationships with much opportunity for two-person conversations, and that hence it was best to avoid including a third person except under special circumstances. Nevertheless they were told:

> Don't use 'strategy'. Don't try to 'treat' the boy or offer explanations for his emotional aches and growing pains. Remember that you are not a professional. Just be as honest with yourself and the boy as possible. Counsellors who are genuine with their boys usually create the best relationships. (p. 56)

Goodman commented that early on students were often worried about the lack of 'deep' problem-oriented discussions with their boys, and doubted whether benefit could come from simply being a friend—being like a 'glorified babysitter' as some put it. They were reassured that companionship might be helpful through offering the boy an opportunity to try out new ways of being with people, and Goodman reported that this became less of a concern as time went on. The interchangeable use of the expressions, 'companions' 'activity counselors', or simply 'counselors' is an indication of the likely role confusion for the students taking part in this or similar projects, and indeed for many non-professionals taking part in helping projects of one kind or another.

Certainly much emphasis was placed on activity which included such things as active sports and games, having a meal together, visiting the companion's home, hiking or taking a walk, and sightseeing. Simply talking was a popular activity and topics of conversation included plans for future visits, school or school work, activities of the present or a past visit, the child's skills, personality and behaviour, and family (Dicken, Bryson and Kass, 1977).

Evaluation was comprehensive, involving assessments before, after and at follow-up, and including parents, teachers and school peers. On the whole, comparing the total group of companion boys with control boys, evidence for the effectiveness of a companionship programme was limited, although retrospective accounts of change by parents were more positive for the companionship group, and there were some differential improvements in ratings by school peers. Of the participating boys, 95 per cent said that companionships could change boys, the most frequently mentioned areas of change being interpersonal relations, skill acquisition, social awareness, and self-concept. Almost all (97 per cent) of their parents said that if they could go back they would join the project again.

Because of the use of a factorial design and careful matching between companion and control groups it was possible to test a number of hypotheses about differential effects for sub-groups, and a number of these were positive. In particular, black boys did particularly well and their relationships with their white companions were described as particularly enjoyable, empathic, and open. Roughly a third of the boys were without fathers and they tended to do well as did, rather to Goodman's surprise, those who were the most disturbed to start with. In addition companions who were initially rated as outgoing produced better results than 'quiet' companions, and the least successful combination was a 'quiet' companion paired with a boy with 'quiet' type problems (passive, withdrawn as opposed to temper tantrums, easily annoyed, irritable, etc.). Less favourable results for 'quiet' companions, particularly when paired with children with 'quiet' type problems, were also found by Dicken, Bryson and Kass (1977) when they replicated Goodman's work, this time with girls and boys, aged between 6 and 13 years.

In the Dicken, Bryson and Kass study once again, however, overall comparisons did not produce a picture of clear superiority for the companionship group, the most positive results being in terms of ratings provided by parents, with teacher ratings showing little change. Despite these mixed results, Dicken, Bryson and Kass recommended the continued use of companionship therapy on the grounds that it was well received by the community and participants, that it could promote personal communication across social strata, that companions gained significantly (Goodman documented how students became more confident, realistic, and open), and that there was no evidence that arranged companionships were harmful.

NEW CAREERS FOR THE DISADVANTAGED

A very different tradition is represented by the *New Careers Movement* (Pearl and Riessman, 1965) and the more recent use of *indigenous paraprofessionals* in community mental health (Tarail, 1985). The theory behind this use of paraprofessionals is that by employing workers from poor, underprivileged, perhaps ethnic minority communities served by an agency, the quantity and quality of service provision to previously neglected groups could be increased, whilst at the same time new career pathways in human service work could be created for people whose opportunities for advancement through conventional educational and professional channels are limited. These were the laudable aims of the series of employment and training programmes funded by the US Federal Government, starting in the 1960s, as part of the new careers movement. These resulted in an enormous increase in the number of paraprofessionals working in such fields as education, probation, social service, and mental and physical health, but results have been mixed and experience has led to a greater appreciation of the pitfalls that await the unwary in this type of work (Pearl and Riessman, 1965; Blanton and Alley, 1977; Durlak, 1982; Alley, Blanton and Feldman, 1985). Many of these useful points of guidance for training and working with paraprofessionals are relevant to most programmes whether or not they share all the aims of the new careers or indigenous paraprofessional movements.

One of the dangers outlined by these writers is that of playing safe in the selection of paraprofessionals, erring on the side of selecting those who are most similar to the professionals, and hence discriminating against the very groups which the new careers movement aimed to enrol in human service occupations. Indeed Blanton and Alley (1977) found that of the 11 new careers projects which they studied those that were more successful in achieving their service delivery and education/training goals tended to be those that selected 'high-risk trainees'. The latter tended to have a poorer record of continuous employment and to have had more time on welfare in recent years; although they also had higher levels of academic attainment. Looking at the individual projects in more detail it appeared that those who took these risks in selection were selecting individuals who had faced poverty and unemployment themselves, and who were concerned to improve mental health services to the poor and to minorities. Furthermore, the project staff saw those selected as people who could help change the agency rather than simply help maintain its current activities.

Also related to achievement of project goals was a positive attitude towards the new careerists as fully-fledged employees with a lot to offer to clients rather than simply as students who had little to offer until their training was completed. This factor undoubtedly relates to the more general problem of appropriate roles for paraprofessionals, a problem highlighted by all these authors. All had seen the danger that paraprofessionals would be exploited by the professionals they worked with, or by their political masters, and would be given the most difficult or the most mundane jobs to do, or alternatively would always be asked to see the poorest and most underprivileged clients, hence creating two classes of service provision. Although differences in pay and status exist and should not be denied (Pearl and Riessman, 1965) their harmful effects can be mitigated by good team work and the valuing of what paraprofessionals can offer to help provide a new and different service.

One illustration of what can be done is provided by a particularly encouraging breakdown of the roles played by paraprofessionals in the Maimonides Community Mental Health Centre in Brooklyn in New York (Tarail, 1985). A number of these roles relate to the social distance hypothesis of paraprofessional effectiveness (Rappaport, Chinsky and Cowen, 1971) which supposes that indigenous workers representing the local community (which is often not the case for professional workers, particularly in poor urban areas) can relate better to clients and groups from this same community. Tarail outlined the way in which indigenous, paraprofessional community mental health workers could represent the needs and views of the community within the service; could liaise and advocate on behalf of clients both within the agency and with other authorities; how they could be more successful than the professionals in reaching and attracting the customers for secondary prevention projects and for primary prevention mental health education; and how they could be effective in training community leaders and in facilitating self-help groups which then go on to take effective action in the community. As examples of the latter type of activity, Tarail cited organising a self-help group of mothers to discuss daily living problems, which went on to campaign successfully for a new day care centre; organising gangs and other youths into a self-advocacy group that successfully persuaded the city government to renovate a swimming pool and park; and organising a tenants' group that successfully put pressure on landlords to remove lead paint. Nor did Tarail exclude the role of participating in clinical treatment services under supervision.

A further danger, widely seen, is that paraprofessionals will out-professionalise the professionals, adopt pseudo-professional attitudes and characteristics, or become so coopted by the professionals that they lose their natural helping skills and commitment to and identification with the community. The specific dangers foreseen include adopting complex, technical professional jargon, concentrating on the use of psychotherapy as the main modality of treatment, and becoming preoccupied with hierarchy and competition with other disciplines (Tarail, 1985).

All stress the need for good training, both academic and on the job, with the two components closely linked so that academic teaching is seen to be highly relevant, and with the provision of continued supervision which is consistent with and builds upon initial training. Blanton and Alley (1977) found a close link between the academic and the on-the-job components of paraprofessionals' education and training to be one of the factors that was related to the achievement of programme goals. Since these two components are often provided by different people, this provides yet another illustration of the importance of Bronfenbrenner's (1979) meso-level system in operation.

Providing good, well-coordinated training and experience is not the same, however, as providing a career structure, and it is here that many of the new careers and indigenous paraprofessional programmes appear to have fallen down (Durlak, 1982). Sometimes this may have been the result of lack of coordination between academic education and the jobs available—the one did not prepare trainees for the other—but often it must have been a lack of the necessary funding, commitment at all levels, and sheer hard work required to put in place some of the necessary structures described by Tarail (1985). In the Maimonides CMHC these included a five-year salary scale with a five-step classification scheme between minimum and maximum earnings; the possibility of promotion to Senior CMH worker or Team Leader; continued in-service training leading to a certificate on successful completion; special training programmes for those undertaking specific areas of work (for example with older people, with children, activity therapy, home visiting); and the arrangement of work-study programmes with local community colleges and universities so that paraprofessionals could graduate in courses in social work, special education, mental health, and psychology, with credit given for life experience, work experience, and in-service training, and with work scheduled in such a way that study could be fitted in.

Finally, there is general agreement that the engagement of paraprofessionals can meet with resistance from professionals who may 'put down' paraprofessionals and oppose paraprofessional training programmes and view the involvement of paraprofessionals with unwarranted scrutiny or criticism. As a solution Durlak (1982) recommended that the professionals in their own training should receive much better orientation towards training and working with paraprofessionals He cited evidence from the mid-1970s showing that only a minority of advanced graduate students in clinical and community psychology in the USA had had field work experiences related to this area of work and that over half of these believed that their experiences were not adequate. In addition more than half of over 200 psychologists working in 55 community mental health centres spent no time training and supervising paraprofessionals. He suggested that before any paraprofessional programme went ahead both the need and the support for it should be firmly established, and relationships between professionals and paraprofessionals and any alteration to the working of professionals should be fully discussed and agreed upon at the outset.

SELF-HELP

Many of the same issues, including lack of awareness and understanding on the part of professionals, arise in the case of self-help. The second half of the twentieth century has seen a phenomenal growth in self-help organisations, in the USA, Britain, Canada, Australia, West Germany and many other countries (Robinson and Henry, 1977; Levine and Perkins, 1987; Borkman,

1990), to the point at which they now provide collectively one of the principal resources for the prevention and treatment of psychological distress. It is vital that human service providers know of the existence of self-help organisations of relevance to their work, that they appreciate their philosophies and how they work, and that they know how to make use of the resources self-help provides and how to be of service to self-help organisations if and when required.

There now exists a vast array of self-help organisations designed to meet different needs. Sagarin (1969) suggested that there were, broadly speaking, two types. The first were those whose primary, and often exclusive, aim was to help members—and this often involved promoting desirable kinds of changes in members (e.g. stopping drinking, adjusting to bereavement, coping better with chronic illness in the family). Secondly, there were those that had, as a principal aim, the changing of public attitudes towards a stigmatised or disadvantaged group. Organisations campaigning for civil rights, women's rights, the rights of gay people, and the rights of the disabled, are perhaps amongst the most prominent examples of the latter, but many other self-help organisations campaign for improvements to public services or for changes in public and professional attitudes. It is important to be aware of this twin aspect of the self-help movement. Katz and Bender (1976, cited by Borkman, 1990) considered friendly societies, consumer cooperatives and early trade unions to be the forerunners of modern self-help, and in Chapter 11 we shall consider some modern community 'self-help' organisations that have had a clearly political purpose.

Sagarin's division of self-help organisations into two broad groups does not do justice to the range of groups which presently exist, however. Levine and Perkins (1987) suggest five types. The first type involves people whom society believes not to be 'normal' in some way, and who are hence subject to, 'social isolation, stigmatisation, scorn, pity, or social punishment' (Levine and Perkins, p. 240). This is a large group and others would distinguish those with life-long physical characteristics (little people—dwarfs—for example), those with chronic medical conditions (such as cancer patients or those with colostomies), those with psychological reasons for joining a self-help group (e.g. the 'nervous persons' or former psychiatric patients who make up the membership of Recovery Inc.), those whose task is personal behaviour change (as in Alcoholics Anonymous, Narcotics Anonymous and Gamblers Anonymous), and those who belong to social or minority groups subject to social discrimination or disadvantage (Borman, 1982; Maton, 1988).

A second large group is made up of family members or associates of people with physical, psychological or stigmatising conditions, and who themselves may suffer stigma or social isolation, stress, and uncertainty about how to cope (Borman, 1982; Levine and Perkins, 1987; Orford, 1987b). Gottlieb (1982) refers to such groups as 'one step removed groups'.

A third group is made up of organisations for people who have experienced a loss, or whose current life circumstances give them needs which can at least partly be met through a self-help group. This category includes groups for widows, groups for single parents, and groups such as Compassionate Friends for bereaved parents (Videka-Sherman, 1982).

The fourth of Levine and Perkins' types consists of mutual assistance groups organised along ethnic, religious or racial lines, and the fifth type of organisation exists for the preservation of specific interests and includes civic and community groups, often formed to meet a particular problem or threat to a community (see Chapter 11).

Like all typologies in community psychology this provides a useful but crude 'map' of the diversity that exists, but many self-help organisations will not fit neatly into a single category. Another way of depicting the impressive range of groups which exists is to point to their effective coverage of the complete life-cycle. As Katz and Hermalin (1987) have pointed out, there are self-help groups—they were writing about the USA but the same applies to Britain and many other countries—for people who are infertile, who have had caesarean deliveries, who have abused their children or who feel in danger of doing so, who have a disabled child, who have adolescent problems, who have any one of numerous problems of adult life, who are experiencing the transition to retirement, and who are adjusting to older age.

It is difficult to formulate a definition of self-help which does justice to this rich diversity of organisations. One which is widely quoted and which is broad enough to do justice to most cases, is that of Katz and Bender (1976):

> Self-help groups are voluntary, small group structures for mutual aid and the accomplishment of a special purpose. They are usually formed by peers who have come together for mutual assistance in satisfying a common need, overcoming a common handicap or life-disrupting problem, and bringing about desired social and/or personal change. The initiators and members of such groups perceive that their needs are not, or cannot be, met by or through existing social institutions. Self-help groups emphasise face-to-face social interactions and the assumption of personal responsibility by members. They often provide material assistance, as well as emotional support; they are frequently 'cause'-oriented, and promulgate any ideology or values through which members may attain an enhanced sense of personal identity. (cited by Katz and Hermalin, 1989, p. 155)

THE FUNCTIONS OF SELF-HELP

What are the needs that so many people appear to have that they find are met in self-help groups and not elsewhere? The functions served by self-help have been discussed by many authors (e.g. Lipson, 1982; Gottlieb, 1982; Hinrichsen, Revenson and Shinn, 1985; Katz and Hermalin, 1987; Levine, 1988; Maton, 1988). Table 17 lists the eight functions which recur in these writings. It is interesting to compare this list with the main functions of social support generally which were listed in Table 5 in Chapter 4. It seems clear that the strength of self-help lies in the fact that it provides most of the social

Table 17. Eight functions of self-help organisations

1. Emotional support	5. Ideas about ways of coping
2. The provision of role models	6. The opportunity to help others
3. A powerful ideology	7. Social companionship
4. Relevant information	8. A sense of mastery and control

support functions for people who have special reasons to be in need of them. It is possible that because of members' special knowledge of their shared problem, different types of social support can be provided in appropriate ways at appropriate times (Vachon and Stylianos, 1988, and see Chapter 4).

Emotional support is probably the function of self-help that is most frequently referred to. Levine (1988) claims that when self-help groups are working well, the group setting is more supportive than that to be found in professionally led therapy groups. Comstock (1982) provided vivid descriptions of the supportive atmosphere that existed at the meetings of Parents Anonymous (for parents who physically abuse their children or who are at risk for child abuse) which she observed. *Informational support* is greatly valued, often neglected by service providers, and collected and disseminated to members by self-help groups. For example in the case of caesarean support groups, information is provided on such subjects as, 'types of anaesthesia, medications and incisions; potential complications; the possibilities and risk of vaginal delivery following a caesarean; hospital procedures and local policies; and current research on the effects of caesarean birth on the infant' (Lipson, 1982). In addition, many self-help groups fulfil the *social companionship* function. For example, Robinson (1979) described how the majority of British Alcoholics Anonymous members surveyed in his research had made new friends through AA. A third regularly had other AA members to their homes, and a further third did so occasionally. Of the major functions of social support discussed in Chapter 4, only instrumental or material support is missing from the list in Table 17. It is rarely mentioned in writings about modern self-help organisations even though Katz and Bender (1976) made specific mention of it in their definition of self-help, and it remains an interesting question to what extent members of self-help groups do in fact provide each other with material aid.

As well as demonstrating the general support functions of self-help, Table 17 also suggests that many groups have some additional, important features which are not well represented in the general literature on social support. This may be a good illustration of Levine's (1988) point that the study of self-help may lead to an increase in knowledge about social support generally. For example, one ingredient of self-help which is repeatedly mentioned by those who have studied the subject is the *provision of role models*. This refers to the impact of sharing experiences with others who have experienced and overcome the same problems, handicaps, disadvantages or social rejection. This is a powerful mechanism for instilling hope and positive thinking. One good illustration is provided by Ablon (1982) in her description of Parents' Auxiliary of Little People of America, a self-help organisation for families with a child who is of low stature. Ablon described the sense of acceptance which parents gradually develop through meeting other low-stature children and their families and being reassured that they are normal and can lead happy lives.

Self-help organisations all have their own philosophies. Sometimes these constitute *powerful ideologies* or ways of understanding members' problems. As in all organisations, there is terminology which members learn to use, and frequently there is literature, held in high esteem by the organisation, in the form of books, articles, newsletters and pamphlets written by founder members. Indeed Levine (1988) goes so far as to suggest that an individual benefits from membership to the extent that she or he accepts and identifies with the organisation's ideology. This is a testable proposition but it would, of course, run up against our familiar problem of deciding whether a correlation indicates cause (acceptance of the ideology leads to benefit) or selection (those who do not accept the ideology or who are less likely to do so tend to drop out of the organisation more quickly). Ideologies may be derived from professional theories and be consonant with much professional theory. They may, on the other hand, be much out of line with a great deal of current, professional thinking on the subject, and this is then likely to be one of the sources of tension between self-help and professionals. The ideology of one organisation may appear to be quite contrary to that of another as Levine (1988) points out in the case of Alcoholics Anonymous and Recovery Inc. The former stresses the need to accept powerlessness over alcohol (a useful antidote to years of battling to control alcohol consumption) whilst the latter emphasises the power of the 'will' (an antidote to feelings of lack of personal control over symptoms of psychological distress).

The literature on social support has, with notable exceptions (e.g. Tolsdorf, 1976), neglected the giving as opposed to the receiving of support. This is something that has not been overlooked by those who have studied the self-help movement, however. Indeed, just because *help is reciprocal*, some prefer the expression 'mutual aid' to 'self-help' (e.g. Levine, 1988). One of the best examples is Alcoholics Anonymous, with its 'twelfth stepping'—a reference to the all-important twelve steps of the AA programme, the last of which exhorts the member to carry the message of the programme to other 'alcoholics'—and its system of 'sponsoring' of new members by existing ones (Robinson, 1979). In his study of Compassionate Friends, Multiple Sclerosis groups, and Overeaters Anonymous (15 groups and 144 members in all) Maton (1988) found that it was those members whom he termed 'bidirectional supporters' (i.e. those high on both receiving and providing support) who reported more positively about the group and about their own well-being. Maton suggested three possible reasons for this finding. First, and most obviously, there might be benefits to providing as well as receiving support. These include increased meaning and purpose through helping others, social reinforcement of helping, increased feelings of self-worth and efficacy, and the cognitive rehearsal of coping strategies involved in advising others. The second possible explanation involves the psychological costs, perhaps in terms of feelings of inferiority or indebtedness, of non-reciprocally receiving without giving support to others. The third explanation is the familiar selection hypothesis, namely that psychological well-being is a precondition for, rather than consequence of, bidirectional supporting.

Widely referred to is the function of self-help groups in transmitting to members *ideas about ways of coping*. These would appear to include both of the major types of coping with stress identified by Folkman and Lazarus (1980)—problem-focused coping (i.e. coping by dealing with the source of the stress) and emotion—focused coping (i.e. dealing with the emotions engendered by the stress). The former includes finding out about the stress, confronting it and planning how to solve it. The latter includes achieving the appropriate 'emotional distance' from the stress or its source—for example members of Al-Anon are advised to 'detach with love' in order to be able to cope effectively with living with someone with a drinking problem without becoming totally overwhelmed and incapacitated by worry, anger and self-blame (Harwin, 1982).

Finally, it has been said that feelings of powerlessness are characteristic of nearly all new members of self-help groups and that one of the most general properties of self-help is the fostering of *empowerment* through an increased sense of mastery and control over the problems that have brought a member to a group (Katz and Hermalin, 1987). This may extend to a more assertive, consumer-oriented approach to relevant professional services (Lipson, 1982). Self-help is, thus, a form of collective action for reducing powerlessness (see Chapter 5).

From this list of common functions of self-help organisations the enormous potential of self-help can be appreciated. It can also be understood that self-help, although it may overlap with professionally led services to some degree, in fact serves some quite different functions and should therefore not be judged by the same criteria. But does self-help achieve the positive gains for members that this impressive list of functions suggests it might? There have been relatively few evaluations of self-help—Vachon, Lyall, Rogers, Freedman-Letofsky and Freeman's (1980) study of a widow-to-widow programme is one. Questions and cautions have often been raised about self-help. How many people can accommodate to the group approach which is almost universal (Levine, 1988)? Can a single organisation cater to the needs of a membership which is often very heterogeneous in terms of variables such as age, stage and severity of need (Hinrichsen, Revenson and Shinn, 1985)? Is it possible that some of the events occurring to other members—for example the death of another member's child in a group for parents of children with chronic physical illness (Eiser, 1987)—may be emotionally upsetting rather than supportive? Is it not the case that branches of a self-help organisation differ in quality markedly from one to another (Palmer, Marshall and Oppenheimer, 1987)? And could some groups not be positively harmful if group leaders lack sufficient knowledge of group processes (Hinrichsen, Revenson and Shinn, 1985; Gilhooly, 1987; Moffat, 1987)?

In his study of three different types of self-help group (see above), Maton (1988) found support for his hypothesis that certain characteristics of groups as organisations would be correlated with members' appraisals of the groups and their own well-being. He assessed three group characteristics and found strong support for the hypothesis in each case. The three organisational features were: role differentiation, order and organisation, and the capabilities of group leaders. Role differentiation was high when relatively many members held relevant roles (e.g. as phone counsellor, newsletter editor, or being on the door to greet members). It was assessed using questionnaire items such as: 'Are different members in charge of different aspects of group functioning?'. The finding that this aspect of a group's functioning was positively related to appraisal of the group and member well-being is in line with predictions from behaviour setting and responsibility theory (see Chapter 2).

The second potentially important group characteristic was the degree of order and organisation at group meetings. The hypothesis, again strongly supported, was that some minimal set of rules and norms is necessary to maintain a flow of sharing, discussion and support at meetings, and in order to avoid maladaptive group processes such as monopolisation of discussion, negative or judgemental feedback, or discontinuity in focus of discussion. Order and organisation is one of the principal dimensions of climate or atmosphere in any setting according to Moos' scheme (1974, and see Chapter 2) and was assessed in this study using items from one of the Moos scales.

The perceived capability of group leaders was the third characteristic assessed, in this case by means of questionnaire items such as: 'The group leaders are somewhat lacking in organisational skills and know-how'. This factor was particularly strongly related to members' satisfaction with the group.

Many writers on the subject of self-help have stressed the vital importance of good leadership. A good illustration is provided by Ablon (1982) in her description of the vigorous recruiting and supportive work carried out by one particular coordinator of a branch of Parents' Auxiliary of Little People of America. As Ablon put it: 'The significance of the persistence and enthusiasm of the coordinator cannot be overestimated in understanding the success of this group or in the planning of other groups' (p. 43). Katz and Hermalin (1987) provide a useful description of the process and tasks of setting up a self-help group, and they too stress the importance of there being a founder member with certain attributes. The latter include:

willingness to devote personal time ...; ability to network successfully with organisations, agencies and groups to recruit membership/resources; skill in the development of fliers, brochures and media announcements; ability to seek out and obtain a cost-effective meeting place; skill in group process development; ability to help the group define relevant goals, objectives, and action strategies; psychological capacity to be flexible and tolerant of a diversity of opinion; ability to take charge and act as facilitator, mediator and arbiter (at least during the group's formative stages); yet have the capacity to surrender control of the group as the group process evolves. (p. 175)

These are demanding requirements of a leader in any setting. Founding and running a self-help group appears to require considerable flexibility and willingness to change as the group forms and develops. Contingency models of leadership were discussed in Chapter 5, but in the case of self-help it seems that leaders must change their styles rapidly to accommodate to the stage of development or state of organisation of the group.

THE ROLE OF PROFESSIONALS IN SELF-HELP

This leads us on to what must surely be a central question for service planners and providers—What should be the role of professionals, if any, in self-help organisations? Many such organisations have been founded or greatly assisted by professionals (Borman, 1982). Because of the range of tasks and skills required to set up and maintain a successful self-help organisation, it may be that Levine (1988) is correct when he states that, 'many mutual assistance organisations seem to thrive best with a professional hand in the background' (p. 180). Many different roles for professionals have been described.

At one extreme are programmes where the initiative has come from professionals and where ideas and leadership continue to come from that direction. These include programmes to improve the social networks of people returning to live in the community after psychiatric hospitalisation (Edmunson, Bedell and Gordon, 1984), mental health promotion groups for older adults (Bliwise and Lieberman, 1984) and anxiety management groups led by former clients of a professional mental health service (Milne, Jones and Walters, 1989). Some such programmes have more in common with those discussed earlier in this chapter which involve the use of paraprofessionals in professionally led services, but others have tried to come to terms with the inevitable tension between professional leadership and genuine self-help. The Community Network Development Project described by Edmunson, Bedell and Gordon is a good example. They believed that partnership with professionals was necessary:

mental-health clients have strengths and abilities that enable them to take an active part not only in their own rehabilitation, but in the rehabilitation of their peers as well. The type of help provided by a peer is more personal, spontaneous, flexible, and enduring than the help that can be provided by a professional. However, self-help or mutual-aid activities that exist outside the realm of professional influence have proven susceptible to a variety of ills. They may lack sufficient structure and organisation, they may fail to link with professional systems of care, they may even assume an anti-professional stance, or they may develop over time undesirable dogma and norms. (p. 197)

In their programme:

natural helpers would be allowed to function within the network, maintaining their special characteristics and unique helping roles. Professional staff would be responsible for tasks that require high levels of training, knowledge, or professional expertise. (p. 198)

Their organisation consisted of a hierarchical arrangement with paid, professional Staff Area Managers who were responsible for training part-time, modestly paid Community Area Managers who in turn coordinated Member Leaders and Member Volunteers in their localities. Hence, as well as any success the programme may have had in networking ex-hospital patients, it provided a number of responsible roles for participants.

The evaluation that was carried out is a rather good example of combining summative and formative evaluation (see Chapter 6). On discharge from hospital, 80 clients were randomly assigned to the programme or to a control group. Otherwise the two groups received the same, normal after-care. At follow-up, on average 10 months later, half as many of the network development project group had been rehospitalised (17.5 per cent versus 35 per cent) and twice as many were functioning without any professional mental health service treatment (52.5 per cent versus 26 per cent). The formative part of the evaluation was based upon interviews with Community Area Managers and Member Leaders. This confirmed the importance of assuming a responsible, helping role amongst these groups, but it also exposed the tension that was felt to exist between the professional staff and the peer leaders. It was concluded that there was a need for greater clarity about the boundary between the tasks of these two groups, and that more input to policy was required from peer leaders so that they should feel a greater investment in any changes that took place (Edmunson, Bedell and Gordon, 1984).

Another organisation intermediate between the professionally led and self-help, is the organisation of SAGE (Senior Actualisation and Growth Exploration) groups described by Bliwise and Lieberman (1984). Initially, these groups, each consisting of 10–15 older people who met weekly over a nine-month period, were exclusively led by mental health professionals and the philosophy was based upon ideas of human potential and growth derived from the professional literature. Partly as a result of the growing demand for such groups the professional leaders began to train 'peer leaders' who had taken part in such groups themselves and who received further training as leaders from the professionals.

The question that Bliwise and Lieberman asked themselves was: 'Can a professionally conceived and implemented help system successfully adopt a self-help orientation?' (p. 219). Using a multiple comparison group type of quasi-experimental design (see Chapter 6), and an analysis of covariance to correct for any initial differences between groups, they compared professionally led, peer-led, and mixed groups with each other and with a waiting list comparison. Results for all groups compared favourably with the waiting list comparison, and there were no differences between groups in terms of physical health outcomes. There were differences in favour of self-esteem outcome, however, with the professionally led groups producing the better results. These authors believed that they had been only partially successful in shifting the programme to a self-help model:

> By remaining in a professional setting, preserving a professional system of supervision and retaining ideological constraints on group behavior that were closely tied to the professional-treatment model, SAGE may only have succeeded in converting peers into less well-trained professionals. Perhaps if the SAGE members were left to pursue goals of personal growth and development under some structure based on their own devices outcome results for the peer leaders would have matched those of the professionals. (p. 232)

The foregoing are examples of 'bridges' between professionally organised services and self-help, and they do not qualify as fully fledged self-help organisations according to Katz and Bender's (1976) definition. An example of a self-help organisation which collaborates closely with professionals is Parents Anonymous. PA was formed through a collaboration between a parent and a social worker and this collaboration has been built into the organisation's rules for running groups. These are normally facilitated by a parent as chairperson and a professional (often but not always a social worker) as 'sponsor'. The latter's role is to provide guidance and encouragement for the group, but particularly to provide support—emotional and informational—for the parent chairperson (Comstock, 1982; Willen, 1984).

In his study of members of three different types of self-help group, Gottlieb (1982) asked members to rate the appropriateness of seven different professional roles in relation to their own groups. All roles received average ratings above the mid-point on a scale from 'inappropriate' to 'very appropriate' indicating that the idea of professional involvement was generally well accepted. However, the roles that received the highest ratings were those suggesting more *indirect* participation in the form of consultant, referral agent, or initiator (helping to start and organise new groups). The more direct, group leader, role for professionals was thought to be somewhat less appropriate, especially by members of 'one step removed' groups. Thus, although members generally supported some involvement of professionals, they were endorsing the idea of self-help organisations as autonomous bodies who could consult with professionals on their own terms. As Katz and Hermalin (1987) put it:

> *Autonomy* is thus a key functional characteristic of the self-help group; that is self-direction from within members, rather than direction from outsiders, for example professionals. (p. 156 their emphasis)

They warn of the possibility of negative professional impact on self-help groups. Control can become an issue because some professionals overstep their roles as consultants or advisers. They may adopt a hierarchical, clinical model rather than a peer egalitarian one. They may not be sufficiently acquainted with the philosophy, goals, objectives and history of the self-help movement. Mowrer (1984) has also warned of the danger of professional 'cooptation' masquerading as professional collaboration. He wrote of the way in which drug rehabilitation projects in the USA, founded and run in their early days by ex-drug users, had been taken over by professional treatment philosophies, funding, and systems of accreditation. Changes of language were a good indication of the cooptation that had occurred:

> It was particularly strange to hear residents speaking about their 'counsellors' or 'therapists', terms that were never used a few years ago and could have come into currency only because there are now staff members designated by these terms. In the 'good old days', residents had 'role models' and talked about 'going through changes', but they *never* spoke of 'therapy'. (pp.141–142, his emphasis)

As was discussed fully in Chapter 7, the idea of an egalitarian relationship between consultant and consultee is central to the theory of consultation, and the latter thus provides one model for the role of professionals in relation to self-help groups. One account of an apparently successful consultation exercise was that carried by Wollert, Knight and Levy (1984) for one chapter of Make Today Count, an organisation for cancer patients and their families. Although Wollert, Knight and Levy made the first approach to this group in order to learn more about MTC for their research on self-help groups, this led to a collaboration that appears to have been productive for the group itself. Initial observations suggested that the group was not flourishing. A low percentage of group attenders were cancer patients themselves, there was difficulty in recruiting new members, meetings lacked a cohesive format, questions about the group's aims and objectives were frequently left unresolved, and the frequency of meetings had been reduced from twice to once a month. On the basis of their observations, and their accumulating knowledge of the purposes, techniques and strengths of self-help groups generally, Wollert, Knight and Levy first made a general presentation to the group about self-help, and later made specific suggestions about clarifying aims and objectives, introducing a more structured format for meetings, and using techniques which facilitated group discussion. Feedback from group members, plus later observations of group functioning, suggested dramatic improvement. The frequency of meetings had increased once more, attendance was greater, the proportion of cancer patients had increased, and meetings were now organised, and warm and enthusiastic in climate in contrast to the previously disorganised, restrained and rather dismal meetings.

Throughout, Wollert, Knight and Levy emphasised that their role was consultative and resisted requests to take on roles such as discussion leader. They believed that professionals' contacts with self-help groups were often, 'hurried and evaluative, focussed on the professional, and asserted the professional's superior status'. Their own contact, by contrast, was, 'long-term, nonevaluative, group-centred, and characterised by a respect for the group's right to accept or reject our input' (p. 136). They suggested that a successful collaboration depended upon a number of conditions. One was the adoption of a consultation model. A second was a rapport-building approach which conveyed respect and acceptance of the group's ways of doing things and which de-emphasised status differentials. One of the most important conditions, however, was an adequate knowledge, on the professionals' part, of the workings of self-help groups.

Appreciating and respecting that the ideology of a self-help organisation may be very different from that of his or her own service organisation or professional group, is one of the hardest tests for the professional. Katz and Hermalin (1987) and Levine (1988) point out that the self-help model should not be confused with a treatment model. For one thing self-help is not time-limited like most treatments. Professionals often point to the length of time that members remain in organisations such as Alcoholics Anonymous, and criticise them for producing a new form of dependency or 'addiction'. This is to misunderstand the philosophy of self-help. As Levine (1988) put it: 'We make "visits" to a treatment setting, we "belong" to a mutual assistance group' (p. 178). Borkman (1990) believes that the self-help approach should be taught to professionals, 'as member-owned self-determining voluntary associations ... the educational programme about SHGs would include teaching professionals respect for SHGs and how to relate to them without cooptation or control' (p. 330).

Being prepared to change one's customary professional role, in response to the needs of a self-help group, is another hard task. Colleagues of the present author have reported how difficult it is to resist being drawn into a familiar counselling or treatment role, and how difficult it can be to justify even to oneself, let alone to one's managers, the fact that a collaborative role with a self-help group may involve a professional in a wide range of activities from the specialised to the mundane. For example, in working with the Miscarriage Association, Vickers (1987) assisted by collecting information available on the subject locally and nationally, by helping develop a pack of written materials, by helping to link the association with local health education resources and with local radio, and by finding information about sources of finance. Some of the most useful information discovered was about the rights of women over such matters as a proper burial for their babies, and the most useful written information for the pack consisted of women's own accounts of their experiences. She also found herself looking for suitable places to meet, and spending a lot of time helping out in printing.

The foregoing discussion still makes the assumption that the professional is the 'consultant' and that the direction of helpful influence is from professional to self-help group. A more radical view, which Katz (1984) suggested may be more prevalent in Europe than in North America, is that by offering alternative models and by pointing out deficiencies in services, self-help organisations may be a source for changing the professional, formal health care and other human service systems (Borkman, 1990). This is one of the themes of the following chapter.

11   Empowering the Community

We saw in the previous chapter how important it is for most self-help groups that they retain autonomy. This is true even of those self-help groups that collaborate closely with professionals and which aim principally to provide support for members or help to one another in making behavioural changes. It is even more the case for those organisations which aim to campaign for member's rights, to change public attitudes, or to expose and correct gaps in services (Sagarin, 1969). Thus, self-help organisations represent pockets of alternative, collective power in their communities, and working with them requires of professionals a departure from their traditional way of working.

In this final chapter, we shall approach this topic of empowering the community from a slightly different angle—that of the development of services in the community—and will go still further down the path towards community autonomy and non-traditional practice in the application of psychology.

COMMUNITY ALTERNATIVES TO PSYCHIATRIC HOSPITAL

Two major, randomised controlled trials have compared what appears to have been good, thorough community-based treatment for a virtually unselected group of psychiatric patients, with good, standard-care treatment based on psychiatric hospitalisation and after-care. The first was carried out in Wisconsin USA, using an approach termed Training in Community Living (Stein and Test, 1980). The second, based upon the Stein and Test approach, was carried out in Sydney, Australia (Hoult, Rosen and Reynolds, 1984).

In both studies the patients involved received a wide range of diagnoses (only those with neurological disorders or addictions were excluded). Approximately half in each study were diagnosed as suffering from schizophrenia. The large majority had been hospitalised previously, most a number of times. The US and Australian studies involved 130 and 120 patients, respectively, who were seeking admission at the psychiatric hospital. Half in each study were randomly assigned to receive intensive treatment from a mental health team *outside* the hospital. Treatment was continuously available for up to approximately one year. Others received standard care.

Several aspects of this community training approach are highlighted in the reports of these studies. One is the intensive nature of the support given to patient and family when they initially sought admission for the patient: often several hours were spent at the initial interview with frequent visits or continuous periods of time spent with patient and family in the first few days. Hoult and Reynolds (1984) remark that a strong alliance was frequently formed at that stage and that patients and their relatives often, 'learned to regard the illness in quite a different light and learned new ways of managing it' (p. 362). The emphasis was on resuming normal functioning and routine as quickly as possible, and on taking advantage of patients' strengths rather than pathology. An ingredient that was highly stressed was the full involvement of relatives and/or other caretakers, and the need to provide them, where appropriate, with information, support, guidance and counselling. It is a sad fact that, when these studies were being carried out, this wholehearted involvement of families was the exception rather than the rule, since much professional theorising and practice has tended to keep relatives at arm's length, or worse, to view them as a significant part of the patient's pathology (Orford, 1987b). Again we see an example of the way in which opportunities for the constructive use of a meso-system (Bronfenbrenner, 1979)—patient, relative, mental health worker, in this case—can be neglected or taken full advantage of.

Also considered to be vitally important was the provision of consistent care by the one team, with one individual case manager taking principal responsibility in each case, the availability of help 24 hours a day and seven days a week, and the continual rather than time-limited availability of this help to patients and families. The basic principle used by Stein and Test, and followed by Hoult, Rosen and Reynolds, was that patients should get the help that they need, when they need it, and in the place where it would do most good. Hence, programmes were individually tailored, took place in patients' homes, places of work or other community locations, and involved assistance in activities of daily living (e.g. laundry, upkeep, shopping, cooking, grooming, budgeting, and use of transportation), help with job-finding (contact then being maintained with employers or supervisors), use of leisure time, development of social skills, and provision of support, information and advice on management for relatives or other carers. Both the American and Australian teams believed that community mental health workers should be 'assertive' in maintaining contact, whilst at the same time not being overly intrusive. They contrast their approach with the typical community mental health or after-care approach which is comparatively passive, leaving the onus of responsibility for re-establishing contact, if it is broken, with the patient.

The results of both studies were impressive. The major findings are summarised in Table 18. Each study demonstrated that treatment could be provided for often quite severely disturbed patients, largely outside hospital, in a way that met with greater approval from the users of the service, and which

Table 18. Major findings of two studies comparing community care and standard hospital care (based on Stein and Test, 1980 and Hoult, Rosen and Reynolds, 1984)

	Wisconsin (Stein and Test)		Sydney (Hoult, Rosen and Reynolds)	
	Community (C)	Standard (S)	Community (C)	Standard (S)
Time in hospital	2.6% vs	15.3%	8.4 days vs	53.5 days
Time unemployed	29.0% vs	57.5%		
Average income	747 vs	388 dollars		
Contact with 'trusted friends'	Sig. greater for C group at 12 months			
Satisfaction with life				
Use of leisure time				
Symptoms	Sig. greater for S group in the case of six of eleven symptoms (others n.s.)		29% vs 43% at 12 months had sufficient symptoms for a diagnosis of psychosis	
Present state examination			Sig. greater total PSE score for S group	
Use of medication	C group more compliant with anti-psychotic medication at 12 months			
'Very satisfied' with advice and information			60% vs	29%
'Very satisfied' with support and help			65% vs	33%
'Very pleased' with admission or non-admission			71% vs	32%
Relatives satisfied with support and information			88% vs	39%
Relatives thought they had coped better			70% vs	28%

produced significantly greater improvement on at least some measured outcome variables. Although some of the community group required hospitalisation during the year (40 per cent in the Hoult, Rosen and Reynolds study for example), these admissions were short and rarely repeated. Almost all standard-care patients were admitted, often more than once. Nor is there any evidence that the greater amount of time spent in the community was at the expense of quality of life or increased symptomatology. The reverse was, if anything, the case. A number of looked-for differences did not emerge, however, including a measure of leisure time activity, and use of psychoactive medication.

As Table 18 shows, Hoult and his colleagues also provided considerable data on user satisfaction. These data uniformly showed that patients and families in the community treatment group were more satisfied. Stein and Test employed an additional, quasi-experimental, element in their study. After a year the experimental community treatment was withdrawn and by 14 months all patients and their families had been transferred to standard care. Almost all the significant gains made in the first year, in comparison with standard care, had been lost by the end of the second year.

In 1982, Kiesler reviewed 10 studies which by then had reported the results of randomly assigning psychiatric patients either to in-patient care or to some alternative non-hospital method of treatment. The Stein and Test study was one of them. Although the type of non-hospital treatment varied widely, including hostel placement, family crisis therapy, and day care, it was Kiesler's judgement that all involved some 'active' form of non-institutional treatment, and that almost all included severely ill patients. The intent of Kiesler's review was to assess the value of hospital admission, rather than to evaluate the effectiveness of particular forms of community treatment. He found that, although results varied, they were never overall in favour of hospital treatment, and where differences existed they always favoured the community form of provision. Furthermore, a period of hospitalisation was itself predictive of further hospitalisations. Although costs also varied widely, in no case was the cost of the community alternative greater than that of hospital care. In their later study, Hoult, Rosen and Reynolds found that hospital treatment was approximately 20 per cent more expensive than their community alternative. It should be pointed out, however, that they only included patients living within two districts of Sydney, and that a community service in a rural area would be likely to be much more expensive. Even in their, urban-based, study differences in costs were not great, and they and most others who have commented on the subject have made the point that active community alternatives of the kind which they described and have shown to be effective, should not be set up with the expectation that they will save money. Stein and Test (1980) also pointed out the profound influence on shaping services of the system of reimbursing certain types of treatments and not others under an insurance-based health care system. If the kind of

Training in Community Living approach which they pioneered is not publicly funded or reimbursable then it is unlikely to be implemented on a wide scale, however effective.

These studies took place during an era in which the resident population of mental hospitals in most industrialised countries was, in any event, falling quite dramatically. Various reasons for this fall have been put forward, and different authors have emphasised different factors. The introduction of anti-psychotic and anti-depressant drugs may have played a part, but probably so too have: (a) sociological and social psychiatric studies of psychiatric institutions (e.g. Goffman, 1961; Wing and Brown, 1970); (b) exposés of and enquiries into conditions in mental hospitals; (c) what Ramon (1988) calls the 'psychologisation of everyday life' and changing attitudes towards normality and abnormality; and (d) prevailing economic conditions which, at a time of relatively full employment following a world war, raised the value of the mentally ill in the labour market (Warner, 1985). Against this changing climate a number of countries, notably the USA and Italy, have passed legislation requiring that community services be set up as alternatives to psychiatric hospitals. Much has been written about the new community mental health services in those two particular countries, and the following section will highlight some of the points that are most important from the perspective of community psychology, and will compare developments in those countries with more recent innovations in Britain.

ALTERNATIVES TO HOSPITAL IN THE USA

Amongst the many who have commented upon the community mental health movement in the USA are Jeger and Slotnick (1982) who examine it from the perspective of their own behavioural-ecological perspective, and Mangen (1988) who takes the US and Italian developments as two case studies of how community care may be implemented. Each refers to the provision of federal funding for community mental health centres in all localities across the United States, following the report of the Joint Commission on Mental Illness and Health in 1961, and President Kennedy's message to Congress on the national policy towards mental illness and mental retardation in 1963, and the passing of the Community Mental Health Centers Construction Act later in the same year. This Act and subsequent amendments that were passed during the 1970s required that such centres should provide a wide range of services (in-patient, out-patient, day hospital, crisis, rehabilitative, halfway houses, consultation, and prevention via community education) for a variety of different client groups including children, the elderly, those with alcohol or drug problems, and those with long-term needs. In addition, 2 per cent of operating budgets were required to be allocated to programme evaluation.

Most commentators report that the movement in the US has fallen short of expectations in a number of respects. One factor about which many agree is that the goals set for community mental health centres (CMHCs) were too many and too ambitious, and that such high expectations inevitably gave rise to disillusionment (Feldman, 1978; Mollica, 1980). The evidence suggests that CMHCs: (a) have engaged in very little consultation and preventive education (see Chapters 1 and 7); (b) that the involvement of non-professional workers has been more problematic than predicted (see Chapter 10); (c) that the expected involvement of community members in decision-making about services (one of Bloom's, 1977, 10 hallmarks of community mental health) has hardly occurred at all and when it has it has been confined to an élite; and (d) that programme evaluation has tended to be downplayed, contracted out to outside agencies, and its results rarely acted upon to make changes in CMHC practice (Jeger and Slotnick, 1982).

The major criticism, however, has been on the grounds of CMHCs' relative neglect of those with long-term disabilities and needs arising from mental distress or disorder (the *continuing care users* of the service) and particularly those users who are older. There appear to have been a number of reasons for this. One is the drift, which can so easily occur in all forms of human service work, towards those clients whose problems appear to be the most amenable to change—the relatively young middle-income client suffering from mild to moderate distress—and away from those whose needs are greatest. Another appears to have been the difficulty of establishing close working relationships between hospitals and CMHCs. These are vital for the appropriate use of hospitals and the integration of the two components which would be necessary if community mental health teams were to function in the ways the teams operated in the Stein and Test (1980) and Hoult, Rosen and Reynolds (1984) experiments. Another was the failure to set up the range of alternative residential facilities that experience has shown are necessary: not just transitional halfway houses, but also unstaffed group homes and other forms of sheltered accommodation, as well as relatively highly staffed community houses for those less able to function independently. A variety of such provision is necessary if the right fit between a person's capabilities and the independence and support provided is to be achieved, and *normalisation* maximised. Without such a network of provision, CMHCs in the US have not done as much as was hoped towards reducing admissions to psychiatric hospitals, or towards preventing what some have termed 'transinstitutionalisation' whereby many clients with continuing needs are either transferred to environments, such as large nursing homes or even prisons, cheap hotels or a life of homelessness, which do not maximise their potential or provide a decent quality of life, or are apparently 'integrated' into the community but without emotional support (Kennedy, 1989).

Failure to provide enough, good community care, coupled with social class differences in rates of psychiatric disorder and access to services (discussed in Chapter 3), can lead to the kind of picture provided by Mollica and Milic's (1986) survey of the use of psychiatric in-patient facilities in South-Central

Connecticut. This was the same area in which Hollingshead and Redlich (1958) had carried out their classic study of *Social Class and Mental Illness*. They had discovered marked disparities in types of psychiatric treatment received by members of different social classes. Mollica and Milic concentrated on the use of private versus public in-patient facilities and demonstrated changes that had occurred in the 25 years intervening between the two studies. These years saw a growth in private hospital provision so that, whereas in 1950 private hospitals were largely used by class I and a minority of class II, by 1975 the large majority of classes I, II, III and almost half of IV were using private hospitals, leaving in the state hospital a large concentration of people in the lowest occupational/educational class group (they used the Hollingshead two-factor index of social position which is based on both occupation and education). Independently of social class, however, marital status, gender, race and diagnosis differentiated those using private and public services—the separated and divorced, women, blacks, and those diagnosed as suffering from schizophrenia, alcohol or drug problems, or organic brain conditions, were all more likely to be found in the public hospitals. Mollica and Milic conclude:

> Deinstitutionalization and the shift of patients towards the private sector over the past 25 years have left the state hospital as a reservoir for the region's most socially and psychiatrically debilitated patients ... one survey reveals that all measures of social function are dramatically reduced among the state hospital in-patients. These patients are primarily class V chronically unemployed and unskilled workers who would probably be unable to achieve future occupational stability. (p. 110)

Two thousand CMHCs were envisaged for the USA by 1980. In practice the number of CMHCs in the USA is considerably less than one thousand. Jeger and Slotnick (1982) believe that there was an inherent contradiction in the philosophy behind CMHCs. On the one hand they were to provide an alternative to hospitalisation. On the other hand they persisted with a medical model of mental health problems as their underlying conceptual framework. Instead of a genuinely alternative philosophy of community psychology or community mental health with an emphasis on environmental and societal determinants, and the valuing of the user's participation and the non-professional's contribution, CMHCs in the US, at least according to Jeger and Slotnick, perpetuated a system which emphasised diagnosis and which overvalued treatments by experts, particularly medical and individual treatments such as psychoactive medication and psychotherapy. The medical profession continued to remain the encompassing profession (see Chapter 9).

ALTERNATIVES TO HOSPITAL IN ITALY

The same could not be said to be true of the Italian psychiatric reform spearheaded by the left-wing organisation Psichiatria Democratica (Ramon

1985; Jones and Poletti, 1986; Mangen, 1988). Ramon (1985) suggests that there were three guiding principles in PD's campaign for reform:

> de-segregation of the mentally ill and re-integration in the community; a more equal distribution of power among staff in multi-disciplinary settings; and greater flexibility of therapeutic role according to the specific needs of individual clients, rather than to pre-determined standards of any one professional group. (pp. 176 – 177)

Thus, as well as being concerned with de-segregation and normalisation of previously segregated and stigmatised groups, the movement has been very explicitly concerned with questions of power and dominance: dominance of the mental hospital system over the lives of those who lived in them, as well as the dominance of the medical model and the medical profession over other models and professions. Although the US CMHC movement took place at a time of growing awareness of and concern with issues such as poverty and race, the Italian reform was much more overtly political and was linked, for example, with the student and worker movements of the late 1960s in Europe.

It seems that the Italian psychiatric hospital system was particularly ripe for change, characterised as it was by poor conditions and a high proportion of compulsory admissions. Innovations had already been taking place in a number of towns and cities, particularly in Northern and Central Italy, most notably in Trieste. As a result of campaigning by PD and parliamentary support by the small Radical Party, the relevant legislation, Law 180, was passed in 1978. At around the same time, the whole Italian health system was undergoing change, with the formation of a National Health Service. The new law forbade the building of new psychiatric hospitals, severely curtailed their use especially for new admissions, radically altered the procedure for compulsory admissions, and encouraged the discharge of patients and the setting up of community services.

CMHCs form the centrepiece of these new services. Visitors to the centres in Trieste—including those, like Jones, who have been critical of the Italian reform generally—are impressed by the atmosphere. Jones and Poletti (1986) wrote:

> The relationships between staff and patients (called 'users') are warm and caring; there are no white coats, no appointments, and no queues of patients waiting to be seen. The atmosphere is more like that of a club than a medical centre. In the centres in the city, patients come when they like, talk to whom they like, stay as long as they like, and leave when they like. Some treat the centres as lunch clubs, some come seeking the help of the staff (psychiatrists and nurses, with a psychologist and a social worker), and some work there part-time or full-time, helping with the cooking and cleaning. This is not the traditional kind of patient labour, which is considered exploitative: there are cooking, cleaning, and agricultural co-operatives, which patients join; by an arrangement with the trades unions in the city, these pay full union rates. The health district budget provides the money on contract if the co-operative's tender is accepted. (p. 145)

Ramon (1985) also describes the informal atmosphere in the centres with staff lending a hand with manual tasks such as cleaning and preparing meals, and users being involved in answering the phone and other administrative tasks. Lack of private offices for staff, absence of secretarial support or a formal appointment system, or formalised case notes, all encourage this sense of informality.

As allowed for in the Act each centre has a small number of back-up beds in a psychiatric Diagnosis and Cure (D and C) unit in the general hospital. According to Jones and Poletti, patients stay in the Trieste unit only for a few hours before being referred to a centre. A variety of types of accommodation is available for service users ranging from small homely apartments to large apartments with full-time nursing staff. CMHCs provide a wide range of services including support, counselling, medication (but not ECT), and help in securing accommodation, education and employment (Ramon, 1985). It seems that the Italian movement, perhaps unlike that in the USA, may have been successful in substituting a genuinely alternative model of mental distress and illness. Amongst the several positive outcomes of the reform, Ramon (1985) includes the following:

> The attention now paid to social factors in the aetiology of psychiatric disorders, and in clinical practice, redresses the previous imbalance in which the relevance of these factors was underestimated. However, this has not led to the neglect of psychological, biochemical and organic factors. (p. 197)

From all accounts it would appear that at least in Trieste and some other towns and cities it has been possible to create an entirely new style of service with a much greater degree of integration of service users with the rest of the community, far less use of hospital admission, virtually no compulsory admissions, and much greater egalitarianism both between users and staff and amongst different staff groups.

There is also general agreement, however, that there are many remaining problems and shortcomings. One of these, about which all agree, is the simple fact that the spread of the reform through Italy has been limited and patchy. The regions are highly autonomous with different traditions of psychiatric health care, and most places do not share Trieste's advantage of having had a declining population and the ready availability of relatively low-cost housing with which to set up alternative residential facilities. The reform was followed by a period of cuts in public health spending, and in many places, particularly in the South of the country, mental health services remain traditional and unsatisfactory. Private practice psychiatry flourishes in many areas, creating the familiar 'two-tier' mental health service which has already been mentioned in the discussion of mental health services in the USA.

There is also agreement that the desire to cast off an individual, private conceptualisation of mental distress, and to move away from formal professionalism, has led to a neglect of individual psychotherapy and the insight which models of individual therapy can bring. Commentators have pointed to a neglect of professional training, an absence of formal evaluation and the means of disseminating findings about practices which have been successful or unsuccessful, and some (e.g. Jones and Poletti, 1986) say there has been far too much reliance on rhetoric in supporting the reform. Jones and Poletti believe that the claims of success may have been exaggerated even in Trieste. Their observations were that the old mental hospital, although officially closed and totally changed in many ways, still housed the CMHC, a work cooperative, an arts centre, administration, an alcohol dependence unit, a locked ward for patients suffering from senile dementia, and a considerable number of long-stay psychiatric patients and severely mentally handicapped young people. Ramon (1985) also made an important point when she referred to the prevailing attitudes towards family members of adult clients of the new community services. Her point here is that, although family members are expected to support the client and carry on with their lives as usual, they and their needs are rarely considered. She comments: 'It seems that the identification with the index client is probably the main factor which limits the perception of family members as persons in need in their own right' (p. 199).

ALTERNATIVES TO HOSPITAL IN BRITAIN

In Britain the same general move to reduce the mental hospital population, to close some hospitals altogether, and to develop alternative community services has taken place slowly and gradually over the course of the last 20 to 30 years. Although these general aims have been the policy of the British government's health department throughout that time, there has been no major legislation or radical reform movement as in the USA or Italy. Summarising developments in Britain, over that time, Ramon (1988) is critical of the lack of vision amongst most professionals working in the field, and the absence of recognition in government policy statements that new ways of working might be required, that staff might need retraining, that the communities from which those with long-term mental health needs had previously been segregated might need reorienting, or that a different model of mental health and illness might be required.

Pace of change has varied greatly from district to district. Hospitals have closed or are closing in a number of areas, and CMHCs or mental health resource or advice centres have been set up (McAusland, 1985). There has, sadly, been very little evaluation of these new services, but collections of the early experiences of those who have operated such facilities, such as the collection edited by McAusland for the Kings Fund Centre are valuable. It appears that some of the same mistakes that were noted above when discussing US CMHCs are being made again in Britain. For example, there is a tendency to take on too many tasks, and a tendency in practice to neglect consultative and preventive work, as well as work with families, and work encouraging and developing social support networks and self-help groups, in favour of individual and group therapy. In at least one instance, however, a service has been established with a clear, alternative philosophy not unlike that which has underpinned the Italian reform (Milroy and Hennelly, 1989). The intention in this centre, in North Derbyshire, was not to impose professional ideas and values, or to carry out individual therapeutic work, but rather to run a therapeutic community, a social support club, a range of mental health volunteer groups, a day centre for older people run by a voluntary organisation, an occupational workshop, and an employment scheme. This innovative service was set up as part of the local authority's social services department, and the local health authority would not assist in funding it. The fact that the needs of the 'continuing care' service user fall within the provinces of both social services and health has bedevilled service planning for this group both in Britain and in a number of other countries (Mangen, 1988; Ramon, 1988). At the time of writing the British government is in the process of shifting responsibility for continuing care more clearly than hitherto in the direction of social service departments.

THE CONCEPT OF NORMALISATION

One group of human service users about whom professional thinking *has* changed radically in recent years consists of people with learning disabilities. The aim of differentiating members of this group from others in terms of scores on norm-referenced tests of ability has given way to the aim of *normalisation* (Wolfensberger, 1972) and the objective of integrating with rather than segregating from the rest of the community in education, housing, work and leisure (Sinha, 1986). Achievements are more likely to be assessed in terms of criterion-referenced scales of individual development, or in terms of quality of life (see Chapter 3). There has been increasing recognition of the role of exo- and macro-systems, such as the school system with its divisive emphasis upon 'brightness' and examinations, and prevailing public language and attitudes (witness the shift in terminology from 'mental retardation' to 'mental handicap' to 'learning disabilities').

The concept of 'normalisation' arose in the USA in the late 1960s, based upon Scandinavian developments in the provision of services for people with learning disabilities. It has become a leading concept for service development in that field mainly through the writings of Wolfensberger (e.g. Wolfensberger, 1972; Wolfensberger and Thomas, 1983). Central to the principle of normalisation is the idea of role and the idea that some groups in a community are undervalued or devalued relative to others. Members of such groups, which have included people with learning disabilities, tend to occupy less valued roles. The aim of those using the principle of normalisation is, 'to enable, establish and/or maintain valued social roles for people'

(Wolfensberger and Thomas, 1983, p. 23). Indeed 'social role valorisation' was a later alternative to the term 'normalisation'.

Underlying the general principle of normalisation are the seven core themes described by Wolfensberger and Thomas (1983) and shown here in Table 19. These are attractive notions for community psychology for two separate reasons. For one thing the concept of normalisation and that of valued role upon which it is based meet the most important criterion for a useful concept for community psychology, namely that it should deal with person-in-context. They are concerned with the person—for example with his or her self-concept and level of competence—but are as much concerned with settings and with the interaction between person and setting. In fact one of the most important developments from the principle of normalisation has been a way of evaluating settings in which people with learning disabilities find themselves,

Table 19. Normalisation: seven core themes (based on Wolfensberger and Thomas, 1983)

1. The role of (un)consciousness in human services
   People who work in human services may be unaware of the social devaluation experienced by the people they are trying to serve, and some of the ways in which the organisations they work for perpetuate this state of affairs
2. The relevance of role expectancy and role circularity to deviancy-making and deviancy-unmaking
   Roles are powerful, and human services should do all they can to minimise devalued roles for people (as object, burden, sick person, child-like, etc.) and to create roles that are valued and age-appropriate and which give people status
3. The 'conservatism corollary' to the principle of normalisation
   Because people with disabilities that are apparent to others are vulnerable to being devalued, it may be necessary to take more than normal steps to enhance status (e.g. by dressing smartly when there is a choice of smart or casual attire)
4. The developmental model, and the importance of personal competency enhancement
   A commitment to personal development, growth and increased competence for people with handicaps
5. The power of imitation
   Imitation should be capitalised upon by exposing people who are in otherwise devalued groups to models of appropriate functioning rather than, as happens when people are segregated, to predominantly abnormal models
6. The dynamics and relevance of social imagery
   The symbols and images historically associated with devalued people are negative, and any features of the human service that can convey an image about its clients should be positive
7. The importance of personal social integration and valued social participation
   Socially devalued people are often rejected and segregated, but normalisation requires that they should have the greatest possible opportunity to be integrated into the valued life of society in terms of housing, education, work, recreation, worship, shopping, and in all other normal activities

particularly service settings, in terms of the goals of normalisation. This is the Programme Analysis of Service Systems' Implementation of Normalisation Goals (PASSING). This evaluates a setting in terms of the degree to which it enhances the social image and personal competencies of an otherwise devalued group of people. This takes us a long way from the assessment of cognitive deficits, with which psychology was preoccupied at one time. The recognition that characteristics of behaviour settings are all-important, and the use of a guiding set of principles for understanding and assessing settings, have produced nothing less than a major paradigm shift in thinking about the provision of services for people with learning disabilities.

The second attractive feature of normalisation is its potential general applicability. Although it has had relatively little application outside the field of learning disabilities to date, it does concern devalued groups in general. Whether it could fill the gap, detected by Ramon (1988), in new thinking to guide community services of people with psychiatric difficulties remains to be seen. There is clearly a great deal of overlap between the core themes of normalisation, on the one hand, and the ideas that have guided the Italian psychiatric reforms on the other hand.

Normalisation has not been without its critics, however. One line of criticism has been that proponents of the concept have been strong on ideology, even to the point of, 'excessive zealotry, proselytising and evangelising' (Baldwin, 1989, p. 306), and short on empirical testing of the theory. For example, Rapley (1990) has considered the first two of the core themes shown in Table 19 and concludes that neither is well supported by the evidence yet available. Others have questioned the overall thrust of the normalisation argument. For example, Szivos and Griffiths (1990) ask whether the advocates of normalisation are right to prescribe certain do's and don'ts, such as that the aim should be for people with learning disabilities not to travel, live or socialise together in easily identified and stigmatised groups, but rather to integrate with and disperse amongst other people. Perhaps this is to ignore individual choice. Perhaps consciousness-raising of learning-disabled people as a distinct group with special needs but equal rights would be a better principle? It seems likely that the principle of normalisation has served a valuable function during a time of very considerable change in thinking about services for this one undervalued group but the details of the theory will now come under much closer scrutiny and test.

ADVOCACY AND USERS' GROUPS

A service development concept that has given rise to some important and innovative practical developments has been that of advocacy. Here we shall examine the emergence of this concept and of special roles such as ally or advocate for people who might otherwise be relatively powerless, such as those with long-term psychiatric care needs or with learning disabilities. For example, in Exeter a number of clinical psychologists have developed the role of 'professional ally' towards groups of the mental illness service users, both by helping to set up a Users' Group, and by working with MIND, the national voluntary association for mental health (Williams, 1985; Temple, personal communication). This work has involved the psychologists in a range of tasks, some familiar and some new. A major aim has been to help users identify their own wishes and wants, rather than to have professionals identifying problems and prescribing remedies. The professionals need to show flexibility and commitment about ordinary, but vital, considerations such as times and places for meetings and transport to and from meetings. To maximise the involvement and sense of ownership on the part of users, professionals find themselves operating out of hours and out of their usual roles. Their skills as listeners, analysers, group facilitators, and presenters of information, are, however, used to the full. For example, a knowledge of intra-group processes may help to enable everyone to participate, including those who are having the most difficulty in expressing themselves and whose views might otherwise be rejected as invalid. Similarly such knowledge and skill may help in preventing the leadership role in a group becoming stuck with one or a few dominant individuals even though a number of members may wish this. Other relevant skills include those of someone who facilitates the collection in written form of members' ideas, and the analysis and subsequent presentation of these digested and summarised. These are, in essence, the skills of qualitative analysis and action research (see Chapters 6 and 9) although they may often not be recognised as such.

In the Exeter work with the Users' Group psychologists have pursued the ally or advocate role by, for example, broadcasting on local radio with group members, assisting where necessary in the production of a group newsletter and a 'constitution' or bill of rights for users, holding joint public meetings, accompanying users on visits to acute admission wards in the local psychiatric hospital and helping to set up facilities which were identified by users as facilities that were lacking—such as a cafe club in the town.

Inherent in this kind of work is the idea of a conflict of interests between groups that are relatively powerful in a community (in this case service providers who have expertise, information, and financial and other resources) and another group (the service users) who have the major stake in service provision but who are, nevertheless, relatively powerless. Any professionals who aim to engage in this conflict as allies or advocates for members of the relatively powerless group will be bound to find themselves caught up in the conflict in one way or another. At times they are bound to be seen by service managers or even by their own professional colleagues as being misguided, unprofessional, or breaking ranks. Nor will they always be seen by the users themselves as being on their side, but will be seen as being in a compromised position. It is with this potential conflict of interests very much in mind that an alternative form of advocacy—*citizen advocacy*—has developed as an alternative to the kind of *professional advocacy* which we have been discussing or *self-advocacy* practised by many self-help organisations.

Citizen advocacy began in Britain in the early 1980s with the formation of the Advocacy Alliance in London and other projects have started since in areas such as Sheffield and Avon. A crucial aspect of this type of advocacy is that both the advocates themselves and the agency which recruits and trains them, matches them with their 'partners', and continues to support them, are as independent as possible from those agencies that provide the services that partners need access to. Thus, those who write about citizen advocacy are adamant that advocates should not be professionals working for relevant service agencies and that the advocacy agency and its offices should be independent in its location, administration, and preferably in its funding also (Butler, 1987; Line, Personal Communication). One of the central roles for an advocate is to represent the interests of his or her partner as if they were his or her own. For this to work well the advocate must be as free as possible from potential conflicts of interest. As is the case with self-help groups, professionals who have embraced the advocacy concept may, nevertheless, play influential parts in setting up an advocacy service, and by continuing to provide support and advice.

It is no accident that the concept of advocacy, at least in Britain, has had its main application in relation to people with learning disabilities. For this is a group who, by virtue of their handicaps and the way they have been treated and the ways in which services have been organised for them in the past, have been in a very powerless and devalued position.

However, advocacy services may be relevant for any groups who have a stake in the provision of human services but who, for whatever reason, have difficulty in expressing their wishes or whose voices are not heard by those who plan or provide such services. As well as with people with learning disabilities the concept has been particularly used in relation to people with long-term psychiatric disabilities, but it is equally applicable to others such as those with physical disabilities, people suffering from Alzheimer's disease and those who do not speak the major language spoken locally.

A principle adopted by most advocacy agencies is that advocates should be voluntary and unpaid and should be prepared to commit themselves to develop an important relationship with their partners. These relationships may be long-term and even life-long. The notion that a non-disabled person should voluntarily enter into a relationship with one who is disabled, and that the latter should have this on-going contact with someone who is neither disabled him or herself nor in the role of someone who is paid to be with the disabled person, is consistent with the general principle of normalisation.

The actual roles which advocates fulfil towards their partners, as observed by those who work in advocacy agencies (Line, Personal Communication) correspond to the major categories of social support which were discussed in

Chapter 4. One is *expressive advocacy*. This involves a commitment on a personal level, and may include sharing friendship, love, warmth, family and friends, interests and hobbies. The role of *instrumental advocate*, on the other hand, may involve being an adviser, helper, and spokesperson on material issues such as finding paid work, overcoming official opposition to marriage, finding a good place to live, social benefits and finances, legal matters, making purchases, making complaints, and helping gain access to medical and dental treatment, education, and other services. Inevitably this sometimes brings the advocate and partner into conflict with professionals and those in official positions. If we were to add to these two roles that of helping the partner obtain important information or knowledge, which seems a very likely accompaniment to the Citizen Advocacy role, then virtually the complete gamut of social support functions is represented.

NEIGHBOURHOOD NETWORKING

Providing someone with an advocate may add a vitally important element to a person's social support network, but it does not consider characteristics of the network as a whole, nor does it consider community or neighbourhood in the sense of a geographically defined group of settings or systems. The remainder of this chapter will address these community issues under the headings of neighbourhood networking, coping with community disasters, and community development.

In psychology, approaches to networking have ranged from the more individualistic to the more socio-cultural. At the first extreme are those who have seen the importance of social support for individuals or families in therapy. For example, Parry (1988) has advocated an approach to therapy with individuals which makes a person's social support one of the principal foci of therapy aiming to enhance the use that the individual makes of his or her informal social network by altering cognition and behaviours which may be hindering such use. In her discussion of ways of mobilising social support, Parry (1988) refers to *family networking* as another, potentially powerful method. Although it has not yet been well evaluated, it has been used, particularly in the USA, with the networks of individuals with apparently very difficult and professional-time-consuming adolescent or adult mental health problems (Schoenferd, Halevy-Martine, Hemley-Van Der Velden and Ruhf, 1985, cited by Parry) including problems of alcohol and drug dependence (Treadway, 1989). The method consists of bringing together as many members as possible of the family and friendship social network. The aim of the process, sometimes referred to as 're-tribalisation', is to facilitate open communication and sharing of information (many members of the network may not have been fully in the picture), to bring about a renewed sense of cohesiveness and hope, and to identify specific resources in the network which may assist in solving the problem.

Nearer to the socio-cultural or macro- end of the micro- to macro-dimension are projects which attempt to modify whole networks. One such project was carried out in a 450-room, single-room occupancy hotel in Manhattan that largely housed older people and former psychiatric patients (Cohen, Adler and Mintz, 1983, cited by Chapman and Pancoast, 1985). Although active social networks within such hotels were not immediately obvious, previous fieldwork had discovered and described such networks. The goal of this project was to sensitise human service workers to the existence of networks in this hotel, to assist staff in understanding residents' behaviour in the context of their social network, and to attempt to deal with all problems raised by clients through the social network rather than through direct assistance. During the 15 months that this project ran, staff worked with over 150 hotel residents on a total of over 500 problems. Interventions involving the informal social network were attempted for almost half of these problems, and in approximately a third of these instances the network interventions were successfully activated. The principal reason for non-activation was the failure to identify a network member who might be able to help with the problem concerned.

Similar was the Tenderloin Project (Minkler, 1981, cited by Parry, 1988). This represents another way of enhancing informal networks amongst the residents of a single-room occupancy hotel in a high-crime area. In this instance increased social contact and mutual aid were facilitated by health workers setting up a health-screening and blood-pressure stall in the hotel lobby. Socialising and mutual help with tasks such as shopping increased, and this process eventually gave rise to the organisation of meetings to discuss rent and living conditions. Parry reports that the project eventually included eight houses linked by a self-help organisation which liaised with the police and city officials in providing protection from crime.

Applied social support work of this kind is clearly still in its infancy and there are many problems to be thought about and solutions to be worked out before it can be said to be firmly established. This line of work is, for a start, based on a number of assumptions: for example that artificially stimulated social support is acceptable to people; that it can substitute for and be as effective as naturally occurring social support; and that it has no harmful effects (Rook and Dooley, 1985). For example, Chapman and Pancoast (1985) pointed out, with reference to the Manhattan project that they described, that some older people were determined *not* to have to rely upon others, and for these people any intervention that attempted to stimulate help from the informal social network would run the risk of being quite contrary to the wishes of those it was aiming to help. Chapman and Pancoast (1985) in addition referred to a number of factors to do with the way agencies them-selves are organised which make this type of work more difficult. One of these is the difficulty encountered with agencies whose work is largely individual person-centred and limited to providing direct services to specific clients. To reorient such agencies to work in a very different way, and with a very different underlying philosophy, is often very difficult. This is, of course, a general theme that recurs regularly throughout the field of community psychology (see Chapter 1).

A point made by several writers on this subject—and again this is a very general point that applies to most of the work described in this book—is that any attempted intervention in a complex social system is likely to have a number of effects, some of them indirect and difficult to predict, and some of them, perhaps, unintended and harmful (Rook and Dooley, 1985; Parry, 1988). Quite apart from possible, unintended, harmful effects upon the person whose social network is being mobilised, there also has to be considered the possibility of harm to individual members of the network in the form of the increased burden which may fall upon them (Rook and Dooley, 1985). Hence there is a responsibility, as in all community psychology, to base any intervention on solid prior understanding of the social systems concerned, and to set the intervention within the framework of an evaluation which is sensitive to detecting both the hoped for benefits and possible harms (Brownell and Shumaker, 1985).

COPING WITH COMMUNITY DISASTERS

A different perspective on neighbourhood networks has been gained by those who have become involved in communities in the aftermath of a collective disaster. These are events that affect the whole of a neighbourhood or community because they are public, there are a large number of casualties within the one area, many people become involved in different capacities, and very many people continue to be distressed afterwards. In Britain, the Aberfan coaltip disaster, the Bradford football stadium fire, and the Hungerford shooting are examples. One such disaster which has been written about in some detail was the Kansas City hotel disaster in which over 100 people were killed and more than 200 injured when two aerial walkways spanning the hotel lobby collapsed in the middle of a crowded tea dance (Gist and Stolz, 1982). These dances were regular and highly popular events and virtually all the victims were local. Most residents of the area either knew at least one person who had been killed or knew someone else who did. Including non-injured guests at the dance, family and friends, other hotel guests, hotel workers, fire fighters, police, doctors, nurses, 'paramedics', volunteers, and media employees, it was estimated at the time that 5000 people might be at immediate risk of adverse psychological consequences.

Although Gist and Stolz presented no formal evaluative data, it appears from their account that an effective strategy to prevent serious, longer-term adverse reactions was very quickly mounted. The disaster occurred on a Friday evening, and by the following Monday local organisations with an interest in mental health, including the area's community mental health centres, had combined to produce a three-point strategy. One component was the provision of support group activities in community mental health centres throughout the area. It was made clear that these services were given free of charge and that those attending would not be enrolled as centre clients. The second element was the mounting of training, given by CMHC staff and University faculty, for all those who might be called upon to provide care or support. The third component was what appears to have been a very thorough and maintained media campaign which aimed to publicise the availability of services and to put across a consistent message about the normality of expected reactions such as shock and disbelief, a period of automatic action, a period characterised by a sense of accomplishment and exhaustion, and an extended period of assessment and integration during which the total impact of the tragedy is finally felt. It was also stressed that such feelings should be shared and accepted in others. Kits were prepared for the media covering all these points and emphasising the availability of services, a phone line was set up, data press releases and broadcast interviews were held, and a major event was held for purposes of mutual support exactly one week after the tragedy. The media campaign continued for several weeks. In the month following the incident, Gist and Stolz reported that more than 500 people had been served by the CMHCs' support groups and almost 200 psychologists, clergy, counsellors, social workers and nurses had attended training programmes. In the nine months following the event, the numbers requesting direct clinical services on account of delayed reactions were reported to be far below that predicted on the basis of previous studies.

Fleming and Baum (1985) discussed the kind of disaster which they term 'technological catastrophe'. The Chernobyl nuclear power station disaster in the USSR and the Bhopal chemical plant catastrophe in India would be major examples of recent years. More has been written from a community psychology perspective, however, about the Three Mile Island nuclear power station catastrophe and the Love Canal chemical dump leakage, both of which occurred in the USA. Such catastrophes are particularly likely to lead to lasting uncertainties over long-term health risks and over the future safety of the plant or waste dump involved (Fleming and Baum, 1985). They are also particularly likely to lead to feelings of loss of control over events in the community which have a major impact on people's lives. They are also likely to bring individual residents into conflict with those who represent officialdom or the vested interests of big business. Trotter (1981) is amongst the many who have discussed the way in which road development, as well as more subtle influences such as public housing policy or lack of private investment, have destroyed neighbourhoods, and how neighbourhood organisations have flourished as antidotes to these anti-neighbourhood policies and trends. According to Trotter, the common thread in these organisations, which often start with concern about a single issue but evolve to become organisations involved in a number of issues, is that,

> their focus is on everyday, immediate, and immediately recognisable problems *as those problems are defined by the people involved.* Defining the problem means owning it, and that is the first step in taking collective responsibility for dealing with it. Pre-packaged remedies are not dictated by distant bureaucrats; clients are not 'serviced' by experts and professionals ... these groups have arisen largely because of the obvious failures of both representative democracy and governmentally mandated citizen participation to meet the needs of the non-rich. (Trotter, 1981, pp. 270, 272, original emphasis)

One of the best documented examples of successful local action over a specific issue was the formation of the Love Canal Homeowner's Association. This association, formed of residents of a small community in New York State, came into being when it was acknowledged by the authorities that the housing estate had been built on the site of a chemical dump which was leaking toxic fumes. Local schools were closed and residents were recommended to restrict the use of their basements and to avoid eating homegrown vegetables. It was revealed that miscarriage rates were higher than normal in the area, and it was suggested that pregnant women, and children under the age of 2, who lived close to the hazard should be moved temporarily (Stone and Levine, 1985). The subsequent history of the association is a success story of neighbourhood activism. The membership consisted of over 500 families, the core 'activists' threw themselves into a highly demanding schedule of campaign work, and the success of the organisation in gaining acceptance as a representative group, fighting bureaucracy, and gaining concessions for residents, was acknowledged both locally and nationally.

In this case local collective action appears to have been more effective than professional mental health intervention, although the local community mental health centre was involved in coordinating agencies to provide services to local residents, and did obtain State funding to employ three outreach workers who were sited in an office within the neighbourhood itself (Hess and Wandersman, 1985). Not that this kind of crisis work was seen as irrelevant. Indeed counsellors appear to have been overworked in attempting to handle the multitude of problems that arose for residents. There appears also to have been a delay in setting up the centre and a lack of coordination between the State government and these local resources.

A published conversation between the President of the Love Canal Homeowner's Association, Lois Gibbs, and a consultant to the crisis centre, Richard Valinsky, is very revealing concerning the coexistence of these two very different forms of response to such a technological disaster—residents' community association and professional crisis centre—and the misperceptions that can arise (Hess and Wandersman, 1985). The professional 'counselling team' that was set up did much to try and dissociate the centre from the 'mental health' tag. They involved local people in training staff, and by no means confined themselves to a structured or traditional counselling format in their work—for example they would run residents to appointments and help residents fill out government forms or deal with a government agency. Nevertheless, it was clearly impossible for them to totally rid themselves of the image of a group who were there to *react* to the results of stress amongst residents rather than to challenge the source of the stress *proactively*. As Lois Gibbs said subsequently:

> Even though the [mental health] sign was taken down, people had filtered through and identified the table as a place to go if you were 'crazy'... . It was sad but it was the reality... . We as a community were told numerous times that this chemical or this disease or this problem was all in our heads, that it was all psychosomatic, and that we were acting out of emotions and hysteria rather than out of logic and reality... even those people who recognised they needed help would call the association and say that they were not going to see anybody because they would just be told that it was all in their heads and was not really deforming children or creating disease. (Hess and Wandersman, 1985, pp. 114–116)

In a study of Love Canal 'activist' and 'non-activist' families, Stone and Levine (1985) found that activists were significantly less likely to report negative personal changes as a result of the crisis and were much more likely to believe that they had had an influence on decisions made about Love Canal. They speculated that for activists, involvement provided a means of feeling more in control of otherwise uncontrollable events, and that the association also served as a self-help group, reducing the worry and anxiety of active residents through shared activities and interpretations of the experience. Many activists were surprised at the extent to which their active membership had entailed a change in personal behaviour and the taking on of new roles and activities. This 'personal growth' that can come about through involvement in citizens' groups is a frequent accompaniment to disasters and their aftermath, particularly for women: engagement in new activities outside the home during World Wars I and II are well known examples, and from the 1980s activism in women's neighbourhood groups in Central Mexico City in the aftermath of the 1985 earthquake, and involvement in community support activities during the coalminers' strike of 1984/85 in Britain, are examples of the same phenomenon.

Stone and Levine were as interested, however, in the non-activists, who were more likely to be older, longer-standing residents, more often renting their properties, with lower incomes, and including more non-white residents. These groups did not benefit personally from their own involvement in the citizens' organisations, and Stone and Levine's general conclusion was that, 'it is not realistic to assume that any one approach to providing helping services, whether by spontaneous citizen groups, or by professional helpers, will be effective for all members of a community in crisis' (1985, p. 176).

COMMUNITY DEVELOPMENT

In his paper, 'From communities to neighbourhoods', Baldwin (1987) recommends a form of neighbourhood work in which people with disabilities are integrated into much smaller geographical areas (up to a few thousand) than are usually implied by the terms 'community' and 'community care'. This is done on the basis of detailed local knowledge, and with the participation of service users and neighbourhood members. He refers to techniques such as: (1) obtaining users' perceptions of their neighbourhoods by asking them to draw maps of the area including their own home (for a useful introduction to the topic of perceptual maps in social geography, see Jones and Eyles, 1977); (2) compiling a neighbourhood resources directory which may include data about housing, other aspects of the physical environment, parks and recreation facilities, churches, clubs and organisations, communications, services, even jumble sales, plus qualitative aspects such as appearance and upkeep, social interaction and networks, values, power and leadership; and (3) the compiling of a neighbourhood workers' directory which lists those key people in the neighbourhood who hold informal and/or formal positions and who may serve as 'gatekeepers' to services or provide substantial amounts of services themselves. He recommends, further, that an agreed plan or contract should be written for each neighbourhood. This should specify both short- and long-term goals, and the principle of consultation and partnership with users and residents should be built into this statement. Baldwin recognises that conflicts of interest are inevitable and suggests that neighbourhood workers should be encouraged to recognise their own needs and to consider their own positions with respect to their employers and their client group.

Baldwin's emphasis upon empirical work, and upon the varying levels at which such neighbourhood work occurs, places his approach squarely within the community psychology tradition:

> A commitment to data collection and hypothesis-testing is ... an essential component of neighbourhood work. This investment in comparative methods and evaluative research is a major departure from the woolly concepts of the so-called community care approach, which does not commit staff to evaluative work ....
>
> Successful neighbourhood work requires a tactical understanding of systems and an appreciation of human behaviour at many levels. ... Units of analysis included for consideration in evaluation research should not fail to include data about individual clients, as well as at the level of the neighbourhood itself. It is this multiple focus upon individuals, groups of users and the neighbourhood itself that provides a major strength of this approach to human services. (Baldwin, 1987, pp. 48–49)

One line of investigation which is particularly relevant to Baldwin's idea of neighbourhood and to issues surrounding community care for people with disabilities of various kinds, is of course the study of quality of life (QOL) which was considered in Chapter 3.

In urban areas in the USA it has been argued that the 'block' is the appropriate unit for community development (Perkins, Florin, Rich, Wandersman and Chavis, 1990). Indeed it was citizen participation in block associations in Nashville and New York which formed the substance of work reported by Chavis and Wandersman (1990) and Perkins *et al.* (1990). A leading concept for this group of community psychologists was that of 'empowerment'.

Empowerment can be defined as: 'A process by which individuals gain mastery or control over their own lives and democratic participation in the life of their community' (Zimmerman and Rappaport, 1988, cited by Chavis and Wandersman, 1990). Note that this definition refers to individuals and the community. It is, thus, another concept—vital for community psychology—which links person and context. As with all such concepts—social support was another (see Chapter 4)—there is the danger that empowerment will be given largely individualistic connotations (Chavis and Wandersman, 1990). Perkins *et al.* (1990) feel:

> that empowerment, even at the psychological level, should have a clear communitarian, or collectivist, orientation. This would have the conceptual benefit of distinguishing empowerment from self-efficacy and internal locus of control. It might also have the practical benefit of focussing interventions on collective action, which is likely to be more effective than individual action in solving collective problems. (p. 108)

Nevertheless, the concept of empowerment and the issue of participation in block associations provides an ideal setting for studying multilevel person–environment interactions and reciprocal influences over time (Florin and Wandersman, 1990)—just the kinds of things that are so difficult to study but which have come up repeatedly throughout this book.

Like Stone and Levine (1985) at Love Canal, Chavis and Wandersman (1990) were interested in determining who participated in community action, in this case in block associations in urban Nashville. In an initial, cross-sectional study, they found support for a path model suggesting that a felt 'sense of community' (Do you feel a sense of community with others on this block? How important is it to you to feel a sense of community with the people on the block?) was of central importance in predicting level of participation in block associations (non-member versus member versus worker versus leader) and that this influence was mediated by 'neighbouring relations' (e.g. How many people who live on your block would you recognise? How many people on this block do you see socially at least three or four times a year? With how many people on your block would you feel comfortable talking about a personal problem? Asking to watch your house while you are away?). In a second study that involved repeat interviews one year later, the reciprocal influence of felt sense of community, and participation became apparent: participation at time 1 was strongly predictive of change in felt sense of community, as was sense of community at time 1 predictive of change in participation.

The foregoing analysis remains at the individual level. Perkins *et al.*'s (1990) analysis of participation was at the block level. They were interested in differences in the activity levels of different block associations in certain chosen neighbourhoods in New York. They found activity levels to be associated with both permanent and transient physical features of the block environment and aspects of the social climate as experienced by block residents. For example, activity level was lower when the block area contained trees and gardens and when there were physical barriers such as fences on (rather than round the edge of) the property, but was greater when the general level of satisfaction with the block was higher. These same researchers were involved in the Block Booster Project in which they collaborated with block associations and with a 'community technical assistance organisation' whose purpose was to support and promote the efforts of volunteer neighbourhood groups in New York. The aim of the collaboration was to understand the role of block associations in community development and crime control, and to develop techniques to help voluntary organisations of this kind (Prestby, Wandersman, Florin, Rich and Chavis, 1990). In an interesting article, Kaye (1990), a community organiser working for the technical assistance organisation involved in this collaboration, has written about the advantages and difficulties of such a research-practice link in community work. She describes how fruitful this collaboration was in developing training for community leaders and in developing ideas about the ways community groups could be best facilitated. On the negative side, she writes of the way in which research findings, as they became available, took on an 'untouchable' and difficult-to-challenge quality, seeming to take precedence over many years of wisdom accumulated by community development practitioners. The presence of researchers in the organisation's office itself, and the researchers' sensitivity to this and other such issues contributed to the maintenance of the collaboration.

For further advances in psychological theory and practice applied to community organisation and development we may need to look to developing countries. In such countries the existence of continuing rather than time-limited crises, the relative scarcity of advanced health, education and other human services for individuals and families, and the inappropriateness of much existing psychological theory and practice, are all more starkly obvious than in the 'developed' countries where most psychological research and writing has been carried out. Mexico will serve as an example since it is a country with which the author is familiar and which possesses a number of characteristics that lend themselves to the development of an active community psychology. The following draws heavily upon a review of community social psychology in Mexico by Reid and Aguilar (1991).

Although Mexico's economy strengthened greatly up to the 1970s, the 1980s was a decade of economic crisis, massive devaluation of the currency, and crippling foreign debt. The major earthquake of November 1985 contributed to a worsening of morale and the economy. As well as migration across the border into the USA to seek work or higher wages, there has been massive internal migration to the cities, and hence phenomenal changes to communities in and around the main urban areas. The government has not had the resources to invest sufficiently in public services such as housing, health and education, and there still exist massive inequalities in standards of living and access to services and resources. Added to this is a growing consciousness of the country's rich and mixed heritage—both native pre-colonial and colonial European—and of the deprived conditions and status of the country's large minority of indigenous peoples (Bonfil Batalla, 1987; Reid and Aguilar, 1991).

It is against this background that a form of community psychology is developing in a number of parts of the country, usually based upon university departments of psychology working with a local community and simultaneously developing new theories and style of practice which support this work. A number of such joint university-community development projects are described by Reid and Aguilar (1991) in their review. Other examples are to be found in two volumes of proceedings of conferences on social psychology in Mexico, held in 1986 and 1988 (LaPsicología Social en México, 1986; 1988).

One of the main principles that emerges from this work is the importance of community members themselves making their own evaluation of their community and its problems, and of coming to their own understanding (the process of *autodiagnostico*). This is a process already familiar to us in the form of action research (see Chapter 9) and is the same point discussed above in relation to Love Canal in the USA. In Mexico, according to Reid and Aguilar, this has often meant a shift in research methods, towards more participant and more qualitative methods, and sometimes a more radical deprofessionalising of research and the sharing of research skills with community members.

One of the best known Mexican community projects, which has achieved international recognition since it started in the early 1970s, is the collaboration between the people of San Miguel Tzinacapan, a small Nahuat village in the Sierra Norte in the State of Puebla, and the faculty of psychology at the National Autonomous University of Mexico (UNAM) in Mexico City (Almeida, Sanchez, Soto, Felix, Perez, Osorio and Morales, 1986; Reid and Aguilar, 1991). The work of the project, which involves a small number of urban professionals who live in the village, is coordinated by a non-governmental village-based organisation organisation called PRADE (Project of Dynamisation and Development) and a number of other local organisations that have been set up under the aegis of the project for special purposes (e.g. a society for rural production). The achievements of the project appear to have been very considerable, and there is no doubt that it has attracted much attention. Of central importance has been the growth of a now considerable group (around 20) of local researchers, plus the full way in which the project has been documented in the form of analyses of formal and informal group discussions and through other special means such as diaries of events and group autobiographies (*autobiografías razonades*) (Almeida *et al.*, 1986). As in other community projects in Mexico, the exploration, through special workshops, of oral and documented tradition, has contributed an important historial element.

Other community projects include the action research programme operated by the University of Coahuila in part of the industrial urban area of Saltillo in the north of Mexico. Four independent, self-sufficient urban community centres, run by non-government organisations with the university's support, have grown from this project (Reid and Aguilar, 1991). The programme covers five areas: health and nutrition, family planning, sex education, work and ecology. It involves 10 professionals, 6 university students, 14 community coordinators who are recruited from the communities and receive 18 months training, and a total of over 200 local voluntary community promoters.

Discovering the collective history of the area, as well as of ethnic minority groups included amongst its present-day residents, has been an important part of many of these projects. It also figured large in an innovative project focused on the mental health of women living on a housing estate in west London. The project is described by Holland (1988), whose unusual background as both psychotherapist and someone with experience of community action in another part of London gave her the basis for helping to set up a mental health service with a rare mixture of ingredients.

The housing estate concerned was stigmatised as, 'the end-of-the-line for people who have failed to find anywhere better: the homeless, displaced immigrants, unemployed, single mothers, black and ethnic minority people, as well as the original English families who first moved in when the estate was a "showcase" for the white working classes' (p. 134). Amongst the women residents there was a high rate of depression which was generally viewed in a highly individualised way and treated with psychoactive medication upon which they had often become dependent. The project that Holland describes combined, 'intensive focal psychotherapy, group work, mental health education and the stimulation of mutual-help initiatives within the neighbourhood' (p. 131). Women move from an initial period of a few months engagement in individual therapy to an involvement in groups which aim to locate women's mental health within the context of family and society. From this has developed collective social action in which women have been effective in changing things in their local environment and raising mental health as a *social* issue within the estate.

The women are seen as moving from a position in which they view their private troubles in terms of individual symptoms, through a stage at which they question the origins of their mental health difficulties, to a further stage at which they ask what changes they desire of themselves and for others, and finally to a radical structuralist position at which they are able to engage in social action to alter conditions that make them and others vulnerable to psychological difficulties. As Holland puts it: 'This progression within a neighbourhood therapy programme, could be described in terms of trying to move the depressed women through psychic space into social space and so into political space' (p. 134). Like Ramon (1988), she is critical of the recent British community mental health movement for failing to take on new models such as these:

> none of the issues concerning the effects on mental health of the environment, work, housing, poverty, racism, sexism, ageism, are considered to be appropriate subjects for preventive action. (p. 127)
>
> Prevention must ... be addressed to both the internalised social structures of the human psyche and the external social structures of society and state. The prescriptions of 'treatment' which follow from such a model include both psychotherapeutic intervention at the psychic level, and political action at the structural level. (p. 126)

The data necessary to evaluate this highly innovative and attractive approach are not available, but there can be little doubting its relevance for the development of community psychology theory and practice. Its main theme, that of reconciling the psychic and the social, the private and the public, the person and her social context, has recurred throughout this book and is the central issue for community psychology.

References

Ablon J. (1982). The parents' auxiliary of little people of America: a self-help model of social support for families of short-statured children. In: *Helping People to Help Themselves: Self-Help and Prevention. Prevention in Human Services*. New York: Haworth, 1 (3), pp. 31–46.

Albee G. (1968). Conceptual models and manpower requirements in psychology. *Amer. Psychol.*, **23**, 317–320.

Allen G., Chinsky J., Larcen S., Lockmann J. and Selinger H. (1976). *Community Psychology and the Schools: A Behaviorally Oriented Multilevel Preventive Approach*. Hillsdale, NJ: Erlbaum.

Allen L. and Britt D. (1983). Social class, mental health, and mental illness: the impact of resources and feedback. In: R. Felner, L. Jason, J. Moritsugu and S. Farber (Eds) *Preventive Psychology: Theory, Research and Practice*. New York: Pergamon, pp. 149–161.

Alley S., Blanton J. and Feldman R. (Eds) (1985). *Paraprofessionals in Mental Health: Theory and Practice*. New York: Hum. Sci. Press, Ch. 10.

Almeida E., Sanchez M., Soto B., Felix L., Perez V., Osorio M. and Morales J. (1986). La Investigación Participativa y sus efectos en una región de la sierra norte de Puebla. In: *La Psicología Social en México*, Vol. I. Mexico City: Asociación Mexicana de Psicología Social.

Anderson C., Hogarty G., Bayer T. and Needleman R. (1984). Expressed emotion and social networks of parents of schizophrenic patients. *Brit. J. Psychiat.*, **144**, 247–255.

Andrews F. and Inglehart R. (1979). The structure of subjective well-being in nine western societies. *Soc. Indicators Res.*, **6**, 73–90.

Andrews F. and Withey S. (1976). *Social Indicators of Well-Being*. New York: Plenum Press.

Aneshensel C. and Frerichs R. (1982). Stress, support and depression: a longitudinal causal model. *J. of Community Psychol.*, **10**, 363–376.

Apte R. (1968). *Halfway Houses: a New Dilemma in Institutional Care*. London: Bell.

Argyris C., Putnam R. and Smith D. (1985). *Action Science*. San Francisco: Jossey-Bass.

Asher H. (1983). *Causal Modeling*. Beverly Hills: Sage.

Atkinson T., Liem R. and Liem J. (1986). The social costs of unemployment: implications for social support. *J. of Health and Soc. Behav.*, **27**, 317–331.

Bachrach P. and Baratz M. (1962). The two faces of power. *Amer. Polit. Sci. Rev.*, **56**, 947–952 (cited by Wrong, 1979).

Bagley C. (1968). The evaluation of a suicide prevention scheme by an ecological method. *Soc. Sci. and Med.*, **2**, 1–14.

Baldwin S. (1987). From communities to neighbourhoods—I. *Disability, Handicap & Society*, **2**, 41–59.

Baldwin S. (1989). Applied behaviour analysis and normalization: new carts for old horses? A commentary. *Behav. Psychother.*, **17**, 305–308.

Banks M. and Ullah P. (1988). *Youth Unemployment in the 1980s: its Psychological Effects*. London: Croom Helm.

Barker R. (1968). *Ecological Psychology: Concepts and Methods for Studying the Environment of Human Behaviour*. Stanford, California: Stanford University Press.

Barker R. and Associates (1978). *Habitats, Environments, and Human Behavior*. San Francisco: Jossey-Bass.

Barker R. and Gump P. (Eds) (1964). *Big School, Small School*. Stanford, California: Stanford University Press.

Barlow D., Hayes S. and Nelson R. (1984). *The Scientist Practitioner: Research and Accountability in Clinical and Educational Settings*. New York: Pergamon.

Barrera M. and Ainlay S. (1983). The structure of social support: a conceptual and empirical analysis. *J. of Community Psychol.*, **11**, 133–143.

Barton L. (1986). The politics of special educational needs. *Disability, Handicap and Society*, **1**, 273–290.

Barton R. (1959, third edition 1976). *Institutional Neurosis*. Bristol: Wright.

Bebbington P., Hurry J., Tennant C., Sturt E. and Wing J. (1981). Epidemiology of mental disorders in Camberwell. *Psychol. Med.*, **11**, 561–579.

Bechtel R. (1984). Patient and community: the ecological bond. In: W. O'Connor and B. Lubin (Eds) *Ecological Approaches to Clinical and Community Psychology*. New York: Wiley, Ch. 10.

Bender M. (1976). *Community Psychology*. London: Methuen.

Bennett L., Wolin S. and Reiss D. (1988). Deliberate family process: a strategy for protecting children of alcoholics. *Brit. J. of Addict.*, **83**, 821–829.

Berkman L.F. (1985). The relationship of social networks and social support to morbidity and mortality. In: S. Cohen and S. Syme (Eds) *Social Support and Health*. New York: Academic Press, pp. 241–262.

Berrueta-Clement J., Schweinhart L., Barnett W., Epstein A. and Weikart D. (1984). *Changed Lives: the Effects of the Perry Preschool Program on Youths through Age 19*. Ypsilanti, MI: High/Scope Press (cited by Levine and Perkins, 1987).

Biernacki P. (1986). *Pathways from Heroin Addiction*. Philadelphia, PA: Temple University Press.

Birchwood M. and Smith J. (1987). Schizophrenia and the family. In: J. Orford (Ed.) *Coping with Disorder in the Family*. London: Croom Helm, Ch. 2.

Blackburn H., Luepker R., Kline F. *et al.* (1982). The Minnesota heart health program: a research and demonstration project in cardiovascular disease prevention. In: *Handbook of Psychology and Health*, Ch. 86.

Blanton J. and Alley S. (1977). Models of program success in new careers programs. *J. of Community Psychol.*, **5**, 350–371.

Bliwise N. and Lieberman M. (1984). From professional help to self-help: an evaluation of therapeutic groups for the elderly. In: A Gartner and F. Riessman (Eds) *The Self-Help Revolution*. New York: Human Sciences Press, Ch. 17.

Bloom B. (1968). The evaluation of primary prevention programs. In: L. Roberts, N. Greenfield and M. Miller (Eds) *Comprehensive Mental Health: The Challenge of Evaluation*. Madison: University of Wisconsin Press.

Bloom B. (1977). *Community Mental Health: a General Introduction*. Monterey, California: Brooks/Cole.

Bloom B., Asher S. and White S. (1978). Marital disruption as a stressor: a review and analysis. *Psychol. Bull.*, **84**, 867–894.

Bloom B. and Asher S. (1982). Patient rights and patient advocacy: a historical and conceptual appreciation. In: B. Bloom and S. Asher (Eds) *Psychiatric Patient Rights and Patient Advocacy*. Vol. VII. Community Psychol. Series.

de Board R. (1978) *The Psychoanalysis of Organizations: a Psychoanalytic Approach to Behaviour in Groups and Organizations*. London: Tavistock.

Bolton W. and Oatley K. (1987). A longitudinal study of social support and depression in unemployed men. *Psychol. Med.*, **17**, 453–460.

Bonfil Batalla G. (1987). *México Profundo: una Civilización Negada*. Mexico City: Secretaria de Educación Pública Centro de Investigaciones y Estudios Superiores en Antropología.

Borkman T. (1990). Self-help groups at the turning point: emerging egalitarian alliances with the formal health care system: *Amer. J. of Community Psychol.*, **18**, 321–332.

Borman L. (1982). Introduction. In: *Helping People to Help Themselves: Self-Help and Prevention. Prevention in Human Services*. New York: Haworth, 1 (3), pp. 3–15.

Boss R. (1979). It doesn't matter if you win or lose, unless you're losing: organizational change in law enforcement agency. *J. of App. Behav. Sci.*, **15**, 198–220 (cited by Gallessich, 1982).

Bowey A.M. (1980). Approaches to organisational theory. In: M. Lockett and R. Spear (Eds) *Organisations as Systems*. Milton Keynes: Open University Press.

Boyce, W. (1985). Social support, family relations, and children. In: S. Cohen and S. Syme (Eds) *Social Support and Health*. San Francisco: Academic Press.

Boyce W., Kay M. and Uitti C. (1988). The taxonomy of social support: an ethnographic analysis among adolescent mothers. *Soc. Sci. and Med.*, **26**, 1079–1985.

Brenner S-O. and Starrin B. (1988). Unemployment and health in Sweden: public issues and private troubles. *J. Soc. Issues*, **44**, 125–140.

Briner R. and Hockey G. (1988). Operator stress and computer-based work. In: C. Cooper and R. Payne (Eds) *Causes, Coping and Consequences of Stress at Work*. Chichester: Wiley.

Bromley D. (1986). *The Case-Study Method in Psychology and Related Disciplines*. Chichester: Wiley.

Bronfenbrenner U. (1979). *The Ecology of Human Development: Experiments by Nature and Design*. Cambridge, Massachusetts: Harvard University Press.

Brown A. (1984). *Consultation: an Aid to Successful Social Work*. London: Heinemann.

Brown B. (1986). Services for adolescents. In: H. Koch (Ed.) *Community Clinical Psychology*. London: Croom Helm, Ch. 2.

Brown, G., Birley J. and Wing J. (1972). Influence of family life on the course of schizophrenic disorders: a replication. *British Journal of Psychiatry*, **121**, 241–258.

Brown G. and Harris T. (1978). *The Social Origins of Depression*. London: Tavistock.

Brown G. and Prudo R. (1981). Psychiatric disorder in a rural and an urban population: 1. Etiology of depression. *Psychol. Med.*, **11**, 581–599.

Brownell A. and Shumaker S. (1985). Where do we go from here? The policy implications of social support. *J. of Soc. Issues*, **41**, 111–121.

Bryman A., Bresmen M., Beardsworth A. and Keil T. (1988). Qualitative research and the study of leadership. *Hum. Relat.*, **41**, 13–30.

Buckley W. (1980). Systems. In: M. Lockett and R. Spear (Eds) *Organisations as Systems*. Milton Keynes: Open University Press.

Butler K. (1987). Citizen advocacy in action. *New Society*, 24 April.

Campbell A., Converse P. and Rodgers W. (1976). *The Quality of American Life*. New York: Russel Sage Foundation.

Campbell D. and Stanley J. (1963). Experimental and quasi-experimental designs for research on teaching. In: N. Gage (Ed.) *Handbook of Research on Teaching*. Chicago: Rand McNally.

Campbell E., Cope S. and Teasdale J. (1983). Social factors and affective disorder: an investigation of Brown and Harris' model. *Brit. J. of Psychiat.*, **143**, 548–553.

Caplan G. (1964). *Principles of Preventive Psychiatry*. New York: Basic Books.

Caplan G. (1970). *The Theory and Practice of Mental Health Consultation*. London: Tavistock.

Cartwright A. (1980). The attitudes of helping agents towards the alcoholic client: the influence of experience, support, training and self-esteem. *Brit. J. of Addict.*, **75**, 413–431.

Cassell S. (1965). Effect of brief puppet therapy upon the emotional responses of children undergoing cardiac catheterization. *J. of Consulting Psychol.*, **29**, 1–8 (cited by Heller *et al.*, 1984).

Catalano R. and Dooley D. (1980). Economic change in primary prevention. In: R. Price, R. Ketterer, B. Bader and J. Monahan (Eds) *Prevention in Mental Health: Research Policy and Practice*. London: Sage.

Caudill W. (1958). *The Psychiatric Hospital as a Small Society*. Harvard: Harvard University Press.

Chapman N. and Pancoast D. (1985). Working with the informal helping networks of the elderly: the experiences of three programs. *J. of Soc. Issues*, **41**, 47–64.

Chavis D. and Wandersman A. (1990). Sense of community in the urban environment: a catalyst for participation and community development. *Amer. J. of Community Psychol.* **18**, 55–82.

Cherniss C. (1980a). *Professional Burnout in Human Service Organisations*. New York: Praeger.

Cherniss C. (1980b). Human service programs as work organisations: using organizational design to improve staff motivation and effectiveness. In R. Price and P. Politser (Eds), *Evaluation and Action in the Social Environment*. New York: Academic Press.

Cicirelli V., Cooper W. and Granger R. (1969). The impact of Head Start: An evaluation of the effects of Head Start experience on children's cognitive and affective development. Athens, OH: Westinghouse Learning Corporation and Ohio University (cited by Lloyd and Bettencourt, 1986).

Clark A. (1976). *Experimenting with Organisational Life: the Action Research Approach*. New York: Plenum (cited by Ketterer *et al.*, 1980).

Clement S. (1987). The Salford experiment: an account of the community alcohol team approach. In: T. Stockwell and S. Clement (Eds) *Helping the Problem Drinker: New Initiatives in Community Care*. London: Croom Helm, Ch. 6.

Clement S. (1989). The Community Drug Team: lessons from alcohol and handicap services. In: G. Bennett (Ed.) *Treating Drug Abusers*. London: Tavistock/Routledge.

Cobb S. (1976). Social support as a moderator of life stress. *Psychosomatic Med.*, **38**, 300–314.

Cochrane R. (1983). *The Social Creation of Mental Illness*. London: Longman.

Cochrane R. and Stopes-Roe M. (1980). Factors affecting the distribution of psychological symptoms in urban areas of England. *Acta Psychiat. Scand.*, **61**, 445–460.

Cohen C., Adler A. and Mintz J. (1983). Network interventions on the margin: a service experiment in a welfare hotel. In: D. Pancoast, P. Parker and C. Froland (Eds) *Rediscovering Self-Help: Its Role in Social Care*. Beverly Hills, California: Sage, pp. 67–88.

Cohen S. and Syme S. (Eds) (1985). *Social Support and Health*. New York: Academic Press.

Cohen S. and Wills T. (1985). Stress, social support and the buffering hypothesis. *Psychol. Bull.*, **98**, 310–357.

The Community Psychologist (1987). A survey of graduate education in community psychology. *The Community Psychologist* (official publication of Division 27 of the American Psychological Association), **20**, Summer.

Comstock C. (1982). Preventive processes in self-help groups: parents anonymous. In: *Helping People to Help Themselves: Self-Help and Prevention. Prevention in Human Services*. New York: Haworth, 1 (3), pp. 47–53.

Cook T. and Campbell D. (1979). *Quasi-experimentation: Design and Analysis Issues for Field Settings*. Chicago: Rand McNally.

Cope D. (1981). *Organisation Development and Action Research in Hospitals*. Aldershot, Hants: Gower.

Corrie M. and Zaklukiewicz S. (1978). Qualitative research and case-study approaches: an introduction. In: J. Bynner and K. Stribley (Eds) *Social Research: Principles and Procedures*. London: Longman/Open University, Ch. 7.

Costello C. (1982). Social factors associated with depression: a retrospective community study. *Psychol. Med.*, **12**, 329–339.

Cowen E. (1980). The Community Context. In: P. Feldman and J. Orford (Eds) *Psychological Problems: the Social Context*. Chichester: Wiley, Ch. 11.

Cowen E. (1982). Help is where you find it. *Amer. Psychol.*, **37**, 385–395.

Cowen E., Pederson A., Babigian H., Izzo L. and Trost M. (1973). Long-term follow-up of early detected vulnerable children. *J. of Consult. and Clin. Psychol.*, **41**, 438–446.

Cronkite R., Moos R. and Finney J. (1984). The context of adaptation: an integrative perspective on community and treatment environments. In: W. O'Connor and B. Lubin (Eds) *Ecological Approaches to Clinical and Community Psychology*. New York: Wiley, Ch. 9.

Cubbon J. (1984). The emergence of mental handicap registers. *Mental Handicap*, **12**, 137–138.

Cubbon J. (1985). Integrating mental handicap registers with service provision. *Mental Handicap*, **13**, 60–61.

Dahl R. (1957). The concept of power. *Behav. Sci.*, **2**, 201–215 (cited by Ng, 1980).

Dahrendorf R. (1959). *Class and Class Conflict in Industrial Society*. Stanford, California: Stanford University Press (cited by Wrong, 1979).

Dahrendorf R. (1968). *Essays on the Theory of Society*. Stanford, California: Stanford University Press (cited by Wrong, 1979).

Daniels V., Somers M., Orford J. and Kirby B. (1991). Can risk drinking amongst medical patients be reduced? The effectiveness of computer screening and feedback and a self-help book. *Behav. Psychoth.* (in press).

Darlington R., Royce J., Snipper A., Murray H. and Lazar I. (1980). Preschool programs and later school competence of children from low income families. *Science*, **208**, 202–204.

D'Aunno T., Klein D. and Susskind E. (1985) Seven approaches for the study of community phenomena. In: E. Susskind and D. Klein (Eds) *Community Research: Methods, Paradigms and Applications*. New York: Praeger, Ch. 10.

Davidson S. (1976). Planning and co-ordination of social services in multi-organisational contexts. *Soc. Ser. Rev.*, **50**, 117–137 (cited by M. Payne, 1982).

Davis K. and Moore W. (1945). Some principles of stratification. *Amer. Sociol. Rev.*, **10**, 242–249. (cited by Ragan and Wales, 1980).

Deflem M. (1989). From anomie to anomia and anomic depression: a sociological critique on the use of anomie in psychiatric research. *Soc. Sci. and Med.*, **29**, 627–634.

Delaney J., Seidman E. and Willis G. (1978). Crisis intervention and the prevention of institutionalisation. *Amer. J. Community Psychol.*, **6**, 33–45.

Dicken C., Bryson R. and Kass N. (1977) Companionship Therapy: a replication in experimental community pychology. *J. of Consult. and Clin. Psychol.*, **4**, 637–646.

Dixon D., Heppner P., Petersen, C. and Ronning R. (1979). Problem-solving workshop training. *Journal of Counseling Psychology*, **26**, 133–139 (cited by Durlak, 1983).

Dobash R. and Dobash R. (1987). Violence towards wives. In: J. Orford (Ed.) *Coping with Disorder in the Family*. London: Croom Helm, Ch. 8.

Dohrenwend B.P. and Dohrenwend B. (1969). *Social Status and Psychological Disorder: a Causal Inquiry*. New York: Wiley (cited by Bebbington *et al.*, 1981).

Dooley D. (1985). Causal inference in the study of social support. In: S. Cohen and S. Syme (Eds) *Social Support and Health*. New York: Academic Press, pp. 109–128.

Dooley D. and Catalano R. (1988). Recent research on the psychological effects of unemployment. *J. of Soc. Issues*, **44**, 1–12.

Durkheim E. (1952). *Suicide: a Study in Sociology* (translated by Simpson G.). Glencoe Illinois: The Free Press (originally published in 1897, cited by Deflem, 1989).

Durlak J. (1979). Comparative effectiveness of para-professional and professional helpers. *Psychol. Bull.*, **86**, 80–92.

Durlak J. (1981). Evaluating comparative studies of para-professional and professional helpers: a reply to Nietzel and Fisher. *Psychol. Bull.*, **89**, 566–569.

Durlak J. (1982). Training programs for para-professionals: guidelines and issues. In: A. Jeger and R. Slotnick (Eds) *Community Mental Health and Behavioral Ecology: Handbook of Theory, Research and Practice*. New York: Plenum Press.

Durlak J. (1983). Social problem-solving as a primary prevention strategy. In: R. Felner, L. Jason, J. Moritsugu and S. Farber (Eds) *Preventive Psychology: Theory, Research and Practice*. New York: Plenum, Ch. 3.

Dustin D. and Blocher D. (1984). Theories and models of consultation. In: S. Brown and R. Lent (Eds) *Handbook of Counseling Psychology*. New York: Wiley.

Duverger M. (1966). *The Idea of Politics: the Uses of Power in Society*. London: Methuen (cited by Ng, 1980).

D'Zurilla, T. and Goldfried, M. (1971). Problem solving and behaviour modification. *J. Abnorm. Psychol.*, **78**, 107–126.

Edmundson E., Bedell J. and Gordon R. (1984). The community network development project: bridging the gap between professional aftercare and self-help. In: A. Gartner and F. Riessman (Eds) *The Self-Help Revolution*. New York: Human Sciences Press, Ch. 15.

Egbert L., Battit G., Welch C. and Bartlett M. (1964). Reduction of post-operative pain by encouragement and instruction of patients. *New England J. of Med.*, **270**, 825–827 (cited by Heller *et al.*, 1984).

Eiser C. (1987) Chronic disease in childhood. In: J. Orford (Ed.) *Coping with Disorder in the Family*. London: Croom Helm, Ch. 10.

Elias M., Gara M., Ubriaco M., Rothbaum P., Clabby J. and Schuyler T. (1986). Impact of a preventive social problem solving intervention on children's coping with middle-school stressors. *Amer. J. of Community Psychol.*, **14**, 259–276.

Endler N. and Magnusson D. (1976). Toward an interactional psychology of personality. *Psychol. Bull.*, **83**, 956–974.

Fairweather G. (Ed.) (1964). *Social Psychology in Treating Mental Illness*. New York: Wiley.

Fairweather G., Sanders D., Maynard H. and Cressler D. (1969). *Community Life for the Mentally Ill: an Alternative to Institutional Care*. Chicago: Aldine.

Fairweather G., Sanders D. and Tonatsky L. (1974). *Creating Change in Mental Health Organisations*. New York: Pergamon.

Farber S., Felner R. and Primavera J. (1985). Parental separation/divorce and adolescents: an examination of factors mediating adaptation. *Amer. J. of Community Psychol.*, **13**, 171–186.

Faris R. and Dunham W. (1939). *Mental Disorders in Urban Areas*. Chicago: University of Chicago Press.

Farquhar J., Fortmann S., Maccoby N. *et al.* (1982). The Stanford Five City Project: an overview. In: *Handbook of Psychology and Health*, Ch. 84.

Farquhar J., Maccoby N. and Wood P. *et al.* (1977). Community education for cardiovascular health. *Lancet*, **1**, 1192–1195.

Feiger S. and Schmitt M. (1979). Collegiality in interdisciplinary health teams: its measurement and its effects. *Soc. Sci. and Med.*, **13**, 217–229.

Feldman S. (1978). Promises, promises or community mental health services and training: ships that pass in the night. *Community Ment. Health J.*, **14**, 83–91.

Fiedler F. (1967). *A Theory of Leadership Effectiveness*. New York: McGraw Hill (cited by Katz and Kahn, 1978).

Figg J. and Ross A. (1981). Analysing a school system: a practical exercise. In: B. Gillham (Ed.) *Problem Behaviour in the Secondary School*. London: Croom Helm, Ch. 10.

Fiore J., Coppel D., Becker J. and Cox G. (1986). Social support as a multifaceted concept: examination of important dimensions for adustment. *Amer. J. of Community Psychol.*, **14**, 93–112.

Fiorelli J. S. (1988). Power in work groups: team members' perspectives. *Hum. Rel.*, **41**, 1–12.

Fleming I. and Baum A. (1985). The role of prevention in technological catastrophe. In: A. Wandersman and R. Hess (Eds) *Beyond the Individual: Environmental Approaches and Prevention*. New York: Haworth Press.

Florin P. and Wandersman A. (1990). An introduction to citizen participation, voluntary organizations, and community development: insights for empowerment through research. *Amer. J of Community Psychol.*, **18**, 41–54.

Folkman S. and Lazarus R. (1980). An analysis of coping in a middle-aged community sample. *J. of Health and Soc. Behav.*, **21**, 219–239.

Frazier P. and Horowitz A. (1986). Prevention of oral disease. In: B. Edelstein and L. Michelson (Eds) *Handbook of Prevention*. New York: Plenum Press.

Freeman H. (1984a). Housing. In: H. Freeman (Ed.) *Mental Health and the Environment*. London: Churchill Livingstone, Ch. 7.

Freeman H. (1984b). The scientific background. In: H. Freeman (Ed.) *Mental Health and the Environment*. London: Churchill Livingstone, Ch. 2.

French J. and Raven B. (1960). The bases of social power. In: D. Cartwright and A. Zander (Eds) *Group Dynamics: Research and Theory*. New York: Row, Peterson, second edition, pp. 607–623.

French J., Rogers W. and Cobb S. (1981) A model of person-environment fit. In: L. Levi (Ed.) *Society, Stress and Disease*. Vol. 5. *Ageing and Old Age*. Oxford: Oxford University Press.

Furnell J., Flett S. and Clark D. (1987). Multi-disciplinary clinical teams: some issues in establishment and function. *Hospital and Health Service Rev.*, 15–18.

Gallessich J. (1982). *The Prevention and Practice of Consultation*. San Francisco: Jossey-Bass.

Ganster D. and Victor B. (1988). The impact of social support on mental and physical health. *Brit. J. of Med. Psychol.*, **61**, 17–36.

Garbarino J. (1982). *Children and Families in the Social Environment*. New York: Aldine.

Gath G., Cooper B., Gattoni F. and Rockett D. (1977). *Child Guidance and Delinquency in a London Borough*. London: Oxford University Press.

Geller E. (1986). Prevention of environmental problems. In: B. Edelstein and L. Michelson (Eds) *Handbook of Prevention*. New York: Plenum Press.

Georgiades N. and Phillimore L. (1975). The myth of the hero-innovator and alternative strategies for organizational change. In: C. Kiernan and E. Woodford (Eds) *Behaviour Modification with the Severely Retarded*. Amsterdam: Elsevier.

Gilhooly M. (1987). Senile dementia and the family. In: J. Orford (Ed.) *Coping with Disorder in the Family*. London: Croom Helm, Ch. 7.

Gillham B. (Ed.) (1981). *Problem Behaviour in the Secondary School*. London: Croom Helm.

Gist R. and Stolz S. (1982). Mental health promotion and the media: community response to the Kansas City hotel disaster. *Amer. Psychol.*, **37**, 1136–1139.

Glaser B. and Strauss A. (1967). *The Discovery of Grounded Theory*. Chicago: Aldine.

Goffman E. (1961). *Asylums: Essays on the Social Situation of Mental Patients and Other Inmates*. New York: Anchor Books, Doubleday & Co.

Goldberg D. and Huxley P. (1980). *Mental Illness in the Community: the Pathway to Psychiatric Care*. London: Tavistock.

Goldstein H. (1980). Review of Fifteen Thousand Hours by M. Rutter *et al. J. of Child Psychol. and Psychiat.*, **21**, 364–365.

Goldthorpe J. and Hope K. (1974). *The Social Grading of Occupations: A New Approach and Scale*. London: Oxford University Press (cited by Bebbington *et al.*, 1981).

Good D. and Watts F. (1989). Qualitative Research. In: G. Parry and F. Watts (Eds) *Behavioural and Mental Health Research: a Handbook of Skills and Methods*. Hove and London: Lawrence Erlbaum.

Goodman G. (1972). *Companionship Therapy: Studies in Structured Intimacy*. San Francisco: Jossey-Bass.

Goodman S. (1984a). Children of disturbed parents: a research based model for intervention. In: B. Cohler and J. Musick (Eds) *Interventions with Psychiatrically Disturbed Parents and their Young Children*. San Francisco: Jossey-Bass.

Goodman S. (1984b). Children of disturbed parents: the interface between research and intervention. *Amer. J. of Community Psychol.*, **12**, 663–688.

Gottlieb B. (1982). Mutual-help groups: members' views of their benefits and of roles for professionals. In: *Helping People to Help Themselves: Self-Help and Prevention. Prevention in Human Services*. New York: Haworth, Vol. 1(3), 55–67.

Gottlieb B. (1985). Social support and community mental health. In: S. Cohen and S. Syme (Eds) *Social Support and Health*. New York: Academic Press, pp. 303–326.

Gove W. (1972) Sex roles, marital roles and mental illness. *Social Forces*, **51**, 34–44.

Grygier T. (1975). Measurement of treatment potential: its rationale, method and some results in Canada. In: J. Tizard, I. Sinclair and R. Clarke (Eds) *Varieties of Residential Experience*. London: Routledge and Kegan Paul, Ch. 7.

Guest D. (1984) Social psychology and organizational change. In: M. Gruneberg and T. Wall (Eds) *Social Psychology and Organizational Behaviour*. Chichester: Wiley, Ch. 8.

Gurin G., Veroff J. and Feld S. (1960). *Americans View their Mental Health: a Nationwide Interview Survey*. New York: Basic Books.

Gutkin T. (1981). Relative frequency of consultee lack of knowledge, skills, confidence, and objectivity in school settings. *J. of School Psychol.*, **19**, 57–61 (cited by Dustin and Blocher, 1984).

Hall A. and Wellman B. (1985). Social networks and social support. In: S. Cohen and S. Syme (Eds) *Social Support and Health*. New York: Academic Press, pp. 23–42.

Hammer M. (1983). Core and extended social networks in relation to health and illness. *Soc. Sci. and Med.*, **17**, 405–411.

Hannay D. (1981). Mental health and high flats. *J. of Chronic Diseases*, **34**, 431–432 (cited by Freeman, 1984a).

Hartnoll R., Daviaud E., Lewis R. and Mitcheson M. (1985). *Drug Problems: Assessing Local Needs—a Practical Manual for Assessing the Nature and Extent of Problematic Drug Use in a Community*. Drug Indicators Project, Department of Politics and Sociology, Birkbeck College, London.

Harwin J. (1982). The excessive drinker and the family: approaches to treatment. In: J. Orford and J. Harwin (Eds) *Alcohol and the Family*. London: Croom Helm, Ch. 11.

Hattie J., Sharpley C. and Rogers H. (1984). Comparative effectiveness of professional and para-professional helpers. *Psychol. Bull.*, **95**, 534–541.

Hawks D. (1973). Conceptual models and manpower requirements in clinical psychology. *Bulletin of The Brit. Psychol. Soc.*, **26**, 207–209.

Heartbeat Wales (1985). Take Heart: a consultative document on the development of community based heart health initiatives within Wales. *Heartbeat Wales, Technical Report* No. 1.

Heber F. (1978). Research in the prevention of sociocultural mental retardation. In: D. Forgays (Ed.) *Primary Prevention of Psychopathology 2. Environmental Influences*. Hanover, New Hampshire: University Press of New England, pp. 39–62.

Heller K. (1989). The return to community. *Amer. J. of Community Psychol.*, **17**, 1–16.

Heller K. and Monahan J. (1977). *Psychology and Community Change*. Homewood, Illinois: Dorsey.

Heller K., Price R., Reinharz S., Riger S., Wandersman A. and D'Aunno T. (1984). *Psychology and Community Change: Challenges for the Future*. Homewood, Illinois, Dorsey.

Henderson S., Byrne D., Duncan-Jones P., Scott R. and Adcock S. (1980). Social relationships, adversity and neurosis: a study of associations in a general population sample. *Brit. J. Psychiat.*, **136**, 574–583.

Hess R. and Wandersman A. (1985). What can we learn from Love Canal?: a conversation with Lois Gibbs and Richard Valinsky. In: A. Wandersman and R. Hess (Eds) *Beyond the Individual: Environmental Approaches and Prevention*. New York: Haworth Press.

Hetherington E. (1972). The effects of father absence on personality development in daughters. *Developmental Psychology*, **7**, 313–326.

Hetherington E. (1979). Divorce: a child's perspective. *Amer. Psychol.*, **34**, 851–858.

Hinrichsen G., Revenson T. and Shinn M. (1985). Does self-help help? An empirical investigation of scoliosis peer support groups. *J. of Soc. Issues*, **41**, 65–88.

Hirsch, B. (1981). Social networks and the coping process. Creating personal communities. In: B. Gottlieb (Ed.) *Social Networks and Social Support*. Beverly Hills, California: Sage.

Holahan C. (1972). Seating patterns and patient behavior in an experimental dayroom. *J. of Abnorm. Psychol.*, **80**, 115–124.

Holahan C. and Moos R. (1981) Social support and psychological distress: a longitudinal analysis. *J. of Abnorm. Psychol.*, **90**, 365–370.

Holahan C. and Saegert S. (1973). Behavioral and attitudinal effects of large-scale variation in the physical environment of psychiatric wards. *J. of Abnorm. Psychol.*, **82**, 454–462.

Holding T., Buglass D., Duffy J. and Kreitman N. (1977). Parasuicide in Edinurgh—a seven-year review 1968–74. *Brit. J. Psychiat.*, **130**, 534–43.

Holland S. (1988). Defining and experimenting with prevention. In: S. Ramon and M. Giannichedda (Eds) *Psychiatry in Transition: The British and Italian Experiences*. London: Pluto, Ch. 11.

Hollingshead A. and Redlich F. (1958). *Social Class and Mental Illness*. New York: Wiley.

Holroyd K., Penzien D. and Holm J. (1986). Behavioural medicine. In: H. Koch (Ed.) *Community Clinical Psychology*. London: Croom Helm, Ch. 11.

Hoult J. and Reynolds I. (1984). Schizophrenia: a comparative trial of community orientated and hospital orientated psychiatric care. *Acta Psychiat. Scand.*, **69**, 359–372.

Hoult J., Rosen A. and Reynolds I. (1984). Community orientated treatment compared to psychiatric hospital orientated treatment. *Soc. Sci. and Med.*, **18**, 1005–1010.

House J. (1981). *Work Stress and Social Support*. Reading, Mass.: Addison-Wesley (cited by Leavy, 1983).

House J. and Mortimer J. (1990). Social structure and the individual: emerging themes and new directions. *Soc. Psychol. Quarterly*, **53**, 71–80.

Hunt J. and Orford J. (1988). The world's listeners: a study of the natural caregiving activities of hairdressers and bartenders: an English replication and extension of the work of E. Cowen. Unpublished MS, University of Exeter.

Hurry L. (1989). Social factors in health service use. Unpublished PhD thesis, University of London.

Ineichen B. and Harper D. (1974). Wives' mental health and children's behaviour problems in contrasting residential areas. *Soc. Sci. and Med.*, **8**, 369–374 (cited by Freeman, 1984a).

Iversen L. and Sabroe S. (1988). Psychological well-being among unemployed and employed people after a company closedown: a longitudinal study. *J. of Soc. Issues*, **44**, 141–152.

Jackson S. (1983). Participation in decision making as a strategy for reducing job-related strain. *J. of Appl. Psychol.*, **68**, 3–19.

Jacobson D. (1986). Types and timing of social support. *J. of Health and Soc. Behav.*, **27**, 250–263.

Jahoda G. (1982). *Psychology and Anthropology: A Psychological Perspective*. London: Academic Press.

Jahoda M. (1979). The impact of unemployment in the 1930s and 1970s. *Bull. of the Brit. Psychol. Soc.*, **32**, 309–314.

Jahoda M. (1988). Economic recession and mental health: some conceptual issues. *J. of Soc. Issues*, **44**, 13–24.

Jaques E. (1978) (Ed.) *Health Services: their Nature and Organisation and the Role of Patients, Doctors, Nurses and the Complementary Professions*. London: Heinemann.

Jason L. (1980). Prevention in the schools: behavioural approaches. In: R. Price, R. Ketterer, B. Bader, and J. Monahan (Eds) *Prevention in Mental Health: Research, Policy, and Practice*. Beverly Hills, California: Sage.

Jeger A. and Slotnick R. (1982). *Community Mental Health and Behavioral Ecology: a Handbook of Theory, Research and Practice*. New York: Plenum Press.

Jennings C., Barraclough D. and Moss J. (1978). Have the Samaritans lowered the suicide rate? A controlled study. *Psychol. Med.*, **8**, 413–422.

Jilek W. (1974). *Salish Indian Mental Health and Culture Change. Psychohygienic and Therapeutic Aspects of the Guardian Spirit Ceremonial*. Toronto: Holt, Rinehart and Winston (cited by Deflem, 1989).

Joffe J. and Albee G. (1981). Powerlessness and psychopathology. In: J. Joffe and G. Albee (Eds) *Prevention through Political Action and Social Change*. Hanover: University Press of New England, pp. 321–325.

Jones E. and Eyles J. (1977). *An Introduction to Social Geography*. Oxford: Oxford University Press.

Jones K. and Poletti A. (1986). The Italian experiences reconsidered. *Brit. J. of Psychiat.*, **148**, 144–150.

Jouvenel, B. de (1958). Authority: the efficient imperative. In: Friedrich (Ed.) *Authority*. Cambridge, Massachusetts, pp. 159–169 (cited by Wrong, 1979).

Justice B. (1982). Primary prevention: fact or fantasy? In: M. Wagenfeld, P. Lemkau and B. Justice (Eds) *Public Mental Health: Perspectives and Prospects.* Beverly Hills, California: Sage, Ch. 10.

Kahn R. and Antonucci T. (1980). Convoys over the life course: attachments, roles, and social support. In: P. Baltes and O. Brim (Eds) *Life-Span Development and Behavior*, Vol. 3. New York: Academic Press.

Kane R. (1975). Interprofessional teamwork. Manpower Monograph No. 8. Syracuse University School of Social Work (cited by Noon, 1988).

Kasl S., Gore S. and Cobb S. (1975). The experience of losing a job: reported changes in health, symptoms and illness behavior. *Psychosomatic Med.*, **37**, 106–122.

Kasl S. and Wells J. (1985). Social support and health in the middle years: work and the family. In: S. Cohen and S. Syme (Eds) *Social Support and Health*. New York: Academic Press, pp. 175–198.

Kasl S., White M., Will J. and Marcuse P. (1982). In: A. Baum and J. Singer (Eds) *Advances in Environmental Psychology*. Vol. 4. *Environment and Health*. Boston: Lawrence Erlbaum (cited by Freeman, 1984a).

Katz A. (1984). Self-help groups: an international perspective. In: A. Gartner and F. Riessman (Eds) *The Self-Help Revolution*. New York: Human Sciences Press, Ch. 18.

Katz A. and Bender E. (1976). (Eds) *The Strength in Us*. New York: Franklin Watts.

Katz A. and Hermalin J. (1987). Self-help and prevention. In: J. Hermalin and J. Morell (Eds) *Prevention Planning in Mental Health*. Newbury Park, CA: Sage, Ch. 6.

Katz D. and Kahn R. (1978). *The Social Psychology of Organizations*. New York: Wiley (second edition).

Kaye G. (1990). A community organizer's perspective on citizen participation research and the researcher-practitioner partnership. *Amer. J. of Community Psychol.*, **18**, 151–158.

Kennedy C. (1989) Community integration and well-being: toward the goals of community care. *J. of Soc. Issues*, **45**, 65–78.

Kessler R. and McLeod J. (1985). Social support and mental health in community samples. In: S. Cohen and S. Syme (Eds) *Social Support and Health*. New York: Academic Press, pp. 219–240.

Ketterer R. (1981). *Consultation and Education in Mental Health*. Beverly Hills, California: Sage.

Ketterer R., Price R. and Politser P. (1980). The action research paradigm. In: R. Price and P. Politser (Eds) *Evaluation and Action in the Social Environment*. New York: Academic Press.

Keys C. and Frank S. (1987) Community psychology and the study of organisations: a reciprocal relationship. *Amer. J. of Community Psychol.*, **15**, 239–251.

Kiesler C. (1982). Mental hospitals and alternative care. Noninstitutionalization as potential public policy for mental patients. *Amer. Psychol.*, **37**, 349–360.

Kiesler C. (1985). Policy implications of research on social support and health. In: S. Cohen and S. Syme (Eds) *Social Support and Health*. New York: Academic Press, pp. 347–364.

Kiesler D. (1983). The 1982 interpersonal circle: a taxonomy for complementarity in human transactions. *Psychol. Rev.*, **90**, 185–214.

Kilmann R. (1983). A typology of organization topologies: toward parsimony and integration in the organizational sciences. *Hum. Relat.*, **36**, 523–548.

King R., Raynes N. and Tizard J. (1971). *Patterns of Residential Care: Sociological Studies in Institutions for Handicapped Children*. London: Routledge and Kegan Paul.

Klein D. and Ross A. (1960). Kindergarten entry: a study of role transition. *Orthopsychiatry and the School*, 60–69 (cited by D'Aunno *et al.*, 1985).

Kobasa S., Maddi S., Puccetti M. and Zola M. (1985). Effectiveness of hardiness, exercise and social support as resources against illness. *J. of Psychosomatic Res.*, **29**, 525–533.

Koch H. (Ed.) (1986). *Community Clinical Psychology*. London: Croom Helm.

Kuhn T. (1970). *The Structure of Scientific Revolutions*, 2nd Ed. Chicago: University of Chicago Press.

Kurdek L. (1981). An integrative perspective on children's divorce adjustments. *Amer. Psychol.*, **36**, 856–866.

La Psicología Social en México Vol. I (1986). Asociación Mexicana de psicología social. Proceedings of the 1st Mexican Congress of Social Psychology that took place in Trinidad, Tlaxcala, 22–24 October.

La Psicología Social en México Vol. II (1988). Asociación Mexicana de psicología social. Proceedings of the 2nd Mexican Congress of Social Psychology that took place in Metepec, Puebla, 19–21 October.

Lasater T., Abrams D., Artz L. *et al.* (1982). Lay volunteer delivery of a community-based cardiovascular risk factor change program: the Pawtucket experiment. In: *Handbook of Psychology and Health*, Ch. 85.

Leach E. (1976). *Culture and Communication*. Cambridge: Cambridge University Press (cited by Jahoda, 1982).

Leary T. (1957). *Interpersonal Diagnosis of Personality*. New York: Ronald.

Leavy R. (1983). Social support and psychological disorder: a review. *J. of Community Psychol.*, **11**, 3–21.

Lehman A. (1983). The well-being of chronic mental patients: assessing their quality of life. *Arch. Gen. Psychiat.*, **40**, 369–373.

Lehman A., Ward N. and Linn L. (1982). Chronic mental patients: the quality of life issue. *Amer. J. Psychiat.*, **139**, 1271–1276.

Lenski G. (1966). *Power and Privilege: A Theory of Social Stratification*. New York: McGraw-Hill (cited by Ragan and Wales, 1980).

Levi L. (1981). Prevention of stress-related disorders. *Int. J. of Mental Health*, **9**, 9–26.

Levine M. (1988). An analysis of mutual assistance. *Amer. J. of Community Psychol.*, **16**, 167–188.

Levine M. and Perkins D. (1987). *Principles of Community Psychology: Perspectives and Applications*. New York: Oxford University Press.

Lewin K. (1951). *Field Theory in Social Science*. New York: Harper.

Lewin K. (1952). In: D. Cartwright (Ed.) *Field Theory in Social Science*. London: Tavistock (cited by Ottaway, 1983).

Lightfoot P. and Orford J. (1986). Helping agents' attitudes towards alcohol-related problems. Situations vacant? A test and elaboration of a model. *Brit. J. of Addict.*, **81**, 749–756.

Lin N., Woelfel M. and Light S. (1985). The buffering effect of social support subsequent to an important life event. *Journal of Health and Social Behavior*, **26**, 247–263.

Lindsey A., Norbeck J., Carrieri V. and Perry E. (1981). Social support and health outcomes in post mastectomy women: a review. *Cancer Nursing*, October, 377–384.

Line J. (1988). Personal Communication.

Link B., Dohrenwend B. and Skodol A. (1986). Socio-economic status and schizophrenia: noisome occupational characteristics as a risk factor. *Amer. Sociol. Rev.*, **51**, 242–258.

Lipson J. (1982). Effects of a support group on the emotional impact of caesarean child-birth. In: *Helping People to Help Themselves: Self-help and Prevention. Prevention in Human Services.* New York: Haworth, 1 (3) pp. 17–29.

Lloyd J. and Bettencourt L. (1986). Prevention of achievement deficits. In: B. Edelstein and L. Michelson (Eds) *Handbook of Prevention.* New York: Plenum Press.

Lounsbury J., Cook M., Leader D. and Mears E. (1985). A critical analysis of community psychology research. In: E. Susskind and D. Klein (Eds) *Community Research: Methods, Paradigms and Applications.* New York: Praeger, Ch. 2.

Lukes S. (1974). *Power: A Radical View.* London: Macmillan (cited by Wrong, 1979).

Luria A. (1976). *Cognitive Development: Cultural and Social Foundations.* Cambridge, MA: Harvard University Press.

Maccoby N. and Alexander J. (1979). Reducing heart disease risk using the mass media: comparing the effects of three communities. In: R. Munoz, L. Snowden and J. Kelly *et al.* (Eds) *Social and Psychological Research in Community Settings.* San Francisco: Jossey-Bass.

Mangen S. (1988). Implementing community care: an international assessment. In: A. Lavender and F. Holloway (Eds) *Community Care in Practice.* Chichester: Wiley, Ch. 3.

Mansell J. (1986). The Natural History of the Community Mental Handicap Team. Paper given at Workshop on the community mental handicap team, Centre for Research in Social Policy and British Institute for Mental Handicap, University of Loughborough, September.

Manz C. and Gioia D. (1983). The interrelationship of power and control. *Hum. Rel.,* **36**, 459–476.

Marsella A. (1984). An interactional model of psychopathology. In: W. O'Connor and B. Lubin (Eds) *Ecological Approaches to Clinical and Community Psychology.* New York: Wiley, Ch. 11.

Martin P. and Turner B. (1986). Grounded theory and organisational research. *J. of Appl. Psychol.,* **22**, 141–157.

Maton K. (1988). Social support, organizational characteristics, psychological well-being, and group appraisal in three self-help group populations. *Amer. J. of Community Psychol.,* **16**, 53–78.

Matson N. (1991). Coping with caring: a study of the influence of coping on the distress experienced by carers of stroke victims and carers of older confused people. Unpub. PhD thesis, University of Exeter.

Matthews S. (1986). *Friendships through the Life Course: Oral Biographies in Old Age.* Beverly Hills, California: Sage.

Mazis S. and Canter D. (1979). Physical conditions and management practices for mentally retarded children. In: D. Canter and S. Canter (Eds) *Designing for Therapeutic Environments: a Review of Research.* Chichester: Wiley, pp. 119–158.

McAusland T. (Ed.) (1985). *Planning and Monitoring Community Mental Health Centres.* London: Kings Fund Centre.

McAusland T. and Patel Y. (1987). When people think you are mad they start behaving in very odd ways. Unpub. report, Evaluation Team, Exeter Health Authority.

McCarthy B. and Saegert S. (1978). Residential density, social control and social withdrawal. *Hum. Ecol.,* **6**, 253–272.

McCluskey-Fawcett K., Meck N. and Harris M. (1986). Prevention during prenatal and infant development. In: B. Edelstein and L. Michelson (Eds) *Handbook of Prevention.* New York: Plenum Press.

MacMillan D. and Chavis D. (1976). Sense of community: a definition and theory. *J. of Community Psychol.,* **14**, 6–22.

Medway F. and Updyke J. (1985). Meta-analysis of consultation outcome studies. *Amer. J. of Community Psychol.*, **13**, 489–506.

Mehrabian A. and Russell J. (1974). *An Approach to Environmental Psychology.* Cambridge, Massachusetts: MIT.

Merton R. (1938). Social structure and anomie. *Amer. Sociol. Rev.*, **3**, 672–682 (cited by Deflem, 1989).

Miles A. (1977). Staff relations in psychiatric hospitals. *Brit. J. Psychiat.*, **130**, 84–88.

Miller E. and Gwynne G. (1972). *Life Apart: a Pilot Study of Residential Institutions for the Physically Handicapped and the Young Chronic Sick.* London: Tavistock.

Miller G. (1969). Psychology in the Promotion of Human Welfare. Presidential address to the American Psychological Association.

Miller P. and Ingham J. (1976). Friends, confidants and symptoms. *Soc. Psychiat.*, **11**, 51–58.

Mills C. (1956). *The Power Elite.* New York: Oxford University Press (cited by Wrong, 1979).

Milne D., Jones R. and Walters, P. (1989). Anxiety management in the community: a social support model and preliminary evaluation. *Behavioural psychotherapy*, **17**, 221–236.

Milroy A. and Hennelly R. (1989). Changing our professional ways. In: A. Brackx and C. Grimshaw (Eds) *Mental Health Care in Crisis.* London: Pluto, pp. 175–189.

Minkler M. (1981). Application of social support theory to education: Implications for work with the elderly. *Health Education Quart.*, **8**, 147–165 (cited by Parry, 1988).

Minkler M. (1985). Social support and health of the elderly. In: S. Cohen and S. Syme (Eds) *Social Support and Health.* New York: Academic Press, pp. 199–218.

Mitchell A. (1986). Achieving autonomy: evaluation of the effectiveness of group work with young adults who have physical disabilities and their parents. Unpublished MSc Dissertation, University of Exeter.

Mitchell R. and Moos R. (1984). Deficiencies in social support among depressed patients: antecedents or consequences of stress? *J. of Health and Soc. Behav.*, **25**, 438–452.

Mitchell C., Davidson W., Chodakowski J. and McVeigh J. (1985). Intervention orientation: quantification of 'person-blame' versus 'situation-blame' intervention philosophies. *Amer. J. of Community Psychol.*, **13**, 543–552.

Moffat N. (1987). Brain damage and the family. In: J. Orford (Ed.) *Coping with Disorder in the Family.* London: Croom Helm, Ch. 11.

Mollica R. (1980). Community mental health centres: an American response to Kathleen Jones. *J. of the Royal Society of Med.*, **73**, 863–870.

Mollica R. and Milic M. (1986). Social class and psychiatric inpatient care: a twenty-five year perspective. *Soc. Psychiat.*, **21**, 106–112.

Moos R. (1974). *Evaluating Treatment Environments: a Social Ecological Approach.* New York: Wiley.

Morgan H., Pocock H. and Pottle S. (1975). The urban distribution of non-fatal deliberate self-harm. *Brit. J. of Psychiat.*, **126**, 319–328.

Morgan M., Patrick D. and Charlton J. (1984). Social networks and psychosocial support among disabled people. *Soc. Sci. and Med.*, **19**, 489–497.

Moscovici S. (1976). *Social Influence and Social Change.* London: Academic Press (cited by Ng, 1980).

Moscovici S. (1981). On social representations. In: J. Forgas (Ed.) *Social Cognition: Perspectives on Everyday Understanding.* London: Academic Press.

Mowrer O. (1984). The mental health professions and mutual help programs: co-optation or cooperation. In: A. Gartner and F. Riessman (Eds) *The Self-Help Revolution.* New York: Human Sciences Press, Ch. 11.

Mulvey A. (1988). Community psychology and feminism: tensions and commonalities. *J. of Community Psychol.*, **16**, 70–83.

Munroe S. and Steiner S. (1986). Social support and psychopathology: interrelations with preexisting disorder, stress and personality. *J. of Abnorm. Psychol.* **95**, 29–39.

Murphy E. (1982). Social origins of depression in old age. *Brit. J. of Psychiat.*, **141**, 135–142.

Murphy R. (1971). *The Dialectics of Social Life: Alarms and Excursions in Anthropological Theory.* London: Allen and Unwin (cited by Jahoda, 1982).

Nadler D. (1977). *Feedback and Organization Development: Using Data-Based Methods.* Reading, Massachusetts: Addison-Wesley (cited by Gallessich 1982).

Newton J. (1988). *Preventing Mental Illness.* London: Routledge and Kegan Paul.

Ng S. (1980). *The Social Psychology of Power.* London: Academic Press.

Nietzel M. and Fisher S. (1981). Effectiveness of professional and para-professional helpers: a comment on Durlak. *Psychol. Bull.*, **89**, 555–565.

Nietzel M. and Himelein M. (1986). Prevention of crime and delinquency. In: B. Edelstein and L. Michelson (Eds) *Handbook of Prevention.* New York: Plenum.

Noon M. (1988). Do multidisciplinary teams provide a coordinated approach to healthcare or are they unworkable? *The Health Service Journal*, October, 1160–1161.

O'Donnell C. (1980). Environmental design and the prevention of psychological problems. In: P. Feldman and J. Orford (Eds) *Psychological Problems: the Social Context.* Chichester: Wiley, Ch. 10.

Orford J. (1986). The rules of interpersonal complementarity: does hostility beget hostility and dominance, submission? *Psychol. Rev.*, **93**, 365–377.

Orford J. (1987a). The need for a community response to alcohol-related problems. In: T. Stockwell and S. Clement (Eds) *Helping the Problem Drinker: New Initiatives in Community Care.* London: Croom Helm, Ch. 1.

Orford J. (1987b). *Coping with Disorder in the Family.* London: Croom Helm.

Orford J. (1988). An Enquiry into the Closure of the Berkshire Council on Alcoholism (BCA). A report prepared for the Association of Directors of Councils on Alcoholism (UK).

Orford J., Natera G., Casco M., Nava A. and Ollinger E. (1990). Coping with alcohol and drug use in the family: Report of a Mexican feasibility study. A report prepared for the World Health Organisation, Division of Mental Health, Geneva.

Orford J., Oppenheimer E., Egert S., Hensman C. and Guthrie S. (1976). The cohesiveness of alcoholism-complicated marriages and its influence on treatment outcome. *Brit. J. of Psychiat.*, **128**, 318–339.

Orford J., Rigby K., Tod A., Miller T., Bennett G. and Velleman R. (1991). Coping with excessive drug use in the family: a study of 50 close relatives (paper submitted for publication).

Orford J. and Stockwell T. (1988). The first five years of a District Community Alcohol Team: a case study in community psychology. In: J. West and P. Spinks (Eds) *Case Studies in Clinical Psychology.* London: Butterworths.

Orford J. and Velleman R. (1990). Offspring of parents with drinking problems: drinking and drug-taking as young adults. *Brit. J. of Addict.*, **85**, 779–794.

O'Sullivan M., Peterson P., Cox G. and Kirkeby J. (1989). Ethnic populations: community mental health services ten years later. *Amer. J. of Community Psychol.*, **17**, 17–30.

Ottaway R. (1983). The change agent: a taxonomy in relation to the change process. *Hum. Relat.*, **36**, 361–392.

Otto S. and Armstrong F. (1978). The Action Research Experiment: a Report of Two Years Work by the Consortium Action Research Team, 1975–7. London: South East London Consortium.

Otto S. and Orford J. (1978). *Not Quite Like Home: Small Hostels for Alcoholics and Others*. Chichester: Wiley.

Palmer R., Marshall P. and Oppenheimer R. (1987). Anorexia and the family. In: J. Orford (Ed.) *Coping with Disorder in the Family*. London: Croom Helm, Ch. 6.

Pancer S. and Westhues A. (1989). A developmental stage approach to program planning and evaluation. *Eval. Rev.*, **13**, 56–77.

Parry G. (1988). Mobilizing social support. In: F. Watts (Ed.) *New Developments in Clinical Psychology*, Vol. 2. Chichester: Wiley.

Parry G. and Shapiro D. (1986). Social support and life events in working class women. Stress buffering or independent effects? *Arch. of Gen. Psychiat.*, **43**, 315–323.

Payne M. (1982). *Working in Teams*. London: Macmillan.

Pearl A. and Riessman F. (1965). *New Careers for the Poor: the Nonprofessional in Human Service*. London: Collier Macmillan.

Pedro-Carroll J. and Cowen E. (1985). The children of divorce intervention program: an investigation of the efficacy of a school-based prevention program. *J. of Consult. and Clin. Psychol.*, **53**, 603–611.

Pedro-Carroll J., Cowen E., Hightower A. and Guare J. (1986). Preventive intervention with latency-aged children of divorce: a reflective study. *Amer. J. of Community Psychol.*, **14**, 277–290.

Perkins D., Florin P., Rich R., Wandersman A. and Chavis D. (1990). Participation and the social and physical environment of residential blocks: crime and community context. *Amer. J of Community Psychol.*, **18**, 83–116.

Peterson C. and Stunkard A. (1989). Personal control and health promotion. *Soc. Sci. and Med.*, **28**, 819–828.

Pettigrew A. (1975). Strategic aspects of the management of specialist activity. *Personnel Review*, **4**, 5–13.

Plant M. (1975). *Drugtakers in an English Town*. London: Tavistock.

Platt S. and Kreitman N. (1985). Parasuicide and unemployment among men in Edinburgh 1968–1982. *Psychological Medicine*, **15**, 113–123. (cited by Jahoda, 1988).

Plaut T. (1980). Prevention policy: the federal perspective. In: R. Price, R. Ketterer, B. Bader and J. Monahan (Eds) *Prevention in Mental Health: Research, Policy, and Practice*. Beverly Hills, California: Sage.

Posovac E. and Carey R. (1985). *Program Evaluation: Methods and Case Studies* (second edition). Englewood Cliffs, New Jersey: Prentice-Hall.

President's Commission on Mental Health (1978). Report to the President from the President's Commission on Mental Health, 1 and 4. Washington DC: US Government Printing Office (cited by Catalano and Dooley, 1980).

Prestby J., Wandersman A., Florin P., Rich R. and Chavis D. (1990). Benefits, costs, incentive management and participation in voluntary organizations: a means to understanding and promoting empowerment. *Amer. J. of Community Psychol.*, **18**, 117–150.

Puska P. (1982). Community-based prevention of cardiovascular disease: the North Karelia project. In: *Handbook of Psychology and Health*, Ch. 82.

Puska P., Salonen J., Nissinen A. *et al.* (1983). Change in risk factors for coronary heart disease during 10 years of a community intervention programme (North Karelia Project). *Brit. Med. Journal*, **287**, 1840–1844.

Ragan P. and Wales J. (1980). Age stratification and life course. In: J. Birren and R. Sloane (Eds) *Handbook of Mental Health and Aging*. Englewood Cliffs, NJ: Prentice-Hall.

Ramon S. (1985). The Italian psychiatric reform. In S. Mangen (Ed.) *Mental Health Care in the European Community*. London: Croom Helm.

Ramon S. (1988). Community Care in Britain. In: A. Lavender and F. Holloway (Eds) *Community Care in Practice*. Chichester: Wiley, Ch. 2.

Rapley M. (1990). Is normalisation a scientific theory? *Clinical Psychology Forum*, **29**, 16–20.

Rapoport R. (1960). *Community as Doctor: New Perspectives on a Therapeutic Community*. London: Tavistock.

Rapoport R. (1970). Three dilemmas of action research. *Hum. Rel.*, **23**, 499–513 (cited by Susman and Evered, 1978).

Rappaport J. (1977). *Community Psychology: Values, Research and Action*. New York: Holt, Rinehart and Winston.

Rappaport J., Chinsky J. and Cowen E. (1971). *Innovations in Helping Chronic Patients*. New York: Academic Press.

Raush H. (1965). Interaction sequences. *J. of Pers. and Soc. Psychol.*, **2**, 487–499.

Reid A. and Angel Aguilar M. (1991). Constructing Community Social Psychology in Mexico. *Applied Psychology: An International Review*, **40**(2).

Repucci N. (1987). Prevention and ecology: teenage pregnancy, child sexual abuse and organised youth sports. *Amer. J. of Community Psychol.*, 15, 1–22.

Reynolds D. and Sullivan M. (1981). The effects of schools: a radical faith restated. In: B. Gillham (Ed.) *Problem Behaviour in the Secondary School*. London: Croom Helm, Ch. 3.

Rice A. (1958). *Productivity and Social Organisations: the Ahmedabad Experiment*. London: Tavistock (cited by de Board, 1978).

Richman N. (1974). Effects of housing on preschool children and their mothers. *Developmental Medicine and Child Neurology*, 10, 1–9 (cited by Freeman, 1984a).

Robertson L. (1986). Injury. In: B. Edelstein and L. Michelson (Eds) *Handbook of Prevention*. New York: Plenum Press.

Robinson D. (1979). *Talking out of Alcoholism: The Self-Help Process of Alcoholics Anonymous*. London: Croom Helm.

Robinson D. and Henry S. (1977). *Self-Help and Health*. London: Martin Robertson.

Rodin J. (1983). Behavioural medicine: beneficial effects of self-control training in ageing. *Int. Review of Appl. Psychol.*, **32**, 153–181 (cited by Newton, 1988).

Rook K. and Dooley D. (1985). Applying social support research: theoretical problems and future directions. *J. of Soc. Issues*, **41**, 5–28.

Rosenfield S. (1989). The effects of women's employment: personal control and sex differences in mental health. *J. of Health and Soc. Behav.*, **30**, 77–91.

Rossi P. and Freeman H. (1986). *Evaluation: A Systematic Approach* (third edition). Beverly Hills, California: Sage.

Rowbottom R. and Billis D. (1978). The stratification of work and organisational design. In: E. Jaques (Ed.) *Health Services: their Nature and Organisation and the Role of Patients, Doctors, Nurses and the Complementary Professions*. London: Heinemann, Ch. 7.

Rowbottom R. and Bromley G. (1978). The future of child guidance: a study in multi-disciplinary team-work. In: E. Jaques (Ed.) *Health Services: their Nature and Organisation and the Role of Patients, Doctors, Nurses and the Complementary Professions*. London: Heinemann, Ch. 10.

Rowbottom R. and Hey A. (1978). Organisation of Services for the Mentally Ill. Brunel University Institute of Organisation and Social Studies Working Paper (cited by Furnell, Flett and Clark, 1987).

Russell D., Altmaier E. and Van Velzen D. (1987). Job-related stress, social support, and burnout among classroom teachers. *J. Appl. Psychol.*, **72**, 269–274.

Rutter M., Maughan B., Mortimore P. and Ouston J. (1979). *Fifteen Thousand Hours*. London: Open Books.

Ryan W. (1971). *Blaming the Victim*. New York: Random House.

Safilios-Rothschild C. (1970). The study of family power structure: a review 1960–1969. *Journal of Marriage and the Family*, **32**, 539–551.

Sagarin E. (1969). *Odd Man In: Societies of Deviants in America*. Chicago: Quadrangle.

Salonen J., Puska P., Kottke T., Tuomilehto J. and Nissinen A. (1983). Decline in mortality from coronary heart disease in Finland from 1969 to 1979. *Brit. Med. Journal*, 1857–1860.

Sarason S. (1974). *The Psychological Sense of Community: Perspectives for Community Psychology*. San Francisco: Jossey-Bass.

Schoenferd P., Halevy-Martine J., Hemley-Van Der Velden E. and Ruhf L. (1985). Network therapy: an outcome study of twelve social networks. *J. of Community Psychol.*, **13**, 281–287 (cited by Parry, 1988).

Schulz R. and Rau M. (1985). Social support through the life course. In: S. Cohen and S. Syme (Eds) *Social Support and Health*. New York: Academic Press, pp. 129–150.

Seidman E. (1988). Back to the future, community psychology: unfolding a theory of social intervention. *Amer. J. of Community Psychol.*, **16**, 3–24.

Shapiro D. A. and Shapiro D. (1982). Meta-analysis of comparative therapy outcome studies: a replication and refinement. *Psychol. Bull.*, **92**, 581–604.

Shaw S., Cartwright A., Spratley T. and Harwin J. (1978). *Responding to Drinking Problems*. London: Croom Helm.

Shepherd G. and Richardson A. (1979). Organization and interaction in psychiatric day centres. *Psychol. Med.*, **9**, 1–7.

Shure M. and Spivack G. (1979). Interpersonal cognitive problem solving and primary prevention. Programming for pre-school and kindergarten children. *J. of Clin. Child Psychol.*, **8**, 89–94.

Shure M. and Spivack G. (1982). Interpersonal problem-solving in young children: a cognitive approach to prevention. *Amer. J. of Community Psychol.*, **10**, 341–356.

Sinha C. (1986). Psychology, education and the ghost of Kaspar Hauser. *Disability, Handicap and Society*, **1**, 245–260.

Skipper J. and Leonard R. (1968) Children, stress, and hospitalization: a field experiment. *J. of Health and Soc. Behav.*, **9**, 275–287 (cited by Justice, 1982).

Smith M. and Glass G. (1977). Meta-analysis of psychotherapy outcome studies. *Amer. Psychol.*, **32**, 752–760.

Solomon D. and Maccoby N. (1982). Communication as a model for health enhancement. In: *Handbook of Psychology and Health*, Ch. 13.

Solomon Z. and Bromet E. (1982). The role of social factors in affective disorder: an assessment of the vulnerability model of Brown and his colleagues. *Psychol. Med.*, **12**, 123–130.

Sommer R. and Ross H. (1958). Social interaction on a geriatric ward. *Int. J. of Soc. Psychiat.*, **4**, 128–133.

Spector J. (1984). Clinical psychology and primary care: some ongoing dilemmas. *Bull. of The Brit. Psychol. Society*, **37**, 73–76.

Spivack G. and Shure M. (1974). *Social Adjustment of Young Children. A Cognitive Approach to Solving Real-Life Problems*. San Francisco: Jossey-Bass (cited by Durlak, 1983).

Spratley T. (1987). Consultancy as part of community alcohol team (CAT) work. In: T. Stockwell and S. Clement (Eds) *Helping the Problem Drinker: New Initiatives in Community Care*. London: Croom Helm, Ch. 7.

Srole L., Langner T., Michael S., Kirkpatrick P., Opler M. and Rennie T. (1978). *Mental Health in the Metropolis: The Midtown Manhattan Study* (revised and enlarged edition). New York: New York University Press.

Stein, B. and Kanter, R. (1980). Building the parallel organization: creating mechanisms for permanent quality of work life. *J. Appl. Behav. Sci.*, **16**, 371–388 (cited by Gallessich, 1982).

Stein L. and Test M. (1980). Alternative to mental hospital treatment. I. Conceptual model, treatment program and clinical evaluation. *Arch. Gen. Psychiat.*, **37**, 392–397.

Stockwell T. (1988). Community alcohol teams: a review of studies evaluating their effectiveness with special reference to the experience of other community teams. London: Department of Health.

Stockwell T. (1989). *The Exeter Home Detoxification Project: Final Report to the Department of Health and Social Security.* London: DHSS.

Stockwell T., Bolt L., Milner I., Pugh P. and Young I. (1990). Home detoxification for problem drinkers: acceptability to clients, relatives, general practitioners and outcome after 60 days. *Brit J. Addict.*, **85**, 61–70.

Stone R. and Levine A. (1985). Reactions to collective stress: correlates of active citizen participation at Love Canal. In: A. Wandersman and R. Hess (Eds) *Beyond the Individual: Environmental Approaches and Prevention.* New York: Haworth Press.

Stotland E. and Cobler A. (1965). *Life and Death of a Mental Hospital.* Seattle: University of Washington Press.

Strachan A., Leff J., Goldstein M., Doane J. and Burtt C. (1986). Emotional attitudes and direct communication in the families of schizophrenics: a cross-national replication. *British Journal of Psychiatry*, **149**, 279–287.

Strauss A. (1987). *Qualitative Analysis for Social Scientists.* Cambridge: Cambridge University Press.

Strong S. and Hills H. (1986). *Interpersonal Communication Rating Scale.* Richmond: Virginia Commonwealth University.

Strong S., Hills H. and Nelson B. (1988). *Interpersonal Communication Rating Scale.* Richmond: Virginia Commonwealth University.

Susman G. and Evered R. (1978). An assessment of the scientific merits of action research. *Admin. Sci. Quart.*, **23**, 582–603.

Swan H., Press A., and Briggs S. (1985). Child sexual abuse prevention: does it work? *Child Welfare*, **64**, 395–405.

Swift C. (1980). Primary prevention: policy and practice. In: R. Price, R. Ketterer, B. Bader and J. Monahan (Eds) *Prevention in Mental Health. Research, Policy and Practice.* Beverly Hills, California: Sage.

Swift M. and Weirich T. (1987). Prevention planning as social and organisational change. In: J. Hermalin and J. Morell (Eds) *Prevention Planning in Mental Health.* Beverly Hills, California: Sage, Ch. 2.

Syrotuik J. and D'Arcy C. (1984). Social support and mental health: direct, protective and compensatory effects. *Soc. Sci. and Med.*, **18**, 229–236.

Szivos S. and Griffiths E. (1990). Consciousness raising and social identity theory: a challenge to normalisation. *Clinical Psychology Forum*, **28**, 11–15.

Tannenbaum A. (1974). *Hierarchy in Organisations.* San Francisco: Jossey-Bass (cited by Katz and Kahn, 1978).

Tarail M. (1985). The Community Mental Health Worker: The role and function of indigenous paraprofessionals in a comprehensive community mental health center. In: S. Alley, J. Blanton and R. Feldman (Eds) *Paraprofessionals in Mental Health: Theory and Practice.* New York: Human Sciences Press, Ch. 10.

Tellis-Nayak M. and Tellis-Nayak V. (1984). Games that professionals play: the social psychology of physician-nurse interaction. *Soc. Sc. and Med.*, **18**, 1063–1069.

Temple H. (1987). Personal Communication.

Thoits P. (1982). Conceptual, methodological and theoretical problems in studying social support as a buffer against life stress. *J. of Health and Soc. Behav.*, **23**, 145–149.

Thornton D., Curran L., Grayson D. and Holloway V. (1984). *Tougher Regimes in Detention Centres: Report of an evaluation by the Young Offender Psychology Unit*. London: HMSO.

Tizard B. (1980). Review of *Fifteen Thousand Hours* by M. Rutter *et al*. *J. of Child Psychol. and Psychiat.*, **21**, 363–364.

Tizard J. (1976). Psychology and social policy (Presidential address to the BPS, April 1976) *Bull. of the Brit. Psychol. Society*, **29**, 225–234.

Tizard J., Sinclair I. and Clarke R. (Eds) (1975). *Varieties of Residential Experience*. London: Routledge and Kegan Paul.

Tolsdorf C. (1976). Social networks, support, and coping: an exploratory study. *Fam. Proc.*, **15**, 407–417.

Towell D. and Harries C. (1979). *Innovations in Patient Care*. London: Croom Helm.

Townsend P. (1979). *Poverty in the United Kingdom*. Harmondsworth: Penguin.

Townsend P. and Davidson N. (1982). *Inequalities in Health Care: The Black Report*. Harmondsworth: Penguin.

Treadway D. (1989). *Before It's Too Late: Working with Substance Abuse in the Family*. New York: Norton.

Triandis H. (1977). Subjective culture and interpersonal relations across cultures. *Annals of the N.Y. Acad. of Sci.*, **285**, 418–434.

Trist E. and Bamforth K. (1951). Some social and psychological consequences of the longwall method of coal-cutting. *Hum. Rel.*, **4**, 3–38 (cited by de Board, 1978).

Trist E., Higgen G., Murray H. and Pollock A. (1963). *Organisational Choice*. London: Tavistock (cited by de Board, 1978).

Trochim W. (1984). *Research Design for Program Evaluation: the Regression-Discontinuity Approach*. Beverly Hills, California: Sage.

Trotter S. (1981). Neighborhoods, politics and mental health. In: J. Joffe and G. Albee (Eds) *Prevention through Political Action and Social Change*. Hanover: University Press of New England.

Tuckman B. (1965). Developmental sequence in small groups. *Psychol. Bull.*, **63**, 384–399 (cited by Payne M., 1982).

Turner B. (1981). Some practical aspects of qualitative data analysis: one way of organising the cognitive processes associated with the generation of grounded theory. *Quality and Quantity*, **15**, 225–247.

Turner B. (1983). The use of grounded theory for the qualitative analysis of organisational behaviour. *J. of Management Studies*, **20**, 333–348.

Turner J. and Oakes P. (1986). The significance of the social identity concept for social psychology with reference to individualism, interactionism and social influence. *Brit. J. of Soc. Psychol.*, **25**, 237–252.

Turner R. (1981). Social support as a contingency in psychological well-being. *J. of Health and Soc. Behav.*, **22**, 357–367.

Turner R., Grindstaff C. and Phillips N. (1990). Social support and outcome in teenage pregnancy. *J. of Health and Soc. Behav.*, **31**, 43–57.

Twining T. (1986). The elderly. In: H. Koch (Ed.) *Community Clinical Psychology*. London: Croom Helm, Ch. 12.

Ullah P., Banks M. and Warr P. (1985). Social support, social pressures and psychological distress during unemployment. *Psychol. Med.*, **15**, 283–295.

Vachon M., Lyall W., Rogers J., Freedman-Letofsky K. and Freeman S. (1980). A controlled study of self-help intervention for widows. *Amer. J. of Psychiat.*, **137**, 1380–1384.

Vachon M. and Stylianos S. (1988). The role of social support in bereavement. *J. of Soc. Issues*, **44**, 175–190.

Vetere A. and Gale A. (1987). *Ecological Studies of Family Life*. Chichester: Wiley.

Vickers E. (1987). Resourcing a self-help group for women who have lost a baby through miscarriage or stillbirth. Unpublished project report, University of Exeter.

Videka-Sherman L. (1982). Effects of participation in a self-help group for bereaved parents: compassionate friends. In: *Helping People to Help Themselves: Self-Help and Prevention. Prevention in Human Services.* New York: Haworth, 1 (3), pp. 69–77.

Warner R. (1985). *Recovery from Schizophrenia: Psychiatry and Political Economy.* London: Routledge and Kegan Paul.

Warr P. (1987). *Work, Unemployment and Mental Health.* Oxford: Clarendon.

Warr P., Jackson P. and Banks M. (1988). Unemployment and mental health: some British studies. *J. of Soc. Issues,* **44,** 47–68.

Webb A. and Hobdell M. (1980). Coordination and teamwork in the health and personal social services. In: S. Lonsdale *et al. Teamwork in the Personal Social Services and Health Care.* London: Croom Helm (cited by Noon, 1988).

Weber M. (1947). *The Theory of Social and Economic Organization.* New York: Oxford University Press (cited by Ng, 1980).

Weiss R. (1976). Transition states and other stressful situations: their nature and programs for their management. In: G. Caplan and M. Killilea (Eds) *Support Systems and Mutual Help: Multi-disciplinary Explorations.* New York: Grune and Stratton, pp. 213–232 (cited by Jacobson, 1986).

Weissberg R. and Allen J. (1986). Promoting children's social skills and adaptive inter-personal behaviour. In B. Edelstein and L. Michelson (Eds) *Handbook of Prevention.* New York: Plenum Press.

Weissberg R., Gesten E., Rapkin B., Cowen E., Davidson E., de Apodaca R. and McKim B. (1981). The evaluation of a social problem-solving training program for suburban and inner-city third-grade children. *Journal of Consulting and Clinical Psychology,* **49,** 251–261.

Wellman B. and Leighton B. (1979). Networks, neighborhoods, and communities. Approaches to the study of the community question. *Urb. Affairs Quart.,* **14,** 363–390.

Wethington E. and Kessler R. (1986). Perceived support, received support, and adjustment to stressful life events. *J. of Health and Soc. Behav.,* **27,** 78–89.

Whittle P. (1984). Study of a social services community observation and assessment team. Unpublished MSc Dissertation, University of Exeter, UK.

Wicker A. (1969). Size of church membership and members' support of church behaviour settings. *J. of Pers. and Soc. Psychol.,* **13,** 278–288.

Wiesenfeld A. and Weiss H. (1979). Hairdressers and helping: influencing the behavior of informal caregivers. *Prof. Psychol.,* **10,** 786–792.

Willems E. (1967). Sense of obligation to high school activities as related to school size and marginality of student. *Child Dev.,* **38,** 1247–1260.

Willen M. (1984). Parents Anonymous: the professional's role as sponsor. In: A. Gartner and F. Riessman (Eds) *The Self-Help Revolution.* New York: Human Sciences Press, Ch. 8.

Williams D. (1990). Socioeconomic differentials in health: a review and redirection. *Soc. Psychol. Quart.,* **53,** 81–99.

Williams J. (1984). Women and mental illness. In: J. Nicholson and H. Beloff (Eds) *Psychology Survey 5.* Leicester: Brit. Psychol. Society.

Williams J. (1985). Unheard voices: women in a mental hospital talk about their lives. Presented at the Women in Psychology British Psychological Society Conference, Cardiff.

Wills T. (1985). Supportive functions of interpersonal relationships. In: S. Cohen and S. Syme (Eds) *Social Support and Health.* New York: Academic Press, pp. 61–82.

Wing J. and Brown G. (1970). *Institutionalism and Schizophrenia: A Comparative Study of Three Mental Hospitals, 1960–68.* Cambridge: Cambridge University Press.

Wing J. and Hailey A. (1972). *Evaluating a Community Psychiatric Service: the Camberwell Register 1964–1971.* London: Oxford University Press.

Wiseman J. (1970). *Stations of the Lost: The Treatment of Skid Row Alcoholics.* Englewood Cliffs, NJ: Prentice-Hall.

Wiseman J. (1978). The research web. In: J. Bynner and K. Stribley (Eds) *Social Research: Principles and Procedures.* London: Longman/Open University.

Wolfensberger W. (1972). *The Principle of Normalization in Human Services.* Toronto: National Institute on Mental Retardation.

Wolfensberger W. and Thomas S. (1983). *PASSING: Program Analysis of Service Systems Implementation of Normalization Goals: Normalization Criteria and Ratings Manual* (second edition). US National Institute on Mental Retardation.

Wollert R., Knight B. and Levy L. (1984). Make Today Count: a collaborative model for professionals and self-help groups. In: A. Gartner and F. Riessman (Eds) *The Self-Help Revolution.* New York: Human Sciences Press, Ch. 10.

World Health Organisation (Europe) (1984). Health Promotion: a discussion document on the concept and principles. World Health Organisation, Supplement to *Europe News*, No. 3.

Wortman C. and Conway T. (1985). The role of social support in adaptation and recovery from physical illness. In: S. Cohen and S. Syme (Eds) *Social Support and Health.* New York: Academic Press, pp. 281–302.

Wrong D. (1979). *Power: Its Forms, Bases and Uses.* Oxford: Basil Blackwell.

Yates P. (1989). Personal Communication.

Yetton P. (1984). Leadership and Supervision. In: M. Gruneberg and T. Wall (Eds) *Social Psychology and Organisational Behaviour.* Chichester: Wiley, Ch. 2.

Young M. and Willmott P. (1957). *Family and Kinship in East London.* London: Routledge and Kegan Paul.

Yule W. (1980). Handicap. In: P. Feldman and J. Orford (Eds) *Psychological Problems: the Social Context.* Chichester: Wiley, Ch. 8.

Zax M. and Specter G. (1974). *An Introduction to Community Psychology.* New York: Wiley.

Zimmerman M. and Rappaport J. (1988). Citizen participation, perceived control, and psychological empowerment. *Amer. J. of Community Psychol.*, **16**, 725–750 (cited by Chavis and Wandersman, 1990).

Index